Northern Tanzania

with Kilimanjaro & Zanzibar

the Bradt Safari Guide

Philip Briggs

www.bradtguides.com

Bradt Travel Guides Ltd, UK
The Globe Pequot Press Inc, USA

edition
2

UGANDA

Lake Victoria

BUKOBA

MUSOMA

Ukara Island

Ukerewe Island

Speke Gulf

Bunda

Rubondo Island
NP

Kome I

MWANZA

Geita

Serengeti
National Park

S e r e n g e t i   P l a i n

Ngorongoro
Conservation
Area

Mto

Ngorongoro
3187m

Lake Manyara
National Park

Lake
Eyasi

SHINYANGA

L. Kitangiri

Nzega

Mount
Hanang
3418m

Babati

Katesh

Kondoa
Rock Art
Reserve

SINGIDA

KONDOA

TABORA

Ugalla River
Wildlife Reserve

Sikonge

Ugalla

DODOMA

Rungwa

Rungwa

Nfahbe

KEY
Capital city ■
Main town ●
Village ○
Airport ✈ ✈
Mountain ▲
Main road (tarmac)
Main road
Other road
Railway
International boundary

KENYA

Lake Natron & Ol Doinyo Lengai
page 189

Mount Kilimanjaro National Park
page 145

N

Bradt

Lake
Natron

Namanga

▲ Kilimanjaro
5888m
Mt
Kilimanjaro
NP

Mount Meru
4566m
▲ Arusha
NP

MOSHI

ARUSHA

Arusha National Park
page 119

Mkomazi
National
Park
Pare
Mountains

Same

Pangani

angire
tional
ark

Maasai
Steppe

Usumbara
Mountains
LUSHOTO

Amani
Nature
Reserve

Mombo

Korogwe

Muheza

Weto

Pemba Island

Chake Chake

TANGA

PANGANI

Saadani
National
Park

ZANZIBAR

Zanzibar Island

Kizimkazi

BAGAMOYO

Chalinze

DAR ES SALAAM

MOROGORO

Uluguru Mountains

Great Ruaha

0   100km
0   150 miles

Northern Tanzania

Don't miss...

African elephant
Loxodonta Africana
(AVZ) page 272

Black rhino
Diceros bicornis
(AVZ) page 272

Lion
Panthera leo
(AVZ) page 263

African buffalo
Syncerus caffer
(AVZ) page 273

Leopard
Panthera pardus
(AVZ) page 263

left Elephants are present in Tarangire National Park all year round (AVZ) page 161

below Sunset over the Serengeti – arguably the finest game reserve anywhere in Africa (AVZ) page 207

bottom Reaching an altitude of 5,895m (19,340ft), Kilimanjaro is the highest mountain in Africa (AVZ) page 145

AUTHOR

Philip Briggs is a travel writer specialising in Africa.
Raised in South Africa, where he still lives, Philip first
visited east Africa in 1986 and has since spent an
average of six months annually exploring the highways
and back roads of the continent. His first Bradt Travel
Guide, to South Africa, was published in 1991, and he
has subsequently written Bradt guides to Tanzania,
Uganda, Ethiopia, Malawi, Mozambique, Ghana,
Rwanda and East African wildlife. Philip has
contributed to more than a dozen other books about
Africa, and his work regularly appears in magazines
such as *Africa Geographic*, *Travel Africa* and *Wanderlust*.

CONTRIBUTORS

Ariadne Van Zandbergen, who took most of the photographs in this book and
did much of the research for sections on Kilimanjaro and Ol Doinyo Lengai, is a
Belgian-born freelance photographer who first travelled through Africa from
Morocco to South Africa in 1994–95 and is now resident in Johannesburg. She has
visited more than 25 African countries and her photographs have appeared in
numerous travel and wildlife guides, coffee-table books, magazines, newspapers,
maps and pamphlets. She runs an online photo library www.africaimagelibrary.com.

Chris McIntyre is co-author of Bradt's *Zanzibar: The Bradt Travel Guide*, which
has been thoroughly revised and expanded for a new seventh edition. Chris started
writing Bradt guides in 1990, and since then has written all the successive guides
for Bradt on Namibia, Botswana and Zambia – as well as numerous articles. Chris
now runs the specialist tour operator, *Expert Africa*, where he leads a team of
dedicated Africa-addicts who provide impartial advice and great safaris to Africa,
including Tanzania.

Susan McIntyre is co-author of Bradt's *Zanzibar: The Bradt Travel Guide*. Having
joined the travel industry professionally in 1999, Susan sought a career focusing on
African travel, the area about which she is most passionate. She has acted as a
consultant for *Expert Africa* and has co-ordinated media campaigns for a number of
southern Africa's finest independent safari camps and boutique hotels. She spends
several months each year in Africa with Chris, and many more encouraging the
press and public to visit.

Emma Thomson is an editorial project manager at Bradt Travel Guides. She has
spent time living with the Rangi, Chagga and Maasai communities in northern
Tanzania, where she became a trustee of Serian UK (*www.serianuk.org.uk*),
established to promote and preserve indigenous peoples. Her work has been
published by a clutch of travel magazines, including *Travel Africa*, *Songlines* and
Msafiri. She is a Fellow of the Royal Geographical Society and a Junior Fellow of
the Royal Anthropological Institute.

Hilary Bradt

Over 30 years ago George and I spent two fruitless days trying to hitchhike through the Serengeti. We were also bitten to distraction by mosquitoes in Mto wa Mbu ('River of Mosquitoes') and arrested in Tabora because, the official said, it was illegal to take photographs in Tanzania without a permit. George sourly wrote in *Backpacker's Africa* (1977): 'We hope someday it will all come together and be the most enlightened and productive country in Africa, but that's not going to happen for a while.' It's happened. The Northern Safari Circuit in Tanzania is widely considered to be the best in east Africa, with an excellent infrastructure and some of the most friendly and welcoming people in Africa. In the introduction of his full-length guide to Tanzania, Philip wrote: 'I've visited most corners of Tanzania … and I have to confess that were my time in the country limited to a couple of weeks, then my first priorities would undoubtedly be the Serengeti, Ngorongoro and Zanzibar. They are very special places.' In his tenth Bradt guide Philip has been able to indulge himself – and his fans – with the detailed descriptions that these special places deserve.

Second edition June 2009   First published February 2006
Bradt Travel Guides Ltd, 23 High Street, Chalfont St Peter, Bucks SL9 9QE, England
www.bradtguides.com
Published in the USA by The Globe Pequot Press Inc, 246 Goose Lane,
PO Box 480, Guilford, Connecticut 06475-0480

Text copyright © 2009 Philip Briggs
Maps copyright © 2009 Bradt Travel Guides Ltd
Town maps content © 2009 Philip Briggs
Illustrations © 2009 Individual photographers and artists

British Library Cataloguing in Publication Data
A catalogue record for this book is available from the British Library
ISBN-13: 978 1 84162 292 7

Photographs Ariadne Van Zandbergen (AVZ), Nick Garbutt (NG)
Front cover Lion (AVZ)
Back cover Elephant (AVZ), Barabaig man (AVZ)
Title page Zebras (AVZ), Hadza woman (AVZ), Red and yellow barbet (AVZ)
Illustrations Annabel Milne
Maps Alan Whitaker, Dave Priestley (colour map)

Typeset from the author's disk by Wakewing
Printed and bound in Aegean Offset Printers, India

Acknowledgements

I received an enormous amount of assistance from within the safari industry during the course of researching both editions of this book, as well as earlier editions of the Bradt Guide to Tanzania, and I would like to express my gratitude to the many safari companies and airlines that have helped ferry us around Tanzania, and to the myriad lodges, hotels and camps that have accommodated us over the years – this would be a poor guidebook indeed were it not for the support and hospitality that has made it possible for me to explore the region so thoroughly. I am also indebted to my wife, travel companion and photographic collaborator Ariadne Van Zandbergen; to Zanzibar experts Chris McIntyre and Susan McIntyre for writing that section of the guide; to Kim Wildman for her collaboration on the sixth edition of Bradt's Tanzania guide; to my parents Roger and Kay Briggs for shuttling us to and from O R Tambo Airport so many times I've lost count; to Reggie Matemu of African Dream Safaris for his driving skills and enthusiasm over the long days on safari; and to various Bradt staffers past and present, notably Tricia Hayne, Adrian Phillips and Emma Thomson.

TANZANIA UPDATES WEBSITE

For the latest travel news about Tanzania, please visit the new interactive Bradt Tanzania update website: http://bradttanzania.wordpress.com.

Administered by *Northern Tanzania* author, Philip Briggs, this website will supplement the printed Bradt guidebook, providing a forum whereby the latest travel news can be publicised online with immediate effect.

This update website is a free service for readers of Bradt's *Northern Tanzania* – and for anybody else who cares to drop by and browse – but its success will depend greatly on the input of those selfsame readers, whose collective experience of Tanzania's tourist attractions and facilities will always be more broad and divergent than those of any individual author.

So if you have any comments, queries, grumbles, insights, news or other feedback, you're invited to post them directly on the website, or to email them to Philip at philari@hixnet.co.za.

We go back a bit, do Tanzania and I. Our first stilted encounter was back in 1986, when as a nervous novice traveller heading from Kenya to Zambia, I'd heard so much about the nightmarish black market, appalling public transport and obtuse officials that I decided to nip through Tanzania in less than a week, stopping only to catch my breath in the spectacularly rundown port of Dar es Salaam.

Two years later, I returned to Tanzania on a less intimidated footing, and followed a more adventurous route that incorporated side trips to somnambulant Tanga and the fabulous ferry ride down Lake Tanganyika. But I guess the real romance began in 1992, when I spent four unforgettable months bussing the length and breadth of Tanzania to research what would become the first dedicated guidebook to this extraordinarily diverse – and at the time vastly underrated – country.

Updating duties have recalled me to Tanzania regularly since then, and every time I'm struck afresh at how much it has blossomed over the course of our acquaintance. The Tanzania I first encountered in 1986 was seemingly stuck in inextricable economic decline, with every aspect of its infrastructure – from roads and public transport to electricity and water supplies – tottering on the verge of collapse. Meanwhile, manufacture had ground to a standstill – simply tracking down a warm beer in Dar was an exercise that could take on epic proportions.

Back then, tourist facilities, such as they existed, were barely functional. And an insane fixed exchange rate ensured that travel was dominated by a risky black market. Had anybody suggested that Tanzania might one-day rank as the most diverse, the most friendly, and arguably the best safari destination anywhere in Africa, I'd have thought they were insane.

And how wrong I'd have been… for today, almost 25 years on, that's exactly what Tanzania is!

Contents

NOTE ABOUT MAPS

Several maps use grid lines to allow easy location of sites. Map grid references are listed in square brackets after listings in the text, with page number followed by grid number, eg: [156 C3].

LIST OF MAPS

Introduction

Tanzania is a statistician's dream. Within its borders lie Africa's highest and fifth-highest mountains, the world's largest intact volcanic caldera, what is widely agreed to be Africa's greatest national park, as well as the lion's share of the continent's most expansive lake. Yet this vast east Africa country also boasts a litany of evocative place names to touch the heart of any poet: Kilimanjaro, Serengeti, Ngorongoro Crater, Olduvai Gorge, Lake Victoria, Zanzibar, the Indian Ocean, the Great Rift Valley, the Maasai Steppes ...

More remarkable still is that this enviable list of landmarks – with the exception of offshore Zanzibar – is concentrated within a mere 10% of the country's surface area abutting the border with Kenya. And here too, bookended by Lake Victoria in the west and Kilimanjaro in the east, a bloc of contiguous national parks, game reserves and other conservation areas forms what is almost certainly the most expansive safari circuit in Africa, and arguably the finest.

At the heart of this near-pristine ecosystem lies the Serengeti National Park and adjacent Ngorongoro Conservation Area, possibly the most publicised pair of game reserves in the world. And justifiably so: the Serengeti Plains host Africa's greatest wildlife spectacle, the annual migration of perhaps two million wildebeest and zebra, while also supporting remarkably dense populations of predators such as lion, cheetah, leopard and spotted hyena. The floor of the spectacular Ngorongoro Crater is if anything even more densely packed with large mammals, and is the best place in east Africa to see the endangered black rhino.

Less celebrated components of this safari circuit include Lake Manyara and Tarangire national parks, the former protecting a shallow but expansive lake on the Rift Valley floor, the latter a tract of dry acacia woodland notable for its innumerable ancient baobabs and dense elephant population. Then there is the caustic expanse of alkaline water known as Lake Natron, breeding site to millions of flamingoes. There is east Africa's most active volcano, the fiery Ol Doinyo Lengai. There is remote Lake Eyasi, its hinterland home to the region's last remaining hunter-gatherers. And dotted amid the savanna, there is jungle-covered Rubondo Island on Lake Victoria, lush montane forest rising in Arusha National Park, and sodden groundwater forest rising from the shores of lakes Duluti and Manyara. And, when the clouds lift, towering above the twin safari capitals of Arusha and Moshi stand the jagged peaks of Mount Meru and the even taller Kilimanjaro itself.

In short, northern Tanzania is the Africa you have always dreamed about: vast plains teeming with wild animals; rainforests alive with cackling birds and monkeys; Kilimanjaro's snow-capped peak rising dramatically above the flat scrubland; colourful Maasai herding their cattle alongside herds of grazing wildebeest; perfect palm-lined beaches lapped by the clear warm waters of the Indian Ocean stretching as far as the eye can see – all supported by a tourist infrastructure that has recovered from an immediate post-independence economic freefall to rank as one of the finest anywhere in Africa.

Northern Tanzania has always boasted an incomparable natural abundance. And these days it is serviced by a selection of genuinely world-class game lodges, bush camps and beach resorts. But travel isn't simply about ticking off the sights in comfort. When you spend time in a country, your feelings towards it are determined more than anything by the mood of its inhabitants. And I have no hesitation in saying that, on this level, my affection for Tanzania is greater than for any other African country I have visited. Tanzania is an oasis of peace and egalitarianism in a continent stoked up with political and tribal tensions, its social mood embodying all that I respect in African culture. Its people, as a rule, are polite and courteous, yet also warm and sincere, both among themselves and in their dealings with foreigners.

The one thing I can say with near certainty is that you will enjoy Tanzania. Whether you decide to stick to the conventional Serengeti–Ngorongoro–Zanzibar tourist circuit or strike out to the more offbeat likes of lakes Natron and Eyasi; whether you visit the mysterious rock art of Kolo or track chimps through the remote forests of Rubondo Island, you will find Tanzania to be a truly wonderful country.

KEY TO SYMBOLS

International boundary	Hotel, inn, guesthouse etc	Archaeological site
National park	Campsite	Hospital/clinic
Forest park/reserve	Resthouse or hut	Pharmacy
Tarred roads (town plans)	Bank/ATM	Theatre/cinema
Tarred roads (regional maps)	Bar	Garden
Other roads (regional maps)	Restaurant, etc	Stadium (track)
Tracks/4x4 (regional maps)	Nightclub/casino	Telephone
Railway	Post office	Woodland feature
Railway station	Internet access	Snorkel/scuba diving
Urban market	Church/cathedral	Summit (heights in metres)
Urban park	Hindu temple	Crater
Airport	Mosque	Glacier
Airstrip/emergency airstrip	Sikh temple	Escarpment (rift valley)
Pedestrian ferry & route	Museum	Footpath
Bus station	Statue/monument	Barrier/gate
Filling station/garage	Castle/fortification	Marsh
Tourist information	Important/historic building	Coral
	Shopping mall/dept store	

Other map symbols are sometimes used. These are normally explained in separate keys on individual maps.

Part One

GENERAL INFORMATION

TANZANIA AT A GLANCE

Location East Africa, between 1° and 11°45'S, and 29°20' and 40°35'E
Size 945,166km²
Climate Tropical along coast; temperate in the highlands
Status Republic
Ruling party Chama Cha Mapinduzi (CCM)
President Jakaya Kikwete
Population 40,000,000 (2009 estimate)
Life expectancy 50.71
Capital Dodoma
Largest city Dar es Salaam
Major exports Coffee, cotton, cashew nuts, sisal, tobacco, tea, diamonds, gold
Languages KiSwahili and English; over 100 regional variations
Religion 35% Muslim, 35% indigenous beliefs; 30% Christian; Zanzibar 99% Muslim
Currency Tanzanian shilling (Tsh)
Exchange rate £1 = Tsh1,988, US$1 = Tsh1,335, €1 = Tsh1,770 (May 2009)
International telephone code +255
Time GMT + 3 hours
Electrical voltage 230v (60Hz). Round or square three-pin British-style plugs
Weights and measures Metric
Flag Blue and green, with diagonal black-and-yellow stripe
Public holidays 1 January, 12 January, 5 February, 26 April, 1 May, 7 July, 8 August, 14 October, 9 December, 25–26 December. See also page 73.

Background Information

GEOGRAPHY

The bulk of east Africa is made up of a vast, flat plateau rising from a narrow coastal belt to an average height of about 1,500m. This plateau is broken dramatically by the 20-million-year-old Great Rift Valley, which cuts a trough up to 2,000m deep through the African continent from the Dead Sea to Mozambique. The main branch of the Rift Valley bisects Tanzania. A western branch of the Rift Valley forms the Tanzania–Congo border. Lakes Natron, Manyara, Eyasi and Nyasa/Malawi are all in the main rift, Lake Tanganyika lies in the western branch, and Lake Victoria lies on an elevated plateau between them.

East Africa's highest mountains (with the exception of the Ruwenzori Mountains in Uganda) are volcanic in origin, created by the same forces that caused the Rift Valley. Kilimanjaro is the most recent of these: it started to form about one million years ago, and was still growing as recently as 100,000 years ago. Mount Meru is older. Ngorongoro Crater is the collapsed caldera of a volcano that would once have been as high as Kilimanjaro is today. The only active volcano in Tanzania, Ol Doinyo Lengai, rises from the rift floor to the north of Ngorongoro.

SIZE AND LOCATION The United Republic of Tanzania came into being in 1964 when Tanganyika on the African mainland united with the offshore state of Zanzibar, the latter comprising the Indian Ocean islands of Unguja (Zanzibar) and Pemba. It lies on the east African coast between 1° and 11°45'S and 29°20' and 40°35'E, and is bordered by Kenya and Uganda to the north, Rwanda, Burundi and the Democratic Republic of the Congo to the west, and Zambia, Malawi and Mozambique to the south. The country extends over 945,166km² (364,929 square miles), making it one of the largest countries in sub-Saharan Africa, covering a greater area than Kenya and Uganda combined. To place this in a European context, Tanzania is more than four times the size of Britain, while in an American context it's about 1.5 times the size of Texas.

This book concentrates mostly on the northeast of Tanzania, running southward from the Kenyan border to a latitude of around 4°, and between 31.5° and 37.5°E, a total area of around 120,000km², about half the size of Britain.

CAPITAL Dodoma was earmarked as the future capital of Tanzania in 1973. It has subsequently displaced Dar es Salaam as the official national capital, and is also where all parliamentary sessions are held. Some government departments, however, are still based in Dar es Salaam, which remains the most important and largest city in the country, and is the site of the main international airport, many diplomatic missions to Tanzania, and most large businesses. The main commercial centre and unofficial safari capital of northern Tanzania is the town of Arusha at the southern base of Mount Meru.

ARUSHA	Jan	Feb	Mar	Apr	May	Jun	Jul	Aug	Sep	Oct	Nov	Dec
Max (°C)	29	29	28	25	22	21	20	22	25	27	28	28
Min (°C)	10	12	12	14	11	10	10	9	9	10	10	10
Rain (mm)	50	85	180	350	205	20	10	15	15	20	105	100

MOSHI	Jan	Feb	Mar	Apr	May	Jun	Jul	Aug	Sept	Oct	Nov	Dec
Max (°C)	36	35	34	30	29	29	28	30	31	32	34	34
Min (°C)	15	15	15	16	14	13	12	12	13	14	14	15
Rain (mm)	50	60	120	300	180	50	20	20	20	40	60	50

CLIMATE

The northern safari circuit as a whole is far cooler than many visitors expect. Lying at an elevation of roughly 2,300m, the Ngorongoro Crater rim in particular tends to be chilly at night and misty in the morning, and it also receives a sufficiently high annual rainfall to support a belt of montane rainforest. The crater floor and Serengeti Plains are warmer but, since they lie above the Rift Valley escarpment at elevations of well over 1,000m, they are far from being oppressively hot and can be quite chilly in the early morning and after dark. Tarangire and Lake Manyara national parks lie at lower elevations and are considerably warmer, with Tarangire in particular sometimes becoming seriously hot in the afternoon. Both areas cool down after dusk, however, and most visitors to Manyara will sleep at one of the lodges on the cool, breezy escarpment. Alpine conditions and sub-zero temperatures are characteristic of the higher slopes of Mount Meru and especially Kilimanjaro after dark.

Tanzania is too near the Equator to experience the sort of dramatic contrast between summer and winter experienced in much of Europe or North America, but the months between October and April are marginally hotter than May to September. The rainy season is generally split into the short rains or *mvuli*, over November and December, and the long rains or *masika* from late February to early May, though the exact timing of these seasons varies considerably from one year to the next.

HISTORY

Tanzania has a rich and fascinating history, but much of the detail is highly elusive. Specialist works often contradict each other to such an extent that it is difficult to tell where fact ends and speculation begins, while broader or more popular accounts are commonly riddled with obvious inaccuracies. This is partly because there are huge gaps in the known facts; partly because much of the available information is scattered in out-of-print or difficult-to-find books; and partly because once an inaccuracy gets into print it tends to spread like a virus through other written works. For whatever reason, there is not, so far as I am aware, one concise, comprehensive and reliable book about Tanzanian history in print.

The following account attempts to provide a reasonably comprehensive and readable overview of the country's history. It is, to the best of my knowledge, as accurate as the known facts will allow, but at times I have had to decide for myself the most probable truth among a mass of contradictions, and I have speculated freely where speculation seems to be the order of the day. My goals are to stimulate

MWANZA	Jan	Feb	Mar	Apr	May	Jun	Jul	Aug	Sep	Oct	Nov	Dec
Max (°C)	33	34	33	31	31	30	29	29	30	32	32	31
Min (°C)	15	16	16	16	14	13	12	13	15	16	15	15
Rain (mm)	105	110	165	160	100	20	15	25	30	45	105	120

ZANZIBAR TOWN	Jan	Feb	Mar	Apr	May	Jun	Jul	Aug	Sep	Oct	Nov	Dec
Max (°C)	32	32	33	30	29	28	27	28	29	30	31	31
Min (°C)	25	25	26	26	25	24	23	23	23	25	25	26
Rain (mm)	50	65	140	310	290	45	25	25	35	60	180	135

the visitor's interest in Tanzanian history, and to give easy access to information that would have greatly enhanced my formative travels in Tanzania. Many of the subjects touched on in this general history are given more elaborate treatment elsewhere in the book, under regional history sections or in tinted boxes.

PREHISTORY OF THE INTERIOR The part of the Rift Valley passing through Ethiopia, Kenya and northern Tanzania is almost certainly where modern human beings and their hominid ancestors evolved. Hominids are generally divided into two genera, called *Australopithecus* and *Homo*, the former extinct for at least a million years, and the latter now represented by only one species – *Homo sapiens* (modern man). The paucity of hominid fossils collected before the 1960s meant that for many years it was assumed the most common Australopithecine fossil, *A. africanus*, had evolved directly into the genus *Homo* and was thus man's oldest identifiable ancestor.

This neat linear theory of human evolution became blurred when Richard and Mary Leakey, who were excavating Olduvai Gorge in northern Tanzania, discovered that at least two Australopithecine species had existed. Carbon dating and the skeletal structure of the two species indicated that the older *A. robustus* had less in common with modern man than its more lightly built ancestor *A. africanus*, implying that the *Australopithecus* line was not ancestral to the *Homo* line at all. This hypothesis was confirmed in 1972 with the discovery of a two-million-year-old skull of a previously undescribed species *Homo habilis* at Lake Turkana in Kenya, providing conclusive evidence that *Australopithecus* and *Homo* species had lived alongside each other for at least one million years. As more fossils have come to light, including older examples of *Homo erectus* (the direct ancestor of modern humans), it has become clear that several different hominid species existed alongside each other in the Rift Valley until perhaps half a million years ago.

In 1974, Donald Johansen discovered an almost complete hominid skeleton in the Danakil region of northern Ethiopia. Named Lucy (the song 'Lucy in the Sky with Diamonds' was playing in camp shortly after the discovery), this turned out to be the fossil of a 3.5-million-year-old Australopithecine of an entirely new species dubbed *A. afarensis*. Lucy's anatomy demonstrated that bipedal hominids (or rather semi-bipedal, since the length of Lucy's arms suggest she would have been as comfortable swinging through the trees as she would have been on a morning jog) had evolved much earlier than previously assumed.

In the 1960s it was widely thought that humans and apes diverged around 20 million years ago. Recent DNA evidence has shown, however, that modern man and chimpanzees are far more closely related than previously assumed – to the

5

extent that less biased observers might place us in the same genus. It is now thought that the hominid and chimpanzee evolutionary lines diverged from a common ancestor between four and six million years ago. In 2001, it was announced that the candidate for the so-called 'missing link' between humans and chimps had been discovered in northern Ethiopia: the fossilised remains of a 5.8-million-year-old hominid that has been assigned to a new genus *Arpipithecus*, with clear affiliations to both chimpanzees and humans.

The immediate ancestor of modern man is *Homo erectus*, which appeared about 1.5 million years ago. *Homo erectus* was the first hominid to surmount the barrier of the Sahara and spread into Europe and Asia, and is credited with the discovery of fire and the first use of stone tools and recognisable speech. Although modern man, *Homo sapiens*, has been around for at least half a million years, only in the last 10,000 years have the African races recognised today more or less taken their modern form. Up until about 1000BC, east Africa was populated exclusively by hunter-gatherers with a physiology, culture and language similar to the modern-day Khoisan (or Bushmen) of southern Africa. Rock art accredited to these hunter-gatherers is found throughout east Africa, most notably in the Kondoa-Irangi region of central Tanzania.

The pastoralist and agricultural lifestyles that were pioneered in the Nile Delta in about 5000BC spread to parts of sub-Saharan Africa by 2000BC, most notably to the Cushitic-speaking people of the Ethiopian Highlands and the Bantu-speakers of west Africa. Cushitic-speakers first drifted into Tanzania in about 1000BC, closely followed by Bantu-speakers. Familiar with Iron Age technology, these migrants would have soon dominated the local hunter-gatherers. By AD1000, most of Tanzania was populated by Bantu-speakers, with Cushitic-speaking pockets in areas such as the Ngorongoro Highlands.

There is no detailed information about the Tanzanian interior prior to 1500, and even after that details are sketchy. Except for the Lake Victoria region, which supported large authoritarian kingdoms similar to those in Uganda, much of the Tanzanian interior is too dry to support large concentrations of people. In most of Tanzania, an informal system of *ntemi* chiefs emerged. The *ntemi* system, though structured, seems to have been flexible and benevolent. The chiefs were served by a council and performed a role that was as much advisory as it was authoritarian. By the 19th century there are estimated to have been more than 200 *ntemi* chiefs in western and central Tanzania, each with about 1,000 subjects.

The *ntemi* system was shattered when southern Tanzania was invaded by Ngoni exiles from what is now South Africa, refugees from the rampantly militaristic Zulu Kingdom moulded by Shaka in the early 19th century. The Ngoni entered southern Tanzania in about 1840, bringing with them the revolutionary Zulu military tactics based on horseshoe formations and a short stabbing-spear. The new arrivals attacked the resident tribes, destroying communities and leaving survivors no option but to turn to banditry. Their tactics were observed and adopted by the more astute *ntemi* chiefs, who needed to protect themselves, but had to forge larger kingdoms to do so. The situation was exacerbated by the growing presence of Arab slave traders. Tribes controlling the areas that caravan routes went through were able to extract taxes from the slavers and to find work with them as porters or organising slave raids. This situation was exploited by several chiefs, most notably Mirambo of Unyamwezi and Mkwawa of the Uhehe, charismatic leaders who dominated the interior in the late 19th century.

THE COAST TO 1800 There have been links between the Tanzanian coast and the rest of the world for millennia, but only the barest sketch is possible of events before AD1000. The ancient Egyptians believed their ancestors came from a southerly land called Punt. In about 2500BC an explorer called Sahare sailed off in search of this mysterious land. Sahare returned laden with ivory, ebony and myrrh, a booty that suggests he had landed somewhere on the east African coast. There is no suggestion that Egypt traded regularly with Punt, but they did visit it again. Interestingly, an engraving of the Queen of Punt, made after an expedition in 1493BC, shows her to have distinctly Khoisan features. The Phoenicians first explored the coast in about 600BC. According to the 1st-century *Periplus of the Ancient Sea* they traded with a town called Rhapta, which is thought to have lain upriver of a major estuary, possibly the Pangani or the Rufiji Delta.

Bantu-speakers arrived at the coast about 2,000 years ago. It seems likely they had trade links with the Roman Empire: Rhapta gets a name check in Ptolemy's 4th-century *Geography*, and a few 4th-century Roman coins have been found at the coast. The fact that the Romans knew of Kilimanjaro, and of the great lakes of the interior, raises some interesting questions. One hypothesis is that the coastal Bantu-speakers were running trade routes into the interior and that these collapsed at the same time as the Roman Empire, presumably as a result of the sudden dearth of trade partners. This notion is attractive and not implausible, but the evidence seems rather flimsy. The Romans could simply have gleaned the information from Bantu-speakers who had arrived at the coast recently enough to have some knowledge of the interior.

Historians have a clearer picture of events on the coast from about AD1000, by which time trade between the coast and the Persian Gulf was well established. The earliest known Islamic buildings on the coast, which stand on Manda Island off Kenya, have been dated to the 9th century AD. Items sold to Arab ships at this time included ivory, ebony and spices, while a variety of oriental and Arabic goods were imported for the use of wealthy traders. The dominant item of export, however, was gold, mined in the Great Zimbabwe region, transported to the coast at Sofala (in modern-day Mozambique) via the Zambezi Valley, then shipped by local traders to Mogadishu, where it was sold to the Arab boats. The common assumption that Swahili language and culture was a direct result of Arab traders mixing with local Bantu-speakers is probably inaccurate. KiSwahili is a Bantu language, and although it did spread along the coast in the 11th century, most of the Arabic words that have entered the language did so at a later date. The driving force behind a common coastal language and culture was almost certainly not the direct trade with Arabs, but rather the internal trade between Sofala and Mogadishu.

More than 30 Swahili city-states sprung up along the east Africa coast between the 13th and 15th century, a large number of which were in modern-day Tanzania. This period is known as the Shirazi era after the sultans who ruled these city-states, most of whom claimed descent from the Shiraz region of Persia. Each city-state had its own sultan; they rarely interfered in each other's business. The Islamic faith was widespread during this period, and many Arabic influences crept into coastal architecture. Cities were centred on a great mosque, normally constructed in rock and coral. It has long been assumed that the many Arabs who settled on the coast before and during the Shirazi era controlled the trade locally, but this notion has been questioned in recent years. Contemporary descriptions of the city-states suggest that Africans formed the bulk of the population. It is possible that some African traders claimed Shirazi descent in order to boost their standing both locally and with Shirazi ships.

In the mid 13th century, probably due to improvements in Arab navigation and ship construction, the centre of the gold trade moved southward from Mogadishu to the small island of Kilwa. Kilwa represented the peak of the Shirazi period. It had a population of 10,000 and operated its own mint, the first in sub-equatorial

Saharan Africa. The multi-domed mosque on Kilwa was the largest and most splendid anywhere on the coast, while another building, now known as Husuni Kubwa, was a gargantuan palace, complete with audience courts, several ornate balconies and even a swimming pool.

Although Mombasa had possibly superseded Kilwa in importance by the end of the 15th century, coastal trade was still booming. It came to an abrupt halt in 1505, however, when the Portuguese captured Mombasa, and several other coastal towns, Kilwa included, were razed. Under Portuguese control the gold trade collapsed and the coastal economy stagnated. It was dealt a further blow in the late 16th century when a mysterious tribe of cannibals called the Zimba swept up the coast to ransack several cities and eat their inhabitants before being defeated by a mixed Portuguese and local army near Malindi in modern-day Kenya.

In 1698, an Arabic naval force under the Sultan of Oman captured Fort Jesus, the Portuguese stronghold in Mombasa, paving the way for the eventual Omani takeover of the coast north of modern-day Mtwara. Rivalries between the new Omani and the old Shirazi dynasties soon surfaced, and in 1728 a group of Shirazi sultans went so far as to conspire with their old oppressors, the Portuguese, to overthrow Fort Jesus. The Omani recaptured the fort a year later. For the next 100 years an uneasy peace gripped the coast, which was nominally under Omani rule, but dominated in economic terms by the Shirazi Sultan of Mombasa.

SLAVERY AND EXPLORATION IN THE 19TH CENTURY The 19th century was a period of rapid change in Tanzania, with stronger links established between the coast and the interior as well as between east Africa and Europe. Over the first half of the 19th century, the most important figure locally was Sultan Seyyid Said of Oman, who ruled from 1804 to 1854. Prior to 1804, Britain had signed a treaty with Oman, and relations between the two powers intensified in the wake of the Napoleonic Wars, since the British did not want to see the coast fall into French hands. In 1827, Said's small but efficient navy captured Mombasa and overthrew its Shirazi sultan, to assert unambiguous control over the whole coast, with strong British support.

Having captured Mombasa, Sultan Said chose Zanzibar as his east African base, partly because of its proximity to Bagamoyo (the terminus of a caravan route to Lake Tanganyika since 1823) and partly because it was more secure against attacks from the sea or the interior than any mainland port. Said's commercial involvement with Zanzibar began in 1827 when he set up a number of clove plantations there, with scant regard for the land claims of local inhabitants. Said and his fellow Arabs had come to totally dominate all aspects of commerce on the island by 1840, the year in which the sultan permanently relocated his personal capital from Oman to Zanzibar.

The extent of the east African slave trade prior to 1827 is unclear. It certainly existed, but was never as important as the gold or ivory trade. In part, this was because the traditional centre of slave trading had always been west Africa, which was far closer than the Indian Ocean to the main markets of the Americas. In the early 19th century, however, the British curbed the slave trade out of west Africa, leaving the way open for Said and his cronies. By 1839, over 40,000 slaves were being sold from Zanzibar annually. These came from two sources: the central caravan route between Bagamoyo and the Lake Tanganyika region, and a southern route between Kilwa Kivinje and Lake Nyasa.

The effects of the slave trade on the interior were numerous. The Nyamwezi of the Tabora region and the Yua of Nyasa became very powerful by serving as porters along the caravan routes and organising slave raids and ivory hunts. Weaker tribes were devastated. Villages were ransacked; the able-bodied men and women were taken away while the young and old were left to die. Hundreds of thousands of slaves were sold in the mid 19th century. Nobody knows how many more died of disease or exhaustion between being captured and reaching the coast. Another long-term effect of the slave trade was that it formed the driving force behind the second great expansion of KiSwahili, which became the lingua franca along caravan routes.

Europeans knew little about the African interior in 1850. The first Europeans to see Kilimanjaro (Rebmann in 1848) and Mount Kenya (Krapf in 1849) were ridiculed for their reports of snow on the Equator. The Arab traders must have had an intimate knowledge of many parts of the interior that intrigued Europeans, but, oddly, at least in hindsight, nobody seems to have thought to ask them. In 1855, a German missionary, James Erhardt, produced a map of Africa, based on third-hand Arab accounts, which showed a large slug-shaped lake in the heart of the continent. Known as the Slug Map, it was wildly inaccurate, yet it did serve to fan interest in a mystery that had tickled geographers since Roman times: the source of the Nile.

The men most responsible for opening up the east African interior to Europeans were David Livingstone, Richard Burton, John Speke and, later, Henry Stanley. Livingstone, who came from a poor Scots background and left school at the age of ten, educated himself to become a doctor and a missionary. He arrived in the Cape in 1841 to work in the Kuruman Mission, but, overcome by the enormity of the task of converting Africa to Christianity, he decided he would be of greater service opening up the continent so that other missionaries could follow. Livingstone was the first European to cross the Kalahari Desert, the first to cross Africa from west to east and the first to see Victoria Falls. In 1858, Livingstone stumbled across Africa's third-largest lake, Nyasa. Later in the same year, on a quest for the source of the Nile funded by the Royal Geographical Society, Burton and Speke were the first Europeans to see Lake Tanganyika, and Speke continued north to Lake Victoria. Speke returned to the northern shore of Lake Victoria in 1863 and concluded – correctly, though it would be many years before the theory gained wide acceptance – that Ripon Falls in modern-day Uganda formed the source of the Nile.

Livingstone had ample opportunity during his wanderings to witness the slave caravans at first hand. Sickened by what he saw – the human bondage, the destruction of entire villages, and the corpses abandoned by the traders – he became an outspoken critic of the trade. He believed the only way to curb it was to open up Africa to the three Cs: Christianity, commerce and civilisation. Though not an imperialist by nature, Livingstone had seen enough of the famine and misery caused by the slavers and the Ngoni in the Nyasa area to believe the only solution was for Britain to colonise eastern Africa.

In 1867, Livingstone set off from Mikindani to spend the last six years of his life wandering between the great lakes, making notes on the slave trade and trying to settle the Nile debate. He believed the source of the Nile to be Lake Bangweulu (in northern Zambia), from which the mighty Lualaba River flowed. In 1872, while recovering from illness at Ujiji, Livingstone was met by Henry Stanley and became the recipient of perhaps the most famous words ever spoken in Africa: 'Dr Livingstone, I presume.' Livingstone died near Lake Bangweulu in 1873. His heart was removed and buried by his porters, who then carried his cured body over 1,500km via Tabora to Bagamoyo, a voyage as remarkable as any undertaken by the European explorers.

Livingstone's quest to end the slave trade met with little success during his lifetime, but his death and highly emotional funeral at Westminster Abbey seem to have acted as a catalyst. Missions were built in his name all over the Nyasa region, while industrialists such as William Mackinnon and the Muir brothers invested in schemes to open Africa to commerce (which Livingstone had always believed was the key to putting the slavers out of business).

In the year Livingstone died, John Kirk was made the British Consul in Zanzibar. Kirk had travelled with Livingstone on his 1856–62 trip to Nyasa. Deeply affected by what he saw, he had since spent years on Zanzibar hoping to find a way to end the slave trade. In 1873, the British navy blockaded the island and Kirk offered Sultan Barghash full protection against foreign powers if he banned the slave trade. Barghash agreed. The slave market was closed and an Anglican church built over it. Within ten years of Livingstone's death, the volume of slaves was a fraction of what it had been in the 1860s. Caravans reverted to ivory as their principal trade, while many of the coastal traders started up rubber and sugar plantations, which turned out to be just as lucrative as their former trade. Nevertheless, a clandestine slave trade continued on the mainland for some years – 12,000 slaves were sold at Kilwa in 1875 – and even into the 20th century, only to be fully eradicated in 1918, when Britain took control of Tanganyika.

THE PARTITIONING OF EAST AFRICA The so-called scramble for Africa was entered into with mixed motives, erratic enthusiasm and an almost total lack of premeditation by the powers involved. Britain, the major beneficiary of the scramble, already enjoyed a degree of influence on Zanzibar, one that arguably approached informal colonisation, and it was quite happy to maintain this mutually agreeable relationship unaltered. Furthermore, the British government at the time, led by Lord Salisbury, was broadly opposed to the taking of African colonies. The scramble was initiated by two events. The first, the decision of King Leopold of Belgium to colonise the Congo Basin, had little direct bearing on events in Tanzania. The partitioning of east Africa was a direct result of an about-face by the German premier, Bismarck, who had previously shown no enthusiasm for acquiring colonies and probably developed an interest in Africa in the hope of acquiring pawns to use in negotiations with Britain and France.

In 1884, a young German metaphysician called Carl Peters arrived inauspiciously on Zanzibar, then made his way to the mainland to sign a series of treaties with local chiefs. The authenticity of these treaties is questionable, but when Bismarck announced claims to a large area between the Pangani and Rufiji rivers, it was enough to set the British government into a mild panic. Britain had plans to expand the Sultanate of Zanzibar, its informal colony, to include the fertile lands around Kilimanjaro. Worse, large parts of the area claimed by Germany were already part of the sultanate. Not only was Britain morally bound to protect these, it also did not want to surrender control of Zanzibar's annual import–export turnover of two million pounds.

Despite pressure put on the British government by John Kirk, angry that his promises to Barghash would not be honoured, there was little option but to negotiate with Germany. A partition was agreed in 1886, identical to the modern border between Kenya and Tanzania. (You may read that Kilimanjaro was part of the British territory before Queen Victoria gave it to her cousin, the Kaiser, as a birthday present. This amusing story, possibly dreamed up by a Victorian satirist to reflect the arbitrariness of the scramble, is complete fabrication.) In April 1888, the Sultan of Zanzibar unwillingly agreed to lease Germany the coastal strip south of the Umba River. Germany mandated this area to Carl Peters's German East Africa Company (GEAC), which placed agencies at most of the coastal settlements north of Dar es Salaam. These agents demanded heavy taxes from traders and were encouraged to behave high-handedly in their dealings with locals.

The GEAC's honeymoon was short. Emil Zalewski, the Pangani agent, ordered the sultan's representative, the Wali, to report to him. When the Wali refused, Zalewski had him arrested and sent away on a German war boat. In September 1888, a sugar plantation owner called Abushiri Ibn Salim led an uprising against the GEAC. Except for Dar es Salaam and Bagamoyo, both protected by German war boats, the GEAC agents were either killed or driven away. A horde of 20,000 men gathered on the coast, including 6,000 Shambaa who refused to relinquish their right to claim tax from caravans passing the Usambara. In November, the mission at Dar es Salaam was attacked. Three priests were killed and the rest captured. The coast was in chaos until April 1889 when the Kaiser's troops invaded Abushiri's camp and forced him to surrender. The German government hanged Abushiri in Pangani; they withdrew the GEAC's mandate and banned Peters from ever setting foot in the area.

The 1886 agreement only created the single line of partition north of Kilimanjaro. By 1890, Germany had claimed an area north of Witu, including Lamu, and there was concern in Britain that they might try to claim the rich agricultural land around Lake Victoria, thereby surrounding Britain's territory. Undeterred by the debacle at Pangani (and with a nod and a wink from Bismarck), Carl Peters decided to force the issue. He slipped through Lamu and in May 1890, after a murderous jaunt across British territory, he signed a treaty with the King of Buganda entitling Germany to most of what is now southern Uganda. This time, however, Peters's plans were frustrated. Bismarck had resigned in March of the same year and his replacement, Von Kaprivi, wanted to maintain good relations with Salisbury's government. In any case, Henry Stanley had signed a similar treaty with the Baganda when he passed through the area in 1888 on his way from rescuing the Emin Pasha in Equatoria.

Germany had its eye on Heligoland, a small but strategic North Sea island that had been seized by Britain from Denmark in 1807. To some extent, German interest in Africa had always been related to the bargaining power it would give them in Europe. In 1890, Salisbury and Von Kaprivi knocked out the agreement that created the modern borders of mainland Tanzania (with the exception of modern-day Burundi and Rwanda, German territory until after World War I). In exchange for an island of less than 1km^2 in extent, Salisbury was guaranteed protectorateship over Zanzibar and handed the German block north of Witu, and Germany relinquished any claims it might have had to what are today Uganda and Malawi.

GERMAN EAST AFRICA The period of German rule was not a happy one. In 1891, Carl Peters was appointed governor. Peters had already proved himself an unsavoury and unsympathetic character: he boasted freely of enjoying killing Africans and, under the guise of the GEAC, his lack of diplomacy had already instigated one uprising. Furthermore, the 1890s were plagued by a series of natural disasters: a rinderpest epidemic at the start of the decade, followed by an outbreak of smallpox, and a destructive plague of locusts. A series of droughts brought famine and disease in their wake. Many previously settled areas reverted to bush, causing the spread of tsetse fly and sleeping sickness. The population of Tanganyika is thought to have decreased significantly between 1890 and 1914.

It took Peters a decade to gain full control of the colony. The main area of conflict was in the vast central plateau where, led by Mkwawa, the Hehe had become the dominant tribe. In 1891, the Hehe ambushed a German battalion led by Emil Zalewski. They killed or wounded more than half Zalewski's men, and made off with his armoury. Mkwawa fortified his capital near Iringa, but the Germans razed it in 1894. Mkwawa was forced to resort to guerrilla tactics, which he used with some success until 1898, when he shot himself rather than face capture by the Germans.

The word 'tribe' has fallen out of vogue in recent years, and I must confess that for several years I rigorously avoided the use of it in my writing. It has, I feel, rather colonial connotations, something to which I'm perhaps overly sensitive having lived most of my life in South Africa. Some African intellectuals have argued that it is derogatory, too, in so far as it is typically applied in a belittling sense to non-European cultures, where words such as 'nation' might be applied to their European equivalent.

All well and good to dispense with the word tribe, at least until you set about looking for a meaningful substitute. 'Nation', for instance, seems appropriate when applied in a historical sense to a large and cohesive centralised entity such as the Zulu or Hehe, but rather less so when you're talking about smaller and more loosely affiliated tribes. Furthermore, in any modern sense, Tanzania itself is a nation (and proud if it), just as are Britain and Germany, so that describing, for instance, the modern Chagga as a nation would feel as inaccurate and contrived as referring to, say, the Liverpudlian or Berliner nation.

It would be inaccurate, too, to refer to most African tribes in purely ethnic, cultural or linguistic terms. Any or all of these factors might come into play in shaping a tribal identity, without in any sense defining it. All modern tribes contain individuals with a diverse ethnic stock, simply through intermarriage. Most modern Ngoni, for instance, belong to that tribe through their ancestors having been assimilated into it, not because all or even any of their ancestors were necessarily members of the Ngoni band who migrated up from South Africa in the 19th century. And, for sure, when the original Bantu-speaking people moved into present-day Tanzania thousands of years ago, local people with an entirely different ethnic background would have been assimilated into the newly established communities. Likewise, the linguistic and cultural differences between two neighbouring tribes are often very slight, and may be no more significant than dialectal or other regional differences within either tribe. The Maasai and Samburu, for instance, share a long common history, are of essentially the same ethnic stock, speak the same language, and

Germany was determined to make the colony self-sufficient. Sugar and rubber were well established on parts of the coast; coffee was planted in the Kilimanjaro region, a major base for settlers; and cotton grew well around Lake Victoria. The colony's leading crop export, sisal, was grown throughout the rest of the country. In 1902, Peters decided that the southeast should be given over to cotton plantations. This was an ill-considered move: the soils were not suitable for the crop and the scheme was bound to cause great hardship. It also led to the infamous and ultimately rather tragic Maji-Maji rebellion, which proved to be perhaps the most decisive event in the colony during German rule.

Carl Peters was fired from the colonial service in 1906. He believed his African mistress had slept with his manservant, so he flogged her close to death then hanged them both. After that, the German administration introduced a series of laws protecting Africans from mistreatment. To the disgust of the settler community, it also created an incentive-based scheme for African farmers. This made it worth their while to grow cash crops and allowed the colony's exports to triple in the period leading up to World War I.

When war broke out in Europe, east Africa also became involved. In the early stages of the war, German troops entered southern Kenya to cut off the Uganda Railway. Britain responded with an abortive attempt to capture Tanga. The balance of power was roughly even until Jan Smuts led the Allied forces into German territory in 1916. By January 1918, the Allies had captured most of German East Africa and the German commander, Von Lettow, retreated into Mozambique. The war disrupted food production, and a serious famine ensued. This was particularly are culturally almost indistinguishable. Yet they perceive themselves to be distinct tribes, and are perceived as such by outsiders.

A few years ago, in mild desperation, I settled on the suitably nebulous term ethno-linguistic group as a substitute for tribe. Clumsy, ugly and verging on the meaningless it might be, but it does sound impressively authoritative, without pinning itself exclusively on ethnicity, language or culture as a defining element, and it positively oozes political correctness. It's also, well, a little bit silly! Just as Tanzanians are unselfconscious about referring to themselves as black and to *wazungu* as white, so too do they talk about their tribe without batting an eyelid. For goodness sake, at every other local hotel in Tanzania, visitors are required to fill in the 'Tribe' column in the standard-issue guesthouse visitors' book! And if it's good enough for Tanzanians, well, who am I to get precious about it?

More than that, it strikes me that even in an African nation as united as Tanzania certainly is, the role of tribe in shaping the identity of an individual has no real equivalent in most Western societies. We may love – or indeed loathe – our home town, we might fight to the death for our loved ones, we might shed tears when our football team loses or our favourite pop group disbands, but we have no equivalent to the African notion of tribe. True enough, tribalism is often cited as the scourge of modern Africa, and when taken to fanatical extremes that's a fair assessment, yet to damn it entirely would be rather like damning English football, or its supporters, because of the actions of a fanatical extreme. Tribalism is an integral part of African society, and pussyfooting around it through an overdeveloped sense of political correctness strikes me as more belittling than being open about it.

So, in case you hadn't gathered, Tanzania's 120 ethno-lingual-cultural groupings are tribes for this edition of the guide, a decision that will hold at least for so long as I'm expected to fill in my tribe – whatever that might be – every time I check into a Tanzanian guesthouse!

devastating in the Dodoma region. The country was taken over by the League of Nations. The Ruanda-Urundi District, now the states of Rwanda and Burundi, was mandated to Belgium. The rest of the country was renamed Tanganyika and mandated to Britain.

TANGANYIKA The period of British rule between the wars was largely uneventful. Tanganyika was never heavily settled by Europeans so the indigenous populace had more opportunity for self-reliance than it did in many colonies. Nevertheless, settlers were favoured in the agricultural field, as were Asians in commerce. The Land Ordinance Act of 1923 secured some land rights for Africans, otherwise they were repeatedly forced into grand but misconceived agricultural schemes. The most notorious of these, the Groundnut Scheme of 1947, was an attempt to convert the southeast of the country into a large-scale mechanised groundnut producer. The scheme failed through a complete lack of understanding of local conditions; it caused a great deal of hardship locally and cost British taxpayers millions of pounds. On a political level, a system of indirect rule based around local government encouraged African leaders to focus on local rivalries rather than national issues between the wars. A low-key national movement called the Tanganyika Africa Association (TAA) was formed in 1929, but it was as much a cultural as a political organisation.

Although it was not directly involved in World War II, Tanganyika was profoundly affected by it. The country benefited economically. It saw no combat so food production continued as normal, while international food prices rocketed.

Tanganyika's trade revenue increased sixfold between 1939 and 1949. World War II was a major force in the rise of African nationalism. Almost 100,000 Tanganyikans fought for the Allies. The exposure to other countries and cultures made it difficult for them to return home as second-class citizens. They had fought for non-racism and democracy in Europe, yet were victims of racist and non-democratic policies in their own country.

The dominant figure in the post-war politics of Tanganyika/Tanzania was Julius Nyerere (1922–99). Schooled at a mission near Lake Victoria, he went on to university in Uganda and gained a master's degree in Edinburgh. After returning to Tanzania in 1952, Nyerere became involved in the TAA. This evolved into the more political and nationalist Tanganyika African National Union (TANU) in 1954. Nyerere became the president of TANU at the age of 32. By supporting rural Africans on grass-roots issues and advocating self-government as the answer to their grievances, TANU gained a strong national following. By the mid 1950s, Britain and the UN were looking at a way of moving Tanganyika towards greater self-government, though over a far longer time-scale than TANU envisaged. The British governor, Sir Edward Twining, favoured a multi-racial system that would give equal representation to whites, blacks and Asians. TANU agreed to an election along these lines, albeit with major reservations. Twining created his own 'African party', the UTC.

In the 1958 election, there were three seats per constituency, one for each racial group. Electors could vote for all three seats, so in addition to putting forward candidates for the black seats, TANU indicated their preferred candidates in the white and Asian seats. Candidates backed by TANU won 67% of the vote; the UTC did not win a single seat. Twining's successor, Sir Richard Turnball, rewarded TANU by scrapping the multi-racial system in favour of open elections. In the democratic election of 1960, TANU won all but one seat. In May 1961, Tanganyika attained self-government and Nyerere was made prime minister. Tanganyika attained full independence on 9 December 1961. Not one life had been taken in the process. Britain granted Zanzibar full independence in December 1963. A month later the Arab government was toppled and in April 1964 the two countries combined to form Tanzania.

TANZANIA At the very core of Tanzania's post-independence achievements and failures lies the figure of Julius Nyerere, who ruled Tanzania until his retirement in 1985. In his own country, where he remains highly respected, Nyerere is called *Mwalimu* – the teacher. In the West, he is a controversial figure, often portrayed as a dangerous socialist who irreparably damaged his country. This image of Nyerere doesn't bear scrutiny. He made mistakes and was intolerant of criticism – at one point Tanzania had more political prisoners than South Africa – but he is also one of the few genuine statesmen to have emerged from Africa, a force for positive change both in his own country and in a wider African context.

In 1962, TANU came into power with little policy other than their attained goal of independence. Tanganyika was the poorest and least economically developed country in east Africa, and one of the poorest in the world. Nyerere's first concerns were to better the lot of rural Africans and to prevent the creation of a money-grabbing elite. The country was made a one-party state, but had an election system which, by African standards, was relatively democratic. Tanzania pursued a policy of non-alignment, but the government's socialist policies and Nyerere's outspoken views alienated most Western leaders. Close bonds were formed with socialist powers, most significantly China, who built the Tanzam Railway (completed in 1975).

Relations with Britain soured in 1965. Nyerere condemned the British government's tacit acceptance of the Unilateral Declaration of Independence

(UDI) in Rhodesia. In return, Britain cut off all aid to Tanzania. Nyerere also gave considerable vocal support to disenfranchised Africans in South Africa, Mozambique and Angola. The ANC and Frelimo both operated from Tanzania in the 1960s.

Nyerere's international concerns were not confined to white supremacism. In 1975, Tanzania pulled out of an Organisation of African Unity (OAU) conference in Idi Amin's Uganda saying: 'The refusal to protest against African crimes against Africans is bad enough … but … by meeting in Kampala … the OAU are giving respectability to one of the most murderous regimes in Africa.' Tanzania gave refuge to several Ugandans, including the former president Milton Obote and the current president Yoweri Museveni. Amin occupied part of northwest Tanzania in October 1978, and bombed Bukoba and Musoma. In 1979, Tanzania retaliated by invading Uganda and toppling Amin. Other African leaders condemned Tanzania for this action, despite Amin having been the initial aggressor. Ousting Amin drained Tanzania's financial resources, but it never received any financial compensation, either from the West, or from any other African country.

At the time of independence, most rural Tanzanians lived in scattered communities. This made it difficult for the government to provide such amenities as clinics and schools and to organise a productive agricultural scheme. In 1967, Nyerere embarked on a policy he called villagisation. Rural people were encouraged to form *Ujamaa* (familyhood) villages and collective farms. The scheme met with some small-scale success in the mid 1970s, so in 1975 Nyerere decided to forcibly re-settle people who had not yet formed villages. By the end of the year 65% of rural Tanzanians lived in *Ujamaa* villages. In many areas, however, water supplies were inadequate to support a village. The resultant mess, exacerbated by one of Tanzania's regular droughts, ended further villagisation. *Ujamaa* is often considered to have been an unmitigated disaster. It did not achieve what it was meant to, but it did help the government improve education and health care. Most reliable sources claim it did little long-term damage to agricultural productivity.

By the late 1970s Tanzania's economy was a mess. There were several contributory factors: drought, *Ujamaa*, rising fuel prices, the border closure with Kenya (to prevent Kenyan operators from dominating the Tanzanian safari industry), lack of foreign aid, bureaucracy and corruption in state-run institutions, and the cost of the Uganda episode. After his re-election in 1980 Nyerere announced he would retire at the end of that five-year term. In 1985, Ali Hassan Mwinyi succeeded Nyerere as prime minister. Nyerere remained chairman of the Chama Cha Mapinduzi (CCM), the party formed when TANU merged with the Zanzibari ASP in 1975, until 1990.

Under President Mwinyi, Tanzania moved away from socialism. In June 1986, in alliance with the IMF, a three-year Economic Recovery Plan was implemented. This included freeing up the exchange rate and encouraging private enterprise. Since then Tanzania has achieved an annual growth rate of around 4% (in real terms). Many locals complain that the only result they have seen is greater inflation. In 1990 attempts were made to rout corruption from the civil service, with surprisingly positive results. The first multi-party election took place in October 1995. The CCM was returned to power with a majority of around 75% under the leadership of Benjamin Mpaka, who stood down in December 2005 following the country's third multi-party election. This, once again, was won by the CCM, which polled more than 80% of the 11.3 million votes under its new leader, Jakaya Kikwete. The next election is scheduled for 2010, and it seems likely that Kikwete – who will turn 60 in the same year – will stand for a second term.

Now well into the fifth decade of the post-independence era, Africa as a whole still suffers from the tribal divisions it had had at the outset. Tanzania is a striking

Region	Capital	Population (millions)	Area (km²)	People (per km²)
Dar es Salaam	Dar es Salaam	2.6	1,393	1,870
Zanzibar & Pemba	Zanzibar	1.0	2,460	406
Mwanza	Mwanza	3.0	19,592	153
Kilimanjaro	Moshi	1.8	13,309	135
Mtwara	Mtwara	1.4	16,707	83
Mara	Musoma	1.5	19,566	76
Tanga	Tanga	2.0	26,808	75
Kagera	Bukoba	2.1	28,388	74
Shinyanga	Shinyanga	2.8	50,781	55
Dodoma	Dodoma	2.0	41,311	48
Mbeya	Mbeya	2.4	60,350	40
Kigoma	Kigoma	1.4	37,037	38
Iringa	Iringa	1.9	56,864	33
Pwani	Bagamoyo	1.0	32,407	31
Morogoro	Morogoro	1.9	70,799	29
Arusha	Arusha	2.1	82,306	25
Singida	Singida	1.2	49,341	24
Tabora	Tabora	1.7	76,151	22
Ruvuma	Songea	1.2	63,498	18
Rukwa	Sumbawanga	1.1	68,635	16
Lindi	Lindi	1.0	66,046	15

exception to this rule, and hindsight demonstrates that Nyerere's greatest achievement was the tremendous sense of national unity he created by making KiSwahili the national language, by banning tribal leaders, by forcing government officials to work away from the area in which they grew up, and by his own example. True, Tanzania remains one of the world's least-developed countries, but most sources agree that the economic situation of the average Tanzanian has improved greatly since independence, with unusually high growth shown over the past ten years, as have adult literacy rates and health care. Tanzania's remarkable political stability and its increasingly pragmatic economic policies form a positive basis for future growth.

Administrative regions Tanzania is divided into 21 administrative regions, each with a local administrative capital. These are listed in the box above in descending order of population density based on the 2002 national census.

ECONOMY

Immediately after independence, Tanzania became one of the most dedicated socialist states in Africa, and its economy suffered badly as a result of a sequence of well-intentioned but misconceived or poorly managed economic policies. By the mid 1980s, Tanzania ranked among the five poorest countries in the world. The subsequent swing towards a free-market economy, making the country more attractive to investors, has resulted in dramatic improvement, and Tanzania today – while hardly wealthy – has managed to ascend out of the list of the world's 20 poorest countries. The mainstay of the economy is agriculture, and most rural Tanzanians are subsistence farmers who might also grow a few crops for sale. The country's major exports are traditionally coffee, cotton, cashew nuts, sisal, tobacco, tea and diamonds, but gold – Tanzania is now the third-largest gold producer in Africa after South Africa and Ghana – and a unique gem called tanzanite are of increasing importance to the export economy. Zanzibar and Pemba are important

TRADITIONAL MUSICAL INSTRUMENTS

Tanzania's tribal diversity has meant that a vast array of very different – and, for that matter, very similar – traditional musical instruments are employed around the country under a bemusing number of local names. Broadly speaking, however, all but a handful of these variants can be placed in one of five distinct categories that conform to the classes of musical instrument used in Europe and the rest of the world.

The traditional music of many Tanzanian cultures is given its melodic drive by a marimba (also called a mbira), a type of instrument that is unique to Africa but could be regarded as a more percussive variant of the familiar keyboard instruments. The basic design of all marimbas consists of a number of metal or wooden keys whose sound is amplified by a hollow resonating box. Marimbas vary greatly in size from one region to the next. Popular with several pastoralist tribes of the Rift Valley and environs are small hand-held boxes with six to ten metal keys that are plucked by the musician. In other areas, organ-sized instruments with 50 or more keys are placed on the ground and beaten with sticks, like drums. The Gogo of the Dodoma region are famed for their marimba orchestras consisting of several instruments that beat out a complex interweave of melodies and rhythms.

The most purely melodic of Tanzanian instruments is the zeze, the local equivalent to the guitar or fiddle, used throughout the country under a variety of names. The basic zeze design consists of between one and five strings running along a wooden neck that terminates in an open resonating gourd. The musician rubs a bow fiddle-like across the strings, while manipulating their tone with the fingers of his other hand, generally without any other instrumental accompaniment, but sometimes as part of an orchestra. Less widespread stringed instruments include the zither-like enanga of the Lake Tanganyika region and similar bango and kinubi of the coast, all of which are plucked like harps rather than stroked with a bow, to produce more defined melodic lines than the zeze.

The most important percussive instrument in African music is the drum, of which numerous local variations are found. Almost identical in structure and role to their European equivalent, most African drums are made by tightly stretching a membrane of animal hide across a section of hollowed tree trunk. A common and widespread type of drum, which is known in most areas as a msondo and is often reserved for important rituals, can be up to 1m tall and is held between the drummer's legs.

Percussive backing is also often provided by a variety of instruments known technically as idiophones. Traditionally, these might include the maraca-like manyanga, a shaker made by filling a gourd with dry seeds, as well as metal bells and bamboo scrapers. A modern variant on the above is the chupa: a glass cold-drink bottle scraped with a piece of tin or a stick.

Finally, in certain areas, horned instruments are also used, often to supply a fanfare at ceremonial occasions. These generally consist of a modified animal horn with a blowing hole cut into its side, through which the musician manipulates the pitch using different mouth movements.

Readers with an interest in traditional music are pointed towards an excellent but difficult-to-locate booklet, The Traditional Musical Instruments of Tanzania, written by Lewis and Makala (Music Conservatoire of Tanzania, 1990), and the primary source of this boxed text.

clove producers. The tourist industry that practically collapsed in the mid 1980s has grown steadily during the last decade or so. Over the past few years, more than 500,000 visitors annually have generated up to US$750 million annually in foreign revenue, a fivefold increase since 1990.

PEOPLE

The total population of Tanzania was estimated at around 40 million in 2009. The most densely populated rural areas tend to be the highlands, especially those around Lake Nyasa and Mount Kilimanjaro, and the coast. The country's largest city is Dar es Salaam, whose population, estimated at 2.5-3 million in 2009, exceeds that of the country's next ten largest towns combined. The only northern Tanzanian towns with a population in excess of 100,000 are Arusha, Moshi and Mwanza.

There are roughly 120 tribes in Tanzania, each speaking their own language, and none of which exceeds 10% of the country's total population. The most numerically significant tribes are the Sukuma of Lake Victoria, Haya of northwest Tanzania, Chagga of Kilimanjaro, Nyamwezi of Tabora, Makonde of the Mozambique border area, Hehe of Iringa and Gogo of Dodoma.

LANGUAGE

More than 100 different languages are spoken across Tanzania, but the official languages are KiSwahili and English. Until recently, very little English was spoken outside of the larger towns, but this is changing rapidly and visitors can be confident that almost anybody involved in the tourist industry will speak passable English. KiSwahili, indigenous to the coast, spread through the region along the 19th-century caravan routes, and is today spoken as a second language by most Tanzanians.

NATURAL HISTORY AND CONSERVATION

There are plenty of good reasons to visit northern Tanzania – the beautiful coastline, fascinating history and magnificent scenery – but for most people one attraction overwhelms all others, and that is the wildlife. Tanzania is Africa's prime

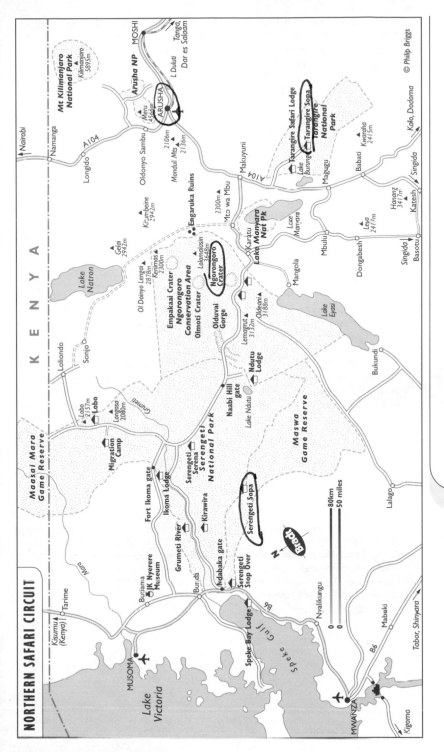

NORTHERN SAFARI CIRCUIT

K E N Y A

© Philip Briggs

game-viewing country, best known for the deservedly well-publicised Serengeti and Ngorongoro Crater, highlights in a mosaic of national parks and other conservation areas that cover almost 25% of the country and protect an estimated 20% of Africa's large mammals.

The phrase Eastern Arc was coined by Dr Jon Lovett as recently as the mid 1980s to encompass a string of 13 ancient east African mountain ranges which, despite being physically isolated from each other, share a very similar geomorphology and ecology. Aside from the Taita Hills in southern Kenya, the crystalline ranges of the Eastern Arc all lie within eastern Tanzania, where – as their name implies – they form a rough crescent running from Pare in the north to Udzungwa and Mahenge in the south. The oldest mountains in east Africa, they formed at least 100 million years ago, along a fault running to the east of the more geologically recent Rift Valley.

The extensive rainforests of the Eastern Arc date back more than 30 million years to a time when Africa was part of a much larger landmass known as Gondwanaland. And, during drier and colder climatic periods when most African rainforests retreated, the Eastern Arc forests flourished thanks to a continuous westerly wind that blew in moisture from the Indian Ocean. It was during one such phase, about ten million years ago, that the Eastern Arc forests became isolated from the lowland rainforests of western and central Africa. More recently, probably, each of the individual forested ranges of the Eastern Arc became a discrete geographical entity, transforming the Eastern Arc into an archipelago of forested islands jutting out from an ocean of low-lying savanna.

Following a pattern characteristic of true islands, the isolated, ancient forests of the Eastern Arc host an assemblage of endemic taxa with few peers anywhere on the planet. The best known of these endemics is the African violet *Saintpaulia ionantha*, first collected in 1892 by Baron Walter von Saint Paul Illaire and now one of the world's most popular perennial pot plants, generating a global trade worth tens of millions of US dollars. In the two Usambara ranges alone, more than 2,850 plant species have been identified, a list that includes 680 types of tree, a greater tally than that of North America and Europe combined. At least 16 plant genera and 75 vertebrate species – including 10 birds and 12 mammals – are endemic to the forests of the Eastern Arc, as are literally thousands of invertebrates. Little wonder, then, that the Eastern Arc Mountains have recently been classified as one of the world's 20 most important biodiversity hotspots, and are frequently referred to as the Galapagos of Africa.

The Eastern Arc endemics fall into two broad categories: old endemics that show little divergence from relict evolutionary lineages, and new endemics representing recently evolved lineages. A clear example of a 'living fossil' in the former category is the giant elephant shrew of the suborder Rhynchocyonidae, represented by four species almost identical in structure to more widespread 20-million-year-old fossils of their ancestors (incredibly, the largest of these four species, endemic to the Udzungwa Mountains, remained unknown to science until it was photographed in 2005). The origins of new endemics are more variable. Some, such as the African violets, probably evolved from an ancestral stock blown across the ocean from Madagascar in a freak cyclone. Others, including many of the birds and flying insects, are essentially locally adapted variants on similar species found in neighbouring savannas or in other forests in east Africa. And four of the endemic birds show sufficient affiliations to Asian species to suggest they may have arrived in Africa at a time when moister coastal vegetation formed a passage around the Arabian peninsula.

The forests of the Eastern Arc Mountains vary greatly in their extent. The natural forest on the vast Udzungwa range extends over some 2,000km², and has yielded previously undescribed bird species and three new monkey taxa in recent years. By contrast,

HABITATS AND VEGETATION The bulk of Tanzania is covered in open grassland, savanna (lightly wooded grassland) and woodland. The Serengeti Plains are an archetypal African savanna: grassland interspersed with trees of the acacia family – which are typically quite short, lightly foliated and thorny. Many have a flat-topped

Kenya's Taita Hills retain a mere 6km² of forest. After Udzungwa, the most significant ranges in terms of biodiversity are the East Usambara and Uluguru, though the Nguru and Rubeho mountains remain relatively unexplored in scientific terms.

The Eastern Arc forests are of great interest to birdwatchers as the core of the so-called Tanzania–Malawi Mountains Endemic Bird Area (EBA). Of 37 described range-restricted bird species endemic to this EBA, all but five occur in Tanzania, and half are confined to the country. In terms of avian diversity, the Udzungwa Mountains are by far the most significant range in the EBA, but Amani Nature Reserve in the Eastern Usambara has the edge over Udzungwa in terms of ease of access to prime birding areas and affordable facilities. The individual distribution patterns of several range-restricted bird species provides clear evidence of the mountains' pseudo-island ecology, with several species widespread on one particular range but absent from other apparently suitable ones. The Usambara akalat, for instance, is confined to the Western Usambara, while Loveridge's sunbird and the Uluguru bush-shrike are unique to the Uluguru Mountains. The most remarkable distribution pattern, however, is that of the long-billed tailorbird or apalis, a poorly known forest-fringe species confined to two ranges situated an incredible 2,000km apart – the Eastern Usambara in northern Tanzania and Mount Namuli in central Mozambique. Stranger still is the case of the Udzungwa partridge: this evolutionary relict, discovered as recently as 1991 and known only from the Udzungwa and Rubeho mountains, evidently has stronger genetic affiliations to the Asian hill partridges than to any other African bird!

For nature lovers, the most accessible and rewarding Eastern Arc add-on to a northern Tanzanian safari is the underrated Amani Nature Reserve in the Eastern Usambara, whose bird checklist of 340 species includes 12 that are globally threatened and 19 endemic to the Eastern Arc Mountains or the east African coastal biome. Formally opened in 1997, this reserve, centred on a former German agricultural research station, protects almost 10,000ha of relatively undisturbed forest. Some of the most productive birdwatching is to be had around Amani village. One of the more conspicuous and alluring residents here is the green-headed oriole, while the flowering gardens attract three of four range-restricted sunbirds associated with the Eastern Usambara, and the rare long-billed tailorbird has been discovered breeding at two sites within the village. In addition to the birds, black-and-white colobus and blue monkey are often seen around the village, as is the outsized Zanj elephant shrew.

Nine walking trails ranging from 3–12km in length are also on offer. The 10km Konkoro Trail, which can be covered on foot or in a vehicle, is good for African violets, while the shorter Turaco and Mbamole hill trails are recommended for montane forest birds such as Usambara eagle owl, southern banded snake eagle, silvery-cheeked hornbill, half-collared kingfisher, African green ibis, Fischer's turaco, African broadbill, East Coast akalat, white-chested alethe, Kenrick's and Waller's starlings, and several forest flycatchers.

Amani lies about six to seven hours' drive from Moshi or Arusha via Muheza on the Tanga road. Entrance to Amani Nature Reserve costs US$30 per person, which – unlike national park fees – is a one-off payment no matter how long you spend in the reserve. The daily guide fee is US$8 per person. Twenty per cent of all fees paid will go towards the development of local communities. Basic but comfortable accommodation is available for around US$5 at two guesthouses run by the nature reserve, as are meals. Camping is permitted too. For more details contact the project management (✆ 053 264 6907; ℮ usambara@twiga.com).

The plight of the mountain gorilla, rhinoceros and elephant has made African conservation a household concern in the West. Despite this, few Westerners have any grasp of the issues. What follows is certainly opinionated, and probably simplistic, but does attempt to clarify the root problem as I see it. You may well disagree...

We often tend to romanticise Africa. An incredible amount of drivel was written about it during the colonial era, and this dominates our perception of the continent. The macho blustering of Hemingway and exaggerated accounts of the Great White Hunters vie in our heads with the nostalgic meandering of *Out of Africa*. For the West, Africa represents wildness and space, vast horizons and shimmering red sunsets: powerful images we do not want shattered by the realities of the 21st century.

It was, of course, European settlers who destroyed the Africa they mythologised. The vast herds that had existed alongside people for millennia were decimated during the colonial era. By the early 1960s, when most of Africa became independent, these herds were by and large restricted to conservation areas that had been set aside by the colonial governments to preserve something of the Africa they loved. Their vision of unspoilt Africa did not include people: when an area was declared a national park, the people who lived there were moved to the fringes. Local people had both hunted and conserved the animals for centuries; now hunting was forbidden and they needed new sources of food.

Areas suitable for national parks are not normally densely populated, since they tend to be relatively infertile. Even if someone succeeded in growing crops on the fringe of an unfenced park, one hungry or angry elephant could wipe out their efforts in the space of minutes. This created a circle of poverty around many game reserves, a scenario that ultimately worked in the interests of ivory and rhino horn traders. People living on the verges of reserves would happily kill an elephant or rhinoceros for what was a fraction of the market price, but a fortune in local terms.

As you are no doubt aware, rhinoceros are close to extinction in most African countries. In Tanzania, there are 20 left in the Ngorongoro Conservation Area and at best a couple of hundred in the Selous. Africa's elephant population is now thought to number about half a million. Tanzania is home to a significant number of these. There are an estimated 60,000 animals in the Selous alone, and probably a similar number scattered across other reserves.

In the late 1980s the elephant situation seemed hopeless. In some reserves, herds had been poached to within 20% of their size ten years previously. In the Selous, up to 20,000 were killed in a two-year period. Most African governments lacked the finance to arrest this process; in some cases they also lacked the will, with strong rumours of

appearance. An atypical acacia, the yellow fever tree, is one of Africa's most striking trees. It is relatively large, has yellow bark and is often associated with water. Combretum is another family of trees typical of many savanna habitats. The dry savanna of central Tanzania can be so barren during the dry season that it resembles semi-desert.

Woodland differs from forest in lacking an interlocking canopy. The most extensive woodland in Tanzania is in the *miombo* belt, which stretches from southern and western Tanzania to Zimbabwe. *Miombo* woodland typically grows on infertile soil, and is dominated by broad-leafed brachystegia trees. You may come across the term mixed woodland: this refers to woodland with a mix of brachystegia, acacia and other species. Many woodland habitats are characterised by an abundance of baobab trees.

True closed canopy forest covers less than 1% of Tanzania's surface area, but it is the country's most ecologically diverse habitat, represented along the northern circuit by the montane forests of Kilimanjaro, Meru, Ngorongoro Crater rim corruption and the involvement of government officials. Anti-poaching units armed with old-fashioned rifles were fighting bands of poachers armed with AK47s, and losing. In 1988, I was driven through a part of Kenya's Tsavo East National Park, one of the worst-hit reserves, where less than a quarter of its 1972 population of 17,000 animals were left. I saw more elephant corpses than I did live animals; those elephants I did see ran off in terror at the approach of a vehicle.

A moratorium on the world ivory trade was implemented in 1989. There is a wide consensus that this ban has worked in east Africa: elephant numbers increased and, without a market, poaching virtually stopped. Southern African countries want this moratorium to be lifted. Herds in South Africa, Botswana and Zimbabwe are stable and growing, and since elephants are extremely destructive when overpopulated, excess animals were until recently culled. This issue was greatly misrepresented in Britain at least, where emotive and irresponsible newspaper columns and television programmes equated culling with murder. Obviously culling is not the ideal solution, but it is difficult to see a practical alternative when populations become unnaturally high, an almost inevitable reality in the fenced reserves of southern Africa. (The suggestion most often put forward is that the animals could be moved. To the Cotswolds? Or somewhere else where African crops can be trampled?)

It has become evident to many conservationists that a complete change of approach is the only chance for the long-term survival of Africa's large animals. Local people must be included in the process. If they benefit from the reserves, they will side with conservationists; if they do not they will side with the poachers. Attempts must be made to ensure that locals benefit from money raised by the reserves, that they are given meat from culled animals, and that, wherever possible, work is found for them within the reserve. In an increasingly densely populated continent, reserves can only justify their existence if they create local wealth.

Africa does not belong to the West. I see no reason why Africans should conserve their wildlife for the sake of Western aesthetics, unless they perceive it to be in their interest to do so. If some gun-happy soul with a Hemingway fixation is idiot enough to pay enough money to support a village for a year in order that he can hunt an elephant, good. If the meat from an elephant can feed a village for a week, and the money from the sale of the ivory be put back into conservation, good. If we Westerners can drop the idealism and allow Africans to both conserve their wildlife and feed their bellies, only then is there a chance that our grandchildren will be able to see the Africa we want them to.

and various lesser mountains, as well as the groundwater forests around Lake Duluti and in Lake Manyara. Other interesting but localised vegetation types are mangrove swamps (common along the coast, particularly around Kilwa) and the heath and moorland found on the higher slopes of Kilimanjaro and Meru.

MAIN CONSERVATION AREAS Almost half of Tanzania's national parks are located in northern Tanzania, from the big names of the Serengeti National Park and Ngorongoro Conservation Area to several less well-known parks and reserves. Here, too, is the dominant grandeur of Mount Kilimanjaro National Park. All the national parks receive detailed coverage in the main part of the guide, as do any other conservation areas that are reasonably accessible, and some that are not. The following potted descriptions are intended to provide an introductory overview to the north's most significant and accessible conservation areas, not to replicate the more extended descriptions in the main body of the guide. The list starts with the Serengeti and runs roughly clockwise from there.

Serengeti National Park This world-famous national park, notable for its million-strong migratory herds of wildebeest and zebra, is the linchpin of the popular northern safari circuit. It also harbours large numbers of predators; it is not unusual to see lion, leopard, cheetah, spotted hyena, bat-eared fox and a couple of jackal and mongoose species in the same day. The Serengeti is so vast that any sense of overcrowding in this popular park is restricted to the Seronera area in the southeast. The northern and western Serengeti have more of a wilderness feel, with surprisingly little tourist traffic around, except when the migration passes through them. Numerous lodges and campsites are dotted around the park.

Ngorongoro Conservation Area This dual-use conservation area – inhabited by the Maasai and their cattle as well as wildlife – protects a large part of Ngorongoro Highlands, including the magnificent Ngorongoro Crater, the largest intact caldera in the world. Ngorongoro Crater supports the world's densest population of lions

ANIMAL TAXONOMY

In this book, I've made widespread use of taxonomic terms such as genus, species and race. Some readers may not be familiar with these terms, so a brief explanation follows.

Taxonomy is the branch of biology concerned with classifying living organisms. It uses a hierarchical system to represent the relationships between different animals. At the top of the hierarchy are kingdoms, phyla, subphyla and classes. All vertebrates belong to the animal kingdom, phylum Chordata, subphylum Vertebrata. There are five vertebrate classes: Mammalia (mammals), Aves (birds), Reptilia (reptiles), Amphibia (amphibians) and Pisces (fish). Within any class, several orders might be divided in turn into families and, depending on the complexity of the order and family, various suborders and subfamilies. All baboons, for instance, belong to the Primate order, suborder Catarrhini (monkeys and apes), family Cercopithecoidea (Old World monkeys) and subfamily Cercopithecidae (cheek-pouch monkeys, ie: guenons, baboons and mangabeys).

Taxonomists accord to every living organism a Latin binomial (two-part name) indicating its genus (plural genera) and species. Thus the savanna baboon *Papio cyenephalus* and hamadrayas baboon *Papio hamadrayas* are different species of the genus *Papio*. Some species are further divided into races or subspecies. For instance, taxonomists recognise four races of savanna baboon: yellow baboon, olive baboon, chacma baboon and Guinea baboon. A race is indicated by a trinomial (three-part name), for instance *Papio cyenephalus cyenephalus* for the yellow baboon and *Papio cyenephalus anubis* for the olive baboon. The identical specific and racial designation of *cyenephalus* for the yellow baboon make it the nominate race – a label that has no significance other than that it would most probably have been the first race of that species to be described by taxonomists.

Taxonomic constructs are designed to approximate the real genetic and evolutionary relationships between various living creatures, and on the whole they succeed. But equally the science exists to help humans understand a reality that is likely to be more complex and less absolute than any conceptual structure used to contain it. This is particularly the case with speciation – the evolution of two or more distinct species from a common ancestor – a gradual process that might occur over many thousands of generations and lack for any absolute landmarks.

Simplistically, the process of speciation begins when a single population splits into two mutually exclusive breeding units. This can happen as a result of geographic isolation (for instance mountain and lowland gorillas), habitat differences (forest and savanna elephants) or varied migratory patterns (the six races of yellow wagtail intermingle as non-breeding migrants to Africa during the northern winter, but they all have discrete Palaearctic breeding grounds). Whatever the reason, the two breeding communities will share an and spotted hyena. It is the last place in Tanzania where black rhinoceros are reasonably easy to see, and is also notable for its magnificent old tuskers, a rare sight today elsewhere in Tanzania. The Ngorongoro Crater is heavily touristed, which does detract from many people's visit. A number of other remote natural landmarks in the Ngorongoro Highlands can be visited by vehicle or on foot. Numerous lodges and campsites are found on the crater rim.

Lake Manyara National Park The most low-key of the triad of reserves situated between Lake Victoria and the main Arusha–Dodoma Road, Lake Manyara has a fabulous situation at the base of the Rift Valley and is a worthy addition to any itinerary taking in the Serengeti and Ngorongoro. The small park's once-famous elephant population suffered badly at the hands of poachers in the 1980s, but it is well on the way to recovery today, and the elephants are perhaps the least jittery in Tanzania. Manyara is also renowned for its tree-climbing

identical gene pool when first they split, but as generations pass they will accumulate a number of small genetic differences and eventually marked racial characteristics. Given long enough, the two populations might even deviate to the point where they wouldn't or couldn't interbreed, even if the barrier that originally divided them was removed.

The taxonomic distinction between a full species and a subspecies or race of that species rests not on how similar the two taxa are in appearance or habit, but on the final point above. Should it be known that two distinct taxa freely interbreed and produce fertile hybrids where their ranges overlap, or it is believed that they would in the event that their ranges did overlap, then they are classified as races of the same species. If not, they are regarded as full species. The six races of yellow wagtail referred to above are all very different in appearance, far more so, for instance, than the several dozen warbler species of the genus *Cisticola*, but clearly they are able to interbreed, and they must thus be regarded as belonging to the same species. And while this may seem a strange distinction on the face of things, it does make sense when you recall that humans rely mostly on visual recognition, whereas many other creatures are more dependent on other senses. Those pesky cisticolas all look much the same to human observers, but each species has a highly distinctive call and in some cases a display flight that would preclude crossbreeding whether or not it is genetically possible.

The gradual nature of speciation creates grey areas that no arbitrary distinction can cover – at any given moment in time there might exist separate breeding populations of a certain species that have not yet evolved distinct racial characters, or distinct races that are on their way to becoming full species. Furthermore, where no conclusive evidence exists, some taxonomists tend to be habitual 'lumpers' and others eager 'splitters' – respectively inclined to designate any controversial taxon racial or full specific status. For this reason, various field guides often differ in their designation of controversial taxa.

Among African mammals, this is particularly the case with primates, where in some cases up to 20 described taxa are sometimes lumped together as one species and sometimes split into several specific clusters of similar races. The savanna baboon is a case in point. The four races are known to interbreed where their ranges overlap. But they are also all very distinctive in appearance, and several field guides now classify them as different species, so that the olive baboon, for instance, is designated *Papio anubis* as opposed to *Papio cynocephalus anubis*. Such ambiguities can be a source of genuine frustration, particularly for birdwatchers obsessed with ticking 'new' species, but they also serve as a valid reminder that the natural world is and will always be a more complex, mysterious and dynamic entity than any taxonomic construct designed to label it.

lions, and the large flocks of flamingo that sometimes congregate on the lake. A recent development at Manyara is a number of adventure activities – canoeing, mountain biking, walking and abseiling – run out of the Serena Hotel. There is one lodge in the park, a lovely campsite at the gate, and accommodation to suit all budgets within 5km of the gate.

Tarangire National Park Lying to the east of Lake Manyara, this excellent national park is included on many northern-circuit itineraries. It preserves a classic piece of dry African woodland studded with plentiful baobabs and transected by the perennial Tarangire River. Best known for the prodigious elephant herds that congregate along the river in the dry season, Tarangire also harbours a rich birdlife and such localised antelope species as fringe-eared oryx and gerenuk. Several lodges are to be found in and around the park.

Arusha National Park This underrated but eminently accessible park lies an hour's drive from Arusha town, the northern 'safari capital', and is best known perhaps for protecting Mount Meru, Africa's fifth-tallest peak. Other attractive features include the Momella Lakes, which host large concentrations of waterbirds including flamingoes, and Ngurdoto Crater, a smaller version of Ngorongoro whose jungle-clad slopes harbour a variety of monkeys and forest birds. It can be visited as a day trip from Arusha, but there is a remote lodge on the northern border and a budget campsite on the southern one.

Mount Kilimanjaro National Park Encompassing the two peaks and higher slopes of Africa's highest mountain, Kilimanjaro is of all the country's national parks the least oriented towards game viewing. Thousands of tourists climb it every year, however, to stand on the snow-capped pinnacle of Africa, and to experience the haunting and somewhat other-worldly Afro-montane moorland habitat of the upper slopes. Accommodation within the park is limited to simple mountain huts and campsites, but several lodges lie outside the boundary.

Amani Nature Reserve This reserve in the Eastern Usambara Mountains, inland of Tanga, protects some of the most important montane forest in Tanzania and a wealth of rare and endemic birds, mammals, butterflies and other creatures. Comfortable and inexpensive accommodation is available within the nature reserve, and a good range of walking trails will keep hikers and birdwatchers busy for days. It's easily accessible on public transport, too.

Saadani National Park This proposed national park (likely to be gazetted very soon) is the only savanna reserve in east Africa to be lapped by the shores of the Indian Ocean. As things stand, it is more accurately characterised as a beach retreat with some wildlife around than as a full-blown safari destination. Boat and walking safaris are a bonus, peace and quiet a given, and the beach really is lovely. One excellent lodge lies on the beach.

Jozani Forest Reserve The main stronghold for the rare Kirk's red colobus, endemic to Zanzibar Island, this small forested reserve is well worth the slight effort required to reach it from Zanzibar Stone Town or the beach resorts of the island's east coast.

Rubondo Island National Park This immensely peaceful national park protects a forested island in Lake Victoria, and is well suited for those who want to explore on foot or by boat. Indigenous fauna includes the sitatunga antelope and

The Prosimian galago family is the modern representative of the most ancient of Africa's extant primate lineages, more closely related to the lemurs of Madagascar than to any other mainland monkeys or apes. With their wide round eyes and agile bodies, they are also – as their alternative name of bushbaby suggests – uniquely endearing creatures, bound to warm the heart of even the least anthropomorphic of observers. And no natural history lover could fail to feel some excitement at the revolution in the taxonomy of the galago family that has taken place over recent years, largely due to research undertaken in the forests of Tanzania by the Nocturnal Primate Research Group of Oxford Brookes University.

In 1975, only six species of galago were recognised by specialists. By 1998, that number had risen to 18, of which ten are confirmed or likely to occur in Tanzania, including three probable endemic species and two with a core range within Tanzania. The reasons behind this explosion of knowledge probably lie in the animals' nocturnal habits, which makes casual identification tricky, particularly in relatively inaccessible forested habitats. Previously biologists based their definition of galago species largely on superficial visual similarities. It has recently been recognised, however, that the distinctive vocal repertoires of different populations, as well as differences in the penile structure, provide a more accurate indicator of whether two populations would or indeed could interbreed given the opportunity – in other words, whether they should be regarded as discrete species.

By comparing the calls, penile structures and DNA of dwarf galago populations around Tanzania, the Nocturnal Primate Research Group has discovered four previously undescribed species since the early 1990s. These are the Mozambique galago *Galagoides granti* (coastal woodland south of the Rufiji River), Matundu galago *Galagoides udzungwensis* (Udzungwa Mountains), Mountain galago *Galagoides orinus* (Uluguru and Usambara mountains) and Rondo galago *Galagoides rondoensis*. The last of these species, initially thought to be confined to the Rondo Plateau inland of Lindi, has recently been discovered living in the Pugu Hills, right outside the country's largest city! It is not so much possible as certain that further galago species await discovery: in east Africa alone populations that require further study are found in southeast Tanzania, in the isolated forests of Mount Marsabit in northern Kenya, and in the mountains along the northern shores of Lake Nyasa-Malawi.

Simon Bearder of the Nocturnal Primate Research Group argues convincingly that the implications of these fresh discoveries in galago taxonomy might extend to other 'difficult' groups of closely related animals. He points out that our most important sense is vision, which makes it easiest for us to separate species that rely primarily on vision to recognise or attract partners. It becomes more difficult for us to separate animals that attract their mates primarily by sound and scent, more so if they use senses we do not possess such as ultrasound or electric impulses. 'Such "cryptic" species,' Bearder writes, 'are no less valid than any other, but we are easily misled into thinking of them as being much more similar than would be the case if we had their kind of sensitivity. The easiest way for us to distinguish between free-living species is to concentrate on those aspects of the communication system that the animals themselves use to attract partners.'

spotted-necked otter – both surprisingly easily observed – and introduced elephant, giraffe and chimps can also be seen. The island offers good birdwatching and game fishing. An upmarket lodge and national park *bandas* (freestanding huts) are found on the island

Mkomazi National Park Gazetted in 2008, the former Mkomazi Game Reserve is a dry-country extension of Kenya's better-known Tsavo West National Park. Gamed densities are still low, but it's a beautiful tract of wilderness, and a good place for eland, lesser kudu, African wild dog and tsessebe. A reintroduced population of black rhino is kept in a large holding pen within the reserve.

WILDLIFE

Mammals More than 80 large mammal species are resident in Tanzania. On an organised safari your guide will normally be able to identify all the mammals you see. For serious identification purposes (or a better understanding of an animal's

---

DANGEROUS ANIMALS

The dangers associated with Africa's wild animals have frequently been overstated since the days of the so-called Great White Hunters – who, after all, rather intensified the risk by shooting at animals that are most likely to turn nasty when wounded – and others trying to glamorise their chosen way of life. Contrary to the fanciful notions conjured up by images of rampaging elephants, man-eating lions and psychotic snakes, most wild animals fear us more than we fear them, and their normal response to human proximity is to flee. That said, many travel guides have responded to the exaggerated ideas of the dangers associated with wild animals by being overly reassuring. The likelihood of a tourist being attacked by an animal is indeed very low, but it can happen, and there have been a number of fatalities caused by such incidents in recent years, particularly in southern Africa.

The need for caution is greatest near water, particularly around dusk and dawn, when hippos are out grazing. Hippos are responsible for more human fatalities than any other large mammal, not because they are aggressive but because they tend to panic when something comes between them and the safety of the water. If you happen to be that something, then you're unlikely to live to tell the tale. Never consciously walk between a hippo and water, and never walk along riverbanks or through reed beds, especially in overcast weather or at dusk or dawn, unless you are certain that no hippos are present. Watch out, too, for crocodiles. Only a very large crocodile is likely to attack a person, and then only in the water or right on the shore.

Near towns and other settlements, you can be fairly sure that any such crocodile will have been consigned to its maker by its potential human prey, so the risk is greatest away from human habitation. It is also near water that you are most likely to unwittingly corner a normally placid terrestrial animal – the waterbuck. The population on Crescent Island in Kenya's Lake Naivasha has acquired a nasty reputation for attacking on close approach, and the riverine-forest-dwelling bushbuck has a reputation as the most dangerous African antelope when cornered.

There are areas where hikers might still stumble across an elephant or a buffalo, the most dangerous of Africa's terrestrial herbivores. Elephants almost invariably mock charge and indulge in some hair-raising trumpeting before they attack in earnest. Provided that you back off at the first sign of unease, they are most unlikely to take further notice of you. If you see them before they see you, give them a wide berth, bearing in mind they are most likely to attack if surprised at close proximity. If an animal charges you, the safest course of action is to head for the nearest tree and climb it. Black rhinos are prone to charging without apparent provocation, but they're too rare in Tanzania to be a cause for concern. Elephants are the only animals to pose a potential danger to a vehicle, and much the same advice applies – if an elephant evidently doesn't want you to pass, then back off and wait until it has crossed the road or moved further away before you try again. In general, it's a good idea to leave your engine running when you are close to an elephant, and you should avoid letting yourself be boxed in between an elephant and another vehicle.

lifestyle and habits) it is worth investing in a decent field guide or a book on animal behaviour. Such books are too generalised to give much detail on distribution in any one country, so the section that follows is best seen as a Tanzania-specific supplement to a field guide. A number of field guides are available (see *Appendix 3, Further information*) and are best bought before you get to Tanzania. For details of individual mammals, see *Appendix 1, Wildlife*.

For most first-time safari-goers, a major goal is to tick off the so-called 'Big Five' – and even if doing so wasn't a priority when you first arrived in Tanzania, your conversations with lion-obsessive driver-guides and with other travellers are likely to make it one. Ironically, given its ubiquity in modern game-viewing circles, the

There are campsites in Tanzania where vervet monkeys and baboons have become pests. Feeding these animals is highly irresponsible, since it encourages them to scavenge and may eventually lead to them being shot. Vervet monkeys are too small to progress much beyond being a nuisance, but baboons are very dangerous and have often killed children and maimed adults with their teeth. Do not tease or underestimate them. If primates are hanging around a campsite, and you wander off leaving fruit in your tent, don't expect the tent to be standing when you return. Chimpanzees are also potentially dangerous, but unlikely to be encountered except on a guided forest walk, when there is little risk provided that you obey your guide's instructions at all times.

The dangers associated with large predators are often exaggerated. Most predators stay clear of humans and are only likely to kill accidentally or in self-defence. Lions are arguably the exception, but it is unusual for a lion to attack a human without cause. Should you encounter one on foot, the important thing is not to run, since this is likely to trigger the instinct to give chase. Of the other cats, cheetahs represent no threat and leopards generally attack only when they are cornered. Hyenas are often associated with human settlements, and are potentially very dangerous, but in practice they aren't aggressive towards people and are most likely to slink off into the shadows when disturbed. A slight but real danger when sleeping in the bush without a tent is that a passing hyena or lion might investigate a hairy object sticking out of a sleeping bag, and you might be decapitated through predatory curiosity. In areas where large predators are still reasonably common, sleeping in a sealed tent practically guarantees your safety – but don't sleep with your head sticking out and don't at any point put meat in the tent.

All manner of venomous snakes occur in Tanzania, but they are unlikely to be encountered since they generally slither away when they sense the seismic vibrations made by a walking person. You should be most alert to snakes on rocky slopes and cliffs, particularly where you risk putting your hand on a ledge that you can't see. Rocky areas are the favoured habitat of the puff adder, which is not an especially venomous snake, but is potentially lethal and unusual in that it won't always move off in response to human foot treads. Wearing good boots when walking in the bush will protect against the 50% of snake bites that occur below the ankle, and long trousers will help deflect bites higher up on the leg, reducing the quantity of venom injected. Lethal snake bites are a rarity (in South Africa, which boasts almost as many venomous snakes as Tanzania, more people are killed by lightning than by snake bites) but some discussion of treatment is included in the *Health* section, pages 60–1.

When all is said and done, the most dangerous animal in Africa, exponentially a greater threat than everything mentioned above, is the Anopheles mosquito, which carries the malaria parasite. Humans – particularly when behind a steering wheel – run them a close second!

term 'Big Five' originated with the hunting fraternity and it refers to those animals considered to be the most dangerous (and thus the best sport) back in the colonial era, namely lion, elephant, buffalo, leopard and rhino. Of these, the first three are likely to be seen with ease on a safari of any significant duration, but leopard are more elusive (the most reliable site in northern Tanzania is the Serengeti's Seronera Valley) and the only part of northern Tanzania where black rhino remain reasonably visible is the Ngorongoro Crater.

Birds Tanzania is a birdwatcher's dream, and it is impossible to do justice to its rich avifauna in the confines of a short introduction. Casual visitors will be stunned at the abundance of birdlife: the brilliantly coloured lilac-breasted rollers and superb

WEAVERS

Placed by some authorities in the same family as the closely related sparrows, the weavers of the family Ploceidae are a quintessential part of Africa's natural landscape, common and highly visible in virtually every habitat from rainforest to desert. The name of the family derives from the intricate and elaborate nests – typically but not always a roughly oval ball of dried grass, reeds and twigs – that are built by the dextrous males of most species.

It can be fascinating to watch a male weaver at work. First, a nest site is chosen, usually at the end of a thin hanging branch or frond, which is immediately stripped of leaves, probably to prevent snakes from reaching the nest undetected. The weaver then flies back and forth to the site, carrying the building material blade by blade in his heavy beak, first using a few thick strands to hang a skeletal nest from the end of a branch, then gradually completing the structure by interweaving numerous thinner blades of grass into the main frame. Once completed, the nest is subjected to the attention of his chosen partner, who will tear it apart if the result is less than satisfactory, and so the process starts all over again.

All but 12 of the 113 described weaver species are resident on the African mainland or associated islands, with at least 45 represented within Tanzania, all but six of which have a range extending into the north of the country. A full 20 of these Tanzanian species are placed in the genus Ploceus (true weavers), which is surely the most characteristic of all African bird genera. Most of the Ploceus weavers are slightly larger than a sparrow, and display a strong sexual dimorphism. Females are with few exceptions drab buff- or olive-brown birds, with some streaking on the back, and perhaps a hint of yellow on the belly.

Most male Ploceus weavers conform to the basic colour pattern of the 'masked weaver' – predominantly yellow, with streaky back and wings, and a distinct black facial mask, often bordered with orange. Seven Tanzanian weaver species fit this masked weaver prototype more or less absolutely, and a similar number approximate it rather less exactly, for instance by having a chestnut-brown mask, or a full black head, or a black back, or being more chestnut than yellow on the belly. Identification of the masked weavers can be tricky without experience – useful clues are the exact shape of the mask, the presence and extent of the fringing orange, and the colour of the eye and the back.

The golden weavers, of which only four species are present in Tanzania, are also brilliant yellow and/or light orange with some light streaking on the back, but they lack a mask or any other strong distinguishing features. Forest-associated Ploceus weavers, by contrast, tend to have quite different and very striking colour patterns, and although sexually dimorphic, the female is often as boldly marked as the male. The most aberrant among these is Vieillot's black weaver, the males of which are totally black except for their eyes, while the extralimital black-billed weaver reverses the prototype by being all black with a yellow face-mask.

starlings, the numerous birds of prey, the giant ostrich, the faintly comic hornbills, the magnificent crowned crane – the list could go on forever. For more dedicated birdwatchers, Tanzania, following an explosion in ornithological knowledge of the country over the past two decades, must now surely rank with the top handful of birding destinations in Africa.

The national checklist, which stood at below 1,000 species in 1980, had risen to 1,130 in 2005, according to a working checklist compiled by Neil and Liz Baker of the Tanzania Bird Atlas Project. This astonishing gain of 13% in 25 years is exaggerated by the Bakers' admitted bias towards splitting controversial species, but it also reflects an unparalleled accumulation of genuine new records. In 1987, the Minziro Forest on the Uganda border yielded 17 additions to the national checklist,

Among the more conspicuous *Ploceus* species in northern Tanzania are the Baglafecht, spectacled, vitelline masked, lesser masked and black-headed weavers – for the most part gregarious breeders forming single- or mixed-species colonies of hundreds, sometimes thousands, of pairs, often in reed beds and waterside vegetation. Most weavers don't have a distinctive song, but they compensate with a rowdy jumble of harsh swizzles, rattles and nasal notes that can reach deafening proportions near large colonies. One more cohesive song you will often hear seasonally around weaver colonies is a cyclic 'dee-dee-dee-Diederik', often accelerating to a hysterical crescendo when several birds call at once. This is the call of the Diederik cuckoo, a handsome green-and-white cuckoo that lays its eggs in weaver nests.

Oddly, while most east African *Ploceus* weavers are common, even abundant, in suitable habitats, seven highly localised species are listed as range-restricted, and three are regarded to be of global conservation concern. These include the Taveta palm weaver, which is restricted to the plains immediately below Kilimanjaro and is most common in the West Kilimanjaro-Amboseli area and around Lake Jipe, and the Usambara and Kilombero weavers, both endemic to a limited number of sites in eastern Tanzania.

Most of the colonial weavers, perhaps relying on safety in numbers, build relatively plain nests with a roughly oval shape and an unadorned entrance hole. The nests of certain more solitary weavers, by contrast, are far more elaborate. Several weavers, for instance, protect their nests from egg-eating invaders by attaching tubular entrance tunnels to the base – in the case of the spectacled weaver, sometimes twice as long as the nest itself. The grosbeak weaver (a peculiar larger-than-average, brown-and-white weaver of reed beds, distinguished by its outsized bill and placed in the monospecific genus *Amblyospiza*), constructs a large and distinctive domed nest, which is supported by a pair of reeds, and woven as precisely as the finest basketwork, with a neat raised entrance hole at the front.

By contrast, the scruffiest nests are built by the various species of sparrow- and buffalo-weaver, relatively drab but highly gregarious dry-country birds that occur throughout northern Tanzania. The most striking bird in the group is the white-headed buffalo-weaver, which despite its name is most easily identified by its unique bright red rump. The endemic rufous-tailed weaver, a close relative of the buffalo-weavers, is a common resident of Tarangire, Serengeti and the Ngorongoro Conservation Area.

and at least 60 new species have been recorded since then. Even if one discounts the controversial splits on the working checklist, Tanzania has almost certainly overtaken Kenya (1,080 species) as the African country with the second most varied avifauna.

Virtually anywhere in Tanzania offers good birding, and species of special interest are noted under the relevant site throughout the main body of this guide. In many areas a reasonably competent novice to east African birds could hope to see between 50 and 100 species in a day. Any of the northern reserves are recommended: Arusha and Lake Manyara national parks are both good for forest and water birds; the Serengeti and Tarangire are good for raptors and acacia and grassland species.

Recent new discoveries now place Tanzania second to South Africa for its wealth of endemic birds – species that are unique to the country. At present, 34 endemic species are recognised, including a couple of controversial splits, three species discovered and described in the 1990s, and four that still await formal description. Six of the national endemics are readily observed on the northern safari circuit, but a greater number are restricted to the Eastern Arc Mountains, together with about 20 eastern forest and woodland species whose core range lies within Tanzania. The forests of the Eastern Arc Mountains must therefore rank as the country's most important bird habitat, with the Amani Nature Reserve the most accessible site for seeing some of the Eastern Arc specials.

Field guides are discussed in *Appendix 3*, page 286. A comprehensive and regularly updated checklist of Tanzania's birds, together with atlas maps for a growing number of species, is posted on the Tanzania Bird Atlas Project website (*www.tanzaniabirdatlas.com*). Experienced birders who wish to fill in species cards for the Atlas Project based on their observations are also welcome to contact them through the website.

Brief details of those confirmed and probable endemics likely to be seen on a northern safari follow.

Grey-breasted spurfowl *Francolinus rufopictus* Game bird with distinctive combination of a red mask under which is a white stripe. Confined to the Serengeti and immediate vicinity, where it is common in scattered woodland in the Seronera area.

Tanzanian red-billed hornbill *Tockus ruahae* Recently 'split' from other red-billed hornbills, from which it can be distinguished by the unique combination of a black (not red) face-mask and pale (not black) eyes, this central Tanzanian endemic is a resident of acacia woodland in the Babati-Kondoa and it may also range into Tarangire National Park.

Fischer's lovebird *Agapornis fischeri* Stunning and colourful parrot-like bird with bright red head and white eye, most often first noticed when a flock passes overhead squawking and screeching. Its natural range is centred on the Serengeti, where it is common. A popular caged bird in Europe, a feral population of this lovebird occurs in Naivasha (Kenya) where it regularly interbreeds with the next species.

Yellow-collared lovebird *Agapornis personatus* Another endemic lovebird – with black rather than red head – that has gone feral in Naivasha, Kenya. Naturally confined to the Maasai Steppes and other semi-arid parts of central Tanzania, the yellow-collared lovebird is common in Tarangire National Park.

Beesley's lark *Chersomanes beesleyi* Recently split from the widespread spike-heeled lark, this endangered species is confined to a single population of fewer than 1,000 individuals in short grasslands west of Kilimanjaro.

Ashy starling *Cosmopsarus unicolor* A drab but nevertheless distinctive member of this normally colourful group of birds, the ashy starling is associated with semi-arid parts of central Tanzania. It's common in Tarangire National Park, and can be seen at the southern end of its range in Ruaha National Park.

Rufous-tailed weaver *Histurgops ruficauda* Large, sturdily built weaver of the central savanna, whose scaly feathering, pale eyes and habit of bouncing around boisterously in small flocks could lead to it being mistaken for a type of babbler, albeit one with an unusually large bill. It is a common and visible resident of the Serengeti, Ngorongoro and Tarangire national parks.

Reptiles
Nile crocodile The order *Crocodilia* dates back at least 150 million years, and fossil forms that lived contemporaneously with dinosaurs are remarkably unchanged from their modern counterparts, of which the Nile crocodile is the largest living reptile, regularly growing to lengths of up to 6m. Widespread throughout Africa, the Nile crocodile was once common in most large rivers and lakes, but it has been exterminated in many areas in the past century – hunted professionally for its skin as well as by vengeful local villagers. Contrary to popular legend, Nile crocodiles generally feed mostly on fish, at least where densities are sufficient. They will also prey on drinking or swimming mammals where the opportunity presents itself, dragging their victim under water until it drowns, then storing it under a submerged log or tree until it has decomposed sufficiently for them to eat. A large crocodile is capable of killing a lion or wildebeest, or an adult human for that matter, and in certain areas such as the Mara or Grumeti rivers in the Serengeti, large mammals do form their main prey. Today, large crocodiles are mostly confined to protected areas within Tanzania.

Snakes A wide variety of snakes are found in Tanzania, though – fortunately, most would agree – they are typically very shy and unlikely to be seen unless actively sought. One of the snakes most likely to be seen on safari is Africa's largest, the rock python, which has a gold-on-black mottled skin and regularly grows to lengths exceeding 5m. Non-venomous, pythons kill their prey by strangulation, wrapping their muscular bodies around it until it cannot breathe, then swallowing it whole and dozing off for a couple of months while it is digested. Pythons feed mainly on small antelopes, large rodents and similar animals. They are harmless to adult humans, but could conceivably kill a small child. A slumbering python might be encountered almost anywhere in northern Tanzania.

Of the venomous snakes, one of the most commonly encountered is the puff adder, a large, thick resident of savanna and rocky habitats. Although it feeds mainly on rodents, the puff adder will strike when threatened, and it is rightly considered the most dangerous of African snakes, not because it is especially venomous or aggressive, but because its notoriously sluggish disposition means it is more often disturbed than other snakes. The related Gabon viper is possibly the largest African viper, growing up to 2m long, very heavily built, and with a beautiful cryptic, geometric gold, black and brown skin pattern that blends perfectly into the rainforest litter it inhabits. Although highly venomous, it is more placid and less likely to be encountered than the puff adder.

Several cobra species, including the spitting cobra, are present in Tanzania, most with characteristic hoods that they raise when about to strike, though they are all very seldom seen. Another widespread family is the mambas, of which the black mamba – which will only attack when cornered, despite an unfounded reputation for unprovoked aggression – is the largest venomous snake in Africa, measuring up to 3.5m long. Theoretically, the most toxic of Africa's snakes is said to be the

33

boomslang, a variably coloured and, as its name – literally tree snake – suggests, largely arboreal snake that is reputed not to have accounted for one known human fatality, as it is back-fanged and very non-aggressive.

Most snakes are in fact non-venomous and not even potentially harmful to any other living creature much bigger than a rat. One of the non-venomous snakes in the region is the green tree snake (sometimes mistaken for a boomslang, though the latter is never as green and more often brown), which feeds mostly on amphibians. The mole snake is a common and widespread grey-brown savanna resident that grows up to 2m long, and feeds on moles and other rodents. The remarkable egg-eating snake lives exclusively on bird eggs, dislocating its jaws to swallow the egg whole, then eventually regurgitating the crushed shell in a neat little package. Many snakes will take eggs opportunistically, for which reason large-scale agitation among birds in a tree is often a good indication that a snake (or small bird of prey) is around.

Lizards All African lizards are harmless to humans, with the arguable exception of the giant monitor lizards, which could in theory inflict a nasty bite if cornered. Two species of monitor occur in east Africa, the water and the savanna, the latter growing up to 2.2m long and occasionally seen in the vicinity of termite mounds, the former slightly smaller but far more regularly observed by tourists, particularly in the vicinity of Lake Victoria. Their size alone might make it possible to fleetingly mistake a monitor for a small crocodile, but their more colourful yellow-dappled skin precludes sustained confusion. Both species are predatory, feeding on anything from bird eggs to smaller reptiles and mammals, but will also eat carrion opportunistically.

Visitors to Tanzania will soon become familiar with the common house gecko, an endearing bug-eyed, translucent white lizard, which as its name suggests reliably inhabits most houses as well as lodge rooms, scampering up walls and upside down on the ceiling in pursuit of pesky insects attracted to the lights. Also very common in some lodge grounds are various agama species, distinguished from other common lizards by their relatively large size of around 20–25cm, basking habits, and almost plastic-looking scaling – depending on the species, a combination of blue, purple, orange or red, with the flattened head generally a different colour from the torso. Another common family are the skinks: small, long-tailed lizards, most of which are quite dark and have a few thin black stripes running from head to tail.

Chameleons Common and widespread in Tanzania, but not easily seen unless they are actively searched for, chameleons are arguably the most intriguing of African reptiles. True chameleons of the family Chamaeleontidae are confined to the Old World, with the most important centre of speciation being the island of Madagascar, to which about half of the world's 120 recognised species are endemic. Aside from two species of chameleon apiece in Asia and Europe, the remainder are distributed across mainland Africa.

Chameleons are best known for their capacity to change colour, a trait that has often been exaggerated in popular literature, and which is generally influenced by mood more than the colour of the background. Some chameleons are more adept at changing colour than others, with the most variable being the common chameleon *Chamaeleo chamaeleon* of the Mediterranean region, with more than 100 colour and pattern variations recorded. Many African chameleons are typically green in colour but will gradually take on a browner hue when they descend from the foliage in more exposed terrain, for instance while crossing a road. Several change colour and pattern far more dramatically when they feel threatened or are confronted by a rival of the same species. Different chameleon species also vary greatly in size, with the largest being Oustalet's chameleon of Madagascar, known to reach a length of almost 80cm.

A remarkable physiological feature common to all true chameleons is their protuberant round eyes, which offer a potential 180° vision on both sides and are able to swivel around independently of each other. Only when one of them isolates a suitably juicy-looking insect will the two eyes focus in the same direction as the chameleon stalks slowly forward until it is close enough to use the other unique weapon in its armoury. This is its sticky-tipped tongue, which is typically about the same length as its body and remains coiled up within its mouth most of the time, to be unleashed in a sudden, blink-and-you'll-miss-it lunge to zap a selected item of prey. In addition to their unique eyes and tongues, many chameleons are adorned with an array of facial casques, flaps, horns and crests that enhance their already somewhat fearsome prehistoric appearance.

In Tanzania, you're most likely to come across a chameleon by chance when it is crossing a road, in which case it should be easy to take a closer look at it, since most chameleons move painfully slowly and deliberately. Chameleons are also often seen on night game drives, when their ghostly nocturnal colouring shows up clearly under a spotlight – as well as making it pretty clear why these strange creatures are regarded with both fear and awe in many local African cultures. More actively, you could ask your guide if they know where to find a chameleon – a few individuals will be resident in most lodge grounds.

The flap-necked chameleon *Chamaeleo delepis* is probably the most regularly observed species of savanna and woodland habitats in east Africa. Often observed crossing roads, the flap-necked chameleon is generally around 15cm long and bright green in colour with few distinctive markings, but individuals might be up to 30cm in length and will turn tan or brown under the right conditions. Another closely related and widespread savanna and woodland species is the similarly sized graceful chameleon *Chamaeleo gracilis*, which is generally yellow-green in colour and often has a white horizontal stripe along its flanks.

Characteristic of east African montane forests, three-horned chameleons form a closely allied species cluster of some taxonomic uncertainty. Typically darker than the savanna chameleons and around 20cm in length, the males of all taxa within this cluster are distinguished by a trio of long nasal horns that project forward from their face. The most widespread three-horned chameleon in Tanzania is *Chamaeleo johnstoni*, while the most localised is the Ngosi three-horned chameleon *Chamaeleo fuelleborni*, confined to the forested slopes of Ngosi Volcano in the Poroto Mountains. Perhaps the most alluring of east Africa's chameleons is the giant chameleon *Chamaeleo melleri*, a bulky dark-green creature with yellow stripes and a small solitary horn, mainly associated with the Eastern Arc forests, where it feeds on small reptiles (including snakes) as well as insects.

Tortoises and terrapins These peculiar reptiles are unique in being protected by a prototypal suit of armour formed by their heavy exoskeleton. The most common of the terrestrial tortoises in the region is the leopard tortoise, which is named after its gold-and-black mottled shell, can weigh up to 30kg, and has been known to live for more than 50 years in captivity. It is often seen motoring along in the slow lane of game reserve roads in northern Tanzania. Four species of terrapin – essentially the freshwater equivalent of turtles – are resident in east Africa, all somewhat flatter in shape than the tortoises, and generally with a plainer brown shell. They might be seen sunning on rocks close to water or peering out from roadside puddles. The largest is the Nile soft-shelled terrapin, which has a wide, flat shell and in rare instances might reach a length of almost 1m.

Butterflies Tanzania's wealth of invertebrate life, though largely overlooked by visitors, is perhaps most easily appreciated in the form of butterflies and moths of the order Lepidoptera. Almost 1,000 butterfly species have been recorded in Tanzania, as compared to roughly 650 in the whole of North America, and a mere 56 on the British Isles. Several forests in Tanzania harbour 300 or more butterfly species, and one might easily see a greater selection in the course of a day than one could in a lifetime of exploring the English countryside. Indeed, I've often sat at one roadside pool in an east African forest and watched 10–20 clearly different species converge there over the space of 20 minutes.

The Lepidoptera are placed in the class Insecta, which includes ants, beetles and locusts among others. All insects are distinguished from other invertebrates, such as arachnids (spiders) and crustaceans, by their combination of six legs, a pair of frontal antennae, and a body divided into a distinct head, thorax and abdomen. Insects are the only winged invertebrates, though some primitive orders have never evolved wings, and other more recently evolved orders have discarded them. Most flying insects have two pairs of wings, one of which, as in the case of flies, might have been modified beyond immediate recognition. The butterflies and moths of the order Lepidoptera have two sets of wings and are distinguished from all other insect orders by the tiny ridged wing scales that create their characteristic bright colours.

The most spectacular of all butterflies are the swallowtails of the family Papilionidae, of which roughly 100 species have been identified in Africa. Named for the streamers that trail from the base of their wings, swallowtails are typically large and colourful, and relatively easy to observe when they feed on mammal dung deposited on forest trails and roads. Sadly, this last generalisation doesn't apply to the African giant swallowtail *Papilio antimachus*, a powerful flier that tends to stick at canopy levels and seldom alights on the ground, but the first two certainly do. With a wingspan known to exceed 20cm, this black, orange and green gem is the largest butterfly on the continent, and possibly the world.

The Pieridae is a family of medium-sized butterflies, generally smaller than the swallowtails and with wider wings, of which almost 100 species are present in Tanzania, several as seasonal intra-African migrants. Most species are predominantly white in colour, with some yellow, orange, black or even red and blue markings on the wings. One widespread member of this family is the oddly named angled grass yellow *Eurema desjardini*, which has yellow wings marked by a broad black band, and is likely to be seen in any savanna or forest fringe habitat. The orange and lemon *Eronia leda* also has yellow wings, but with an orange upper tip, and it occurs in open grassland and savanna countrywide.

The most diverse of African butterfly families is the Lycaenidae, which accounts for almost one-third of the continental tally of around 1,500 recorded species. Known also as gossamer wings, this varied family consists mostly of small to medium-sized butterflies, with a wingspan of 1–5cm, dull underwings, and brilliant violet blue, copper or rufous-orange upper wings. The larvae of many Lycaenidae species have a symbiotic relationship with ants – they secrete a fluid that is milked by the ants and are thus permitted to shelter in their nests. A striking member of this family is *Hypolycaena hatita*, a small bluish butterfly with long tail streamers, often seen on forest paths throughout Tanzania.

Another well-represented family in Tanzania is the Nymphalidae, a diversely coloured group of small to large butterflies, generally associated with forest edges or interiors. The Nymphalidae are also known as brush-footed butterflies, because their forelegs have evolved into non-functional brush-like structures. One of the more distinctive species is the African blue tiger *Tirumala petiverana*, a large black butterfly with about two dozen blue-white wing spots, often observed in forest paths near puddles or feeding from animal droppings. Another large member of this family is the African queen *Danaus chrysippus*, which has a slow, deliberate flight pattern, orange or brown wings, and is as common in forest edge habitats as it is in cultivated fields or suburbia.

The family Charaxidae, regarded by some authorities to be a subfamily of the Nymphalidae, is represented by roughly 200 African species. Typically large, robust, strong fliers with one or two short tails on each wing, the butterflies in this family vary greatly in coloration, and several species appear to be scarce and localised since they inhabit forest canopies and are seldom observed. Rather less spectacular are the 200–300 grass-skipper species of the family Hersperiidae, most of which are small and rather drably coloured, though some are more attractively marked in black, white and/or yellow. The grass-skippers are regarded to form the evolutionary link between butterflies and the generally more nocturnal moths, represented in Tanzania by several families of which the most impressive are the boldly patterned giant silk moths of the family Saturniidae.

2

Practical Information

WHEN TO VISIT

You can visit northern Tanzania at any time of year, as every season has different advantages. For those with the option, there is much to be said for trying to avoid peak tourist seasons, as the parks and other main attractions will be less crowded with tourists. Broadly speaking, tourism arrivals are highest during the northern hemisphere winter, while the low season runs from the end of the Easter weekend until the end of September, though this is distorted by a surge of tourism over June and July, when the wildebeest migration starts its northward surge through the Serengeti.

The rainy season between November and April is a good time to visit the Serengeti; it is when the countryside is greenest, and it offers the best birdwatching, with resident species supplemented by a number of Palaearctic and intra-African migrants. April and May are the official low season, with cheaper rates available at most lodges, yet these months still offer great game viewing, especially in the southern Serengeti. The rainy season is hotter than the period May to October, but in most parts of the country this will only be by a matter of a couple of degrees. The seasonal difference in temperature is most noticeable along the humid coast, which can be rather uncomfortable in the hotter months. The wettest months are March and April, when parts of the country may experience storms virtually on a daily basis.

The dry seasons (December to February or August to September), offer the best trekking conditions on Mount Kilimanjaro and Meru. The dry season is the best time for hiking generally, and for travelling in parts of the country with poor roads. Temperatures at the coast tend to be more bearable during the dry season, which is also considerably safer than the wet season in terms of malaria and other mosquito-borne diseases.

Game viewing in the Ngorongoro Crater and Lake Manyara is not strongly affected by season, and tends to be good at any time of year. The southern Serengeti, the part of the park visited by most tourists, hosts the greatest concentrations of animals between December and April. The western Serengeti is normally best over May to July, while wildlife activity in the far north peaks over September to November. That said, game viewing anywhere in the Serengeti is pretty good at any time of year, and the more remote northern and western areas have the big advantage of being practically bereft of tourists outside of the migration periods. The most seasonal game viewing in the northern circuit is at Tarangire National Park, where animal concentrations generally peak between July and the start of the rains in November or early December.

ITINERARY PLANNING

Tanzania has a well-defined tourist circuit. It would be no exaggeration to say that as many as 90% of visitors divide their time in the country between the northern

39

safari circuit and the island of Zanzibar. If this is what you plan on doing, then any tour operator or safari company in Arusha will be able to put together a package to meet your requirements. A 10–14-day trip is ideal for the Zanzibar/safari combination. You might want to read the section *Organising a safari* below, before making contact with a tour operator. With Zanzibar, the main decision you need to make in advance is whether you want to be based at a hotel in the old Stone Town, or out on one of the beaches, or a combination of the two. For a short trip to Tanzania, it is advisable to fly between Arusha (the springboard for safaris in northern Tanzania) and Zanzibar. If you are really tight for time, you'll get more out of your safari by flying between lodges. A fly-in safari will also be less tiring than the more normal drive-in safari.

After the northern safari circuit and Zanzibar, Tanzania's main tourist attraction is Kilimanjaro, which is normally climbed over five to seven days. A Kilimanjaro climb is one of those things that you either do or don't want to undertake: for a significant minority of travellers, climbing Kilimanjaro is the main reason for visiting Tanzania, but for the majority it is of little interest. If you want to do a Kili climb, it can be organised in advance through any number of tour operators and safari companies, and there is a lot to be said for arranging the climb through the same operator that organises your safari. As with safaris, it is generally possible to get cheaper prices on the spot. To combine a Kili climb with a few days on safari and a visit to Zanzibar, you would need an absolute minimum of two weeks in the country, and even that would be very tight, allowing for no more than two nights on Zanzibar.

ORGANISING A SAFARI There are, in essence, four types of safari package on offer: budget camping safaris, standard lodge-based safaris, exclusive camping safaris and fly-in safaris. Budget camping safaris are generally designed to keep costs to a minimum, so they will make use of the cheapest camping options, often outside the national parks, and clients are normally expected to set up their own tents. Most backpackers and volunteers working in Tanzania go on budget camping safaris, though even with these there is a gap between the real shoestring operators, who'll skimp on everything, and those operators who offer a sensible compromise between affordability and adequate service. These days, high park fees mean that the minimum you are likely to pay for a budget safari is around US$160 per person per day, so it really isn't worth going with a dodgy company to save a few dollars.

Most fly-in tourists go on a standard lodge-based safari, which will generally cost around double the price of a similar budget camping safari. For the extra outlay, you get a roof over your head at night, restaurant food and a far higher level of comfort. If you decide to go on a lodge safari, the probability is that the operator will decide which lodges you stay at. Should you have the choice, however, it's worth noting that the former government 'Wildlife Lodge' chain generally has the best natural settings, while Sopa Lodges are more luxurious and slightly more expensive (but only the Ngorongoro Sopa Lodge has a setting to compare to its wildlife lodge equivalent) and the lodges in the Serena chain are more upmarket still, with modern facilities, good locations and attractive décor.

Camping isn't necessarily a cost-reducing device. Sleeping under canvas and eating under the stars will unquestionably make you feel more integrated into the bush environment than staying at the above chain lodges, which are all of the institutionalised 'hotel in the bush' variety. This is where upmarket camping safaris come into play. At the top end of the range, an ever multiplying number of smaller permanent lodges and seasonal, mobile or semi-permanent tented camps are scattered around the northern safari circuit. These generally offer accommodation in bandas or standing tents and possess a more intimate bush atmosphere than any

The combination of steep national park entrance and camping fees, and the expense of running 4x4 vehicles in northern Tanzania, places the northern safari circuit pretty much out of bounds for travellers on a very tight budget. It is possible, however, to see parts of the circuit relatively cheaply by using public transport and/or hiring vehicles locally.

The most affordable way of traversing the Serengeti National Park is on one of the buses and Land Rovers that run daily along the B142 between Mwanza and Arusha. This route passes through conservation areas for a total of about 250km, firstly the Serengeti's Western Corridor and Seronera Plains, then the plains of the western Ngorongoro Conservation Area and over the Ngorongoro Crater rim. You'd get a good feel of the scenery and landscapes from a bus window, and between November and July you should see plenty of game, including large predators, but of course the vehicle cannot be expected to stop for special sightings. The trip will entail paying US$100 in park entrance fees, over and above the bus fare. In theory, it is possible to make advance arrangements for one of these buses to drop you off at Seronera, and to pick you up at a later stage, but it's difficult to see any reason why anybody would want to do this.

A more satisfying option for travellers who specifically want to see the Serengeti, have time on their hands, and cannot afford a safari of several days' duration, is to approach the park from the western side. This cuts out the long drive and overnight stops coming from Arusha, allowing you to get within 1km of the entrance gate on public transport and to visit the park as a day or overnight trip rather than as part of a longer safari. The best place to set up something like this would be Serengeti Stopover, a private campsite situated right next to the entrance gate to the Serengeti's Western Corridor and alongside the main road between the Lake Victoria ports of Mwanza and Musoma. The Western Corridor itself generally offers good game viewing, particularly when the migration passes through between May and July, and the game-rich Seronera Plains and Campsite are only about two hours' drive from the western entrance gate. Serengeti Stopover charges US$150 per day for a vehicle that can carry up to five people into the park, which means that a day trip would work out at around US$125 per person for two people including park fees, and about US$90 per person for four people. For further details, see page 223.

On the eastern side of the northern safari circuit, affordable local buses run daily from Arusha to Karatu, stopping at the village of Mto wa Mbu near the entrance of Lake Manyara National Park. The Ngorongoro Safari Resort in Karatu rents out 4x4 vehicles seating up to four people, or five at a push, for half/full-day visits to Lake Manyara National Park or the Ngorongoro Crater. Should you want to make advance arrangements, the resort's contact details are included under the *Where to stay* listings for *Karatu*, page 184. Worth noting, too, is that safari vehicles are found in abundance in Mto wa Mbu and Karatu, so there's every chance you could make cheaper private arrangements to hire a vehicle for a day. Were you to do something like this, you should be very clear about what the deal covers and how long you will spend in the game reserve – ambiguities at the negotiating stage often result in frayed tempers later in the day.

Hitching into most of the reserves covered in this chapter is pretty much out of the question. Relatively few private vehicles pass this way, and most safari companies forbid their drivers to pick up hitchhikers. In any case, people who have paid for a safari, or who are in a private vehicle loaded with supplies, are unlikely to want to carry freeloaders. Even if you were to catch a lift, you may well get stuck in the Serengeti or Ngorongoro and although you will see little game from a campsite or lodge, you will still have to pay park fees.

lodge. Yet many are as luxurious as any lodge safari, with top-quality food, a full team of staff, large tents, portable showers and the like.

The cost of a safari like this will depend on your exact requirements, but it will probably cost at least as much as a similar lodge safari. Indeed, the best mobile and tented camps (as operated by the likes of Asilia, Lemala and &Beyond), though absolutely superlative, are often more than twice as expensive as the larger chain lodges, so not within most safari-goers' means. Fortunately, there are also a number of tented camps that offer a bush atmosphere at rates comparable to the chain lodges – Tarangire Safari Lodge, Kirurumu Tented Camp and Ndutu Lodge stand out, as do the mobile camps operated by Wild Frontiers and Tanganyika Wilderness Safaris – and these are highly recommended to those seeking a bush experience at a relatively affordable price.

Regular scheduled flights connect all the main reserves in northern Tanzania, and an increasingly high proportion of safari-goers choose to fly around rather than bump along the long, dusty roads that separate the parks. Flying around will be particularly attractive to those who have bad backs or who tire easily, but it is more expensive and does dilute the sense of magic attached to driving through the vast spaces that characterise this region. Fly-in safaris allow you to see far more wildlife in a shorter space of time, because you don't lose hours on the road.

In all categories of safari, the price you are quoted should include the vehicle and driver/guide, fuel, accommodation or camping equipment and fees, meals and park entrance fees. You are expected to tip the driver and cook. Around US$5–10 per day per party seems to be par, but you should check this with the company. Drivers and cooks are poorly paid; if they have done a good job, be generous.

Group size One factor that all visitors should consider is the size of the group doing the safari. It is almost invariably cheaper to go on safari as part of a group, but it can also ruin things if the people in that group are not compatible. A group safari will be highly frustrating to those who have a special interest such as birding or serious photography. And, frankly, I think it is unfair to impose this sort of interest on other passengers, who will have little interest in identifying every raptor you drive past, or in waiting for two hours at a lion kill to get the perfect shot. Another consideration is that non-stretch Land Rovers can feel rather cramped with four people in the back, especially when the luggage is in the vehicle, and jostling for head room out of the roof can be a nightmare when four cameras are vying for the best position.

A small proportion of companies – generally the large package tour operators – use minibuses as opposed to conventional 4x4s. In my opinion, minibuses have several disadvantages, notably that the larger group size (typically around eight people) creates more of a package tour atmosphere, and that it is difficult for a large group to take proper advantage of the pop-up roofs which are usually found on safari vehicles. In any event, bouncing around rutted roads in a Land Rover is an integral part of the safari experience – it just wouldn't be the same in a minibus.

Finally, there is the question of aesthetics. Without wishing to wax too lyrical, the thrill of being on safari doesn't derive merely from the animals you see. There is an altogether more elusive and arguably spiritual quality attached to simply being in a place as wild and vast and wonderful as the Serengeti, one that is most easily absorbed in silence, whether you travel on your own or with somebody with whom you feel totally relaxed. It isn't the same when one has to make small talk to new acquaintances, crack the rote jokes about who should be put out of the vehicle to make the lion move, decide democratically when to move on, listen to the driver's educational monotones, and observe social niceties that seem at odds with the surrounding wilderness.

Itinerary Your itinerary will depend on how much time and money you have, and also the time of year. There are endless options, and most safari companies will put together the package you ask for. They know the ground well and can advise you on what is possible, but may tend to assume you will want to cover as many reserves as possible. This is not always the best approach.

A typical five- or six-day safari takes in Ngorongoro, Serengeti, Manyara and Tarangire. A typical three-day trip takes in all these reserves except for the Serengeti. In the dry season (July to October) there is little game in the Serengeti; most safari companies will suggest you spend more time in Tarangire.

The distances between these reserves are considerable and the roads are poor; you will have a more relaxed trip if you visit fewer reserves. On a five-day safari, I would drop either the Serengeti or Tarangire. To visit all four reserves, six days is just about adequate, seven or more days would be better.

Three days isn't long enough to get a good feel for Tarangire, Manyara and Ngorongoro; four or even five days would be better. The combination of Ngorongoro and Tarangire would make an unhurried three-day safari. If you are limited to two days, you could either visit Tarangire on its own or do a combined trip to Manyara and Ngorongoro. If your budget is really limited, Tarangire can be visited as a day trip from Arusha; it is less than two hours' drive each way.

At the other end of the time scale, there is enough to see and do in the area to warrant a safari of two weeks in duration, or even longer. You could easily spend a few days exploring the Serengeti alone. In a two-week package, you could also visit Lake Natron and Ol Doinyo Lengai, the Kondoa-Irangi rock art and/or the Lake Eyasi area.

MISCELLANEOUS WARNINGS Malaria is present in most parts of the region, with the notable exception of the Ngorongoro Crater rim, and the normal precautions should be taken. Aside from malaria, there are no serious health risks attached to visiting this area. Tsetse flies are seasonally abundant in well-wooded areas such as Tarangire and the Western Corridor of the Serengeti. Sleeping sickness is not a cause for serious concern, but the flies are sufficiently aggravating that it is worth applying insect repellent to your arms and legs before game drives (though this doesn't always deter tsetse flies) and avoiding the dark clothing that tends to attract them.

Tarangire can be reached via a good tar road, and so too can Lake Manyara and the eastern entrance gate to Ngorongoro Conservation Area. The roads between the Ngorongoro Crater and Serengeti are very rough, for which reason safari-goers with serious back problems or a low tolerance for bumping around in the back of a vehicle might want to consider flying between the reserves. If one member of a safari party has a particular need to avoid being bumped around, they will be best off in the front passenger seat or the central row of seats – the seats above the rear axle tend to soak up the most punishment.

The combination of dust and glare may create problems for those with sensitive eyes. Sunglasses afford some protection against glare and dust, and if you anticipate problems of this sort, then don't forget to pack eye drops. Many people who wear contact lenses suffer in these dusty conditions, so it is a good idea to wear glasses on long drives, assuming that you have a pair. Dust and heat can damage sensitive camera equipment and film, so read over the precautions mentioned in the *Photographic tips* box, pages 76–7.

As is standard practice in many countries, safari drivers earn a commission when their clients buy something from one of the many curio stalls in Mto wa Mbu and elsewhere in the region. There's nothing inherently wrong with this arrangement, but you might find that your safari driver is very keen to stop at a few stalls along the way. If this isn't what you want, then the onus is on you to make this clear the first time it happens – there's no need to be rude or confrontational, just explain gently that this isn't why you're on safari. Even if you do want to buy curios, don't fall into the obvious trap of assuming that you'll get a better deal buying locally. Many of the curios you see in places like Mto wa Mbu probably found their way there from outside, and they will generally be cheaper in Arusha than they will be at roadside stalls dealing exclusively with tourists.

Travellers on a budget camping safari who want to keep down their extra costs should be aware that drinks, although available at all game lodges, are very expensive. A beer at a lodge will typically cost around US$4–5, as opposed to about US$1 in a shop or local bar, and prices of sodas are similarly inflated. It is definitely worth stocking up on mineral water in Arusha (at least one 1.5-litre bottle per person per day), since this will be a lot more expensive on the road. Once in the game reserves, some travellers might feel that it's worth spending the extra money to enjoy the occasional chilled beer or soda at a lodge. Those travellers who don't should ask their driver where to buy drinks to bring back to the campsite – there are bars aimed at drivers near to all the budget safaris' campsites, and the prices are only slightly higher than in Arusha.

Finally, and at risk of stating the obvious, it is both illegal and foolhardy to get out of your safari vehicle in the presence of any wild animal, and especially buffalo, elephant, hippo and lion.

i TOURIST INFORMATION

The Tanzania Tourist Board (TTB) (*www.tanzaniatouristboard.com*) has improved greatly over recent years, and its offices in London, New York, Stockholm, Milan and Frankfurt may be able to supply you with an information pack and leaflets about the country.

There are TTB offices in Dar es Salaam and in Arusha. Both are reasonably helpful and well informed when it comes to tourist-class hotels and major tourist attractions, but neither is generally able to offer much help when it comes to more remote destinations. The TTB in Arusha is a good source of information about the various cultural tourism programmes that have been established in northern Tanzania over the past few years. Its list of registered and blacklisted safari companies is a useful resource for travellers working through cheap safari companies.

Additional online content for the Bradt guide to Tanzania and update information can be accessed at http://bradttanzania.wordpress.com.

TOUR OPERATORS

The following overseas companies specialise in Tanzania. Safari specialists in Tanzania are found under their different regions in *Part Two, The Guide*.

UK

Abercrombie & Kent ☎ 0845 618 2200; e info@ abercrombiekent.co.uk; www.abercrombiekent.co.uk. Tailored safaris.
Africa-in-Focus (UK) ☎ 01803 770956; e info@ africa-in-focus.com; www.africa-in-focus.com. Comfortable mobile camping safaris targeting wildlife enthusiasts, photographers & families.

Africa Select ☎ 01670 787646; e pg@ africaselect.com; www.africaselect.com. Tailor-made itineraries, including tours to safari & mountain destinations.
Africa Travel ☎ 0845 450 1520; f 0845 450 5725; e info@africatravel.co.uk; www.africatravel.co.uk
Aim 4 Africa Ltd ☎ 0114 255 2533; e enquiries@aim4africa.com; www.aim4africa.com

Alpha Travel ☎ 020 8423 0220; e alpha@
alphauk.co.uk; www.arpsafaris.com. Arranges tours
with Ranger Safaris in Tanzania.
Baobab – Alternative Roots to Travel ☎ 0121 314
6011; f 0121 314 6012; e enquiries@
baobabtravel.com; www.baobabtravel.com. An ethical
tour operator specialising in ecotourism in Africa.
Cazenove & Loyd Safaris ☎ 020 7384 2332;
e experts@cazloyd.com; www.caz-loyd.com
Crusader Travel ☎ 020 8744 0474; e info@
crusadertravel.com; www.crusadertravel.com
Explore Worldwide ☎ 0845 013 1537; e hello@
explore.co.uk; www.exploreworldwide.com
Footloose ☎ 01943 604030; e info@
footlooseadventure.co.uk;
www.footlooseadventure.co.uk. Tailor-made tours,
safaris & treks throughout Tanzania, including
Zanzibar.
Gane & Marshall ☎ 01822 600 600; e holidays@
ganeandmarshall.co.uk; www.ganeandmarshall.co.uk
Hartley's Safaris ☎ 01673 861600; e info@
hartleys-safaris.co.uk; www.hartleys-safaris.co.uk.
Safaris to east & southern Africa, as well as diving &
island holidays in the region.
Journeys by Design ☎ 01273 623 790; e info@
journeysbydesign.co.uk; www.journeysbydesign.co.uk

Okavango Tours & Safaris ☎ 020 8347 4030;
e info@okavango.com; www.okavango.com.
Individually tailored holidays to east & southern Africa.
Rainbow Tours ☎ 020 7226 1004; e info@
rainbowtours.co.uk; www.rainbowtours.co.uk
Safari Drive ☎ 01488 71140; e info@
safaridrive.com; www.safaridrive.com. Self-drive &
tailor-made safaris.
Sherpa Expeditions ☎ 020 8577 2717; e sales@
sherpa-walking-holidays.co.uk;
www.sherpaexpeditions.com
Steppes Africa ☎ 01285 880 980; e safaris@
steppesafrica.co.uk; www.steppesafrica.co.uk
Sunvil Africa ☎ 020 8568 4499; e africa@
sunvil.co.uk; www.sunvil.co.uk
Tanzania Odyssey ☎ 020 7471 8780 or (USA) +1
866 356 4691; e info@tanzaniaodyssey.com;
www.tanzaniaodyssey.com. Tailor-made tours
throughout Tanzania.
Tribes Travel ☎ 01728 685971; e bradtanz@
tribes.co.uk; www.tribes.co.uk
Wildlife Worldwide ☎ 0845 130 6982; e sales@
wildlifeworldwide.com; www.wildlifeworldwide.com
World Odyssey ☎ 01905 731373; e info@
world-odyssey.com; www.world-odyssey.com. Tailor-
made safaris.

US
Aardvark Safaris ☎ 1 888 776 0888; e info@
aardvarksafaris.com; www.aardvarksafaris.com. Tailored
trips to southern & northern Tanzania, including
walking safaris.
Abercrombie & Kent ☎ 1 800 554 7016;
www.abercrombiekent.com. A leader in luxury
adventure travel.
Adventure Center ☎ 1 800 228 8747;
www.adventurecenter.com. Provides safaris, treks,
expeditions & active vacations worldwide, with a
focus on value. Represents Explore Worldwide.
Big Five Tours & Expeditions ☎ 1 800 244 3483;
e info@bigfive.com; www.bigfive.com. Family-owned
safari company.
Eco-resorts ☎ 1 866 326 7376; e info@
eco-resorts.com; www.eco-resorts.com. Offers a variety
of safaris. A percentage of the booking fee is used
to support local communities & the environment.
Ker & Downey USA ☎ 1 800 423 4236;
e safari@kerdowney.com; www.kerdowney.com

Micato Safaris ☎ 1 800 642 2861; e inquiries@
micato.com; www.micato.com. Family company, based
in Nairobi but with an office in New York.
Naipenda Safaris ☎ 1 888 404 4499; e jo@
naipendasafaris; www.naipendasafaris.com
Next Adventure ☎ 1 800 562 7298; e safari@
nextadventure.com; www.nextadventure.com. California-
based company with strong ties to Tanzania.
International Expeditions ☎ 1 800 633 4734;
e nature@ietravel.com; www.ietravel.com
Thomson Safaris ☎ 1 800 235 0289; e info@
thomsonsafaris.com; www.thomsonsafaris.com.
Specialising in Tanzania for 20 years, Thomson
operates innovative safaris throughout the country,
including walking tours & adventure camps.
Remote River Expeditions ☎ +261 020 955 2347;
e info@remoterivers.com; www.remoterivers.com
United Travel Group ☎ 1 800 223 6486; e info@
unitedtravelgroup.com; www.unitedtravelgroup.com One
of the oldest safari companies in Africa.

SOUTH AFRICA
Wild Frontiers ☎ 11 702 2035; f 11 468 1655;
e wildfront@icon.co.za; www.wildfrontiers.com. This
excellent Johannesburg-based tour operator has years

of experience arranging general & ornithological
safaris to east Africa, as well as reasonably priced
air tickets.

2

Check well in advance that you have a valid **passport** and that it won't expire within six months of the date on which you intend to leave Tanzania. Should your passport be lost or stolen, it will generally be easier to get a replacement if you have a photocopy of the important pages.

If you want to drive or hire a vehicle while you're in the country, either bring your normal driving licence or organise an **international driving licence** through the AA. You may sometimes be asked at the border or international airport for an **international health certificate** showing you've had a yellow fever shot.

For security reasons, it's advisable to detail all your important information on one sheet of paper, photocopy it, and distribute a few copies in your luggage, your money-belt, and among relatives or friends at home. The sort of thing you want to include are your travellers' cheque numbers and refund information, travel insurance policy details and 24-hour emergency contact number, passport number, details of relatives or friends to be contacted in an emergency, bank and credit card details, camera and lens serial numbers, etc.

For up-to-the-minute advice on travel in Tanzania, also check www.fco.gov.uk/knowbeforeyougo.

VISAS Visas are required by most visitors to Tanzania, including UK and USA passport holders, and cost US$30–60, depending on your nationality. This can be obtained on arrival at any international airport in Tanzania, or at any border post. This is a straightforward procedure: no photographs or other documents are required, but the visa must be paid for in hard currency. The visa is normally valid for three months after arriving in the country, and it allows for multiple crossings into Uganda and Kenya during that period, (but not from neighbouring countries). For current information about visa requirements, visit http://tanzaniatouristboard.com/pages/ttb_visa.php. This page links to a full list of Tanzanian embassies and high commissions abroad.

ⓔ EMBASSIES AND DIPLOMATIC MISSIONS

A selection of embassies and high commissions in Dar es Salaam is listed below. Most are open mornings only and closed at weekends. Typical hours are 09.00 to 12.30, but this varies considerably.

Algeria 34 Ali Hassan Mwinyi Rd; ☎ 022 211 7619; f 022 211 7620; www.mae.dz

Belgium 5 Ocean Rd, Upanga; ☎ 022 211 2688/2503; f 022 211 7621; www.diplomatie.be/dar-es-salaam

Burundi Lugalo Rd, Upanga; ☎ 022 212 6827; f 022 211 5923 ; e burundemb@raha.com

Canada 38 Mirambo St; ☎ 022 216 3300; f 022 211 6897; www.canadainternational.gc.ca

China 2 Kajifcheni St; ☎ 022 266 7475/105; f 022 266 6353; http://tz.china-embassy.org

Denmark Ghana Av; ☎ 022 211 3887/8; f 022 211 6433; www.ambdaressalaam.um.dk

Egypt 24 Ghana Av; ☎ 022 211 3591; f 022 211 2543; e egypt.emb.tz@Cats-net.com

Finland Cnr Mirambo St & Garden Av; ☎ 022 219 6565; f 022 219 6573; www.finland.or.tz

France Ali Hassan Mwinyi Rd; ☎ 022 266 6021/3; f 022 266 8434; www.ambafrance-tz.org

Germany Cnr Mirambo St & Garden Av; ☎ 022 211 7409/15; f 022 211 2944; www.daressalam.diplo.de

Greece 64 Upanga Rd; ☎ 022 211 5895; f 022 260 015

Hungary 204 Chake Chake Rd, Oyster Bay; ☎ 022 266 8573; f 022 266 7214

India Haile Selassie Rd, Masiki; ☎ 022 260 0714/6; f 022 260 0697; www.hcindiatz.org

Ireland 353 Toure Drive; ☎ 022 260 2355; f 022 260 2362; e daressalaamembassy@dfa.ie

Italy 316 Lugalo Rd; ☎ 022 211 5935/6; f 022 211 5938; www.ambdaressalaam.esteri.it

Japan 1081 Ali Hassan Mwinyi Rd; ☎ 022 211 5827/9; f 022 211 5830; www.tz.emb-japan.go.jp

Kenya Old Bagamoyo Rd; ✆ 022 266 8285/6;
f 022 266 8213; www.kenyahighcomtz.org
Malawi Zambia Hse, Ohio/Sokoine Rd; ✆ 022 213
6951; f 022 213 6951
Mozambique 25 Garden Av; ✆ 022 211 6502;
f 022 211 6502
Netherlands Cnr Mirambo St & Garden Av; ✆ 022
211 0000; f 022 211 0044; www.netherlands-
embassy.go.tz
Norway Cnr Mirambo St & Garden Av; ✆ 022 211
3366/3610; f 022 211 6564; www.norway.go.tz
Pakistan 149 Malik Rd; ✆ 022 211 7630; f 022
211 3205
Poland 63 Ali Kahn Rd; ✆ 022 211 5271; f 022
211 5812
Romania 11 Ocean Rd, Upanga; ✆ 022 211 5899;
f 022 211 3866
Russia 73 Ali Hassan Mwinyi Rd; ✆ 022 266
6005/6; f 022 266 6818; www.russianembassy.net

Rwanda 32 Ali Hassan Mwinyi Rd; ✆ 022 213
0119; f 022 211 5888
South Africa Mwaya Rd, Msasani; ✆ 022 260 1800;
f 022 260 1684; e ntombelal@foreign.gov.za
Spain 99B Kinondoni Rd; ✆ 022 266 6936/6018;
f 022 266 6938; e embesptz@mail.mae.es
Sudan 64 Ali Mwinyi Rd; ✆ 022 211 7641; f 022
211 5811
Sweden Cnr Mirambo St & Garden Av; ✆ 022 211
0101; f 022 211 0102; www.swedenabroad.com
Switzerland Kinondoni Rd; ✆ 022 266 6008/9;
f 022 266 6736; www.eda.admin.ch/daressalaam
Uganda Extelcom Bldg, Samora Machel Av; ✆ 022
266 7391; f 022 266 7224
UK Cnr Mirambo St & Garden Av; ✆ 022 211 0101;
f 022 211 0102; http://ukintanzania.fco.gov.uk
USA 686 Old Bagamoyo Rd; ✆ 022 266 8001;
f 022 266 8238; http://tanzania.usembassy.gov
Zambia Cnr Ohio Rd & Sokoine Drive; ✆ 022 211
2977; f 022 211 2977

GETTING THERE AND AWAY

✈ **BY AIR** The following airlines fly to Tanzania from outside Africa: Air India, British Airways, Emirates, Qatar Airways, KLM and Swiss International Airlines. Of the various African airlines that fly to Tanzania, EgyptAir, Kenya Airways, South African Airways and Ethiopian Airlines are all pretty useful in terms of intercontinental connections. Other carriers such as Air Tanzania, Air Malawi, Uganda Air, Rwandair Express and Zambia Airways are generally of interest for intra-African connections only.

There are two international airports on the Tanzanian mainland. Julius Nyerere International Airport in Dar es Salaam is the normal point of entry for international airlines, which is generally convenient for business travellers, but for tourists Dar es Salaam is usually no more than a point of entry, and many people transfer directly onto flights to elsewhere in the country. Kilimanjaro International Airport, which lies midway between Moshi and Arusha, is the more useful point of entry for tourists, and following recent privatisation this airport may catch on with more international airlines. For the meantime, however, the only prominent airlines that run direct flights to Kilimanjaro from outside of Africa are the national carrier Air Tanzania, Ethiopian Airlines, Kenya Airways and KLM.

Budget travellers looking for flights to east Africa may well find it cheapest to use an airline that takes an indirect route. London is the best place to pick up a cheap ticket; many continental travellers buy their tickets there. It is generally cheaper to fly to Nairobi than to Dar es Salaam, and getting from Nairobi to Arusha by shuttle bus is cheap, simple and quick. Be warned, however, that a high proportion of travellers are robbed in Nairobi, so it isn't the greatest introduction to the continent.

Flight specialists
From the UK
Flight Centre 13 The Broadway, Wimbledon SW19
1PS; ✆ 020 8296 8181; f 020 8296 0808;
www.flightcentre.co.uk. An independent flight provider

with over 450 outlets worldwide. They also have offices in Australia, New Zealand, South Africa & Canada.

Quest Travel Stoneham Hse, 17 Scarbrook Rd, Croydon, Surrey CR0 1SQ; ✆ 0845 263 6963; f 020 8406 7255; www.questtravel.com. An independent agent that has been in operation for a decade offering competitive prices, specialising in long-haul flights.
STA Travel 52 Grosvenor Gdns, Victoria, London SW1W 0AG; ✆ 0871 468 0649; f 020 7881 1299; e enquiries@statravel.co.uk; www.statravel.co.uk. STA has 10 branches in London & 30 or so around the country & at different university sites. STA also has several branches & associate organisations around the world.
Trailfinders 194 Kensington High St, London W8 7RG; ✆ 020 7938 3939; f 020 7938 3305; www.trailfinders.com. Has several other offices in the UK. With origins in the discount flight market, Trailfinders now provides a one-stop travel service

including visa & passport service, travel clinic & foreign exchange.
Travel Bag 2–3 High St, Alton, Hants GU34 1TL; ✆ 0207 810 6831; f 01420 82133 & at 373–5 The Strand, London WC2R 0JE; ✆ 0844 880 4436; f 020 7497 2923; www.travelbag.co.uk. Provides tailor-made flight schedules & holidays for destinations throughout the world.
Travel Mood 24 Islington Green, London N1 8DU; ✆ 0844 815 9560; f 0844 815 9561; e sales@travelmood.com; www.travelmood.com. Provides flights & tailor-made holidays.
WEXAS 45–49 Brompton Rd, Knightsbridge, London SW3 1DE; ✆ 020 7589 3315; f 020 7589 8418; e mship@wexas.com; www.wexas.com. More of a club than a travel agent. Membership is around £40 a year, but for frequent fliers the benefits are many.

From the USA

Airtech ✆ 1 212 219 7000; e fly@airtech.com; www.airtech.com. Standby seat broker that also deals in consolidator fares, courier flights & a host of other travel-related services.
Net Fare ✆ (freephone) 1 800 766 3601; e qdmin@netfare.net; www.netfare.net. Provides fares for destinations throughout the world.
Council on International Educational Exchange ✆ 1 207 553 4000; f 1 207 553 4299;

e contact@ciee.org; www.ciee.org. Although the Council focuses on work-exchange trips, it also has a large travel department.
STA Travel ✆ (freephone) 1 800 781 4040; e go@statravel.com; www.statravel.com. Has several branches around the country.
Worldtek Travel ✆ (freephone) 1 800 243 1723; e info@worldtek.com; www.worldtek.com. Operates a network of rapidly growing travel agencies.

From Canada

Flight Centre ✆ (freephone) 1 877 967 5302; www.flightcentre.ca. Has a network of branches around the country.

Travel CUTS ✆ (freephone) 1 866 246 9762; www.travelcuts.com. A Canadian student-based travel organisation with 60 offices throughout Canada.

From Australia

Flight Centre ✆ (freephone) 133 133; www.flightcentre.com.au. An independent flight operator with offices around the country. They also have offices in the UK, New Zealand, South Africa & Canada.

STA Travel ✆ 134 782; www.statravel.com.au. A student travel specialist with network of branches around Australia.

From New Zealand

Flight Centre ✆ 0800 2435 44; www.flightcentre.co.nz. A good starting point for cheap air fares.

From South Africa

Flight Centre ✆ 0860 400 727; www.flightcentre.co.za. Part of the international chain with a number of branches around the country.

Student Flights ✆ 0860 400 700; www.studentflights.co.za. This outfit is linked to the Flight Centre network.

✚ HEALTH *with Dr Felicity Nicholson*

PREPARATIONS Preparations to ensure a healthy trip to Tanzania require checks on your immunisation status: it is wise to be up to date on tetanus, polio and diphtheria (now given as an all-in-one vaccine, Revaxis, that lasts for ten years), and hepatitis A. Immunisations against meningococcus and rabies may also be recommended. Proof of vaccination against yellow fever is needed for entry into Tanzania if you are coming from another yellow fever endemic area and this includes travelling from Tanzania to Zanzibar. There is much debate as to whether yellow fever vaccine is actually needed for Tanzania as there hasn't been a case since 1992. Whether the vaccine is given should be discussed on an individual basis with a doctor who is used to conducting such an assessment. If the vaccine is not suitable for you then an exemption certificate will be needed to cross borders. This can be obtained from your GP or a travel clinic. Immunisation against cholera is no longer required for Tanzania.

Hepatitis A vaccine (Havrix Monodose or Avaxim) comprises two injections given about a year apart. The course costs about £100, but may be available on the NHS; it protects for 25 years and can be administered even close to the time of departure. Hepatitis B vaccination should be considered for longer trips (two months or more) or for those working with children or in situations where contact with blood is likely. Three injections are needed for the best protection and can be given over a three-week period if time is short. Longer schedules give more sustained protection and are therefore preferred if time allows. Hepatitis A vaccine can also be given as a combination with hepatitis B as 'Twinrix', though two doses are needed at least seven days apart to be effective for the hepatitis A component, and three doses are needed for the hepatitis B.

The newer injectable typhoid vaccines (eg: Typhim Vi) last for three years and are about 85% effective. Oral capsules (Vivotif) are currently available in the US (and soon in the UK); if four capsules are taken over seven days it will last for five years. They should be encouraged unless the traveller is leaving within a few days for a trip of a week or less, when the vaccine would not be effective in time. Meningitis vaccine (ideally containing strains A, C, W and Y, but if this is not available then A + C vaccine is better than nothing) is recommended for all travellers, especially for trips of more than four weeks (see *Meningitis*, page 59). Vaccinations for rabies are ideally advised for everyone, but are especially important for travellers visiting more remote areas, especially if you are more than 24 hours from medical help and definitely if you will be working with animals (see *Rabies*, page 60).

Experts differ over whether a BCG vaccination against tuberculosis (TB) is useful in adults: discuss this with your travel clinic.

In addition to the various vaccinations recommended above, it is important that travellers should be properly protected against malaria. For detailed advice, see page 50.

Ideally you should visit your own doctor or a specialist travel clinic (see pages 52–3) to discuss your requirements if possible at least eight weeks before you plan to travel.

Protection from the sun Give some thought to packing suncream. The incidence of skin cancer is rocketing as Caucasians are travelling more and spending more time in the sun. Keep out of the sun during the middle of the day and, if you must be exposed, build up gradually from 20 minutes per day. Be especially careful of sun reflected off water and wear a T-shirt and lots of waterproof SPF15 suncream when swimming; snorkelling often leads to scorched backs of the thighs so wear Bermuda shorts. Sun exposure ages the skin and makes people prematurely wrinkly; cover up with long, loose clothes and wear a hat when you can. The glare and the dust can be hard on the eyes, too, so bring UV-protecting sunglasses and, perhaps, a soothing eyebath.

Long-haul air travel increases the risk of deep vein thrombosis. Although recent research has suggested that many of us develop clots when immobilised, most resolve without us ever having been aware of them. In certain susceptible individuals, though, clots form on clots and when large ones break away and lodge in the lungs this is dangerous. Fortunately this happens in a tiny minority of passengers.

Studies have shown that flights of over five-and-a-half hours are significant, and that people who take lots of shorter flights over a short space of time can also form clots. People at highest risk are:

- Those who have had a clot before – unless they are now taking warfarin
- People over 80 years of age
- Anyone who has recently undergone a major operation or surgery for varicose veins
- Someone who has had a hip or knee replacement in the last three months
- Cancer sufferers
- Those who have ever had a stroke
- People with heart disease
- Those with a close blood relative who has had a clot

Those with a slightly increased risk:

- People over 40
- Women who are pregnant or have had a baby in the last couple of weeks
- People taking female hormones, the combined contraceptive pill or other oestrogen therapy
- Heavy smokers
- Those who have very severe varicose veins
- The very obese
- People who are very tall (over 6ft/1.8m) or short (under 5ft/1.5m)

Malaria prevention There is no vaccine against malaria, but there are other ways to avoid it; since most of Africa is very high risk for malaria, travellers must plan their malaria protection properly. Seek current advice on the best antimalarials to take: usually mefloquine, Malarone or doxycycline. If mefloquine (Lariam) is suggested, start this two-and-a-half weeks (three doses) before departure to check that it suits you; stop it immediately if it seems to cause depression or anxiety, visual or hearing disturbances, severe headaches, fits or changes in heart rhythm. Side effects such as nightmares or dizziness are not medical reasons for stopping unless they are sufficiently debilitating or annoying. Anyone who has been or is being treated for depression or psychiatric problems, has diabetes controlled by oral therapy or who is epileptic (or who has suffered fits in the past) or has a close blood relative who is epileptic, should avoid mefloquine. In the past doctors were nervous about prescribing mefloquine to pregnant women, but experience has shown that it is relatively safe and certainly safer than the risk of malaria. That said, there are other issues, so if you are travelling to Tanzania whilst pregnant, seek expert advice before departure.

Malarone (proguanil and atovaquone) is as effective as mefloquine. It has the advantage of having few side effects and need only be continued for one week after returning. However, it is expensive and because of this tends to be reserved for shorter trips although it is generally accepted that it can be taken for three months. Malarone may not be suitable for everybody so advice should be taken from a

A deep vein thrombosis (DVT) is a blood clot that forms in the deep leg veins. This is very different from irritating but harmless superficial phlebitis. DVT causes swelling and redness of one leg, usually with heat and pain in one calf and sometimes the thigh. A DVT is only dangerous if a clot breaks away and travels to the lungs (pulmonary embolus). Symptoms of a pulmonary embolus (PE) include chest pain that is worse on breathing in deeply, shortness of breath, and sometimes coughing up small amounts of blood. The symptoms commonly start three to ten days after a long flight. Anyone who thinks that they might have a DVT needs to see a doctor immediately who will arrange a scan. Warfarin tablets (to thin the blood) are then taken for at least six months.

PREVENTION OF DVT Several conditions make the problem more likely. Immobility is the key, and factors like reduced oxygen in cabin air and dehydration may also contribute. To reduce the risk of thrombosis on a long journey:

- Exercise before and after the flight
- Keep mobile before and during the flight; move around every couple of hours
- Drink plenty of water or juices during the flight
- Avoid taking sleeping pills and excessive tea, coffee and alcohol
- Perform exercises that mimic walking and tense the calf muscles
- Consider wearing flight socks or support stockings (see *www.legshealth.com*)
- Ideally take a meal each week of oily fish (mackerel, trout, salmon, sardines, etc) ahead of your departure. This reduces the blood's ability to clot and thus DVT risk. It may even be worth just taking a meal of oily fish 24 hours before departure if this is more practical.

If you think you are at increased risk of a clot, ask your doctor if it is safe to travel.

doctor. Paediatric Malarone for children over 11kg and under 40kg is now available in the UK and is given based on weight.

The antibiotic doxycycline (100mg daily) is a viable alternative when either mefloquine or Malarone is not considered suitable for whatever reason. Like Malarone it can be started one or two days before arrival. Unlike mefloquine, it may also be used in travellers with epilepsy, although certain anti-epileptic medication may make it less effective. Users must be warned about the possibility of allergic skin reactions developing in sunlight which can occur in about 1–3% of people. The drug should be stopped if this happens. Women using the oral contraceptive should use an additional method of protection for the first four weeks when using doxycycline. It is also unsuitable in pregnancy and breast feeding or for children under 12 years.

Chloroquine and proguanil are no longer considered to be very effective for Tanzania. However, they may still be recommended if no other regime is suitable.

All prophylactic agents should be taken with or after the evening meal, washed down with plenty of fluid and with the exception of Malarone (see above) continued for four weeks after leaving.

Travellers to remote parts would probably be wise to carry a course of treatment to cure malaria. Experts differ on the costs and benefits of self-treatment, but agree that it leads to over-treatment and to many people taking drugs they do not need; yet treatment may save your life. Discuss your trip with a specialist to determine your particular needs and risks, and be sure you understand when and how to take the cure. If you are somewhere remote in a malarial region you probably have to assume that any high fever (over 38°C) for more than a few hours is due to malaria (regardless of any other symptoms) and should seek treatment. Diagnosing malaria is not easy, which is why consulting a doctor is sensible: there are other dangerous causes of fever in Africa, which require different treatments. Presently Malarone or Co-artemether are the favoured regimes, but check for up-to-date advice on the current recommended treatment. And remember malaria may occur anything from seven days into the trip to up to six months or even one year if you have taken prophylactic medication after leaving Africa.

The risk of malaria above 1,800m above sea level is low. In addition to antimalarial medication, it is important to avoid mosquito bites between dusk and dawn. Pack an insect repellent containing around 50–55% DEET, such as Repel or Expedition Plus. You may also need either a permethrin-impregnated bed net or a permethrin spray so that you can 'treat' bed nets in hotels, unless you are staying in five-star accommodation with air conditioning. Always check the details before you go. Putting on long clothes at dusk means you can reduce the amount of repellent you need to put on your skin, but be aware that malaria mosquitoes hunt at ankle level and will bite through socks, so apply repellent under socks too. Travel clinics usually sell a good range of nets, treatment kits and repellents.

Travel clinics and health information A full list of current travel clinic websites worldwide is available on www.istm.org/. For other journey preparation information, consult www.nathnac.org/ds/map_world.aspx. Information about various medications may be found on www.netdoctor.co.uk/travel.

UK

Berkeley Travel Clinic 32 Berkeley St, London W1J 8EL (near Green Park tube station); ☏ 020 7629 6233; ⊕ 10.00–18.00 Mon–Fri, 10.00–15.00 Sat
Cambridge Travel Clinic 41 Hills Rd, Cambridge, CB2 1NT; ☏ 01223 367362; f 01223 368021; e enquiries@travelcliniccambridge.co.uk; www.travelcliniccambridge.co.uk; ⊕ 10.00–16.00 Mon, 12.00–19.00 Wed–Thu, 11.00–18.00 Fri, 10.00–16.00 Sat
Edinburgh Travel Health Clinic 14 East Preston St, Newington, Edinburgh EH8 9QA; ☏ 0131 667 1030; www.edinburghtravelhealthclinic.co.uk; ⊕ 09.00–19.00 Mon–Wed, 9.00–18.00 Thu & Fri. Travel vaccinations & advice on all aspects of malaria prevention. All current UK-prescribed anti-malaria tablets in stock.
Fleet Street Travel Clinic 29 Fleet St, London EC4Y 1AA; ☏ 020 7353 5678; www.fleetstreetclinic.com; ⊕ 08.45–17.30 Mon–Fri. Injections, travel products & latest advice.
Hospital for Tropical Diseases Travel Clinic Mortimer Market Centre, 2nd Floor, Capper St (off Tottenham Ct Rd), London WC1E 6AU; ☏ 020 7388 9600; www.thehtd.org. Offers consultations & advice, & is able to provide all necessary drugs & vaccines for travellers. Runs a healthline (☏ 020 7950 7799)

for country-specific information & health hazards. Also stocks nets, water purification equipment & personal protection measures.
MASTA (Medical Advisory Service for Travellers Abroad) London School of Hygiene & Tropical Medicine, Keppel St, London WC1 7HT; ☏ 09068 224100; www.masta-travel-health.com. This is a premium-line number, charged at 60p per minute. For a fee, they will provide an individually tailored health brief, with up-to-date information on how to stay healthy, inoculations & what to take.
MASTA pre-travel clinics ☏ 01276 685040. Call for the nearest; there are currently 30 in Britain. They also sell malaria prophylaxis memory cards, treatment kits, bed nets, net treatment kits, etc.
NHS travel website www.fitfortravel.scot.nhs.uk. Provides country-by-country advice on immunisation & malaria prevention, plus details of recent developments, & a list of relevant health organisations.
Nomad Travel Store 3–4 Wellington Terr, Turnpike La, London N8 0PX; ☏ 020 8889 7014; f 020 8889 9528; e turnpike@nomadtravel.co.uk; www.nomadtravel.co.uk; ⊕ 09.15–17.00 Mon–Fri, late night Thu. Walk in or appointments. 6 stores in total countrywide. As well as dispensing health

advice, Nomad stocks mosquito nets & other anti-bug devices, & an excellent range of adventure travel gear.

InterHealth Travel Clinic 157 Waterloo Rd, London SE1 8US; ☎ 020 7902 9000; e askus@ interhealth.org.uk; www.interhealth.org.uk; ⏰ 09.00–17.00 Mon–Fri. Competitively priced, one-stop travel health service, by appointment only.

Trailfinders Immunisation Centre 194 Kensington High St, London W8 7RG; ☎ 020 7938 3999 www.trailfinders.com/travelessentials/travelclinic.htm; ⏰ 09.00–17.00 Mon, Tue, Wed & Fri, 09.00–18.00 Thu, 10.00–17.15 Sat. No appointment necessary **Travelpharm** www.travelpharm.com. The Travelpharm website offers up-to-date guidance on travel-related health & has a range of medications available through their online mini-pharmacy.

Irish Republic

Tropical Medical Bureau Grafton St Medical Centre, Grafton Bldgs, 34 Grafton St, Dublin 2; ☎ 1 671 9200; www.tmb.ie. Useful website specific to tropical destinations.

USA

Centers for Disease Control 1600 Clifton Rd, Atlanta, GA 30333; ☎ (404) 498 1515 or (800) 311 3435; e cdcinfo@cdc.gov; www.cdc.gov/travel. The central source of travel information in the USA. Each summer they publish the invaluable *Health Information for International Travel*.

IAMAT (International Association for Medical Assistance to Travelers) 1623 Military Rd, 279 Niagara Falls, NY 14304-1745; ☎ 716 754 4883; e info@iamat.org; www.iamat.org. A non-profit organisation with free membership that provides lists of English-speaking doctors abroad.

Canada

IAMAT (International Association for Medical Assistance to Travellers) Suite 1, 1287 St Clair Av W, Toronto, Ontario M6E 1B8; ☎ 416 652 0137; www.iamat.org

TMVC Suite 314, 1030 W Georgia St, Vancouver, BC V6E 2Y3; ☎ 905 648 1112; www.tmvc.com. One-stop medical clinic for all your international travel medicine & vaccination needs.

Australia, New Zealand, Thailand

TMVC (Travel Doctors Group) ☎ 1300 65 88 44; www.tmvc.com.au. 22 clinics in Australia, New Zealand & Thailand, including:
Auckland Canterbury Arcade, 170 Queen St; ☎ 9 373 3531
Brisbane Dr Deborah Mills, Qantas Domestic Bldg, 6th Floor, 247 Adelaide St, QLD 4000; ☎ 7 3221 9066; f 7 3321 7076

Melbourne Dr Sonny Lau, 393 Little Bourke St, 2nd floor, Melbourne, VIC 3000; ☎ 3 9602 5788; f 3 9670 8394
Sydney Dr Mandy Hu, Dymocks Bldg, 7th Floor, 428 George St, Sydney, NSW 2000; ☎ 2 221 7133; f 2 221 8401
IAMAT PO Box 5049, Christchurch 5, New Zealand; www.iamat.org

South Africa

SAA-Netcare Travel Clinics e travelinfo@ netcare.co.za; www.travelclinic.co.za or www.malaria.co.za. 12 clinics throughout South Africa.

TMVC NHC Health Centre, Cnr Beyers Naude & Waugh Northcliff; ☎ 0 11 214 9030; www.traveldoctor.co.za. Consult the website for details of clinics.

Switzerland

IAMAT 57 Chemin des Voirets, 1212 Grand-Lancy, Geneva; e info@iamat.org; www.iamat.org

Personal first-aid kit A minimal kit contains:

- A good drying antiseptic, eg: iodine or potassium permanganate (don't take antiseptic cream)
- A few small dressings (Band-Aids)
- Suncream

- Insect repellent; anti-malarial tablets; impregnated bed net or permethrin spray
- Aspirin or paracetamol
- Antifungal cream (eg: Canesten)
- Ciprofloxacin or norfloxacin, for severe diarrhoea
- Tinidazole for giardia or amoebic dysentery (see below for regime)
- Antibiotic eye drops, for sore, 'gritty', stuck-together eyes (conjunctivitis)
- A pair of fine pointed tweezers (to remove hairy caterpillar hairs, thorns, splinters, coral, etc)
- Alcohol-based hand rub or bar of soap in plastic box
- Condoms or femidoms
- A digital thermometer (for those going to remote areas)

IN TANZANIA

Major hazards People new to exotic travel often worry about tropical diseases, but it is accidents that are most likely to carry you off. Road accidents are very common in many parts of Tanzania, so be aware and do what you can to reduce risks: try to travel during daylight hours and refuse to be driven by a drunk. Listen to local advice about areas where violent crime is rife, too.

Common medical problems

Travellers' diarrhoea Travelling in Tanzania carries a fairly high risk of getting a dose of travellers' diarrhoea; perhaps half of all visitors will suffer and the newer you are to exotic travel, the more likely you will be to suffer. By taking precautions against travellers' diarrhoea you will also avoid typhoid, cholera, hepatitis, dysentery, worms, etc. Travellers' diarrhoea and the other faecal-oral diseases come from getting other peoples' faeces in your mouth. This most often happens from cooks not washing their hands after a trip to the toilet, but even if the restaurant cook does not understand basic hygiene you will be safe if your food has been properly cooked and arrives piping hot. The maxim to remind you what you can safely eat is:

PEEL IT, BOIL IT, COOK IT OR FORGET IT.

This means that fruit you have washed and peeled yourself, and hot foods, should be safe but raw foods, cold cooked foods, salads, fruit salads that have been prepared by others, ice cream and ice are all risky. And foods kept lukewarm in hotel buffets are often dangerous. If you are struck, see the box for treatment.

MEDICAL FACILITIES IN TANZANIA

Private clinics, hospitals and pharmacies can be found in most large towns, and doctors generally speak fair to fluent English. Consultation fees and laboratory tests are remarkably inexpensive when compared with most Western countries, so if you do fall sick it would be absurd to let financial considerations dissuade you from seeking medical help. Commonly required medicines such as broad-spectrum antibiotics are widely available and cheap throughout the region, as are malaria cures and prophylactics. It is advisable to carry all malaria-related tablets on you, and only rely on their availability locally if you need to restock your supplies. If you are on any medication prior to departure, or you have specific needs relating to a known medical condition (for instance if you are allergic to bee stings or you are prone to attacks of asthma), then you are strongly advised to bring any related drugs and devices with you.

Dr Jane Wilson-Howarth

It is dehydration that makes you feel awful during a bout of diarrhoea and the most important part of treatment is drinking lots of clear fluids. Sachets of oral rehydration salts give the perfect biochemical mix to replace all that is pouring out of your bottom but other recipes taste nicer. Any dilute mixture of sugar and salt in water will do you good: try Coke or orange squash with a three-finger pinch of salt added to each glass (if you are salt-depleted you won't taste the salt). Otherwise make a solution of a four-finger scoop of sugar with a three-finger pinch of salt in a 500 ml glass. Or add eight level teaspoons of sugar (18g) and one level teaspoon of salt (3g) to one litre (five cups) of safe water. A squeeze of lemon or orange juice improves the taste and adds potassium, which is also lost in diarrhoea. Drink two large glasses after every bowel action, and more if you are thirsty. These solutions are still absorbed well if you are vomiting, but you will need to take sips at a time. If you are not eating you need to drink three litres a day plus whatever is pouring into the toilet. If you feel like eating, take a bland, high carbohydrate diet. Heavy, greasy foods will probably give you cramps.

If the diarrhoea is bad, or you are passing blood or slime, or you have a fever, you will probably need antibiotics in addition to fluid replacement. A dose of norfloxacin or ciprofloxacin repeated twice a day until better may be appropriate (if you are planning to take an antibiotic with you, note that both norfloxacin and ciprofloxacin are available only on prescription in the UK). If the diarrhoea is greasy and bulky and is accompanied by sulphurous (eggy) burps, one likely cause is giardia. This is best treated with tinidazole (four x 500mg in one dose, repeated seven days later if symptoms persist).

Water sterilisation It is rare to get sick from drinking contaminated water but it happens, so try to drink from safe sources.

Water should have been brought to the boil (even at altitude it only needs to be brought to the boil), or passed through a good bacteriological filter or purified with iodine; chlorine tablets (eg: Puritabs) are also adequate although theoretically less effective and they taste nastier. Mineral water has been found to be contaminated in Tanzania but should be safer than contaminated tap water.

Malaria Whether or not you are taking malaria tablets, it is important to protect yourself from mosquito bites (see box, *Malaria in Tanzania*, pages 56–7, and *Malaria prevention*, pages 50–2), so keep your repellent stick or roll-on to hand at all times. Be aware that no prophylactic is 100% protective but those on prophylactics who are unlucky enough to catch malaria are less likely to rapidly get into serious trouble. It is easy and inexpensive to arrange a malaria blood test.

Dengue fever This mosquito-borne disease may mimic malaria but there is no prophylactic medication available to deal with it. The mosquitoes that carry this virus bite during the daytime, so it is worth applying repellent if you see any mosquitoes around. Symptoms include strong headaches, rashes, excruciating joint and muscle pains and high fever. Dengue fever lasts only for a week or so and is not usually fatal. Complete rest and paracetamol are the usual treatment; plenty of fluids also help. Some patients are given an intravenous drip to prevent dehydration. It is especially important to protect yourself if you have had dengue fever before, since a second infection with a different strain can result in the potentially fatal dengue haemorrhagic fever.

Insect bites It is crucial to avoid mosquito bites between dusk and dawn; as the sun is going down, don long clothes and apply repellent on any exposed flesh. This will protect you from malaria, elephantiasis and a range of nasty insect-borne viruses. Otherwise retire to an air-conditioned room or burn mosquito coils (which are widely available and cheap in Tanzania) or sleep under a fan. Coils and fans reduce rather than eliminate bites. During the day it is wise to wear long, loose (preferably 100% cotton) clothes if you are pushing through scrubby country; this will keep ticks off and also tsetse and day-biting Aedes mosquitoes which may spread dengue and yellow fever. Tsetse flies hurt when they bite and are attracted to the colour blue; locals will advise on where they are a problem and where they transmit sleeping sickness.

Minute pestilential biting blackflies spread river blindness in some parts of Africa between 90°N and 170°S; the disease is caught close to fast-flowing rivers since flies breed there and the larvae live in rapids. The flies bite during the day but long trousers tucked into socks will help keep them off. Citronella-based natural repellents do not work against them.

MALARIA IN TANZANIA

Along with road accidents, malaria poses the single biggest serious threat to the health of travellers in most parts of tropical Africa, Tanzania included. The Anopheles mosquito which transmits the parasite is most abundant near marshes and still water, where it breeds, and the parasite is most prolific at low altitudes. Parts of Tanzania lying at an altitude of 2,000m or higher (a category that includes the Ngorongoro Crater rim, Mount Kilimanjaro and Meru, and parts of the Eastern Arc Mountains) are regarded to be free of malaria. In mid-altitude locations, malaria is largely but not entirely seasonal, with the highest risk of transmission occurring during the rainy season. Moist and low-lying areas such as the Indian Ocean coast and the hinterland of lakes Tanganyika, Victoria and Nyasa are high risk throughout the year, but the danger is greatest during the rainy season. This localised breakdown might influence what foreigners working in Tanzania do about malaria prevention, but all travellers to Tanzania must assume that they will be exposed to malaria and should take precautions throughout their trip (see pages 50–2 for advice on prophylactic drugs and avoiding mosquito bites).

Even those who take their malaria tablets meticulously and do everything possible to avoid mosquito bites may contract a strain of malaria that is resistant to prophylactic drugs. Untreated malaria is likely to be fatal, but even strains resistant to prophylaxis respond well to prompt treatment. Because of this, your immediate priority upon displaying possible malaria symptoms – which might include any combination of a headache, flu-like aches and pains, a rapid rise in temperature, a general sense of disorientation, and possibly even nausea and diarrhoea – is to establish whether you have malaria.

The blood test for malaria takes ten minutes to produce a result and costs about US$1 in Tanzania. A positive result means that you have malaria. A negative result suggests that you don't have malaria, but bear in mind that the parasite doesn't always show up on a test, particularly when the level of infection is mild or is 'cloaked' by partially effective prophylactics. For this reason, even if you test negative, it would be wise to stay within reach of a laboratory until the symptoms clear up, and to test again after a day or two if they don't. It's worth noting that if you have a fever and the malaria test is negative, you may have typhoid, which should also receive immediate treatment. Where typhoid testing is unavailable, a routine blood test can give a strong indication of this disease.

Mosquitoes and many other insects are attracted to light. If you are camping, never put a lamp near the opening of your tent, or you will have a swarm of biters waiting to join you when you retire. In hotel rooms, be aware that the longer your light is on, the greater the number of insects will be sharing your accommodation.

Tumbu flies or putsi are a problem where the climate is hot and humid. The adult fly lays her eggs on the soil or on drying laundry and when the eggs come in contact with human flesh (when you put on clothes or lie on a bed) they hatch and bury themselves under the skin. Here they form a crop of 'boils' which each hatches a grub after about eight days, when the inflammation will settle down. In putsi areas either dry your clothes and sheets within a screened house, or dry them in direct sunshine until they are crisp, or iron them.

Jiggers or sandfleas are another flesh-feaster. They latch on if you walk barefoot in contaminated places, and set up home under the skin of the foot, usually at the side of a toenail where they cause a painful, boil-like swelling. They need picking out by a local expert; if the distended flea bursts during eviction the wound should be dowsed in spirit, alcohol or kerosene, otherwise more jiggers will infest you.

It is preferable not to attempt self-diagnosis or to start treatment for malaria before you have been tested. There are, however, many places in Tanzania where you will be unable to test for malaria, for instance in the game reserves and in most of the popular hiking areas. With malaria, it is normal enough to go from feeling healthy to having a high fever in the space of a few hours (and it is possible to die from falciparum malaria within 24 hours of the first symptoms). In such circumstances, assume that you have malaria and act accordingly – whatever risks are attached to taking an unnecessary cure are outweighed by the dangers of untreated malaria.

It is imperative to treat malaria promptly. The sooner you take a cure, the less likely you are to become critically ill, and the more ill you become the greater the chance you'll have difficulty holding down the tablets. There is some division about the best treatment for malaria. Currently Malarone or Co-artemethor are considered the best standby treatments, but other regimes such as a quinine/doxycycline course are usually effective. Alternatively quinine and fansidar can be used if doxycycline is unavailable. And if there is no quinine either then fansidar alone can be used. The latter is widely available in Tanzania. One cure that you should avoid is Halfan, which is dangerous, particularly if you are using Lariam as a prophylactic.

In severe cases of malaria, the victim will be unable to hold down medication, at which point they are likely to die unless they are hospitalised immediately and put on a drip. If you or a travelling companion start vomiting after taking your malaria medication, get to a hospital or clinic quickly, ideally a private one. Whatever concerns you might have about African hospitals, they are used to dealing with malaria, and the alternative to hospitalisation is far worse. Malaria typically takes around two weeks to incubate (minimum time seven days), but it can take much longer, so you should always complete the prophylaxis as recommended after returning home. If you display possible malaria symptoms up to a year later, then get to a doctor immediately and ensure that they are aware you have been exposed to malaria.

Every so often I run into travellers who prefer to acquire resistance to malaria rather than take preventative tablets, or who witter on about homoeopathic cures for this killer disease. That's their prerogative, but they have no place expounding their ill-informed views to others. Travellers to Africa cannot acquire any effective resistance to malaria, and those who don't make use of prophylactic drugs risk their life in a manner that is both foolish and unnecessary.

African ticks are not the rampant disease transmitters they are in the Americas, but they may spread **tick-bite fever** and a few dangerous rarities. In Tanzania tick-bite fever is a flu-like illness that can easily be treated with doxycycline, but as there can be some serious complications it is important to visit a doctor.

Ticks should ideally be removed as soon as possible as leaving them on the body increases the chance of infection. They should be removed with special tick tweezers that can be bought in good travel shops. Failing that you can use your finger nails: grasp the tick as close to your body as possible and pull steadily and firmly away at right angles to your skin. The tick will then come away complete, as long as you do not jerk or twist. If possible douse the wound with alcohol (any spirit will do) or iodine. Irritants (eg: Olbas oil) or lit cigarettes are to be discouraged since they can cause the ticks to regurgitate and therefore increase the risk of disease. It is best to get a travelling companion to check you for ticks; if you are travelling with small children, remember to check their heads, and particularly behind the ears.

Spreading redness around the bite and/or fever and/or aching joints after a tick bite imply that you have an infection that requires antibiotic treatment, so seek advice.

Bilharzia or schistosomiasis *with thanks to Dr Vaughan Southgate of the Natural History Museum, London, and Dr Dick Stockley, The Surgery, Kampala*

Bilharzia or schistosomiasis is a disease that commonly afflicts the rural poor of the tropics. Two types exist in sub-Saharan Africa – *Schistosoma mansoni* and *Schistosoma haematobium*. It is an unpleasant problem that is worth avoiding, though can be treated if you do get it. This parasite is common in almost all water sources in Tanzania, even places advertised as 'bilharzia free'. The most risky shores will be close to places where infected people use water, wash clothes, etc.

It is easier to understand how to diagnose it, treat it and prevent it if you know a little about the life cycle. Contaminated faeces are washed into the lake, the eggs hatch and the larva infects certain species of snail. The snails then produce about 10,000 cercariae a day for the rest of their lives. The parasites can digest their way through your skin when you wade, or bathe in infested fresh water.

Winds disperse the snails and cercariae. The snails in particular can drift a long way, especially on windblown weed, so nowhere is really safe. However, deep water and running water are safer, while shallow water presents the greatest risk. The cercariae penetrate intact skin, and find their way to the liver. There male and female meet and spend the rest of their lives in permanent copulation. No wonder you feel tired! Most finish up in the wall of the lower bowel, but others can get lost and can cause damage to many different organs. *Schistosoma haematobium* goes mostly to the bladder.

Although the adults do not cause any harm in themselves, after about four to six weeks they start to lay eggs, which cause an intense but usually ineffective immune reaction, including fever, cough, abdominal pain, and a fleeting, itching rash called 'safari itch'. The absence of early symptoms does not necessarily mean there is no infection. Later symptoms can be more localised and more severe, but the general symptoms settle down fairly quickly and eventually you are just tired. 'Tired all the time' is one of the most common symptoms among expats in Africa, and bilharzia, giardia, amoeba and intestinal yeast are the most common culprits.

Although bilharzia is difficult to diagnose, it can be tested at specialist travel clinics. Ideally tests need to be done at least six weeks after likely exposure and will determine whether you need treatment. Fortunately it is easy to treat at present.

Avoiding bilharzia

- If you are bathing, swimming, paddling or wading in fresh water that you think may carry a bilharzia risk, try to get out of the water within ten minutes.
- Avoid bathing or paddling on shores within 200m of villages or places where people use the water a great deal, especially reedy shores or where there is lots of water weed.
- Dry off thoroughly with a towel; rub vigorously.
- If your bathing water comes from a risky source try to ensure that the water is taken from the lake in the early morning and stored snail-free, otherwise it should be filtered or Dettol or Cresol added.
- Bathing early in the morning is safer than bathing in the last half of the day.
- Cover yourself with DEET insect repellent before swimming: it may offer some protection.

Skin infections Any mosquito bite or small nick in the skin gives an opportunity for bacteria to foil the body's usually excellent defences; it will surprise many travellers how quickly skin infections start in warm humid climates and it is essential to clean and cover even the slightest wound. Creams are not as effective as a good drying antiseptic such as dilute iodine, potassium permanganate (a few crystals in half a cup of water) or crystal (or gentian) violet. One of these should be available in most towns. If the wound starts to throb, or becomes red and the redness starts to spread, or the wound oozes, and especially if you develop a fever, antibiotics will probably be needed: flucloxacillin (250mg four times a day) or cloxacillin (500mg four times a day). For those allergic to penicillin, erythromycin (500mg twice a day) for five days should help. See a doctor if the symptoms do not start to improve in 48 hours.

Fungal infections also get a hold easily in hot moist climates so wear 100% cotton socks and underwear and shower frequently. An itchy rash in the groin or flaking between the toes is likely to be a fungal infection. This needs treatment with an antifungal cream such as Canesten (clotrimazole); if this is not available try Whitfield's ointment (compound benzoic acid ointment) or crystal violet (although this will turn you purple!).

Eye problems Bacterial conjunctivitis (pink eye) is a common infection in Africa; people who wear contact lenses are most open to this irritating problem. The eyes feel sore and gritty and they will often be stuck closed in the mornings. They will need treatment with antibiotic drops or ointment. Lesser eye irritation should settle with bathing in salt water and keeping the eyes shaded. If an insect flies into your eye, extract it with great care, ensuring you do not crush or damage it otherwise you may get a nastily inflamed eye from toxins secreted by the creature.

Prickly heat A fine pimply rash on the trunk is likely to be heat rash; cool showers, dabbing dry, and talc will help. Treat the problem by slowing down to a relaxed schedule, wearing only loose, baggy, 100% cotton clothes and sleeping naked under a fan; if it's bad you may need to check into an air-conditioned hotel room for a while.

Meningitis This is a particularly nasty disease as it can kill within hours of the first symptoms appearing. The telltale symptoms are a combination of a blinding headache (light sensitivity), a blotchy rash and a high fever. Immunisation protects against the most serious bacterial form of meningitis and the tetravalent vaccine ACWY is recommended for Tanzania. Other forms of meningitis exist (usually viral) but there are no vaccines for these. Local papers normally report localised

Most established tourist beaches in Tanzania can be assumed to be safe for swimming. Elsewhere along the coast, it would be wise to ask local advice before plunging in the water, and to err on the side of caution if no sensible advice is forthcoming, since there is always a possibility of being swept away by strong currents or undertows that cannot be detected until you are actually in the water.

Snorkellers and divers should wear something on their feet to avoid treading on coral reefs, and should never touch the reefs with their bare hands – coral itself can give nasty cuts, and there is a danger of touching a venomous creature camouflaged against the reef. On beaches, never walk barefoot on exposed coral. Even on sandy beaches, people who walk barefoot risk getting coral or urchin spines in their soles or venomous fish spines in their feet.

If you do tread on a venomous fish, soak the foot in hot (but not scalding) water until sometime after the pain subsides; this may be for 20–30 minutes in all. Take the foot out of the water to top up; otherwise you may scald it. If the pain returns, re-immerse the foot. Once the venom has been heat-inactivated, get a doctor to check and remove any bits of fish spine in the wound.

outbreaks. A severe headache and fever should make you run to a doctor immediately. There are also other causes of headache and fever, one of which is typhoid, which occurs in travellers to Tanzania. Seek medical help if you are ill for more than a few days.

Rabies Rabies can be carried by all mammals (beware the village dogs and small monkeys that are used to being fed in the parks) and is passed on to humans through a bite, scratch or a lick of an open wound. You must always assume any animal is rabid (unless personally known to you) and seek medical help as soon as possible. Meanwhile scrub the wound with soap under a running tap or while pouring water from a jug. Find a reasonably clear-looking source of water (but at this stage the quality of the water is not important), then pour on a strong iodine or alcohol solution of gin, whisky or rum. This helps stop the rabies virus entering the body and will guard against wound infections, including tetanus.

If you intend to have contact with animals and/or are likely to be more than 24 hours away from medical help, then pre-exposure vaccination is advised. Ideally three doses should be taken over a minimum of three weeks. Contrary to popular belief, these vaccinations are relatively painless.

If you are exposed as described, treatment should be given as soon as possible, but it is never too late to seek help as the incubation period for rabies can be very long. Those who have not been immunised will need a full course of injections together with rabies immunoglobulin (RIG), but this product is expensive (around US$800) and may be hard to come by. This is another reason why pre-exposure vaccination should be encouraged in travellers who are planning to visit more remote areas.

Tell the doctor if you have had pre-exposure vaccine, as this will change the treatment you receive. And remember that, if you do contract rabies, mortality is 100% and death from rabies is probably one of the worst ways to go.

Snakes Snakes rarely attack unless provoked, and bites in travellers are unusual. You are less likely to get bitten if you wear stout shoes and long trousers when in the bush. Most snakes are harmless and even venomous species will dispense venom in only about half of their bites. If bitten, then, you are unlikely to have received venom; keeping this fact in mind may help you to stay calm. Many so-called first-aid techniques do more harm than good: cutting into the wound is harmful; tourniquets are dangerous; suction and electrical inactivation devices do not work. The only treatment is antivenom. In the event of a bite which you fear may have been from a venomous snake:

- Try to keep calm – it is likely that no venom has been dispensed.
- Prevent movement of the bitten limb by applying a splint.
- Keep the bitten limb BELOW heart height to slow the spread of any venom.
- If you have a crêpe bandage, bind up as much of the bitten limb as you can, but release the bandage every half-hour.
- Evacuate to a hospital which has antivenom.

And remember:

- NEVER give aspirin; you may offer paracetamol, which is safe.
- NEVER cut or suck the wound.
- DO NOT apply ice packs.
- DO NOT apply potassium permanganate.

If the offending snake can be captured without risk of someone else being bitten, take this to show the doctor – but beware since even a decapitated head is able to bite.

SAFETY

Crime exists in Tanzania as it does practically everywhere in the world. There has been a marked increase in crime in Tanzania over recent years, and tourists are inevitably at risk, because they are far richer than most locals, and are conspicuous in their dress, behaviour and (with obvious exceptions) skin colour. For all that, Tanzania remains a lower crime risk than many countries, and the social taboo on theft is such that even a petty criminal is likely to be beaten to death should they be caught in the act. With a bit of care, you would have to be unlucky to suffer from more serious crime while you are in Tanzania.

MUGGING There is nowhere in Tanzania where mugging is as commonplace as it is in, say, Nairobi or Johannesburg, but there are certainly several parts of the country where walking around alone at night would place you at some risk of being mugged. Mugging is generally an urban problem, with the main areas of risk being Dar es Salaam, Arusha and Zanzibar Town. Even in these places, the risk is often localised, so ask local advice at your hotel, since the staff there will generally know of any recent incidents in the immediate vicinity. The best way to ensure that any potential mugging remains an unpleasant incident rather than a complete disaster

SAFE SEX

Travel is a time when we might enjoy sexual adventures, especially when alcohol reduces inhibitions. Remember that the risks of sexually transmitted infection are high, whether you sleep with fellow travellers or locals. About 80% of HIV infections in British heterosexuals are acquired abroad. Use condoms or femidoms to help reduce the risk of transmission. If you notice any genital ulcers or discharge, get treatment promptly since these increase the risk of acquiring HIV. If you do have unprotected sex, visit a clinic as soon as possible; this should be within 24 hours, or no later than 72 hours, for post-exposure prophylaxis.

is to carry as little as you need on your person. If you are mugged in Tanzania, the personal threat is minimal provided that you promptly hand over what is asked for.

CASUAL THEFT The bulk of crime in Tanzania consists of casual theft such as bag-snatching or pickpocketing. This sort of thing is not particularly aimed at tourists (and as a consequence it is not limited to tourist areas), but tourists will be considered fair game. The key to not being pickpocketed is not having anything of value in your pockets; the key to avoiding having things snatched is to avoid having valuables in a place where they could easily be snatched. Most of the following points will be obvious to experienced travellers, but they are worth making:

- Many casual thieves operate in bus stations and markets. Keep a close watch on your belongings in these places, and avoid having loose valuables in your pocket or daypack.
- Keep all your valuables – passport, travellers' cheques, etc – in a money-belt. One you can hide under your clothes has obvious advantages over one of the currently fashionable codpieces that are worn externally.
- Never carry spending money in your money-belt. A normal wallet is fine provided it contains only a moderate sum of money. Better still is a wallet you can hang around your neck. If I plan to visit a risky area such as a busy market, I sometimes wear shorts under my trousers and keep my cash in the pockets of the shorts. In my opinion, it is difficult for somebody to stick a hand in the front pocket of a shirt unobserved, for which reason this is normally my favourite pocket for keeping ready cash.
- Distribute your money throughout your luggage. I always keep the bulk of my foreign currency in my money-belt, but I like to keep some cash and travellers' cheques hidden in various parts of my pack and daypack.
- Many people prefer to carry their money-belt on their person at all times. I think it is far safer to leave it locked away in a bag or safe in your hotel room. It's not impossible for a locked hotel room to be broken into, but I've not heard of it happening in Tanzania, whereas I have met countless people who have been pickpocketed, mugged or had possessions snatched from them on the street. Circumstances do play a part here: in a large city, I would be far happier with my valuables locked away somewhere, whereas in a game lodge the risk of theft from a room has to be greater than that of theft from your person. One factor to consider is that some travellers' cheque companies won't issue refunds on cheques stolen from a hotel room.
- If you have jewellery that is of high personal or financial value, leave it at home.
- If you are robbed, think twice before you chase the thief, especially if the stolen items are of no great value. An identified thief is likely to be descended on by a mob and quite possibly beaten to death. I have met a few travellers who found themselves in the bizarre position of having to save someone who had just ripped them off.

DOCUMENTATION The best insurance against complete disaster is to keep things well documented. If you carry a photocopy of the main page of your passport, you will be issued a new one more promptly. In addition, keep details of your bank, credit card (if you have one), travel insurance policy and camera equipment (including serial numbers).

Keep copies of your travellers' cheque numbers and *a record of which ones you have cashed*, as well as the international refund assistance telephone number and local agent. If all this information fits on one piece of paper, you can keep photocopies on you and with a friend at home.

You will have to report to the police the theft of any item against which you wish to claim insurance.

SECURITY Tanzania is a very secure country, with a proud record of internal stability since independence. The bombing of the US embassies in Dar es Salaam and Nairobi resulted in large-scale cancellations of US tours to Tanzania in late 1998, despite a mass of evidence that would provide any rational human with greater cause to give a wide birth to US embassies than to cancel a holiday in east Africa. Aside from this, the only part of Tanzania where there is currently a security problem is in the remote tract of Maasailand lying between Lake Natron and the Serengeti. The security situation here is the direct result of the recent incursion of a group of armed Somalis from Kenya, and while it has resulted in several deaths locally, the only effect on tourists to date has been an isolated incident in which a safari vehicle was held up along the road west of Natron. The indications are that this is a short-term problem, and it is unlikely that any responsible safari company would risk taking tourists into this area until it is resolved.

Tanzania shares a western border with the troubled countries of the Congo, Rwanda and Burundi, an area that sees very little tourism. So far as I am aware, the recent civil war in the Congo has had little direct effect on Tanzania, probably because Lake Tanganyika divides the two countries. The Rwanda and Burundi border areas have been overrun with refugees at several points over the last few years, a situation that is of some concern to locals, officials and international aid workers, but has had no effect on parts of Tanzania likely to be visited by tourists.

ADVICE FOR DISABLED TRAVELLERS

Gordon Rattray (www.able-travel.com), author of Access Africa: Safaris for People with Limited Mobility *(Bradt Travel Guides)*
Despite the fact that some of the upmarket lodges have accessible rooms, and a few operators claim to have adapted vehicles, Tanzania does not yet have the infrastructure to make a disabled safari a 'walk in the park'.

In general, wheelchair users and less ambulant people will need to compromise and improvise. On the plus side, African people are used to dealing with problems and disability is common, so you will have no shortage of help and useful advice.

- **VEHICLE TRANSFERS** Safari vehicles are higher than normal cars, making transfers more difficult. Drivers/guides are normally happy to help, but are not trained in this skill, so you must thoroughly explain your needs and stay in control of the situation.
- **SEATING** Because distances are large and roads are often bumpy, you need to be extra vigilant to avoid pressure wounds. Place your own pressure-relieving wheelchair cushion on top of (or instead of) the original cushion and, if necessary, pad around knees and elbows.
- **BATHROOMS** Occasionally (more by accident than through design), showers and toilets are wheelchair accessible. Where this is not the case, be prepared to be carried again, or do your ablutions in the bedroom!
- **HEALTH** Doctors will know about 'everyday' illnesses, but you must understand and be able to explain your own medical requirements. African hospitals are often basic, so if possible, take all necessary medication and equipment with you. It is advisable to pack this in your hand luggage during the flight in case your main luggage becomes lost.

WOMEN TRAVELLERS Women travellers in Tanzania have little to fear on a gender-specific level. Over the years, I've met several women travelling alone in Tanzania, and none had any serious problems in their interactions with locals, aside from the hostility that can be generated by dressing skimpily. Otherwise, an element of flirtation is about the sum of it, perhaps the odd direct proposition, but nothing that cannot be defused by a firm 'No'. And nothing, for that matter, that you wouldn't expect in any Western country, or – probably with a far greater degree of persistence – from many male travellers.

It would be prudent to pay some attention to how you dress in Tanzania, particularly in the more conservative parts of the Swahili coast. In areas where people are used to tourists, they are unlikely to be deeply offended by women travellers wearing shorts or other outfits that might be seen to be provocative. Nevertheless, it still pays to allow for local sensibilities, and under certain circumstances revealing clothes may be perceived to make a statement that's not intended from your side.

More mundanely, tampons are not readily available in smaller towns, though you can easily locate them in Dar es Salaam and Arusha, and in game lodge and hotel gift shops. When travelling in out-of-the-way places, carry enough tampons to see you through to the next time you'll be in a large city, bearing in mind that travelling in the tropics can sometimes cause heavier or more regular periods than normal. Sanitary pads are available in most towns of any size.

WHAT TO TAKE

There are two governing principles with regard to packing for Tanzania. The first is to bring everything that you could possibly need and that mightn't be readily available when you need it. The second is to travel as light as possible. Somewhat contradictory directives, so the key is to find the right balance, something that probably depends on personal experience and taste as much as anything. Worth stressing is that most genuine necessities are surprisingly easy to get hold of in the main centres in Tanzania, and that most of the ingenious gadgets you can buy in camping shops are unlikely to amount to much more than deadweight on the road. If it came to it, you could easily travel in Tanzania with little more than a change of clothes, a few basic toiletries and a medical kit.

CARRYING YOUR LUGGAGE Make sure that your suitcase is tough and durable, and that it seals well, so that its contents will survive bumpy, dusty drives to the game reserves. A lock is a good idea, not only for flights, but also for when you leave your case in a hotel room – rare incidents of theft from upmarket hotels in Africa tend to be opportunistic and a locked suitcase is unlikely to be tampered with. A daypack will be useful when on safari, and you should be able to pack your luggage in such a manner that any breakable goods can be carried separately in the body of the vehicle and on your lap when necessary – anything like an mp3 player, laptop or camera will suffer heavily from vibrations on rutted roads. If you are likely to use public transport, then a backpack is the most practical way to carry your luggage.

CAMPING EQUIPMENT On a budget safari or organised Kilimanjaro climb, camping equipment will be provided by the company you travel with. Taken together with the limited opportunities for camping outside of the safari circuit, this means that for most travellers a tent will be deadweight in Tanzania. An all-weather sleeping bag is required on Mount Meru or Kilimanjaro, and you may want to bring your own sleeping bag for any camping safari.

CLOTHES Assuming that you have the space, you ought to carry at least one change of shirt and underwear for every day you will spend on safari. Organising laundry along the way is tiresome, and dusty conditions practically enforce a daily change of clothes. It's a good idea to keep one or two shirts for evening use only.

When you select your clothes, remember that jeans are heavy to carry, hot to wear and slow to dry. Far better to bring light cotton trousers and, if you intend spending a while in montane regions, tracksuit bottoms, which will provide extra cover on chilly nights. Skirts are best made of a light natural fabric such as cotton. T-shirts are lighter and less bulky than proper shirts, though the top pocket of a shirt (particularly if it buttons up) is a good place to carry spending money in markets and bus stations, since it's easier to keep an eye on than trouser pockets. One sweater or sweatshirt will be adequate in most parts of the country, though you will need serious alpine gear for Kilimanjaro and to a lesser degree Mount Meru.

Socks and underwear should be made from natural fabrics. Bear in mind that reusing sweaty undergarments will encourage fungal infections such as athlete's foot, as well as prickly heat in the groin region. As for footwear, genuine hiking boots are worth considering only if you're a serious off-road hiker, since they are very heavy, whether on your feet or in your pack. A good pair of walking shoes, preferably made of leather and with good ankle support, is a good compromise. It's also useful to carry sandals, thongs or other light shoes.

Another factor in deciding what clothes to bring is the sensibilities of Tanzania's large Muslim population. Women can wear shorts at most beach resorts, in game reserves and in Dar es Salaam, Zanzibar Town or Arusha where locals are used to tourists, but probably not in smaller coastal settlements. Trousers may be frowned upon by traditionalists, but they are seen as unconventional rather than offensive. The ideal thing to wear is a skirt that covers your knees and a modest shirt that doesn't expose shoulders or cleavage.

Men, too, should be conscious of what they wear. Shorts seem to be acceptable, but few Tanzanian men wear them and trousers are considered more respectable. Walking around in a public place without a shirt is unacceptable.

OTHER USEFUL ITEMS Your **toilet bag** should at the very minimum include soap (secured in a plastic bag or soap holder unless you enjoy a soapy toothbrush!), shampoo, toothbrush and toothpaste. This sort of stuff is easy to replace as you go along, so there's no need to bring family-sized packs. Men will probably want a **razor**. Women should carry enough **tampons** and/or **sanitary pads** to see them through at least one heavy period, since these items may not always be immediately available. Nobody should forget to bring a **towel**, or to keep handy a roll of **loo paper** which, although widely available at shops and kiosks, cannot always be relied upon to be present where it's most urgently needed.

Other essentials include a **torch**, a **penknife** and a compact **alarm clock** for those early morning starts. You should carry a small **medical kit** (see pages 53–4) and **mosquito nets**. If you wear **contact lenses**, bring all the fluids you need, since they are not available in Tanzania. You might also want to bring a pair of **glasses** to wear on long bus rides, and on safari – many lens wearers suffer badly in dusty conditions. In general, since many people find the intense sun and dry climate irritates their eyes, you might consider reverting to glasses.

Binoculars are essential if you want to get a good look at birds, or to watch distant mammals in game reserves. For most purposes, lightweight 7x21 compact binoculars will be fine, though some might prefer traditional 7x35 binoculars for their larger field of vision. Serious birdwatchers will find a 10x30 or 10x50 magnification more useful, and should definitely carry a good field guide.

The unit of currency is the Tanzanian shilling (pronounced *shillingi*), divided into 100 cents. The Tanzanian shilling comes in Tsh10,000, 5,000, 1,000, 500 and 200 denomination bills. It is often very difficult to find change for larger denomination bills, so try always to have a fair spread of notes available. The bulky small denomination coins are worth considerably less than their weight in whatever leaden metal it is that's used to mint them! At the time of writing the exchange rate of roughly US$1 = Tsh1,150–200 is reasonably stable, but like most African currencies the Tanzanian shilling has steadily devalued against hard currencies in recent years. It is reasonable to expect that a similar trend will persist during the lifespan of this edition. For rates of exchange, see page 2.

Most upmarket hotels and safari companies in Tanzania quote rates in US dollars. Some will also demand payment in this or another prominent hard currency, though some hotels and lodges actually prefer payment in local currency. The situation with national parks and other conservation areas is variable, but if you expect to pay fees directly rather than through an operator, then you'll need enough hard currency to cover the full amount (see box, *Paying park fees*, opposite). These exceptions noted, most things in Tanzania are best paid for in local currency, including restaurant bills, goods bought at a market or shop, mid-range and budget accommodation, public transport and most other casual purchases. Indeed, most service providers geared towards the local economy will have no facility for accepting any currency other than the Tanzanian shilling.

There are three ways of carrying money: hard currency cash, travellers' cheques or a credit card. My advice is to bring at least as much as you think you'll need in the combination of cash and travellers' cheques, but if possible to also carry a credit card to draw on in an emergency. I would strongly urge any but the most denominationally chauvinistic of backpackers to bring their cash and travellers' cheques in the form of US dollars, and to learn to think and budget in this currency.

From the point of view of security, it's advisable to bring the bulk of your money in the form of travellers' cheques, which can be refunded if they are lost or stolen. Best to use a widely recognised type of travellers' cheque such as American Express or Thomas Cook, and to keep your proof of purchase discrete from the cheques, as well as noting which cheques you have used, in order to facilitate a swift refund should you require one. Buy your travellers' cheques in a healthy mix of denominations, since you may sometimes need to change a small sum only, for instance when you're about to cross into another country. On the other hand, you don't want an impossibly thick wad of cheques. Currency regulations and other complications make it practically impossible to break down a large-denomination travellers' cheque into smaller ones in most African countries, so don't bring travellers' cheques in denominations larger than US$100.

In addition to travellers' cheques, you should definitely bring a proportion of your money in hard currency cash, say around US$200–300, since you are bound to hit situations where travellers' cheques won't be accepted, and cash gets a better exchange rate than travellers' cheques, especially large-denomination bills. This would not be much consolation were all your money to be stolen, so I'd strongly advise against bringing cash only, but would suggest that you save what cash you do bring for situations where it will buy you a real advantage. Note that US dollar bills printed before 2002, particularly larger denominations such as US$100 and US$50, will almost certainly be refused by banks, hotels and other foreign exchange outlets.

Carry your hard currency and travellers' cheques as well as your passport and other important documentation in a money-belt that can be hidden beneath your

Prior to October 2007, entrance, camping and other fees for all national parks, game reserves and other conservation areas were payable in hard currency cash or travellers' cheques (ideally US dollars). However, in order to combat staff pilfering, Tanzania National Parks (Tanapa) has now installed electronic payment systems at all entrance gates and other revenue collection centres in the major national parks in the northern safari circuit, ie: Serengeti, Lake Manyara, Tarangire, Kilimanjaro and Arusha national parks. The electronic systems accept fee payment by international MasterCard and Tanapa Card only. No other cards are accepted, nor are travellers' cheques or Tanzania shillings, and in order to discourage hard currency cash payments, Tanapa now also charges a 50% penalty on these – in other words, if you arrive at the Serengeti wanting to pay your daily US$50 entrance fee in US dollars cash, you'll be charged an additional US$25 per day.

This isn't an issue for travellers on organised safaris, as their operator will pay the fees and will most likely have a Tanapa Card that operates much like a credit card. Independent travellers, however, must either pay by MasterCard, or must arrive at the gate with sufficient funds in the form of prepaid Tanapa Cards, which can be bought at any branch of the Exim Bank. There are two such banks in Arusha: the main branch on Sokoine Avenue near the Clock Tower (⊕ 09.00–15.00 Mon–Fri, 09.00–12.30 Sat) and the subsidiary branch in the TFA (Shoprite) Centre at the other end of Sokoine Avenue (⊕ 09.00–16.30 Mon–Fri, 09.00–14.30 Sat). The cards cannot be bought outside these banking hours or on Sunday.

Prepaid Tanapa Cards come in denominations of US$500, US$250, US$100, US$70 and US$50. They are not refundable, so you ideally want to buy exactly the right amount to cover your total stay in all parks that use the electronic system. The tellers who sell the cards aren't so hot when it comes to this sort of calculation, so try to work out the best combination of cards yourself (a couple spending three days in the Serengeti and one each in Tarangire and Manyara but not camping would need prepaid cards to the value of US$440, ie… one US$250 card, one US$50 and two US$70). You can pay for these Tanapa Cards with a MasterCard (not much point, though, as this card would be accepted at the entrance gate anyway), but otherwise your only option is hard currency cash – neither local currency cash nor hard currency travellers' cheques are accepted, and Exim Bank doesn't have the facility to accept other international cards such as Visa or American Express. It's all monumentally user-unfriendly, and injury is added to insult by the levying of a service fee of US$1 per prepaid card (so the example above would cost US$444).

It is important to note that as things stand this system applies only to the five parks listed above. Other national parks covered in this guidebook, eg: Rubondo Island or Mkomazi, still operate as before, taking hard currency cash or travellers' cheques, though this could change during the lifespan of this edition (check www.tanzaniaparks.com for news). Fees for Ngorongoro Conservation Area are also still payable in hard currency cash or travellers' cheques. This payment is treated as a foreign-exchange transaction, which means that if you don't have the exact amount in US dollar bills or travellers' cheques, you will have to exchange a larger denomination and will receive the change in local currency at a poor exchange rate.

Practical Information **MONEY AND BANKING**

2

clothing. Your money-belt should be made of cotton or another natural fabric, and everything inside the belt should be wrapped in plastic to protect it against sweat.

FOREIGN EXCHANGE Foreign currencies can be changed into Tanzanian shillings at any bank or bureau de change (known locally as forex bureaux). Most banks are open from around 09.00 to 12.30 on weekdays and in many larger towns they stay open until 15.00 or later. They open from 09.00 to at least 11.30 on Saturdays. Most private forex bureaux stay open until 16.00 or later. You can normally change money at any time of day at Julius Nyerere International Airport (Dar es Salaam) or Kilimanjaro International Airport (between Arusha and Moshi). Most private forex bureaux deal in cash only, for which reason you'll probably be forced to change your travellers' cheques at a bank. The rate for this is often slightly lower than the cash rate and a small commission is also charged.

Generally, private forex bureaux offer a better rate of exchange than banks, though this is not so much the case as it was a few years ago, and some forex bureaux actually give notably lower rates than the banks. It's worth shopping around before a major transaction. The private bureaux are almost always far quicker for cash transactions than the banks, which might be a more important consideration than a minor discrepancy in the rate they offer. Before you change a large amount of money, check the bank or forex bureau has enough high denomination banknotes, or you'll need a briefcase to carry your local currency.

The legalisation of private forex bureaux has killed off the black market that previously thrived in Tanzania. Private individuals may give you a slightly better rate than the banks, but the official rate is so favourable it seems unfair to exploit this. In Dar es Salaam or Arusha you will be offered exceptionally good rates on the street, but if you are stupid or greedy enough to accept these, you can expect to be ripped off. There are plenty of forged US$100 bills floating around Tanzania, and you can assume that anyone who suggests a deal involving a US$100 bill is trying to unload a forgery.

CREDIT CARDS Only a few years ago, credit cards were practically useless in Tanzania. Today, however, most major international credit cards (especially Visa but also MasterCard and American Express) are widely accepted by the better safari operators, in upmarket hotels and, to a lesser extent, in smarter restaurants and upmarket tourist-oriented shops in Dar es Salaam, Arusha, Moshi and Zanzibar Town. They are also accepted in many but certainly not all game lodges and upmarket beach resorts, and in a handful of city hotels elsewhere in the country. Increasingly, carrying a credit card is a viable alternative to cash or travellers' cheques, since it can be used to draw up to Tsh200,000 daily (about US$200) at 24-hour ATMs (autotellers) outside selected banks in Dar es Salaam, Arusha, Moshi, Mwanza and other large towns.

Having said that, ATM facilities are not available in the national parks, many lodges and beach resorts that accept cash or travellers' cheques only, and some park fees cannot be paid with a card (see box, *Paying park fees*, page 67). Budget travellers can safely assume that hotels and other facilities within their reach cannot process credit-card payments. Although things are changing rapidly, it's still a good idea to carry some of your funds in hard currency cash or travellers' cheques, and carry a credit card primarily as a back-up for emergencies. Tourists on pre-booked holidays will not of course need to carry a vast amount of cash, and can check with their tour operator whether the lodges they are booked into will accept credit-card payments for extras. No matter how long you are travelling, do make sure that you are set up in such a way that you won't need to have money transferred or drafted across to Tanzania.

GETTING AROUND

✈ **BY AIR** Several private airlines run scheduled flights around Tanzania, most prominently Regional Air Services, Precision Air, Coastal Travel and the national carrier Air Tanzania. Between them, these carriers offer reliable services to most parts of the country that regularly attract tourists, including Dar es Salaam, Zanzibar, Pemba, Mafia, Kilimanjaro, Arusha, Serengeti, Ngorongoro, Lake Manyara, Mwanza, Rubondo Island, Kigoma and most of the southern parks. There are also regular flights between Kilimanjaro and the Kenyan cities of Mombasa and Nairobi. Several of the airlines now offer a straightforward online booking service. Contact details are as follows.

Air Tanzania 🔪 022 211 8411; e bookings@ airtanzania.com; www.airtanzania.com
Coastal Travel 🔪 022 211 7959/60; e safari@ coastal.cc; www.coastal.cc

Precision Air 🔪 022 216 8000; m 0787 888408; e contactcentre@precisionairtz.com; www.precisionairtz.com
Regional Air Services 🔪 027 250 2541/4077; e resvns@regional.co.tz; www.regionaltanzania.com

BY PUBLIC TRANSPORT Good express coach services, typically covering in excess of 60km per hour, connect Arusha and Moshi to Dar es Salaam and Nairobi (Kenya). The Scandinavia Coach company is particularly recommended, approaching (though far from attaining) Greyhound-type standards, and with at least one daily service on the country's two most important routes, ie: Dar es Salaam to Arusha and Dar es Salaam to Mbeya. A number of shuttle companies such as Riverside and Impala run twice-daily minibus transfers between Arusha, Moshi and Nairobi. Coaches and shuttles can be booked through reliable tour operators. The alternative to buses on most routes is a *dala-dala* – a generic name that seems to encompass practically any light public transport. On the whole, *dala-dalas* tend to be overcrowded by comparison with buses, and they are more likely to try to overcharge tourists, while the manic driving style results in regular fatal accidents. When you check out bus departure times, be conscious that many Tanzanians will translate Swahili time to English without making the six-hour conversion – in other words, you might be told that a bus leaves at 11.00 when it actually leaves at 05.00 (see *Swahili Time* in *Appendix 2*, page 279).

BY PRIVATE SAFARI AND CAR RENTAL The most normal way of getting around northern Tanzania is on an organised safari by Land Cruiser, Land Rover or any other similarly hardy 4x4 with high clearance. It is standard procedure for safari companies to provide a driver/guide with a fair knowledge of local wildlife and road conditions, as well as some mechanical expertise. Self-drive car hire isn't a particularly attractive or popular option in northern Tanzania, but it is widely available in Zanzibar and Dar es Salaam.

ACCOMMODATION

The volume of hotels in major urban tourist centres such as Zanzibar Town, Arusha, Moshi and Dar es Salaam is quite remarkable. So, too, is the variety in standard and price, which embraces hundreds of simple local guesthouses charging a couple of US dollars a night, as well as fantastic exclusive beach resorts and lodges charging upwards of US$300 per person – and everything in between.

All accommodation listings in this guidebook are placed in one of six categories: exclusive, upmarket, moderate, budget, shoestring, and camping. The purpose of this categorisation is twofold: to break up long hotel listings that span a wide price range, and to help readers isolate the range of hotels that will best suit their budget and taste. The application of categories is not rigid. Aside from an inevitable element of subjectivity, I have categorised hotels on their feel as much as their rates (the prices are quoted anyway), and this might be influenced by the standard of other accommodation options in the same place.

Before going into more detail about the different accommodation categories, it's worth noting a few potentially misleading quirks in local hotel-speak. In Swahili, the word *hoteli* refers to a restaurant while what we call a hotel is generally called a lodging, guesthouse or *gesti* – so if you ask a Tanzanian to show you a hotel you might well be taken to an eatery (see *Appendix 2, Language*). Another local quirk is that most Tanzanian hotels in all ranges refer to a room with an en-suite shower and toilet as being self-contained. Finally, at most hotels in the moderate category or below, a single room will as often as not be one with a three-quarter or double bed, while a double room will be what we call a twin, with two single or double beds. 'B&B' refers to bed and breakfast, 'HB' to half board, 'FB' to full board.

EXCLUSIVE This category does not generally embrace conventional international-style hotels, but rather small and atmospheric tented camps, game lodges and beach resorts catering to the most exclusive end of the market. Lodges in this category typically (but not invariably) contain significantly fewer than 20 accommodation units built and decorated in a style that complements the surrounding environment. The management will generally place a high priority on personalised service and quality food and wine, with the main idea being that guests are exposed to a holistic 24-hour bush or beach experience, rather than just a hotel room and restaurant in a bush/beach location. In several instances, lodges that fall into the exclusive category might be less conventionally luxurious, in terms of air conditioning and the like, than their competitors in the upmarket category. It is the bush experience, not the range of facilities, that lends lodges in this category a quality of exclusivity. Rates are typically upwards of US$250 per person all-inclusive, but many cost twice as much as that (with substantial discounts for operators). This is the category to look at if you want authentic, atmospheric bush or beach accommodation and have few financial restrictions.

UPMARKET This category includes most hotels, lodges and resorts that cater almost entirely to the international tourist or business travel market. Hotels in this range would typically be accorded a two- to four-star ranking internationally, and they offer smart accommodation with en-suite facilities, mosquito netting, air conditioning or fans depending on the local climate, and satellite television in cities and some beach resorts. Hotels in this bracket might charge anything from under US$100 to upwards of US$500 for a double room, depending on quality and location. As a rule, upmarket hotels in areas that see few foreign visitors are far cheaper than equivalent hotels in or around urban tourist centres such as Dar es Salaam or Arusha, which are in turn cheaper than beach hotels and lodges in national parks and game reserves. Room rates for city and beach hotels invariably include breakfast, while at game lodges they will also normally include lunch and dinner. Most package tours and privately booked safaris use accommodation in this range.

MODERATE In Tanzania, as in many African countries, there is often a wide gap in price and standard between the cheapest hotels geared primarily towards tourists and the best hotels geared primarily towards local travellers and budget travellers. For this reason, the moderate bracket is rather more nebulous than other accommodation categories, essentially consisting of hotels which, for one or another reason, couldn't really be classified as upmarket, but equally are too expensive or of too high quality to be considered budget lodgings. Many places listed in this range are superior local hotels that will suffice in lieu of any genuinely upmarket accommodation in a town that sees relatively few tourists. The category also embraces decent lodges or hotels in recognised tourist areas that charge considerably lower rates than their upmarket competitors, but are clearly a notch or two above the budget category. Hotels in this range normally offer comfortable accommodation in self-contained rooms with hot water, fan and possibly satellite television, and they will have decent restaurants and employ a high proportion of English-speaking staff. Prices for moderate city and beach hotels are generally in the US$50–80 range, more in some game reserves. This is the category to look at if you are travelling privately on a limited or low budget and expect a reasonably high but not luxurious standard of accommodation.

BUDGET Hotels in this category are aimed largely at the local market and definitely don't approach international standards, but are still reasonably clean and comfortable, and a definite cut above the basic guesthouses that proliferate in most towns. Hotels in this bracket will more often than not have a decent restaurant attached, English-speaking staff, and comfortable rooms with en-suite facilities, running cold or possibly hot water, fans (but not air conditioning) and good mosquito netting. Hotels in this category typically charge around US$15–30 for a self-contained double room, but they may charge as little as US$5 in relatively out-of-the-way places and more than US$30 in major tourist centres. This is the category to look at if you are on a limited budget, but want to avoid total squalor!

SHOESTRING This category is aimed at travellers who want the cheapest possible accommodation irrespective of quality. In most Tanzanian towns, this will amount to a choice of dozens of small private guesthouses, which are almost exclusively used by locals, are remarkably uniform in design, and generally charge below US$15 for an uncluttered room. The typical guesthouse consists of around ten cell-like rooms forming three walls around a central courtyard, with a reception area or restaurant at the front. Toilets are more often than not long-drops. Washing facilities often amount to nothing more than a lockable room and a bucket of water, though an increasing number of guesthouses do have proper showers, and a few have hot water. There are several cheap church-run guesthouses and hostels in Tanzania, and these are normally also included under the shoestring listings.

CAMPING There are surprisingly few campsites in Tanzania, and those that do exist tend to be in national parks, where camping costs US$20–30 per person. Along the coast north of Dar es Salaam and in Moshi and Arusha, several recently opened private sites cater to backpackers and overland trucks. If you ask at moderate hotels in out-of- the-way places, you may sometimes be allowed to camp in their grounds for a small fee.

✖ EATING AND DRINKING

FOOD Most tourists will eat 90% of their meals at game lodges or hotels that cater specifically to tourists and whose kitchens serve Western-style food, ranging in standard from adequate to excellent. Game lodges tend to offer a daily set menu with a limited selection, so it is advisable to have your tour operator specify in advance if you are a vegetarian or have other specific dietary requirements. First-time visitors to Africa might take note that most game lodges in and around the national parks have isolated locations, and driving within the parks is neither permitted nor advisable after dark, so that there is no realistic alternative to eating at your lodge. You will rarely be disappointed.

Most game lodges offer the option of a packaged breakfast and/or lunch box, so that their guests can eat on the trot rather than having to base their game-viewing hours around set meal times. The standard of the packed lunches is rather variable (and in some cases pretty awful) but if your first priority is to see wildlife, then taking a breakfast box in particular allows you to be out during the prime game-viewing hours immediately after sunrise. Packed meals must be ordered the night before you need them.

When you are staying in towns such as Arusha and Moshi, there is a fair selection of eating-out options. Indian eateries are particularly numerous in most towns, thanks to the high resident Indian population, and good continental restaurants and pizzerias are also well represented. Seafood is excellent on the coast. A selection of the better restaurants in each town is listed in the main part of the guide.

As for the local cuisine, it tends to consist of a bland stew eaten with one of four staples: rice, chapati, *ugali* or *batoke*. *Ugali* is a stiff maize porridge eaten throughout sub-Saharan Africa. *Batoke* or *matoke* is cooked plantain, served boiled or in a mushy heap. In the Lake Victoria region, *batoke* replaces *ugali* as the staple food. The most common stews are chicken, beef, goat and beans, and the meat is often rather tough. In coastal towns and around the great lakes, whole fried fish is a welcome change. The distinctive Swahili cuisine of the coast makes generous use of coconut milk and is far spicier than other Tanzanian food.

Mandaazi, the local equivalent of doughnuts, are tasty when freshly cooked. They are served at *hotelis* and sold at markets. You can eat cheaply at stalls around markets and bus stations. Goat kebabs, fried chicken, grilled groundnuts and potato chips are often freshly cooked and sold in these places.

KiSwahili names for various foods are given in *Appendix 2, Language*.

DRINKS The most widely drunk beverage is *chai*, a sweet tea where all ingredients are boiled together in a pot. Along the coast *chai* is often flavoured with spices such as ginger. In some places *chai* is served *ya rangi* or black; in others *maziwa* or milky. Sodas such as Coke, Pepsi, Sprite and Fanta are widely available, and normally cost less than US$0.50 in outlets geared towards locals, and up to five times that price

TRADITIONAL MBEGE BANANA BEER

Emma Thomson

This party brew is prepared for many different Chagga ceremonies, but it is always drunk from a dried squash plant that has been hollowed out to form an enormous chalice, with the village landlord's clan name engraved upon it. Below is a rough recipe, as the measurements are only approximate.

Ingredients
1kg mashed banana
1 litre water
1kg finger millet

Method
Boil in water until the bananas turn red, and then cover for three days.

Meanwhile, wash the finger millet, cover and leave in a wet, warm and dark place for three to four days until the millet begins to sprout. Then grind the millet into flour.

From this, make porridge by mixing two parts flour to one part water. Next add ten parts of the boiled banana to one part porridge, mix and cover until the next day.

Let the celebrations begin. (The longer you leave it, the stronger the brew.)

in tourist-oriented lodges. In large towns you can often get fresh fruit juice. On the coast and in some parts of the interior, the most refreshing, healthy and inexpensive drink is coconut milk, sold by street vendors who will decapitate the young coconut of your choice to create a natural cup, from which the juice can be sipped. Tap water in Tanzania is often dodgy, and most travellers try to stick to mineral water, which comes in 1.5-litre bottles that cost a few hundred shillings in supermarkets in Arusha but are very overpriced at game lodges – it is advisable to stock up with a dozen bottles or so before your safari leaves Arusha.

The two main alcoholic drinks are beer and *konyagi*. *Konyagi* is a spirit made from sugar cane. It tastes a bit strange on its own, but it mixes well and is very cheap. The local Safari lager used to be appalling, but since the national brewery was taken over by South African Breweries a few years ago there has been a dramatic improvement not only in the quality of Safari, but also in the selection of other brands available. Around ten different lager beers are now available, of which Castle, Kilimanjaro and Serengeti seem to be the most popular. All beers come in 500ml bottles and cost anything from US$1 at a local bar to US$5 at the most upmarket hotels. A variety of imported spirits are available in larger towns. South African wines are widely available at lodges and hotels, and they are generally of a high quality and reasonably priced by international standards.

PUBLIC HOLIDAYS

Tourists visiting Tanzania should take note of public holidays, since all banks, forex bureaux and government offices will be closed on these days. In addition to Good Friday, Easter Monday, Idd-ul-Fitr, Islamic New Year and the Prophet's Birthday, which fall on different dates every year, the following public holidays are taken in Tanzania:

1 January	New Year's Day
12 January	Zanzibar Revolution Day
5 February	CCM Day
26 April	Union Day (anniversary of union between Tanganyika and Zanzibar)
1 May	International Workers' Day
7 July	Saba Saba (Peasants') Day
8 August	Nane Nane (Farmers') Day
14 October	Nyerere Memorial Day
9 December	Independence Day
25 December	Christmas Day
26 December	Boxing Day

SHOPPING

Until a few years ago it was difficult to buy anything much in Tanzania. One of my most vivid memories of Dar es Salaam in 1986 was walking into a general store where a lone shelf of teaspoons was the only stock. Things have improved greatly since then. In Dar es Salaam and most other large towns a fair range of imported goods is available, though prices are often inflated. If you have any very specific needs – unusual medications or slide film, for instance – bring them with you. Toilet roll, soap, toothpaste, pens, batteries and locally produced food are widely available. Shopping hours are normally between 08.30 and 16.30, with a lunch break between 13.00 and 14.00, but dukas, the stalls you see around markets or lining roads, are cheaper than proper shops and stay open for longer hours.

CURIOS A variety of items specifically aimed at tourists is available: Makonde carvings, Tingatinga paintings (see box, page 105), batiks, musical instruments, wooden spoons and various soapstone and malachite knick-knacks. Arusha is the best place to shop for curios, as prices are competitive and the quality is good. Prices in shops are fixed, but you may be able to negotiate a discount. At curio stalls, haggling is necessary. Unless you are good at this, expect to pay more than you would in a shop. The colourful *vitenge* (the singular of this is *kitenge*) worn by most Tanzanian women can be picked up cheaply at any market in the country.

𝒞 MEDIA AND COMMUNICATIONS

NEWSPAPERS The English-language *Daily News* and *Daily Guardian*, available in all major towns, now carry a fair bit of syndicated international news, and the local news can also make for interesting reading. The Kenyan *Daily Nation*, available in Dar es Salaam, Arusha and Mwanza, is slightly better. The excellent *East African* is a weekly newspaper published in Kenya but distributed throughout the three countries to which it dedicates roughly equal coverage, ie: Kenya, Tanzania and Uganda. Stalls and vendors around the Clocktower in Arusha sell *Time* and *Newsweek*, as well as a variety of European, British and American papers.

TELEPHONES

Phone calls If you want to make an international phone call or send a fax, a TCC Extelcomms centre can be found in most large towns. Calls are cheap by international standards, and some Extelcomms centres will receive as well as send faxes. The costlier but more convenient alternative is to phone directly from your lodge or hotel. If you are carrying a mobile phone that receives international calls, the satellite network is pretty good in and around towns but rather less so in more remote parts of the game reserves.

Cell phones If you bring a cell phone with you from home, it's emphatically worth the minor investment in a Tanzanian SIM card (which costs around US$0.30 and gives you a local number) and airtime cards (available in units of Tsh1,000 to 5,000). International text messages are very cheap (US$1 will buy you around a dozen text messages to anywhere in the world) and international calls work out at around US$1 for three to four minutes. By contrast, you'll rack up a hefty bill if you use your home phone number for calls and/or messages, since in most instances these are charged at international rates out of your home country, even when you phone home. SIM and airtime cards can be bought at a specialist Vodacom outlet (there are several in Arusha and Moshi) or at numerous other small shops displaying the ubiquitous Vodacom sticker. Network reception is increasingly widespread in northern Tanzania, even in the national parks. Note that all Tanzanian mobile phone companies have changed their prefixes since the last edition of this guide. The changes are as follows: 0741 is now 0713; 0748 is now 0784; 0745 is now 0755; and 0747 is now 0777 or 0774. Many mobile numbers serve as fixed lines because the land lines are so bad in Tanzania – I read recently that there are almost 100 mobile phones in the country for every landline!

INTERNET AND EMAIL The spread of internet use in Africa has been remarkable over the last decade, and the existence of email represents a real communications revolution on a continent where international lines tend to be unreliable and expensive. Internet and email have caught on particularly quickly in Tanzania, and internet cafés are prolific and affordable in most major urban tourist centres. The servers are usually quite fast, though not comparable to international broadband, and rates are very affordable. Internet access is not available in most game reserves and national parks, and the few game lodges that do offer browsing or email services tend to charge very high rates.

CULTURAL ETIQUETTE

Tanzania has perhaps the most egalitarian and tolerant mood of any African country that I've visited. As a generalisation, Tanzanians tend to treat visitors with a dignified reserve, something that many Westerners mistake for a stand-offish attitude, but in my opinion is more indicative of a respect both for our culture and their own. Granted, dignified probably won't be the adjective that leaps to mind if your first interaction with Tanzanians comes from the pestilence of touts that hang around bus stations in Arusha or Moshi, or somewhere similar. But then in most poor countries, you'll find that people who make a living on the fringe of the tourist industry tend to be pushy and occasionally confrontational in their dealings – from their perspective, they probably have to be in order to make a living. But I do think that anybody who spends time travelling in Tanzania will recognise the behaviour of touts to be wholly unrepresentative of what is essentially a conservative, unhurried and undemonstrative society.

On the whole, you would have to do something pretty outrageous to commit a serious faux pas in Tanzania. But, like any country, Tanzania does have its rules of etiquette, and while allowances will always be made for tourists, there is some value in ensuring that they are not made too frequently!

GENERAL CONDUCT Perhaps the most important single point of etiquette to be grasped by visitors to Tanzania is the social importance of formal greetings. Tanzanians tend to greet each other elaborately, and if you want to make a good impression on somebody who speaks English, whether they be a waiter or a shop assistant (and especially if they work in a government department), you would do well to follow suit. When you need to ask somebody directions, it is rude to blunder straight into interrogative mode without first exchanging greetings. With Tanzanians who don't speak English, the greeting *'Jambo'* delivered with a smile and a nod of the head will be adequate.

Whenever I visit Tanzania after travelling elsewhere in Africa, I am struck afresh by how readily people greet passing strangers, particularly in rural areas. In Tanzania, this greeting doesn't normally take the form of a shrieked *'Mzungu'* (or whatever local term is used for a white person), or a 'Give me money', something that you become accustomed to in some African countries. On the contrary, in Tanzania adults will normally greet tourists with a cheerful *Jambo*, and children with a subdued *Shikamu* (a greeting reserved for elders). I find this to be a very charming quality in Tanzanian society, one that is worth reinforcing by learning a few simple Swahili greetings.

Among Tanzanians, it is considered poor taste to display certain emotions publicly. Affection is one such emotion: it is frowned upon for members of the opposite sex to hold hands publicly, and kissing or embracing would be seriously offensive. Oddly, it is quite normal for friends of the same sex to walk around hand in hand. Male travellers who get into a long discussion with a male Tanzanian shouldn't be surprised if that person clasps them by the hand and retains a firm grip on their hand for several minutes. This is a warm gesture, one particularly appropriate when the person wants to make a point with which you might disagree. On the subject of intra-gender relations, homosexuality is as good as

2

Ariadne Van Zandbergen

EQUIPMENT Although with some thought and an eye for composition you can take reasonable photos with a 'point and shoot' camera, you need an SLR camera with one or more lenses if you are at all serious about photography. The most important component in a digital SLR is the sensor. There are two types of sensor: DX and FX. The FX is a full-size sensor identical to the old film size (36mm). The DX sensor is half size and produces lower quality. Your choice of lenses will be determined by whether you have a DX or FX sensor in your camera as the DX sensor introduces a 0.5x multiplication to the focal length. So a 300mm lens becomes in effect a 450mm lens. FX ('full frame') sensors are the future, so I will further refer to focal lengths appropriate to the FX sensor.

Always buy the best lens you can afford. Fixed fast lenses are ideal, but very costly. Zoom lenses make it easier to change composition without changing lenses the whole time. If you carry only one lens a 24–70mm or similar zoom should be ideal. For a second lens, a lightweight 80–200mm or 70–300mm or similar will be excellent for candid shots and varying your composition. Wildlife photography will be very frustrating if you don't have at least a 300mm lens. For a small loss of quality, teleconverters are a cheap and compact way to increase magnification: a 300 lens with a 1.4x converter becomes 420mm, and with a 2x it becomes 600mm. Note that 1.4x and 2x teleconverters reduce the speed of your lens by 1.4 and 2 stops respectively.

The resolution of digital cameras is improving all the time. For ordinary prints a 6-megapixel camera is fine. For better results and the possibility to enlarge images and for professional reproduction, higher resolution is available up to 21 megapixels.

It is important to have enough memory space when photographing on your holiday. The number of pictures you can fit on a card depends on the quality you choose. You should calculate how many pictures you can fit on a card and either take enough cards or take a storage drive onto which you can download the cards' content. You can obviously take a laptop which gives the advantage that you can see your pictures properly at the end of each day and edit them and delete rejects. If you don't want the extra bulk and weight you can buy a storage device which can read memory cards. These drives come in a variety of different capacities.

Keep in mind that digital camera batteries, computers and other storage devices need charging. Make sure you have all the chargers, cables and converters with you. Most hotels/lodges have charging points, but it will be best to enquire about this in advance. When camping you might have to rely on charging from the car battery.

taboo in Tanzania, to the extent that it would require some pretty overt behaviour for it to occur to anybody to take offence.

It is also considered bad form to show anger publicly. It is difficult to know where to draw the line here, because many touts positively invite an aggressive response, and I doubt that many people who travel independently in Tanzania will get by without the occasional display of impatience. Frankly, I doubt that many bystanders would take umbrage if you responded to a pushy tout with a display of anger, if only because the tout's behaviour itself goes against the grain of Tanzanian society. By contrast, losing your temper will almost certainly be counterproductive when dealing with obtuse officials, dopey waiters and hotel employees, or unco-operative safari drivers.

MUSLIM CUSTOMS Visitors should be aware of the strong Muslim element in Tanzania, particularly along the coast. In Muslim society, it is insulting to use your left hand to pass or receive something or when shaking hands. If you eat with your

DUST AND HEAT Dust and heat are often a problem. Keep your equipment in a sealed bag, and avoid exposing equipment to the sun when possible. Digital cameras are prone to collecting dust particles on the sensor which results in spots on the image. The dirt mostly enters the camera when changing lenses, so you should be careful when doing this. To some extent photos can be 'cleaned' up afterwards in Photoshop, but this is time-consuming. You can have your camera sensor professionally cleaned, or you can do this yourself with special brushes and swabs made for this purpose, but note that touching the sensor might cause damage and should only be done with the greatest care.

LIGHT The most striking outdoor photographs are often taken during the hour or two of 'golden light' after dawn and before sunset. Shooting in low light may enforce the use of very low shutter speeds, in which case a tripod/beanbag will be required to avoid camera shake. The most advanced digital SLRs have very little loss of quality on higher ISO settings, which allows you to shoot at lower light conditions. It is still recommended not to increase the ISO unless necessary.

With careful handling, side lighting and back lighting can produce stunning effects, especially in soft light and at sunrise or sunset. Generally, however, it is best to shoot with the sun behind you. When photographing animals or people in the harsh midday sun, images taken in light but even shade are likely to look nicer than those taken in direct sunlight or patchy shade, since the latter conditions create too much contrast.

PROTOCOL In some countries, it is unacceptable to photograph local people without permission, and many people will refuse to pose or will ask for a donation. In such circumstances, don't try to sneak photographs as you might get yourself into trouble. Even the most willing subject will often pose stiffly when a camera is pointed at them; relax them by making a joke, and take a few shots in quick succession to improve the odds of capturing a natural pose.

Ariadne Van Zandbergen is a professional travel and wildlife photographer specialising in Africa. She runs 'The Africa Image Library'. For photo requests, visit www.africaimagelibrary.co.za or contact her direct (e ariadne@hixnet.co.za).

fingers, it is also customary to use the right hand only. Even those of us who are naturally right-handed will occasionally need to remind ourselves of this (it may happen, for instance, that you are carrying something in your right hand and so hand money to a shopkeeper with your left). For left-handed travellers, it will require a constant effort. In traditional Muslim societies it is offensive for women to expose their knees or shoulders, a custom that ought to be taken on board by female travellers, especially on parts of the coast where tourists remain a relative novelty.

TIPPING AND GUIDES The question of when and when not to tip can be difficult in a foreign country. In Tanzania, it is customary to tip your guide at the end of a safari and/or a Kilimanjaro climb, as well as any cook and porter who accompany you. A figure of roughly US$5–10 per day is accepted as the benchmark, though it is advisable to check this with your safari company in advance. I see no reason why you shouldn't give a bigger or smaller tip based on the quality of service. Bear in mind, however, that most guides, cooks and porters receive nominal salaries, which means that they are largely dependent on tips for their income. It would be mean not to leave a reasonable tip in any but the most exceptional of circumstances.

In some African countries, it is difficult to travel anywhere without being latched onto by a self-appointed guide, who will often expect a tip over and above any agreed fee. This sort of thing is comparatively unusual in Tanzania, but if you do take on a freelance guide, then it is advisable to clarify in advance that whatever price you agree is final and inclusive of a tip. By contrast, any guide who is given to you by a company should most definitely be tipped, as tips will probably be their main source of income. In Zanzibar and Arusha, a freelance guide may insist upon helping you find a hotel room, in which case they will be given a commission by the hotel, so there is no reason for you to provide an additional tip. In any case, from the guide's point of view, finding you a room is merely the first step in trying to hook you for a safari or a spice tour, or something else that will earn a larger commission.

It is not customary to tip for service in local bars and *hotelis*, though you may sometimes want to leave a tip (in fact, given the difficulty of finding change in Tanzania, you may practically be forced into doing this in some circumstances). A tip of 5% would be very acceptable and 10% generous. Generally any restaurant that caters primarily to tourists and to wealthy Tanzania residents will automatically add a service charge to the bill. Since the government claims the lion's share of any formal service charge, it would still be reasonable to reward good service with a genuine tip.

BARGAINING Tourists to Tanzania will sometimes need to bargain over prices, but generally this need exists only in reasonably predictable circumstances, for instance when chartering a private taxi, organising a guide, agreeing a price for a safari or mountain trek, or buying curios and to a lesser extent other market produce. Prices in hotels, restaurants and shops are generally fixed, and overcharging in such places is too unusual for it to be worth challenging a price unless it is blatantly ridiculous.

You may well be overcharged at some point in Tanzania, but it is important to keep this in perspective. After a couple of bad experiences, some travellers start to haggle with everybody from hotel owners to old women selling fruit by the side of the road, often accompanying their negotiations with aggressive accusations of dishonesty. Unfortunately, it is sometimes necessary to fall back on aggressive posturing in order to determine a fair price, but such behaviour is also very unfair on those people who are forthright and honest in their dealings with tourists. It's a question of finding the right balance, or better still looking for other ways of dealing with the problem.

The main instance where bargaining is essential is when buying curios. What should be understood, however, is that the fact a curio seller is open to negotiation does not mean that you were initially being overcharged or ripped off. Curio sellers will generally quote a price knowing full well that you are going to bargain it down (they'd probably be startled if you didn't) and it is not necessary to respond aggressively or in an accusatory manner. It is impossible to say by how much you should bargain the initial price down. Some people say that you should offer half the asking price and be prepared to settle at around two-thirds, but my experience is that curio sellers are far more whimsical than such advice allows for. The sensible approach, if you want to get a feel for prices, is to ask the price of similar items at a few different stalls before you actually contemplate buying anything.

In fruit and vegetable markets and stalls, bargaining is the norm, even between locals, and the most healthy approach to this sort of haggling is to view it as an enjoyable part of the African experience. There will normally be an accepted price band for any particular commodity. To find out what it is, listen to what other people pay and try a few stalls. A ludicrously inflated price will always drop the moment you walk away. When buying fruit and vegetables, a good way to feel out the situation is to ask for a bulk discount or a few extra items thrown in. And bear in mind that when somebody is reluctant to bargain, it may be because they asked a fair price in the first place.

A final point to consider on the subject of overcharging and bargaining is that it is the fact of being overcharged that annoys; the amount itself is generally of little consequence in the wider context of a trip to Tanzania. Without for a moment wanting to suggest that travellers should routinely allow themselves to be overcharged, I do feel there are occasions when we should pause to look at the bigger picture. If you find yourself quibbling over a pittance with an old lady selling a few piles of fruit by the roadside, you might perhaps bear in mind that the notion of a fixed price is a very Western one. When somebody is desperate enough for money, or afraid that their perishable goods might not last another day, it may well be possible to push them down to a lower price than they would normally accept. In such circumstances, I see nothing wrong with erring on the side of generosity.

Practical Information **CULTURAL ETIQUETTE**

2

Part Two

THE GUIDE

3

Arusha

Situated in the fertile southern foothills of Mount Meru, less than 100km from the Kenyan border as the crow flies, the bustling town of Arusha is Tanzania's so-called safari capital, the most popular and convenient springboard from which to explore the legendary northern game-viewing circuit. The town is also an important gateway into Tanzania, the first town visited by travellers coming across the border from Nairobi, and the entry point for a growing number of fly-in tourists thanks to the daily KLM flights that link Europe to the nearby Kilimanjaro International Airport.

First impressions of Arusha are that practically everything there revolves around the safari industry, a perception that is only reinforced by more prolonged exposure. Wander around the old town centre or backroads north of the stadium, and it can feel like every second person you pass has something to sell, be it a safari, a batik or last week's edition of some or other foreign newspaper, while every other vehicle sports a safari company logo.

In reality, Arusha's rare economic vitality is buoyed by several contributory factors, not the least of which is its location in the bountiful Mount Meru foothills, whose drizzly sub-montane microclimate nurtures the rich volcanic soil to agricultural profligacy. There is also the proximity of the Mererani Hills, the only known source of the increasingly popular gemstone tanzanite, while a more ephemeral economic boost has been provided by the presence of UN and other NGO personnel linked to the Rwandan War Crimes Tribunal, which took up residence in the Arusha International Conference Centre some years back and shows no signs of leaving any time soon. For all this, however, one suspects that the lure of the tourist dollar has been the driving force behind Arusha's steady rise from ninth-largest town in Tanzania in 1978 to second largest today.

Situated at an altitude of around 1,500m in the rainshadow of Mount Meru, Arusha makes for a climatically temperate – and, during the rainy season, often downright soggy – introduction to tropical Africa. The town itself is a pleasant enough place to hang out, and these days it boasts a growing number of trendy bars, restaurants and cafés catering to expatriates, tourists and wealthier locals. Away from these few select spots, however, Arusha remains something of an African everytown, where low-rise colonial-era buildings rub shoulders with a small but gradually increasing number of more modern structures. Indeed, it could be argued that the wealth generated by the safari industry serves to accentuate the vast economic gulf between the haves and have-nots and the spectrum of cultural influences that play havoc with those visitors seeking to pigeonhole the 'Real Africa'. Which is it, then: the colourfully dressed Maasai and Arusha women who sell traditional beadwork on the pavement, the suited businessmen who scurry in and out of the International Conference Centre, or the swaggering, sunglass-shrouded wide-boys who scurry about offering cheap safaris, change money, marijuana...?

If nothing else, Arusha is an attractively green town, with its northern skyline – weather permitting – dominated by the imposing hulk of Africa's fifth-highest mountain. And for those who prefer not to stay in the town centre, there are plenty of more rustic options in the immediate area. The 4,556m Mount Meru is the dominant geographical feature in Arusha National Park which, despite its proximity to Arusha and manifold points of interest, attracts little more than a trickle of tourism. Also of interest in the immediate vicinity of Arusha is Lake Duluti, an attractive forest-fringed crater lake that lies immediately south of the Moshi road, and a cluster of attractive farms set on the coffee plantations and forested hills between Arusha and Usa River – many of which offer views to Meru and Kilimanjaro on a clear day.

HISTORY

Little is known about the Arusha area prior to the 17th century, when the Bantu-speaking Meru people – migrants from the west with strong linguistic and cultural affinities to the Chagga of Kilimanjaro – settled and farmed the fertile and well-watered northern foothills of Mount Meru. In 1830 or thereabouts, the southern slopes of the mountain verging on the Maasai Steppes were settled by the Arusha, a Maasai subgroup who lost their cattle and territory in one of the internecine battles characteristic of this turbulent period in Maasailand. The Arusha people speak the same Maa language as the plains Maasai and share a similar social structure based around initiated age-sets, but when they settled in the Mount Meru area they forsook their pastoralist roots, turning instead to agriculture as a primary source of subsistence.

The Arusha economy was boosted by the trade in agricultural produce – in particular tobacco – with the closely affiliated Maasai of the plains. The Arusha also became known as reliable providers of food and other provisions for the Arab slave caravans that headed inland from the Pangani and Tanga area towards modern-day Kenya and Lake Victoria. Invigorated by this regular trade, the Arusha had, by 1880, cleared the forested slopes of Mount Meru to an altitude of around 1,600m to make way for cultivation. As their territory expanded, however, the Arusha people increasingly came into contact with their northern neighbours, the Meru, resulting in several territorial skirmishes and frequent cattle raids between the two tribes.

In 1881, prompted by the need to defend their combined territories against the Maasai and other potential attackers, the incumbent warrior age-sets of the Arusha and Meru united to form a formidable military force. Since they were settled on the well-watered slopes of Mount Meru, and their subsistence was not primarily dependent on livestock, the Arusha and Meru people were less affected than the plains pastoralists by the devastating series of droughts and rinderpest epidemics of the 1880s and early 1890s. As a result, the combined army, known as the Talala – the Expansionists – was able to exert considerable influence over neighbouring Maasai and Chagga territories.

The Talala staunchly resisted German attempts to settle in their territory, killing the first missionaries to arrive there and repelling an initial punitive attack by the colonial army. In October 1896, however, the Arusha and Meru were soundly defeated by a military expedition out of Moshi led by Karl Johannes and consisting of 100 German troopers supported by some 5,000 Chagga warriors. In the aftermath of this defeat, the Germans drove home the point by razing hundreds of Arusha and Meru smallholdings, killing the men, confiscating the cattle and repatriating women of Chagga origin to the Kilimanjaro area.

In 1889, the Germans established a permanent settlement – modern-day Arusha town – on the border of Arusha and Maasai territories, and used forced Arusha and

Maasai labour to construct the Boma that can still be seen on the north end of Boma Road. Relations between the colonisers and their unwilling subjects remained tense, to say the least. During the construction of the fort, a minor dispute led to some 300 labourers being massacred while marching peacefully along present-day Boma Road, and several local chiefs from outlying areas were arbitrarily arrested and taken to Moshi to be hanged in the street.

Following the construction of the Boma, Arusha quickly developed into a significant trading and administrative centre, with about two dozen Indian and Arab shops clustered along what is today Boma Road. John Boyes, who visited Arusha in 1903, somewhat fancifully compared the Boma to 'an Aladdin's Palace transported from some fairyland and dropped down in the heart of the tropics'. The town, he wrote, was 'a real oasis in the wilderness' and 'spotlessly clean', while 'the streets [were] laid out with fine sidewalks, separated by the road from a stream of clear water flowing down a cemented gully'.

At the outbreak of World War I, the small German garrison town was of some significance as a local agricultural and trade centre, but it remained something of a backwater by comparison with Moshi, which lay a week's ox-wagon trek distant at the railhead of the Tanga line. Much of the area around Arusha was, however, settled by German farmers, who had forcibly displaced the original Arusha and Meru smallholders. In 1916, British troops captured Arusha and expelled the German farmers, resulting in some resettlement by indigenous farmers, but the German farmland was eventually re-allocated to British and Greek settlers. The British also set aside large tracts of land around Arusha for sisal plantations, which meant that by 1920, less than 20% of the land around Mount Meru was available to local farmers, most of it on dry foothills unsuited to cultivating the local staple of bananas.

Arusha grew steadily between the wars. The settler economy was boosted by the introduction of coffee, sisal and other export crops, and trade links were improved with the construction of road links to Moshi and Nairobi and the opening of the railway line to Moshi and the coast in 1929. Yet the land issues continued to simmer, eventually coming to a head after World War II, with the eviction of thousands of Meru farmers from north of Mount Meru to make way for a peanut production project overseen by 13 white farmers. The peanut project, aside from being a dismal and costly failure, resulted in the pivotal Meru Land Case, which not only caused great embarrassment to the UN Trusteeship Council, but also proved to be an important catalyst to the politicisation of the anti-colonial movement in Tanganyika.

Prior to independence, Arusha remained a relatively small town whose primary role was to service the surrounding agricultural lands. The official census of 1952 placed the urban population at fewer than 8,000 people, of which more than half were of Asian or European stock. The town has, however, grown markedly since independence, attracting large numbers of domestic migrants from surrounding rural areas and beyond. This can be attributed to a number of factors: the town's short-lived but prestigious role as capital of the east African community in the 1960s, the tanzanite mining boom, and perhaps most of all its strategic location as the springboard for the northern safari circuit. The permanent population of Arusha is estimated at around 300,000 in 2009, with a similar number of tourists passing through annually!

GETTING THERE AND AWAY

BY AIR The main local point of entry is Kilimanjaro International Airport (KIA), which lies roughly two-thirds along the 80km asphalt road that runs eastward from Arusha to Moshi. KIA is connected to Europe by daily KLM flights, eliminating the need to travel to northern Tanzania via Nairobi or Dar es Salaam. Other international carriers that fly to KIA are Kenya Airways, Ethiopian Airlines and South African Airways, while Air Tanzania operates connecting flights there from several destinations via Dar es Salaam, as well as domestic flights to Dar es Salaam, Mwanza, Zanzibar, Pemba, Mafia and Mbeya.

Travellers arriving at or leaving from KIA with Air Tanzania should note that the national carrier offers a free shuttle service between the airport and Arusha, connecting with all flights and dropping you at the central hotel of your choice. It's easy enough to locate the shuttle when you arrive at the airport. Leaving Arusha, ask about departure times at the Air Tanzania office on Boma Road [104 C5]. For KLM flights, the Impala Hotel runs a connecting shuttle between KIA and the town centre, but this costs US$10 per person. Charter taxis are also available at the airport, at a fixed (and rather steep) price of US$50. Travellers with odd flight times might think about booking into the excellent KIA Lodge (see page 115), which lies just 1km from the airport.

Aside from Air Tanzania, most other domestic carriers, such as Regional, Coastal and Precision Air, fly in and out of the smaller Arusha Airport, which lies about 5km out of town along the Serengeti road. There are daily flights from Arusha to all major airstrips on the northern Tanzania safari circuit, including Manyara, Ngorongoro, Seronera, Grumeti and Lobo, as well as to Dar es Salaam and Zanzibar. There are also regular scheduled flights to the likes of Mwanza, Rubondo Island, Mafia Island and the reserves of the southern safari circuit.

Most tourists flying around Tanzania will have made their flight arrangements in advance through a tour operator, and this is certainly the recommended way of going about things, but it is generally possible to buy tickets from Arusha to major destinations such as Dar es Salaam and Zanzibar at short notice.

Airlines The offices of the main domestic and international airlines are mostly dotted along Boma Road in the old town centre. The combined office of Kenya Airways and KLM [104 C4] (✆ 027 254 8062) is situated immediately north of the New Safari Hotel, as is that of Ethiopian Airlines [104 C4] (✆ 027 250 7512), while Precision Air (✆ 027 250 3261; ☉ Mon–Sun) is just to the south. Air Tanzania/South African Airways is closer to the Clocktower [104 C5] (✆ 027 250 3201) alongside Coastal Travels [104 C5] (*Boma Rd;* ✆ 027 250 0087). The Regional Air office is out of town near the Arusha Coffee Lodge so its best to call them at one of the following numbers (✆ 027 250 4164/254 8536 *or* m 0753 500300).

BY ROAD A number of companies run express bus services to and from Dar es Salaam. These generally take around ten hours, stopping only at Moshi to pick up further passengers and at Korogwe for a 20-minute lunch break, and tickets typically cost around Tsh20,000–25,000. Most such buses leave early in the morning, so it is advisable to make enquiries and a booking the afternoon before you want to leave. The best coach at present is the Scandinavia Express (✆ 027 250 0153), which runs three services daily in either direction, leaving between 07.30 or 08.30, depending on whether you use the normal or luxury service. The office and departure point is on Makao Mapya Road [100 A5], a few hundred metres north of Shoprite. Another recommended company is Mtei Coaches (m 0755 717117), which has a compound right next door to Scandinavia, and runs two coaches daily, leaving at the same time. Cheaper bus services between Arusha and Dar es Salaam aren't worth bothering with, as they stop at every town and can take anything from 12 to 15 hours to cover the same distance.

The quickest and most efficient road transport between Arusha and Nairobi are the minibus shuttles run by Riverside (m 0754 474968), Impala Hotel, Bobby (m *0754 960122*), Osa (m *0762 773662*) and a few other operators. These all leave twice daily in either direction at 08.00 and 14.00, and take around five hours, depending on how quickly you pass through immigration and customs at the Namanga border. The Impala Shuttle leaves from the parking lot of the eponymous hotel [89 G7], while all other shuttles leave from a parking area in front of Hotel La Bella on Simeon Road [89 G6], though you can arrange to be picked up elsewhere (and it is unclear whether these shuttles will return to their old terminus in the parking lot of the former Mount Meru Novotel when eventually it reopens as the Arusha Holiday Inn). Tickets officially cost US$20–25 for non-residents, but more often than not walk-in customers will be permitted to pay the cheaper resident's rate. Tickets for the Impala Shuttle can be bought directly from the Impala Hotel, while those for the other shuttles can be bought at kiosks in the foyer of the La Bella, by calling the company directly, or through any safari operator in Arusha. Another option is to travel to Nairobi with Scandinavia Express (see above), which runs two buses daily, leaving at around 15.30 and costing Tsh25,000.

A steady stream of minibuses and buses connect Moshi and Arusha. I would avoid using minibuses along this route due to the higher incidence of accidents, but they are generally quicker than buses. This trip usually takes between one and two hours. There are also regular buses to other relatively local destinations such as Mto wa Mbu, Karatu, Mbulu, Babati and Kondoa; the best company servicing these routes is Mtei (m *0755 717117*). Most other buses and minibuses leave from the main bus station near the football stadium [88 A4 & 101 F4].

ORIENTATION

Unlike Dar es Salaam or Zanzibar's labyrinthine Stone Town, Arusha is not a difficult town to familiarise yourself with. Its most significant geographical features are the Naura and Goliondoi rivers, which run parallel to each other through the town centre, cutting it into two distinct parts. To the east of the rivers lies the 'old' town centre, a relatively smart area whose main north–south thoroughfares – Boma, India and Goliondoi roads – are lined with upmarket hotels, tourist-friendly restaurants, safari companies, curio shops, banks, bookshops and tourist offices. Major landmarks in this part of town include the Clocktower [88 D5 & 104 C5], the Old Boma (now a museum) [89 E4 & 104 C2] and the Arusha International Conference Centre (AICC) [89 E3 & 104 B1].

Connected to the old town centre by Sokoine Road in the south and Makongoro Road in the north, the more bustling modern town centre consists of a tight grid of roads west of the rivers centred on the market and bus station south of the stadium. This area is well equipped with small budget hotels and Indian restaurants, but it boasts few facilities that approach international standards. Similar in feel, though more residential and less commercially orientated, is the suburb of Kaloleni immediately north of the stadium and main bus station.

Another important suburb is Kijenge, which lies to the southeast of the old town centre, and is reached by following Sokoine Road across a bridge over the Themi River to become the Old Moshi Road. Kijenge has a spacious, leafy character and it is dotted with relatively upmarket hotels (notably the Impala) and restaurants, as well as an increasing number of safari company offices.

GETTING AROUND

BY TAXI There are plenty of taxis in Arusha. Good places to pick them up include the market and bus station, the filling station on the junction of Goliondoi Road and the Old Moshi Road, and the open area at the north end of Boma and India

Map labels:

Grid A-D columns, 1-7 rows

- Eland Motel (A1)
- Njake (B1)
- Engen (C1)
- Pub Nless (D1)
- Ilboru Safari Lodge (1.5km) (D, top)
- ARUSHA MOSHI ROAD
- Gapco (A1)
- Triple 'A' Nightclub, Namanga, Nairobi
- Soweto Gardens (B2)
- see pages 100–1
- Golden Rose (A3)
- LEVOLOSI
- ETHIOPIA
- MIDDLETON RD
- Naura
- Goliondoi
- STADIUM
- Stadium (B3)
- MAKONGORO
- MAKONGORO
- Bus station (B4)
- MAKUA
- ZARAMO
- AZIMIO
- SWAHILI
- SETH
- BENJAMIN
- New Safari (D4)
- BOMA
- Equator
- SOMALI
- MARKET
- Market (B4–5)
- GOLIONDOI
- INDIA
- Caltex (C5)
- Clocktower
- NBC
- Arusha (D5)
- Cultural Heritage Centre, Serengeti, Dodoma
- SOKOINE ROAD
- SOKOINE ROAD
- FACTORY ROAD
- BP (B5)
- Metropole Cinema (B5)
- Stanbic (C5)
- CANTONMENT
- Railway station (A6)

© Philip Briggs

88

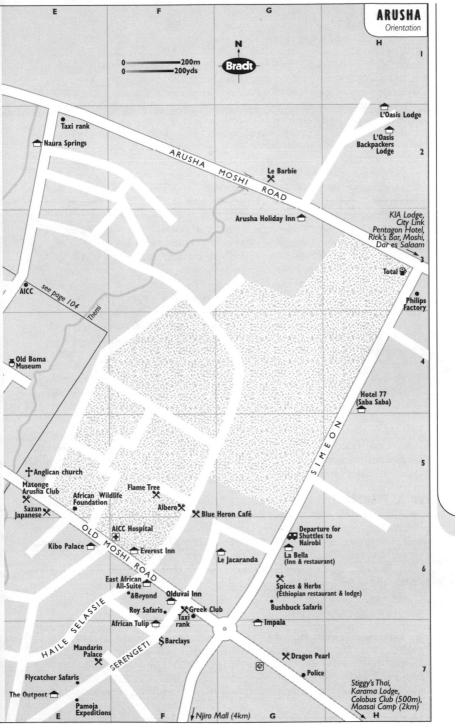

N

Bradt

0 ———— 200m
0 ———— 200yds

E   F   G   H

I

Taxi rank

Naura Springs

L'Oasis Lodge

L'Oasis
Backpackers
Lodge

2

ARUSHA MOSHI ROAD

Le Barbie

Arusha Holiday Inn

KIA Lodge,
City Link
Pentagon Hotel,
Rick's Bar, Moshi,
Dar es Salaam

3

AICC

see page 104

Themi

Total

Philips
Factory

Old Boma
Museum

4

Hotel 77
(Saba Saba)

SIMEON

5

† Anglican church

Matonge
Arusha Club

African Wildlife
Foundation

Flame Tree

Albero

Blue Heron Café

Sazan
Japanese

AICC Hospital

Departure for
Shuttles to
Nairobi

Kibo Palace

Everest Inn

OLD MOSHI ROAD

Le Jacaranda

La Bella
(Inn & restaurant)

6

East African
All-Suite

&Beyond

Olduvai Inn

Spices & Herbs
(Ethiopian restaurant & lodge)

Roy Safaris

African Tulip

Greek Club

Taxi
rank

Impala

Bushbuck Safaris

HAILE SELASSIE

Mandarin
Palace

Barclays

SERENGETI

Dragon Pearl

e

Police

7

Flycatcher Safaris

The Outpost

Stiggy's Thai,
Karama Lodge,
Colobus Club (500m),
Maasai Camp (2km)

Pamoja
Expeditions

E   F   Njiro Mall (4km)   G   H

Arusha can be a daunting prospect on first contact, particularly if you arrive by bus. Competition between budget safari companies is fierce, and 'flycatchers' – the street touts who solicit custom for these companies – know that their best tactic is to hook travellers who don't have a pre-booked safari when they arrive. As a consequence, when you arrive in Arusha by bus you're likely to spend your first few minutes dodging the attention of a dozen yelling touts, all of who will claim to be able to offer you the cheapest safari and room in town. In most cases, the touts probably will show you to a decent room, but allowing this to happen does open the door to your sense of obligation being exploited later in your stay.

Fortunately, once you've run the bus station gauntlet, things do calm down somewhat, though the flock of flycatchers, newspaper vendors and curio sellers who hang around the old town centre can be a nuisance. Unlike in some other parts of Africa, however, it is unusual for such an exchange to descend into something truly unpleasant: most touts here seem capable of taking a good-humoured 'No' for an answer, especially one spoken in Swahili, and they will usually back down at any show of genuine irritation. As for the dodgy money-changers that sometimes hang around with the touts, don't let the offer of a superior rate sucker you in – changing money on the street in Arusha as elsewhere in Tanzania is a definite no-no!

Such annoyances aside, Arusha is not an especially threatening city, though it is certainly not unheard of for tourists to be mugged after dark. The usual commonsense rules apply: avoid walking around singly or in pairs at night, especially on unlit roads and parks, and avoid carrying valuables on your person or taking out significantly more money than you need for the evening. After dark, the dodgiest part of town for muggings is probably the area east of the Themi River, in particular the quiet, unlit road between the Arusha Hotel, and Impala Hotel, and Arusha Holiday Inn. On the whole, Arusha is very safe by day, but do be wary of bag-snatchers and pickpockets in and around the central market.

roads. A taxi ride within the town centre should cost roughly Tsh3,000–4,000, though tourists are normally asked a slightly higher price. A taxi ride to somewhere outside the town centre will cost more.

PUBLIC TRANSPORT A good network of minibus *dala-dalas* services Arusha. A steady flow of these vehicles runs along the length of Sokoine Road, some of which continue west out of town past the Tanganyika Farmers' Association (TFA) centre, while others run east of the clock tower to the Impala Hotel and beyond. There are also regular *dala-dalas* between the town centre and the main Nairobi-Moshi bypass. Fares are nominal, and it's easy enough to hop on or off any passing *dala-dala* heading in your direction.

TOURIST INFORMATION

The **Tanzania Tourist Board** (TTB) office on Boma Road [88 D4 & 104 C4] (✆ *027 250 3842; www.tanzaniatouristboard.com*) is refreshingly helpful and well informed. It stocks a useful colour road map of Tanzania as well as a great street plan of Arusha, both given free of charge to tourists, though this doesn't stop the book vendors out on the street from trying to sell the same maps at a very silly price. If you want to check out a safari company, the TTB office keeps a regularly updated list of all registered safari and trekking companies, as well as those that are blacklisted.

The TTB has been actively involved in the development of cultural tourism programmes in Ng'iresi, Mulala, Mkuru, Longido, Mto wa Mbu, Usambara, North Pare and South Pare, as well as several projects further afield. The Arusha office stocks informative pamphlets about these programmes, and can help out with information on prices and access. Details are also available at the **Cultural Tourism Program** office in the Old Boma (➐ 027 250 0025; f 027 250 8216; e *culturaltourism@habari.co.tz*).

The head office of **Tanzania National Parks** (Tanapa) recently moved to the new Mwalimu J K Nyerere Conservation Centre about 3km out of town along the Serengeti road (*PO Box 3134, Arusha;* ➐ 027 250 1930/4; f 027 250 8216; e *tanapa@habari.co.tz; www.tanzaniaparks.com*), roughly opposite the Cultural Heritage Centre.

The **Ngorongoro Conservation Authority** has recently opened an information office on Boma Road [104 C4] (➐ 027 254 4625; *www.ngorongorocrater.org*) close to the tourist board office. In addition to some worthwhile displays on the conservation area, it sells a good range of books and booklets about the northern circuit.

The **Immigration Office** on Simeon Road [104 A2] (➐ 027 250 6565) will normally extend visas on the spot.

TOUR OPERATORS

The list below is by no means definitive, but it provides a good cross-section of the sort of services that are on offer, and except where otherwise noted, it sticks to companies that have maintained high standards over several years. The listed companies generally specialise in northern circuit safaris, but most can also set up Kilimanjaro and Meru climbs, fly-in safaris on the southern safari circuit, and excursions to Zanzibar.

Africa Dream Safaris m 0752 225551/4 or (US toll free) 877 572 3274; e inquiries@ africadreamsafaris.com; www.africadreamsafaris.com. Emerging as one of the leading upmarket operators in Tanzania, this award-winning outfit specialises in customised safaris aimed at serious wildlife enthusiasts & photographers. The emphasis is on maximising wildlife encounters through early morning & full-day game drives with enthusiastic & knowledgeable driver/guides, avoiding circuits that tend to suffer from overcrowding, taking advantage of seasonal wildlife concentrations, & using intimate tented camps rather than large lodges. It won the 2008 Tanzania Tour Operator Conservation Award, presented by the Tanzania Tourist Board, for its work with the Serengeti Lion Project, was selected Best Safari Outfitter by *National Geographic Adventure* in 2009. The website is helpful for anyone planning a safari in Tanzania.
Asilia ➐ 027 250 4118/9; e enquiries@ sokwe.com; www.sokwe.com. Founded in 1989 under the name Sokwe & affiliated to the eponymous chain of exclusive tented camps, Asilia specialises in top-end safaris in the traditional east African style using luxury, mobile tented camps. The standard of driver/guides is among the very highest in Tanzania, vehicles are well outfitted, & itineraries place high emphasis on escaping standard tour circuits for more untrammelled areas.
Bushbuck Safaris [89 G6] ➐ 027 250 7779/254 4186/254 8924; f 027 254 8293/2954; e bushbuck@yako.habari.co.tz; www.bushbuckltd.com. This reliable company specialises in lodge safaris. It has a large fleet of new & competently maintained 4x4 vehicles, & employs articulate drivers & guides. Prices & service are relatively upmarket, but not extortionate.
Easy Travel & Tours Ltd ➐ 027 250 3929/7322; m 0754 400141/0784 400141; f 027 250 4110; e gm@easytravel.co.tz; www.easytravel.co.tz
Great African Safaris ➐ 027 254 8163; m 0784 493606; f 027 254 4563; e info@ greatafricansafaris.com; www.greatafricansafaris.com. This new Tanzanian-run company offers the usual mid-range safari options as well as Kili climbs using all routes, & an exciting selection of cultural tourism itineraries to Maasailand, the Usambara Mountains & Marangu.

Green Footprint Adventures ↘ 027 254 4635;
m 0784 203000; e info@greenfootprint.co.tz;
www.greenfootprint.co.tz. This environmentally
minded safari company specialises in top-end safaris
that pass over more mainstream circuits in favour
of wilderness areas & low-impact tented camps. The
owner runs a renowned guide-training school
outside Arusha & as such the standard of guiding
is exceptional. It also runs canoeing trips in Arusha
National Park, Lake Duluti & Lake Manyara.
Specialist excursions include 4–5-day walking safaris
in southern Tarangire, 3-day visits to the Hadzabe
& 2–5-day walking safaris in the Serengeti.
Hoopoe Safaris [104 B4] ↘ 027 250 7011; f 027
254 8226; e information@hoopoe.com;
www.hoopoe.com. One of the most highly regarded
safari companies in Arusha, Hoopoe specialises in
personalised luxury camping & lodge safaris. It owns
tented camps outside of Lake Manyara & Tarangire
national parks, as well as a superb private camp in
West Kilimanjaro. It is also one of the best companies
to contact with regard to trekking & walking safaris
in Natron, the Ngorongoro Highlands, & the game-rich
Maasai Plains to the east of the Serengeti. It was
voted the Best Eco Tourism Operator in the World by
Condé Nast Traveller for 2004.
Leopard Tours ↘ 027 250 3603/8441/3;
f 027 250 8219; e leopard@yako.habari.co.tz;
www.leopard-tours.com. One of the largest operators
out of Arusha, Leopard Tours specialises in mid-range
safaris concentrating on the larger lodges & more
established game-viewing areas, & offers a highly
reliable service to those who want to stick firmly to
the beaten track.
Nature Discovery m 0732 971 859; e info@
naturediscovery.com; www.naturediscovery.com. This
eco-friendly operator is widely praised for its high-
quality, top-end Kilimanjaro climbs, & it also arranges
standard northern circuit safaris as well as trekking
expeditions in the Ngorongoro Highlands & elsewhere.
Oreteti Cultural Discovery ↘ 027 250 4961; f 027
250 4962; e info@oreteti.com; www.oreteti.com.
This small, Arusha-based, family company is run by
an English woman & her Maasai husband. They offer
personalised cultural & educational programmes,
combining academic lectures & seminars in
anthropology with a range of walking tours, safaris
or volunteer work camps. Other activities on offer
include visits to Maasai & Chagga villages, short
courses in Maasai beadwork, drumming, dance,
cookery & Swahili hip-hop. They also visit the
Kondoa rock paintings, the Hadza near Lake Eyasi, &
Rangi agro-pastoralist communities in Dodoma

Region. 10% of the profit is donated to community-
based organisations.
Roy Safaris [89 F6] ↘ 027 250 /2115/7940; f 027
254 8892; e roysafaris@intafrica.com;
www.roysafaris.com. Founded in the late 1980s, this
dynamic & efficient company has established itself as
a leading operator when it comes to high quality
but reasonably priced budget & mid-range camping
safaris. Vehicles are always in excellent condition &
the drivers are usually competent & knowledgeable.
It also offers reasonably priced semi-luxury camping
safaris & lodge safaris.
Safari Makers ↘ 027 250 8184/037;
e safarimakers@habari.co.tz; www.safarimakers.com.
Owned & managed by a dynamic hands-on
American–Tanzanian couple, Safari Makers runs
competitively priced camping & lodge safaris, & is
one of the few companies in Arusha committed to
promoting the various cultural programmes in
communities outside Arusha – a recommended first
contact at the budget to mid-range level, & notable
for its flexible & responsive management.
Sunny Safaris [101 F2] ↘ 027 250 7145; m 0754
268475; e info@sunnysafaris.com;
www.sunnysafaris.com. This established company has
long offered the cheapest reliable camping safaris in
Arusha, though rates vary depending on season &
group size. Their cheapest safaris won't involve
camping in national parks, & you might find your
driver inflexible about doing any excursion that puts
extra kilometres on the clock, but otherwise you will
get a thoroughly reliable service, with good vehicles
& drivers. They also organise more upmarket
camping safaris & lodge-based safaris at reasonable
rates. The office is opposite the Golden Rose Hotel.
Tanzania Adventure m 0732 975210; e info@
tanzania-adventure.com; www.tanzania-adventure.com.
Dynamic new joint German–Tanzanian company
offering a wide selection of safaris, including an
extensive walking programme in the Ngorongoro
Highlands & Serengeti border areas. Especially
recommended to German-speakers.
Tropical Trails ↘ 027 250 0358; f 027 250 5578;
e info@tropicaltrails.com; www.tropicaltrails.com.
Based at Maasai Camp, this is a genuinely eco-friendly
company which arranges standard lodge-based &
camping safaris for all budgets, as well as walking
excursions on the fringes of the main national parks,
& Kili climbs along the Machame & Shira routes.
Tropical Trails is especially worth contacting if you
have unusual requirements, or you want to get really
off the beaten track. They also have some experience
in arranging special one-off charity or group events.

TrueAfrica 📞 0784 999 738; e info@trueafrica.com; www.trueafrica.com. This is a new Dutch/Tanzanian run company that specialises in exclusive upmarket safaris using small tented camps & lodges. Personalised tailor-made itineraries include interaction with Maasai communities that are only visited a couple of times per month, & game drives in relatively off-the-beaten-track areas. They can also arrange mountain climbs, beach extensions, & gorilla & chimpanzee treks.

Wild Frontiers 📞 027 250 2668; e bookings.wildfrontiers@habari.co.tz; www.wildfrontiers.com. Founded in South Africa but now with its own ground operation in Arusha, this well-established & flexible company offers a varied range of motorised, walking & combination safaris using standard lodges or its own excellent tented camps in the Serengeti & Ngorongoro Conservation Area (NCA), depending on taste & budget.

Recommended to those seeking a relatively unpackaged safari at a reasonable price. It's good for Kili climbs too.

&Beyond [89 f6] 📞 027 254 8549/8038 or (South Africa) +27 (0)11 809 4447; e inboundsales@andbeyond.com; www.andbeyond.com. Formerly known as CCAfrica, this organisation is lauded throughout Africa for its commitment to genuine ecotourism & superlative lodges, which include top-end units in Serengeti, NCA & Lake Manyara. It arranges fly-in, drive-in (or mixed) safaris throughout northern Tanzania, as well as mobile safaris using seasonal camps in the 'Under Canvas' brand. &Beyond makes no bones about its commitment to high-cost, low-impact tourism, & its Tanzanian properties are notable for their fine attention to detail, informal & personalised service, well-trained guides & rangers, & general air of exclusivity.

WHERE TO STAY

This section concentrates on accommodation located within the city limits. It also includes a handful of individual hotels situated along the Old Moshi and Serengeti roads within 5km of the town centre, but excludes the ever-growing assortment of lodges that flank the Moshi road east of the Arusha Holiday Inn. All hotels in the latter category are covered in *Chapter 4, Around Arusha*, but it is worth noting that most would make a perfectly viable – and, on the whole, more aesthetically pleasing – alternative to staying in the town itself.

EXCLUSIVE (ABOVE US$200)

Arusha Coffee Lodge (18 rooms) 📞 027 254 0630/9; f 027 254 8245; e info@elewana.com; www.elewana.com. Justifiably billed as 'the first truly 5-star hotel in Arusha' when it opened in 2002, the immaculate Arusha Coffee Lodge lays even stronger claims to that accolade following its acquisition by Elewana Lodges & subsequent renovations. It is situated about 5km out of town along the Serengeti

THE ARUSHA HOTEL

Symbolic of Arusha's growing significance in the 1920s was the opening of the New Arusha Hotel in lushly wooded grounds formerly occupied by the small town's only hostelry, the small boarding house operated by the Bloom family since the late 1890s. A 1929 government brochure eulogised the newly opened establishment as having 'hot and cold water in all bedrooms, modern sanitation, teak dancing floor, electric light and really excellent food, as well as golf, tennis, big game and bird shooting'. Less complimentary was the description included in Evelyn Waugh's amusingly acerbic travelogue *A Tourist in Africa* in 1960: it 'seeks to attract by the claim to be exactly midway between Cape Town and Cairo ... I did not see any African or Indian customers. Dogs howled and scuffled under the window at night. Can I say anything pleasant about this hotel? Yes, it stands in a cool place in a well-kept garden and it stocks some potable South African wines in good conditions.' The New Arusha continued its slide, hosting the likes of John Wayne along the way, until finally it closed for overdue renovations a few years back, to reopen in 2004 as the Arusha Hotel, the only five-star establishment in the city centre.

road, close to Arusha Airport, on what is reputedly the largest coffee estate in Tanzania, with a good view of Mount Meru. Accommodation is in stand-alone split-level chalets distinguished by their elegant Victorian décor, hardwood floors, huge balconies & stunning fireplaces & in-room percolators to provide the true aroma of the coffee estate. Designed around the original plantation houses, the excellent restaurant serves a spit-roasted lunchtime grill & a sumptuous à la carte dinner. Facilities include a swimming pool. *US$190/370 sgl/dbl B&B, rising to US$260/450 Jan–Feb & Jun–Oct, dropping to US$150/300 Apr & May.*

⌂ **The Arusha Hotel** [88 D5 & 104 C5] (65 rooms) ➊ 027 250 7777/8870; f 027 250 8889; e marketing@thearushahotel.com; www.thearushahotel.com. Giving Arusha Coffee Lodge a close run for its money is the newly renovated & reopened Arusha Hotel (formerly the New Arusha), which – situated right opposite the Clocktower – now offers the only 5-star accommodation in central Arusha. Situated in large wooded grounds running down towards the Themi River, this stately hotel has an Edwardian feel about the décor, befitting its status as the oldest hostelry in Arusha, & the spacious rooms all come with satellite TV, netting, in-room internet access, smoke detector, electronic safes

UPMARKET (US$90–200)

⌂ **Karama Lodge & Spa** (23 rooms) ➊ 027 250 0359; m 0754 475188; e info@ karama-lodge.com; www.karama-lodge.com. Aptly named after the Swahili word for 'blessing', this fabulous eco-lodge, constructed by Tropical Trails, is remarkable for possessing a genuine bush atmosphere, despite being situated only 3km from central Arusha along the Old Moshi Rd. Perched on the small but densely wooded Suye Hill, the lodge consists of 22 stilted wood-&-*makuti* units with Zanzibar-style beds draped in netting, en-suite shower & toilet, & private balcony facing Kilimanjaro. The brachystegia woodland in the lodge grounds & adjacent forest reserve harbours a wide range of birds (the localised brown-throated barbet prominent among them) as well as small nocturnal mammals such as bushbaby, genet & civet. The restaurant serves tasty snacks & meals, & offers views to Kilimanjaro & Meru on a clear day. A recently opened spa currently offers massage only, but sauna, yoga & other treatments will soon be available. Overall, it's highly recommended as an antidote to the bland city hotels that otherwise characterise Arusha in this price range, though the sloping

& tea/coffee-making facilities. Air-conditioned & non-smoking rooms are available. Facilities include 24hr room service, a business centre, several curio shops, 24hr satellite internet access, a heated swimming pool, 3 bars, 2 restaurants & an airport shuttle service. *Executive rooms US$200/240 sgl/dbl B&B; suites US$400/440.*

⌂ **Arusha Holiday Inn** [89 G3] (168 rooms) ➊ (South Africa) +27 (0)11 442 0488; e pacro@ africansunhotels.com; www.africansunhotels.com. Formerly the government-owned & French-managed Mount Meru Novotel, this high-rise hotel set in large landscaped gardens overlooking the golf course was closed for renovations at the time of writing, but it's set to reopen as the Arusha Holiday Inn in late 2009.

⌂ **Onsea House** (4 rooms) ➊ 0784 833207; e info@onseahouse.com; www.onseahouse.com. Situated on the slopes of Namasi Hill less than 10 mins' drive from central Arusha (along the Moshi Rd), this attractive & intimate boutique hotel has drawn praise from all quarters since it opened in Jul 2006. The large green gardens contain a swimming pool & the restaurant, managed by a Michelin trained Belgian chef, serves superb Afro-European fusion cuisine. *Low season rates are US$145/170 sgl/dbl B&B or US$220/320 FB; whole high season rates are US$175/210 B&B & US$250/360 FB.*

grounds would make it a particularly poor choice for disabled & elderly travellers. *US$87/118 sgl/dbl B&B.*

⌂ **L'Oasis Lodge** [89 H2] (22 rooms) ➊ 027 250 7089; m 0755 749945; f 027 250 7089; e s.broadbent@edi-africa.com; www.loasislodge.com. Set in large green grounds about 500m north of the Moshi road, along a side road signposted opposite the soon-to-reopen Arusha Holiday Inn, this pleasant lodge has recently undergone some major renovations & expansions, but it retains the rustic feel that made it popular in the first place & is easily one of the best-value options in its range in the Arusha area. A variety of comfortable en-suite rooms are available, including some attractive stilted bungalows, while other facilities include a restaurant, a large bar alongside the swimming pool, & the wonderful Lounge at Oasis, whose funky but earthy décor is complemented by a cosmopolitan menu of light snacks, salads, wraps & full meals. *US$79/97/127 sgl/dbl/trpl B&B or US$115/189/235 FB.*

⌂ **East African All-Suite Hotel** [89 F6] (40 rooms) ➊ 027 205 0075; m 0757 600110; e reservations@eastafricanhotel.com; www.eastafricanhotel.com. This slick new hotel on the

Old Moshi Rd doesn't exactly evoke a safari atmosphere, but the accommodation is to a very high standard, consisting of large suites with varied facilities, including flat screen satellite TV, king-size bed, safe, kitchen with stove & fridge, large bathroom with combination tub/shower, AC, & rather bombastic leather furnishing that creates a slightly cluttered effect. The restaurant serves an imaginative selection of contemporary dishes in the Tsh6,000–12,000 range & there's a swimming pool & cigar bar. Good value. *US$145 dbl suite or US$180 presidential suite with 2 bedrooms.*

🏠 **Kibo Palace Hotel** [89 E6] (65 rooms) 📞 027 254 4472; e info@kibopalacehotel.com; www.kibopalacehotel.com. Also situated on the Old Moshi Rd, this smart new 5-storey hotel has an unusual design, centred on a circular lobby with a tall sky-roof above the 5th floor. Comfortable but undistinguished, the rooms have a linoleum faux-wood floor, AC, satellite TV, safe, coffee/tea-making facilities & en-suite combination tub/shower. Facilities include a restaurant & swimming pool surrounded by wrought-iron outdoor furniture. Pleasant enough in its rather sterile manner, it seems a touch overpriced. *US$150/170/180 sgl/dbl/suite.*

🏠 **The African Tulip** [89 F7] (29 rooms) 📞 027 254 3004/5; e info@theafricantulip.com; www.theafricantulip.com. This chic new boutique hotel is set in an attractive suburban garden with a swimming pool along the same road as The Outpost. The rooms are large & attractively decorated with Zanzibar-style wooden furnishing, & good facilities including a safe, minibar, Wi-Fi, satellite TV & large en-suite bathroom with a choice of a tub or shower. There's a well-stocked gift shop on the ground floor, along with the aptly named Zanzibar Bar & promising Baobab Restaurant. *US$135/170 sgl/dbl B&B, US$290 suite.*

🏠 **Impala Hotel** [89 G7] (150 rooms) 📞 027 254 3082/7; m 0754 678678/008448; f 027 254 3088/9; e impala@impalahotel.com; www.impalahotel.com The recently expanded & renovated Impala Hotel, situated in Kijenge about 10 mins' walk from the town centre, is justifiably rated by many tour operators as the best-value hotel in its range in the immediate vicinity of Arusha, & it's certainly one of the largest, busiest, smoothest running & reasonably priced, though somewhat deficient in character. Facilities include 4 restaurants variously specialising in Indian, Italian, Chinese & continental cuisine (the Indian is among the best in town), an internet café, a forex bureau offering good rates, a swimming pool, a gift shop, an inexpensive

shuttle service to Nairobi as well as to KIA, & an in-house safari operator. The rooms are comfortable & attractively decorated, & have satellite TV, hot showers & a fridge. *US$90/110/155 sgl/dbl/trpl B&B; HB & FB rates additional US$12 pp per meal. Executive rooms & suites US$150/230.*

🏠 **Ilboru Safari Lodge** (30 rooms) m 0754 270357/0784 270357; e reservations@ ilborusafarilodge.com; www.ilborusafarilodge.com. Situated in large, leafy grounds among the banana plantations that swathe the Mount Meru foothills some 2.5km north of the town centre, this highly regarded lodge has been offering good-value accommodation for some years, & despite a recent change of ownership, it remains a very pleasant & peaceful retreat, centred on a large swimming pool. Accommodation in comfortable thatched bungalows is very reasonably priced. *US$83/99 sgl/dbl B&B or US$109/151 FB.*

🏠 **New Safari Hotel** [88 D4 & 104 C4] (48 rooms) 📞 027 250 3261/2; e newsafarihotel@habari.co.tz; www.thenewsafarihotel.com. Recently reopened after protracted renovations, this long-serving hotel on Boma Rd, once popular with the hunting fraternity, now seems more geared towards business travellers, with its convenient — though potentially noisy — central location a few minutes from the AICC & a number of government offices & restaurants. Facilities include a ground-floor internet café & a good restaurant. The large, tiled en-suite rooms with digital satellite TV have a modern feel, & seem fair value. *US$85/105 sgl/dbl.*

🏠 **Hotel Equator** [88 D4 & 104 C3] (40 rooms) 📞 027 250 8409/3727/3127; e equator@ars.bol.tz This recently refurbished old hotel on Boma Rd has spacious & well-kept rooms with fridge & TV, but — as with so many former government hotels — the fixtures are as outmoded as the atmosphere is bland & institutional. Still, it's not bad value, especially if you are looking for a central location. *US$80/100 sgl/dbl B&B.*

🏠 **Naura Springs Hotel** [89 E2] (124 rooms) 📞 027 205 0001/8; e naura@nauraspringshotel.com; www.nauraspringshotel.com. Spanning 12 stories & sporting a scary reflective blue exterior, this extrovertly modernistic hotel to the north of the AICC might politely be described as a prominent landmark. The large rooms are more attractive, with wooden floors & décor, 2 dbl beds, flat screen satellite TV, & en-suite shower & jacuzzi, & there's a pleasant swimming pool area, but other public areas are lacking in charm or character. One to avoid. *US$120 dbl.*

3

Situated about 550km southeast of Moshi by road, Dar es Salaam – often referred to as plain 'Dar' – is Tanzania's capital in all but name. With a population estimated at 2.35 million in 2008, it is far and away the country's largest city and most important commercial centre, a lively bustling Indian Ocean port rivalled in regional maritime significance only by Mombasa in Kenya. Unfortunately, however, Dar es Salaam cannot claim to be a tourist centre of any great note. On the contrary, the increasing ease with which one can fly into KIA directly, or fly straight on to Zanzibar or elsewhere after landing at Dar, means that a relatively small proportion of fly-in tourists ever set foot in the city itself.

Whether or not this is a good thing is a matter of opinion. Dar es Salaam is one of those cities that draws extreme reactions from travellers, a real 'love it or hate it' kind of place, and its many detractors would probably regard any Dar-free itinerary through Tanzania to be a highly desirable state of affairs. Personally, however, I enjoy Dar es Salaam more perhaps than any other major east African city, since it boasts all the hustle and bustle of somewhere such as Nairobi, yet has none of that city's underlying aggression or bland architectural modernity.

If nothing else, Dar is imbued with a distinctive sense of place, one derived from the cultural mix of its people and buildings, not to say a torpid coastal humidity that permeates every aspect of day-to-day life. Architecturally, the city boasts German, British, Asian and Arab influences, but it is fundamentally a Swahili city, and beneath the superficial air of hustle, a laid-back and friendly place. People are willing to pass away the time with idle chat and will readily help out strangers, yet tourists are rarely hassled, except in the vicinity of the New Africa Hotel, where a resident brigade of hissing money-changers froths into action every time a *mazungu* (white person) walks past.

If you decide to fly into Dar es Salaam, the international airport is situated 13km from the city centre, a 20-minute taxi ride that costs up to US$25 dependent on how hard you bargain. Long-haul buses out of Dar es Salaam almost all leave from the vast Ubungu Bus Station, situated out of town along the Morogoro road, which enforces a special trip out of town to book tickets a day ahead of departure – a taxi from the city centre to Ubungu will cost up to US$8, depending on how receptive the driver is to negotiation. A notable exception to the above is the excellent Scandinavia Express (✆ 022 218 4833–4/285 0847–9; m 0811 336625/0713 325474; f 022 285 0224; e info@scandinaviagroup.com; www.scandinaviagroup.com), a relatively luxurious coach service whose vehicles leave from a private terminus at the junction of Nyerere and Msimbazi streets on the airport road. These services connect Dar es Salaam to Moshi and Arusha (thrice daily), as well as Nairobi (once daily), Mwanza (once daily) and various towns in the south.

If you need to overnight in Dar, there are plenty of hotels in and around the city to suit all budgets. A few recommendations, in descending order of price and quality, follow.

MODERATE (US$50–90)

⌂ **The Outpost** [89 E7] (23 rooms) 37A Serengeti St; ✆ 027 250 8405; e outpost@bol.co.tz; www.outposttanzania.com Probably the pick in this range, the welcoming & homely Outpost, set in a suburban garden has proved to be consistently popular with travellers seeking the combination of affordability & comfort. Cheap & tasty lunches & dinners are available. To get here from the Clock Tower, head out in the direction of the Impala Hotel for about 1km, then follow a signposted right turn into Serengeti Rd, passing the Roy Safaris office, & you'll reach it after another

300m or so. En-suite rooms with TV US$48/66 sgl/dbl.

⌂ **Hotel Le Jacaranda** [89 G6] (9 rooms) ✆ 027 254 4624; e jacaranda@tz2000com; www.chez.com/jacaranda. Situated in the garden suburbs immediately east of the town centre, not far from The Outpost, this converted colonial-era homestead ranks among the most characterful hotels in Arusha, & it's also exceptionally good value. It lies in prettily overgrown grounds with a mini-golf course & shady & highly rated restaurant/bar area. The large en-suite rooms all

🏠 **Ras Kutani** (12 rooms) ☎ 022 213 4802; f 022 211 2794; e reservations@selous.com; www.selous.com. Closer in spirit & feel to a bush retreat than a typical beach resort, Ras Kutani is a wonderful small lodge situated on a wild & isolated stretch of coast some 35km south of Dar es Salaam. The bandas, constructed almost entirely with organic materials, are set in dense coastal woodland overlooking a small mangrove-lined lagoon & a wide sandy beach. Vervet & blue monkeys & prolific birdlife in the woodland are complemented by good snorkelling & fishing in the nearby reefs. *US$305/365 sgl/dbl FB.*

🏠 **Sea Cliff Hotel** (85 rooms) ☎ 022 260 0380/7; f 022 260 0476; e information@ hotelseacliff.com; www.hotelseacliff.com. Arguably the top hotel within Dar's greater city limits, the Sea Cliff boasts a fabulous seafront location on the Msasani Peninsula, only 15 mins by taxi from the city centre, & should reopen in 2009 after being gutted by fire 2 years before that. *US$170 en-suite non-sea-facing dbl with AC & satellite TV, to US$400 executive suite.*

🏠 **New Africa Hotel** (126 rooms) Cnr Azikiwe & Sokoine Dr; ☎ 022 211 7050/1; f 022 211 6731; e newafricahotel@raha.com. Reopened in 1998 following total renovation, the New Africa is built on the site of the legendary Kaiserhof, the first hotel to open in Dar es Salaam, during the German era. The New Africa in its most recent incarnation is plush & thoroughly modern, with a popular casino & several good restaurants in the building. *US$170/180 sgl/dbl; US$250 suite.*

🏠 **Southern Sun Dar es Salaam** (152 rooms) ☎ 022 213 7575; f 022 213 9070; e reservations@southernsun.co.tz; www.southernsuntz.com. The former Holiday Inn is a smart, centrally located hotel set in lush grounds on the east end of Garden Av. Facilities include a business centre, Wi-Fi, 2 good restaurants, 16hr room service, non-smoking rooms, facilities for the disabled, an on-site travel centre, a good curio & bookshop, a swimming pool & a fitness centre. *US$180/200 sgl/dbl, with suites starting at US$250.*

🏠 **Protea Hotel Oyster Bay** (24 rooms) ☎ 022 266 6665; e proteadar@africaonline.co.tz; www.proteahotels.com/oysterbay. Particularly recommended to business travellers spending a while in Dar es Salaam, this unique modern complex lies about 2km from the city centre on the road to the Msasani Peninsula. The complex contains a swimming pool & restaurant. *Spacious, AC units US$145–185.*

🏠 **Palm Beach Hotel** (32 rooms) ☎ 022 213 0985/212 2931; e info@pbhtz.com; www.pbhtz.com. About 20 mins' walk from the city centre on Ali Hassan Mwinyi Rd, this rambling old 1950s hotel was recently restored to its former Art Deco glory, complete with bright purple exterior, & it retains a time-warped charm. A pleasant garden bar/restaurant serves good meals. En-suite rooms with mini-safe, hot water, TV & internet access are good value. *US$85/110 sgl/dbl.*

🏠 **Econo Lodge** (61 rooms) ☎ 022 211 6048/9; f 022 211 6053; e econolodge@raha.com. This smart new hotel has a convenient central location off Libya St, & is outstandingly good value in the budget range. *En-suite rooms with fans Tsh18/24/30,000 sgl/dbl/trpl; with AC Tsh30/35/40,000.*

have a 4-poster bed with netting & hot water. *US$45/50 sgl/dbl.*

🏠 **La Bella Inn** [89 G6] (12 rooms) m 0732 978013l; e mbegatouristcamp@yahoo.com. Recently acquired by the Mbega Lodge group, this homely hotel lies in large gardens close to the Impala Hotel, & is very convenient for early departures & late arrivals with the Riverside, Bobby & Osa shuttles from Nairobi, all of which depart from the parking lot. There's a good Italian garden restaurant, & live African music 19.00–20.00 Fri–Sun. The neat tiled rooms with net, TV, fan & en-suite hot shower seem good value too. *US$40/50 sgl/dbl.*

🏠 **Everest Inn** [89 F6] (7 rooms) ☎ 027 250 8419; m 0704 255277, e everesttzus@yahoo.com; www.everest-inn.com. This homely guesthouse is attached to an excellent Chinese restaurant set in an old colonial house in a lush garden on the Old Moshi Rd. The small but clean & comfortable en-suite rooms come with TV, hot water & nets, & there's 24hr free internet & Skype. Rooms in the main house are nicer than those out the back. The restaurant serves authentic Chinese food in the Tsh7,000–10,000 range. *US$40/50 sgl/dbl.*

🏠 **Arusha Naaz Hotel** [104 B6] (21 rooms) ☎ 027 250 2087; m 0754 282799;

e arushanaaz@yahoo.com; www.arushaneez.net.
Situated on Sokoine Rd close to the Clock Tower,
this clean, convenient & secure hotel, once a
favourite with budget travellers, now slots more
into the moderate category following extensive
renovations. The en-suite rooms with net, fan, hot
water & satellite TV are on the cramped side, &
can't exactly be described as a bargain, though the
hotel remains a good compromise between price &
comfort in the town centre. There is a good,
inexpensive Indian restaurant on the ground floor
& an internet café & car hire firm on the
premises. *US$30/45 sgl/dbl occupancy.*

⌂ **Arusha Crown Hotel** [101 G4] (38 rooms)
☎ 027 254 4161; e info@arushacrownhotel.com;
www.arushacrownhotel.com. This gleaming new multi-
storey hotel looks decidedly misplaced in the seedy
backroads between the bus station & football
stadium, a location that might well feel mildly
intimidating to the more timid traveller. If you can
get past that, it's not a bad option, albeit with zero
ambience, & the functional & airy en-suite rooms
with tiled floor, digital satellite TV & modern décor
seem fair value. The cafeteria-style restaurant on the
ground floor has meals for around Tsh6,000.
US$65/75 sgl/dbl.

⌂ **Golden Rose Hotel** [88 A2 & 101 F2] (40
rooms) ☎ 027 250 7959/8862; m 0713 510696;

BUDGET (US$25–45)

⌂ **Arusha Resort Centre** [104 C7] (30 rooms)
☎ 027 250 8333; m 0787 830495;
e aruahsresort@habari.co.tz. Situated on a quiet
backroad only 2 mins walk from the central
Clocktower, this is a comfortable & safe albeit rather
institutional double-storey hotel offering clean &
good-value accommodation with discounts for long-
stay visitors. *US$35/45 en-suite sgl/dbl or US$50
self-catering apt.*

⌂ **City Link Pentagon Hotel** (53 rooms) ☎ 027 254
4444; e reservations@hotelcitylink.com;
www.hotelcitylink.com. This eccentrically shaped high-
rise hotel is rather characterless & has an indifferent
location on the Moshi road about 2km past the
Arusha Holiday Inn, but otherwise it seems like very
good value. The large, tiled rooms come with
satellite TV, writing desk & en-suite hot shower, &
there's a pleasant beer garden serving *nyama
choma* & other food. *US$45 twin or dbl.*

⌂ **Olduvai Inn** [89 F6] (15 rooms) ☎ 027 254
3044; m 0732 975362; e magiesaria@yahoo.com.
Set in large gardens on the junction of Serengeti &
Old Moshi roads, this is a great little guesthouse

e goldenrose@habari.co.tz;
www.goldenrosehoteltz.com. This well-known landmark
on the western side of town, the most central
departure point for the Riverside shuttle to Nairobi,
used to be regarded as one of the top hotels in
Arusha. Today, however, the small en-suite rooms
with TV, fan, net & balcony feel rather time-worn &
gloomy, & are indifferent value. *US$40/60 sgl/dbl
B&HB old wing; US$50/70 new wing.*

⌂ **Sinka Court Hotel** [101 H5] (29 rooms)
☎ 027 250 4961; e sinkacourthotel@hotmail.com.
The new multi-storey hotel in the backroads
between the market & the Naura River has cramped
but clean en-suite rooms with satellite TV.
*US$40/50 sgl/dbl; more spacious executive rooms
US$60 dbl.*

⌂ **Hotel Seventy Seven** [89 H4] (120 rooms)
☎ 027 254 3800; m 0744 381047; e hotel77@
tz2000.com; www.seventysevenhotel.netfirms.com. It
once billed itself as 'the largest tourist village in
east Africa', more recently as the 'Geneva of Africa',
yet one could be forgiven for thinking the true
architectural inspiration of this hotel on Nyerere Rd
lay somewhere in Soviet-era Siberia. The '*Saba Saba*'
was closed for renovations in early 2009, but unless
these are truly radical, it is likely to remain an
aesthetically confrontational introduction to a
Tanzanian safari.

offering clean & very reasonably priced en-suite
accommodation with nets, TV & hot shower. There's
internet access onsite & plenty of choice of
restaurants within a few hundred metres. *US$25/30
sgl/dbl B&B.*

⌂ **L'Oasis Backpackers Lodge** [89 H2] (12 rooms)
Contact details as for L'Oasis Lodge, page 94.
Situated opposite L'Oasis Lodge & under the same
management, this offers newcomers to east Africa a
comfortable & reasonably affordable suburban
retreat. The small tree house-like rooms with
wooden floors & screened windows aren't cheap, &
the hot showers & toilets are shared, but this is a
good, safe choice, & the price includes access to the
facilities & restaurant at the main lodge. *US$20 pp
inc full b/fast.*

⌂ **Stereo Hotel** [101 G6] (33 rooms) ☎ 027 250
3995; e aaronm@hormail.com; www.stereohotel.com.
The smart, new 4-storey hotel near the central
market has spotless spacious tiled rooms with queen
or twin beds, phone, satellite TV, nets, & seems
excellent value compared with most other places in
this range. *Tsh35,000/40,000 sgl/dbl.*

⌂ **Hotel Pallson's** [101 F6] (28 rooms) ☎ 027 254 8483; m 0754 400747; e hotel_pallsons@ yahoo.com. This long-serving multi-storey hotel is centrally located on Sokoine Rd a short walk south of the bus station. The rather time-worn en-suite rooms, with satellite TV, fan & hot shower, are adequate value. US$33/43 sgl/dbl B&B.

⌂ **Hotel Fort Des Moines** [101 H5] (20 rooms) ☎ 027 250 0277; e bimel@cybernet.co.tz; www.bimel.co.tz. Pretentious name aside, this clean & reasonably smart new hotel near the market & bus station seems decent enough value. US$20/25 sgl/dbl.

⌂ **Williams Inn** [101 E2] (30 rooms) ☎ 027 250 3578. Part of a cluster of hotels situated along Corner Rd northwest of the stadium, this charges for a clean but spartan dbl with en-suite hot shower & TV, in which 'women of immoral turpitude are strictly not allowed'. US$25 dbl.

SHOESTRING AND CAMPING (UNDER US$25)

⌂ **Arusha Backpackers Hotel** [100 D7] (34 rooms) ☎ 027 2504474; m 0773 377795; e info@ arushabackpackers.co.tz; www.arushabackpackers.co.tz. Affiliated to the long-serving Kindoroko Hotel in Moshi, this new shoestring hotel lies on Sokoine Rd within easy walking distance of the central bus station. It's a safe & reliable set-up, & has quickly established itself as a favourite rendezvous for budget-conscious travellers. The small but clean rooms have a desk & fan, & use common hot showers & toilets. Kindoroko Tours on the ground floor is a reliable bet for budget camping safaris & Kilimanjaro climbs. US$10/16 sgl/dbl B&B or US$6 for a dorm bed, with lunch & dinner an additional US$7 pp.

⋏ **Masai Camp** m 0744 507131/898800; e masaicamp@africamail.com; http://masaicamp.tripod.com. Situated about 2km out of town along the Old Moshi Rd, Masai Camp is one of the best campsites in Tanzania, & it also offers simple accommodation in huts. Facilities include an ablution block with hot water, a pool table, volleyball & a lively 24hr bar, & an excellent safari company called Tropical Trails is onsite. The restaurant is well known for its pizzas, which cost around Tsh4,000. If you're without transport, you can get a taxi here for around Tsh2,000. Camping US$5 pp; rooms US$10 pp.

⌂ **Arusha By Night Annexe** [101 F3] m 0713 485237. For long dauntingly overpriced thanks to its inflated non-resident rates, this stalwart of the Arusha accommodation scene now evidently operates on a one-price-for-all-comers policy. As a result, the slightly faded but spacious rooms with twin or dbl bed, TV, fan, writing desk & en-suite hot shower actually feel like one of the best deals in this range. Tsh16,000 dbl or twin.

⌂ **Bakara Inn** [100 B1] m 0732 978274; e bakarainn@gmail.com. Remote from the main cluster of budget accommodation, this new guesthouse is conveniently located for early departures on the Mtei & Scandinavia buses & the tiled en-suite rooms with fan, TV, hot shower & tea/coffee-making facilities are good value too. Tsh25,000 dbl.

⌂ **Kilimanjaro Villa** [101 G4] ☎ 027 250 8109; m 0713 510696. A long-standing backpacker standby situated close to the market & bus station, the Kilimanjaro Villa is nothing special, but it's friendly, clean & reasonably priced. US$7/10 sgl/dbl using common showers.

⌂ **YMCA** [101 B4] ☎ 027 272 2544. This Arusha institution is looking pretty rundown these days, but it has a conveniently central location on India Rd, & room rates that haven't changed in years mean it is now relatively good value. Tsh11,500/14,500 sgl/dbl.

⌂ **Hotel Flamingo** [101 F4] (9 rooms). ☎ 027 254 8812; m 0744 260309; e flamingoarusha@ yahoo.com. Sensibly priced & conveniently close to the central bus station, this small guesthouse has clean twin rooms with netting, en-suite hot shower & toilet. Tsh20,000/25,000 sgl/dbl.

⌂ **Monje's Guesthouse** [101 G1, 101 G2 & 101 H1] ☎ 027 250 3060. Narrowly the pick of the bottom-of-the-range guesthouses in the backroads north of the stadium, this quiet, family-run affair actually consists of 4 guesthouses running along the same road. All 4 places have clean rooms, friendly staff, hot showers & a vigorously enforced anti-flycatcher policy! Tsh12,000–20,000 depending on room type.

⌂ **Casablanca Mini-lodge** [101 F1] (12 rooms) ☎ 027 250 3419. Also one of the better lodges in the area north of the stadium, this has small but clean rooms with en-suite hot shower. Tsh 15,000.

⋊ WHERE TO EAT

Plenty of good restaurants are dotted around Arusha, with many international cuisines represented and most budgets catered for by a number of places. The following is an alphabetical selection of some long-standing favourites and

ARUSHA
Central West

A

B

C

D

1

Baraka
Inn

MAKAO MAPYA ROAD

N

Bradt

0 ━━━━━ 100km
0 ━━━━━ 100 miles

2

3

✝ Church

M
A
K
A
O

M
A
P
Y
A

R
O
A
D

4

Scandinavia & MTEI
Coach Office

5

WACHAGGA

WASUKOMA

6

● Kiomboro Market

Arusha Coffee Lodge,
Serengeti NP,
Dadoma
←

Meru House Inn 🏠

Gapco

Mt Meru

SOKOINE ROAD

Total

Shanghai

Noble ✕

🏠✕ ⊠
Arusha
Backpackers

HINDI

TFA
(Shoprite)
Shopping Centre

Summit
Shopping Mall

7

© Philip Briggs

A

B

C

D

E   F   G   H

Mashele   Delight GH

MASHELE

Casablanca
Mini-Lodge

NBC
(with ATM)

Bright GH

Williams Inn

Midway

Hotel AM88

Sunny
Safaris

Golden
Rose

Kearsley's Travel

Kitundu

Serenity

Hanang
Guesthouse

African
Queen

LEVOLOSI

Monje's Guesthouse (1)

Monje's 'C'

Pizzarusha

Minja's

Monje's Guesthouse (2)

New Shimba

KANISA

Miami Beach
Guesthouse

STADIUM

COLONEL MIDDLETON ROAD

ETHIOPIA

Arusha By Night
Annexe

STADIUM

Raha Leo

Anglican
church

Arusha Declaration
Museum

MAKONGORO   MAKONGORO Arusha Crown   MAKONGORO

Flamingo

Bus
station

Hotel 7-11

Barclay's
(with ATM)

Aquiline

MAKUA

ZARAMO

MARKET

MOSQUE

SOMALI

Khan's
Barbecue

Robannyson

Silvertouch

Kilimanjaro
Villa

AZIMIO

Uhuru
Monument

SWAHILI

PANGANI

Arusha
Centre Inn

Fort
Des Moines

Sinka
Court

Big Bite

Sarafina

ID

Bookpoint

BENJAMIN

SETH

WAPARE

KITUONI

Pallson's

McMoody's

CRDB

SOKOINE ROAD

BP

Bethal

Town
Guesthouse

Oryx

Dolly's
Patisserie

MAASAI

MARKET

Market

BP

Mukhtar

Coyote GH

Stereo

Sher E
Punjab

AZIMIO

SWAHILI

Taxi rank

SOKOINE ROAD

JACARANDA

Neha Snacks

BP

Mayur

Twin Peaks
Casino

BP

Metropole
Cinema
Green Hut
Burgers

7

E   F   G   H

interesting recent additions, but new places open and close frequently, so don't be afraid to try restaurants that aren't listed.

✗ **Albero Restaurant** [89 F5] Haile Selassie Rd; ☎ 027 254 8987; ⊕ lunch & dinner daily. This new open-air Italian restaurant has a pleasant setting in leafy suburbia & serves a varied selection of pasta dishes & pizzas in the Tsh8,000–10,000 range, while seafood & grills cost Tsh12,000–16,000.

✗ **Arusha Naaz Hotel** [104 B6] Sokoine Rd; ☎ 027 250 2087; ⊕ lunch & dinner daily. The ground-floor restaurant at this popular central hotel offers a great all-you-can-eat Indian buffet lunch at US$7. No alcohol.

✗ **Big Bite** [101 H5] Cnr Swahili & Somali Rd; ⊕ dinner only daily except Tue. This misleadingly named & rather low-key eatery near the market isn't a fast-food outlet but one of the oldest & best north Indian restaurants in Arusha. Mains in the 8,000–12,000 range.

✗ **Blue Heron Coffee & Gift Shop** [89 F5] Haile Selassie Rd; ☏ 0784 505555; ⊕ 09.00–17.00. Combining classic colonial architecture with contemporary décor, this new coffee shop is a great spot for a relaxed open-air lunch, with seating on the veranda & in the green garden. Pasta dishes & salads cost around Tsh6,000 & it serves cheaper sandwiches, cakes & coffee.

✗ **Café Bamboo Restaurant** [104 C4] Boma Rd; ☎ 027 250 6451; ⊕ 07.00–21.00 Mon–Sat. This homely restaurant serves decent coffee, fruit juices, sandwiches, pancakes & snacks, & full meals for around Tsh4,000–6,000. The lunch of the day is usually a bargain. Justifiably packed at lunchtime, but quiet later.

✗ **Chocolate Temptation** [100 A7] TFA Centre, Sokoine Rd; ☏ 0754 696993; ⊕ 09.30–18.00 Mon–Sat. An oasis for the sweet toothed, this has indoor & outdoor seating, a wide range of yummy cakes & ice creams, & strong filter coffee.

✗ **Dolly's Patisserie** [101 F6] Sokoine Rd; ☎ 027 254 4013; ⊕ 09.00–18.00 Mon–Sat. The highly rated bakery sells fresh bread & cakes, along with tasty pastries & sandwiches to take away.

✗ **Everest Inn Chinese Restaurant** [89 F6] Old Moshi Rd; ☏ 0744 377299; ⊕ lunch & dinner. The best Chinese food in Arusha is served at this suburban family-run restaurant, which also caters to vegetarians & charges around Tsh7,000–10,000 for a main course.

✗ **Flame Tree** [89 F5] Haile Selassie Rd; ☏ 0744 377299; ⊕ 12.00–14.00 & 19.00–22.00 Mon–Sat. This is a popular upmarket eatery serving a varied selection of continental fare with Asian & African influences. Main dishes are in the Tsh7,000–12,000 range & a 4-course set menu costs Tsh20,000.

✗ **Greek Club** [89 F6] Old Moshi Rd; ☏ 0754 652747; ⊕ 12.00–14.00 & 17.30–late daily except Mon & Thu. Converted from a stately colonial homestead set in large green gardens, this popular expat hangout has live sports on TV, a busy bar, free Wi-Fi, a wide veranda & a great children's playground. The tasty Greek cuisine is complemented by a selection of sandwiches, salads & baked potatoes, with most meals around Tsh8,000 range.

✗ **Green Hut House of Burgers** [101 H7] Sokoine Rd. Excellent & inexpensive burgers & other greasy fast-food staples & light meals. No alcohol.

✗ **Impala Hotel** [89 G7] Old Moshi Rd; ☎ 027 254 3082/7; www.impalahotel.com. The Indian restaurant in this large hotel is justifiably rated as one of the best in Arusha – & there are 3 other specialist restaurants to choose from if Indian isn't your thing.

✗ **Jambo Coffee House & Makuti Garden** [104 C4] Boma Rd; ⊕ 08.00–22.00. The coffee house serves decent coffee, cooked b/fasts & light snacks. The adjacent Makuti Garden, set in a green courtyard, is one of the best places in the town centre for evening meals – curries & grills in the Tsh7,000–10,000 range.

✗ **Khan's Barbecue** [101 G5] Mosque St; ☏ 0754 652747; ⊕ 18.00–21.00. This singular eatery near the market is a motor spares shop by day & street BBQ in the evening. A mixed grill including beef, chicken & mutton kebabs, with a huge selection of salads, naan bread & the like, costs Tsh7,000. No alcohol.

✗ **McMoody's** [101 F6] Sokoine Rd; ☎ 027 254 4013; ⊕ 10.00–22.00 Tue–Sun. This McDonald's clone serves burgers for around Tsh3,000–4,000 – the plastic décor, like the food, is designed to make fast-food junkies feel at home, & there's a fast internet café attached.

✗ **Milk & Honey Restaurant** [104 B3] Sokoine Rd; ☎ 027 250 2087; ⊕ lunch Mon–Sat. This popular local lunch venue serves a variety of Tanzanian, Indian & Western dishes in the Tsh2,500–4,000 range.

✗ **Patisserie** [104 B6] Sokoine Rd; ☏ 0754 302174; ⊕ 08.30–18.00 Mon–Sat, 08.30–14.00 Sun. This popular backpacker & volunteer hangout near the Clocktower serves fresh loaves, rolls & pastries, adequate light meals & fruit juice, & dismal coffee, but everything else is excellent. Fast internet café attached.

✗ **Pizzarusha Restaurant** [101 H2] Off Mashele Rd; m 0754 366292; ⊕ 09.00–22.00 daily. Recently relocated to Monje's 'C' Guesthouse, this backpacker stalwart serves a range of pizzas, curries & grills in the Tsh4,000–5,000 range & sandwiches for around Tsh2,000. Lacks the atmosphere of the old venue, but still one of the best-value eateries in town.

✗ **Sapporo Restaurant** [100 A7] TFA Centre, Sokoine Rd; m 0787 225224; ⊕ 12.00–14.30 & 19.00–22.00 Mon–Sun. This superb upmarket restaurant serves sushi & other Japanese mains for around Tsh8,000–10,000, or lavish set menus for Tsh22,000–32,000 pp.

✗ **Sazan Japanese Restaurant** [89 E5] Old Moshi Rd; ⊕ lunch & dinner daily. This quirky eatery serves platters of sushi, cooked seafood & other rather greasy Japanese food for around Tsh5,000.

✗ **Sidewalk Bar/Café** [104 B3] India Rd; ⊕ lunch only Mon–Fri This cramped but clean eatery specialises in filled pita bread, sandwiches, burgers & fruit juices. There's also a lunchtime salad buffet on Tues & Thu.

✗ **Spices & Herbs Restaurant** [89 G6] Simeon Rd; m 0754 313163; ⊕ lunch & dinner daily. The oldest & best Ethiopian restaurant in Arusha lies close to the Impala Hotel & serves the distinctive Ethiopian staples such as *kai wat* (a spicy meat or vegetarian stew) served with *injera* (flat round sour bread). There's occasional live music, & an internet café onsite. Most meals are around Tsh6,000–8,000.

✗ **Stiggy's Thai Restaurant** [89 H7] Old Moshi Rd; m 0754 375535; ⊕ 12.00–late Tue–Sun. This has a relaxed informality matched by the Australian-Thai owner/manager's golden touch behind the stove. The Thai & continental cuisine isn't cheap (around Tsh16,000 or more for a main course), but quality & presentation are up to international standards. The bar has a pool table & is a pleasant place to hang out.

✗ **Stiggybucks** [100 A7] TFA Centre, Sokoine Rd; m 0754 375535; ⊕ 09.00–17.00 Mon–Sat. Under the same ownership as Stiggy's, this is an excellent coffee shop that also serves a tempting selection of cakes, bagels, salads, sandwiches & light meals in the Tsh4,000–7,000 range.

✗ **Vama Restaurant** [100 A7] TFA Centre, Sokoine Rd; m 0784 326325; ⊕ 12.00–14.30 & 19.00–22.00 daily. Arusha's top Indian restaurant has a varied selection of meat & vegetarian dishes in the Tsh8,000–10,000 range.

✗ **Via Via Restaurant** [104 C2] Boma Rd; m 0754 384922; http://users.telenet.be/tanzania/via_via_arusha.html; ⊕ 09.30–22.00 Mon–Thu, till later Fri & Sat. This Belgian-owned garden restaurant-cum-bar tucked away behind the Old Boma has a relaxing suburban atmosphere & the most eclectic selection of music in Arusha. It's a nice spot for a drink or sandwich, but cooked meals are unexceptional & portions seem mean for the asking price of around Tsh7,000–10,000. It hosts regular film evenings & cultural events involving artistes from all of Africa, & live music on Thu nights.

ENTERTAINMENT AND NIGHTLIFE

BARS AND NIGHTSPOTS There has been a notable increase in nightspots around Arusha in recent years. The liveliest at the time of writing is the **Colobus Club** [89 H7], which reopened in revamped form in October 2008 after a period of closure. It lies on the Old Moshi Road about 500m past the Impala Hotel, and doubles as a disco, snack bar, boozer and pool hall – it keeps going all night over weekends. Another popular venue is the **Boogaloo Nightclub** in the basement of Njiro Mall [89 F7].

Opposite the Colobus Club, the more sedate **Stiggy's Thai Restaurant** [89 H7] is a popular drinking spot with expatriates. Popular sports bars, all with large screen television, a well stocked bar and pub grub, are the **Greek Club** on Old Moshi Road [89 F6], **Pirate's Cove** in the Njiro Mall [89 F7] and the **Empire Sports Bar** in the TFA Centre [100 A7].

There are several decent bars in the same area as the cluster of guesthouses behind the Golden Rose Hotel. The best place to drink in this part of town is **Soweto Gardens** [88 B2], a relaxed but atmospheric garden bar that often hosts live bands over the weekends. Other good spots for live Tanzanian music include the outdoor restaurant of the **La Bella Hotel** [89 G6] (Friday–Sunday nights), **Via Via** [104 C2] (Thursday night) and **Rick's Bar** [89 H3] on the Moshi road.

3

ARUSHA
Central East

A   B   C   D

1   Arusha International
     Conference Centre

     ✕ Via Via

2   Immigration
     office   Old Boma Museum
                               (Natural History)

                               Municipal buildings

3   Arusha Vision

MAKONGORO

$ Bank of Tanzania   Sidewalk Bar ✕   Total   ♪ Telecomms
                                            New Safari
                        YMCA   Equator

4   Foreigner   Club
     (Bureau de Change) $ Afriko
                                            Medicare   KLM, Air Kenya &
                        Hoopoe Safaris   Pharmacy   Ethiopian Airlines
                                                            Precision Air
                        Tanzanite   Jambo coffee house &
                        Experience   Makuti garden
                                                        i   Tanzania Tourist Board
     Bobby Tours   ✕   Café Bamboo
                                                        i   NCA office
                                                            Kase Bookshop
                        Cybernet
                                                            Air Tanzania
     Kase   Curio &   Coastal Travels
     Bookshop   craft stalls
                                                            Oryx
     Lutheran Church ✝   JAELMAEDA

5   Taxi rank   Kenya   Clocktower   OLD MOSHI
                         Commercial   Supermarket
                                              (& newspaper stall)
                        Fuji Photoshop
                                              $ National   Arusha
                                              Microfinance

     Standard Chartered $ Arusha Naaz
                            Milk &
                            Honey   Patisserie
                        Exim   Services 4U

6   Mawingu ☆   Bradt N

     Vodacom Shop
     Modern
     supermarket

     Mamcho KV
     Garden   0   100km
     $ Stanbic   0   100 miles

7   Arusha
                                             Resort Centre
     $ National Bank
        of Commerce
     Rwandair Express   Mount Meru Curio &   © Philip Briggs
                                             Craft Market (50m)

     A   B   SOKOINE   FIRE   BWALO   C   D

GOLIONDOI   INDIA   BOMA   Themi River

CINEMA The best cinema is the Arusha Cinemax [89 F7] (**m** *0732 102221; www.pigadeal.com/cinemax/nowplaying.php*) in the out-of-town Njiro Mall, whose three screens show a varied selection of reasonably current Hollywood and Bollywood fare. Seats start at Tsh6,000.

SHOPPING

BOOKS Your best bet is one of two branches of Kase Book Shop, which lie on Boma Road next to Café Bamboo [104 C4] and on Jael Marda Road opposite the Kenya Commercial Bank [104 B5]. Both stock a good range of books about Tanzania and a more limited selection of contemporary bestsellers and novels. A few vendors usually hang around the Clocktower [88 D5 & 104 C5] selling the maps and national park booklets at highly inflated prices, and most of the upmarket hotels also sell a limited selection of reading matter in their curio shops. To buy or exchange second-hand novels, there are a couple of stalls dotted around town, one in the alley connecting Boma and India roads and several along Sokoine Rd west of the market.

TINGATINGA PAINTINGS

The brightly coloured paintings of fabulous creatures you might notice at craft stalls in Arusha and elsewhere in the region are Tingatinga paintings, a school of painting that is unique to Tanzania and named after its founder Edward Tingatinga. The style arose in Dar es Salaam in the early 1960s, when Tingatinga fused the vibrant and popular work of Congolese immigrants with art traditions indigenous to his Makua homeland in the Mozambique border area (a region well known to aficionados of African art as the home of Makonde carving). When Tingatinga died in 1972, the accidental victim of a police shoot-out, his commercial success had already spawned a host of imitators, and shortly after that a Tingatinga art co-operative was formed with government backing.

In the early days, Tingatinga and his followers produced fairly simple paintings featuring a large, bold and often rather surreal two-dimensional image of one or another African creature on a monotone background. But as the paintings took off commercially, a greater variety of colours came into play, and a trend developed towards the more complex canvases you see today. Modern Tingatinga paintings typically depict a menagerie of stylised and imaginary birds, fish and mammals against a backdrop of natural features such as Kilimanjaro or an abstract panel of dots and whorls. An offshoot style, reputedly initiated by Tingatinga himself, can be seen in the larger, even more detailed canvases that depict a sequence of village or city scenes so busy you could look at them for an hour and still see something fresh.

Tingatinga painters have no pretensions to producing high art. On the contrary, the style has been commercially driven since its inception: even the largest canvases are produced over a matter of days and most painters work limited variations around favourite subjects. It would be missing the point altogether to talk of Tingatinga as traditional African art. With its bold, bright images – tending towards the anthropomorphic, often subtly humorous, always accessible and evocative – Tingatinga might more appropriately be tagged Africa's answer to Pop Art.

Labels aside, souvenir hunters will find Tingatinga paintings to be a lively, original and surprisingly affordable alternative to the identikit wooden animal carvings that are sold throughout east Africa (and, one suspects, left to gather dust in cupboards all over Europe). Take home a Tingatinga panel, and you'll have a quirky but enduring memento of your African trip, something to hang on your wall and derive pleasure from for years to come.

The Makonde of the Tanzania–Mozambique border area are widely regarded to be the finest traditional sculptors in east Africa, and according to oral tradition the males of this matrilineal society have been practising this craft to woo their women for at least 300 years. Legend has it that this is when the first person on earth, not yet male or female, living alone in the foothills of the Makonde Plateau, carved a piece of wood into the shape of a human figure. The carver left his creation outside his home before he retired for the night, and awoke to find it had been transformed into a living woman. Twice the woman conceived, but both times the child died after three days. Each time, the pair moved higher onto the plateau, believing this would bring them luck. The third child lived, and became the first true Makonde. The mother is regarded to be the spiritual ancestor of all the Makonde, and the legend is sometimes said to be a parable for the difficulty of creation and the necessity to discard unsatisfactory carvings.

In their purest form, the intricate, stylised carvings of the Makonde relate to this ancestral cult of womanhood, and are carried only by men, as a good-luck charm. Traditional carvings almost always depict a female figure, sometimes surrounded by children, and the style was practically unknown outside of Tanzania until a carving workshop was established at Mwenge in suburban Dar es Salaam during the 1950s. Subsequently, like any dynamic art form, Makonde sculpture has been responsive to external influences and subject to changes in fashion, with new styles of carvings becoming increasingly abstract and incorporating wider moral and social themes.

The most rustic of the new styles is the Binadamu sculpture, which depicts traditional scenes such as old men smoking pipes or women fetching water in a relatively naturalistic manner. Altogether more eerie and evocative is the Shetani style, in which grotesquely stylised human forms, sometimes with animal-like features, represent the impish and sometimes evil spirits for which the style is named. Many Makonde and other east Africans leave offerings for Shetani sculptures, believing them to be possessed by ancestral spirits. Most elaborate of all are the naturalistic Ujamaa sculptures, which depict many interlocking figures and relate to the collective social policy of Ujamaa fostered by the late President Nyerere. Also known as People Poles or Trees of Life, these statues sometimes incorporate several generations of the carver's family, rising in circular tiers to be up to 2m high. A newer style called Mawingu – the Swahili word for clouds – combines human figures with abstract shapes to represent intellectual or philosophical themes. Today, the finest examples of the genre fetch prices in excess of US$5,000 from international collectors

The Makonde traditionally shape their creations exclusively from *Dalbergia Melanoxylon*, a hardwood tree known locally as *mpingo* and in English as African blackwood or (misleadingly) African ebony. The carver – always male – will first saw a block of wood to the required size, then create a rough outline by hacking away excess wood with an instrument called an adze. The carving is all done freehand, with hammers, chisels and rasps used to carve the fine detail, before the final sculpture is sanded and brushed for smoothness. A large Ujamaa sculpture can take several months to complete, with some of the carving – appropriately – being undertaken communally. Traditionally, the craft was more or less hereditary, with sons being apprenticed to their fathers from a young age, and different families tending to work specific subjects related to their own traditions.

CRAFTS AND CURIOS Arusha is one of the best places in east Africa to buy Makonde carvings, Tingatinga paintings, batiks, Maasai jewellery and other souvenirs. The curio shops are far cheaper than those in Dar es Salaam and their quality and variety are excellent. Most of the curio shops are clustered between the Clocktower and India Road, though be warned that the outdoor stalls can be full of hassle.

Two places stand out. The Cultural Heritage Centre, about 3km out of town on the road towards the Serengeti, stocks the vastest collection of Tanzanian and other African crafts, ranging from towering carvings to colourful batiks and jewellery and a useful selection of books about Tanzania. It's where the likes of King Harald of Norway and former South African and US presidents Thabo Mbeki and Bill Clinton did their curio shopping in Arusha, and an onsite branch of DHL can arrange shipping to anywhere in the world. It can be visited on the way back from a safari, or as a short taxi trip from Arusha.

Altogether different in atmosphere is Mount Meru Craft & Curio Market – more informally known as the Maasai Market – on Fire Road about 200m south of the Clocktower [88 D5 & 104 C5]. Here, some 50-plus stalls sell Maasai beadwork, Tingatinga and other local paintings, batiks, jewellery and pretty much any other ethno-artefact you might be interested in. Prices are lower than the Cultural Heritage Centre, and very negotiable, but the downside is that there is a bit more hassle, generally of a friendly rather than intimidating nature.

SHOPPING MALLS AND SUPERMARKETS The biggest and best shopping mall is the TFA Centre on the west end of Sokoine Road. It is also often referred to as the **Shoprite Centre** [100 A7], after the eponymous supermarket, a warehouse-sized representative of a major South African chain that stocks a huge range of imported and local goods (including South African wines at a third the price the hotels charge) and is an excellent place to stock up with whatever goodies you need before you head out on safari. Also in the TFA Centre are half a dozen upmarket restaurants and coffee shops, several safari outfitters and a good selection of other clothing and craft shops, hairdressers, banks with ATMs, internet cafés, etc. The more out-of-town **Njiro Mall** [89 F7], 4km south of the Impala Hotel, also boasts several eateries, and Arusha's best cinema, but the selection of shops is limited.

OTHER PRACTICALITIES

FOREIGN EXCHANGE Various private and bank-related bureaux de change are dotted all around Arusha, and it is worth shopping around to find the best rate for US dollars cash. Many bureaux de change won't accept less widely used international currencies or travellers' cheques, but the National Bank of Commerce on Sokoine Road [104 A7] will, as will the bureau de change at the Impala Hotel [89 G7]. Whatever else you do, don't change money on the streets of Arusha, as you are sure to be ripped off. If you are desperate for local currency outside banking hours, Foreigners Bureau de Change on Goliondoi Road [104 A4] is open seven days a week from 07.00 to 18.30, and later than that you will probably have to ask a safari company or hotel to help you out with a small transaction.

There are now numerous ATMs where around US$200 in local currency can be drawn against selected credit cards. For Visa, Maestro and Cirrus card holders, the ATMs at the Standard Chartered Bank on Goliondoi Road [104 A6] and the Barclays Bank on Serengeti Road [89 F7] offer a 24-hour withdrawal service, and there are also ATMs offering similar facilities in the Njiro Mall [89 F7] and TFA Centre [100 A7] on Sokoine Road. By contrast, the ATMs at the two branches of the Exim Bank, one on the junction of Goliondoi and Sokoine Road [104 B6] and the other in the TFA Centre [100 A7], accept MasterCard only. American Express is represented by Rickshaw Travels on Sokoine Road near McMoody's. Travellers heading off on safari should be aware that Arusha will offer the first and last chance to reliably draw money against a credit card.

MEDIA AND COMMUNICATIONS

Internet and email There are numerous internet cafés dotted all over Arusha, generally asking around Tsh500–1,500 per hour, depending largely on the speed of the server. One of the best – not least because so few people seem to know about it or use it, so access is generally very fast – is the Telecom-run internet café on the first floor of the post office building on Boma Road [104 C5]. Also good are the Cybernet Centre on India Road [104 B5], the Patisserie on the east end of Sokoine Road [104 B6] and McMoody's on the west end of the same road [101 F6]. Many hotels also offer internet access but at an inflated rate. The Greek Club on Old Moshi Road [89 F6] offers free Wi-Fi to clients who eat or drink there.

Newspapers A selection of local newspapers is available on the day of publication, as is the *Kenya Nation*, which is generally stronger on international news. You won't need to look for these newspapers, because the vendors who sell them will find you quickly enough. The excellent weekly *East African* is available at several newspaper kiosks. The American weeklies *Time* and *Newsweek* are widely available in Arusha.

Post and telephone The main post office is on Boma Road facing the Clocktower [104 C5]. The telecommunications centre further along Boma Road [104 C3] is a good place to make international phone calls and faxes. If you want to buy a local SIM card for your mobile phone, the best and cheapest place to do so is the Vodacom Shop at the junction of Sokoine and Goliondoi roads [104 A6] – it should cost around Tsh300, though you'll need to buy some pay-as-you-go airtime (Tsh1,000–5,000) to activate it.

MEDICAL The AICC Hospital on the Old Moshi Road [89 F6] (℡ *027 250 2329*) is generally regarded to be the best in Arusha, while the nearby Trinity Clinic on Engira Road (℡ *027 254 4392*) can be recommended for malaria and other tests. For further information, consult your hotel reception or safari company.

SWIMMING The swimming pools at the Ilboru Lodge [88 D1] and Impala Hotel [89 G7] are open to non-residents for a small daily fee.

WHAT TO SEE

Arusha town is better known as a base for safaris and other excursions than as a sightseeing destination in its own right. However, a trio of museums dot central Arusha, none of which could be described as a 'must see', but all worth a passing look if you're in the area.

NATURAL HISTORY MUSEUM [104 C2] (*Boma Rd;* ℡ *027 250 7540;* ⊕ *09.00–17.00; entrance Tsh4,400*) Housed in the old German Boma, this might more accurately be renamed the Archaeological or Palaeontological Museum. The limited displays – you can walk around the museum in one minute – include a selection of animal and hominid fossils unearthed at Olduvai and Laetoli in the Ngorongoro Conservation Area, as well as life-size models of *Australopithecus* hunter-gatherers at play.

ARUSHA DECLARATION MUSEUM [101 G4] (*Uhuru Monument Circle;* ⊕ *08.30– 17.30; entrance Tsh1,000*) Dedicated primarily to 20th-century developments in Tanzania, this has some interesting displays on the colonial and post-independence Nyerere era. It also contains a few decent ethnographic displays.

THE TANZANITE EXPERIENCE [104 B5] (*3rd Floor, Blue Plaza Bldg, India Rd;* ☏ *027 250 5101;* ⏱ *09.00–16.00 Mon–Fri, 09.00–16.00 Sat; no entrance fee*) This recently opened museum, operated by TanzaniteOne, the world's largest tanzanite mining company, provides a fascinating overview of the discovery and extraction of this exquisite blue gem, which occurs in Tanzania only. Imaginative multi-media displays and enthusiastic staff are complemented by many examples of rough and cut tanzanite (and other striking local rocks). There's a coffee shop and buying room attached.

Arusha WHAT TO SEE

3

ARUSHA TO USA RIVER

© Philip Briggs

4

Around Arusha

Arusha's status as Tanzania's safari capital is not in dispute, but, paradoxically, only a small proportion of fly-in safarigoers ever gets to spend a night in town. The reason for this is that, unless you're on a tight budget or you actively want an urban base, there is far more to be said for overnighting at one of the more rustic mid-range to upmarket lodges that lie within a 50km radius of the town centre – along the Moshi road towards Kilimanjaro International Airport, and in the vicinity of Arusha National Park.

The main attraction of these out-of-town lodges is arguably the simple fact that they are out of town. As these things go, Arusha is a pleasant enough urban centre, neither as intimidating nor as sprawling as Nairobi, say, or Dar es Salaam. But equally, it is difficult to imagine that any first-time safari-goer on their first night in Tanzania would regard the modest urban bustle of Arusha as the fulfilment of their African dream. By contrast, the better out-of-town lodges do manage to project a genuinely African feel, and offer a relatively tranquil introduction to the land of safaris – in most cases capped (weather permitting) by sterling views of Mount Meru and the more distant snow-capped peak of Kilimanjaro.

Most visitors perceive Arusha and its immediate environs to be little more than a convenient overnight staging post *en route* to the great game reserves to its west. But the area is well worth exploring in its own right. The main attraction is undoubtedly Arusha National Park, an underrated conservation area that will amply pay back whatever time and effort you choose to invest in it – be it a quick afternoon game drive, a couple of nights at one of the lodges on its periphery or the altogether more challenging ascent of the mighty Mount Meru. Also of interest is Lake Duluti, which lies within walking distance of the main road between Arusha town and the eponymous national park, while a number of low-key ecotourist programmes offer visitors the opportunity to interact with the local Maasai and Wa-Arusha in relatively non-contrived circumstances.

THE MOSHI ROAD

With the exception of Lake Duluti and Arusha National Park, the Moshi road running eastward from Arusha boasts no tourist attractions of note. It's an attractive area, however – lush, fertile and bisected by numerous forest-fringed streams that rise on Mount Meru – and there's no shortage of mid-range to upmarket accommodation flanking the main road between Arusha and the small town of Usa River near the turn-off for Arusha National Park.

TOWARDS LAKE DULUTI The road between Arusha and Lake Duluti gives access to one of the most popular lodges in the Arusha area, Moivaro, set on the coffee plantation of the same name, as well as the newer but equally commendable Kigongoni Lodge. More affordable options include Klub Afriko and the new Songota Falls Lodge.

Where to stay
Upmarket

🏠 **Kigongoni Lodge** (20 units) ☏ 027 255 3087;
e assistant.managers@kigongoni.net;
www.kigongoni.net. Set on a forested hilltop in a
70ha coffee plantation about 10km from Arusha
along the Moshi road, this superb new lodge consists
of 20 large, airy & organic en-suite chalets, all of
which come with a private balcony, 2 dbl beds with
netting, hot shower & bath, & log fire. The countrified
atmosphere of the accommodation is complemented
by superb food & a good wine list, while other
attractions include a swimming pool & plenty of
monkeys & birds in the grounds. A significant portion
of the profits is used to support Sibusiso, a home for
disabled Tanzanian children situated on the same
coffee estate. US$165/230 sgl/dbl B&B or
US$195/330 FB, discounted Mar–Jun & Sep.

🏠 **Moivaro Coffee Plantation Lodge** (20 units)
☏ 027 255 3243; e reservations@moivaro.com;
www.moivaro.com. This elegantly rustic lodge, set on
a 40-acre coffee estate 7km from central Arusha &
1.5km from the Moshi road, has received consistently
good reports from travellers & tour operators since
it opened in the late 1990s. The self-contained
bungalows are set in a circular arrangement around
a clean swimming pool & flowering lawns. The main
dining & reception building has a large patio facing
Mount Meru. Facilities include walking & jogging
paths, internet & a massage room. US$185/250
sgl/dbl B&B or US$230/340 FB, discounted Mar–Jun
& Sep–21 Dec.

Moderate

🏠 **Klub Afriko Hotel** (7 rooms) ☏ 027 250 9205;
m 0744 369475; e info@klubafriko.com;
www.klubafriko.com. The intimate & stylish Klub
Afriko is a newly opened lodge set in compact, neat
grounds on the Moshi road about 3km out of
Arusha. The 6 self-contained chalets have a
traditional African appearance with a bright & airy
interior, while the spacious dining area is decorated
in a more classical style. The accommodation is
excellent value, while 3-course set lunches & dinners
cost Tsh8,000 & 9,000 respectively. US$40/60
sgl/dbl B&B; suites sleeping up to 4 people US$80.

🏠 **Songota Falls Lodge** (5 rooms) m 0744
095576/688806; e joice_kimaro@yahoo.com;

www.songotafallslodge.com. Situated along a
monumentally bad 1.5km dirt road that runs
northward from the Moshi road 2km east of Club
Afriko, Songota Lodge currently consists of a few
unfussy but clean en-suite bungalows overlooking the
large green valley below the Songota Waterfall — to
which guided walks are offered when underfoot
conditions are reasonably dry. It's a refreshingly
unpretentious set-up, owned & managed by a
friendly Tanzanian woman with years of experience
in the hotel trade, & likely to expand its facilities in
due course, but as things stand it feels slightly
overpriced for what you get. US$38/45/68
sgl/dbl/trpl B&B or US$60/89/134 FB.

LAKE DULUTI The small but attractive Lake Duluti lies roughly 10km east of
Arusha and only 2km from the Moshi road near the busy little market town of
Tenguru. Some 62ha in extent, 15m deep and fed by subterranean springs, the lake
is nestled within an extinct volcanic crater whose formation was linked to that of
Mount Meru. Although much of the surrounding area is cultivated and settled, the
steep walls of the crater support a fringing gallery of riparian forest, while the lake
itself is lined with beds of papyrus. The lake is of particular interest to
birdwatchers, as it supports numerous diving and shore birds, as well as seven
kingfisher species and breeding colonies of various weavers. An added attraction is
the good views of Mount Meru and Kilimanjaro from the lakeshore on clear days.

The relatively developed northern lakeshore is open to the public, but the
southern, eastern and western shores are now protected in the 19ha **Lake Duluti
Forest Reserve** (☏ 027 250 9522; e cmisutu@yahoo.co.uk; entrance US$12 pp inc
guided walk; additional photography, camping, fishing & canoeing fees of US$12 pp per
activity). A 60–90-minute walking trail has been established in the reserve, offering
the opportunity to see some of the 50-odd tree species, wildlife such as blue
monkey, vervet monkey and monitor lizard, and an interesting selection of forest
birds including Hartlaub's turaco, crowned and silvery-cheeked hornbills, Narina

trogon, brown-breasted and white-eared barbets, Africa broadbill, little greenbul, black-throated wattle-eye, paradise flycatcher, white-starred robin and black-breasted apalis. Canoe trips on the crater lake are operated by Green Footprint Adventures (🕿 027 254 4635; m 0784 203000; e info@greenfootprint.co.tz; www.greenfootprint.co.tz) out of the nearby Serena Mountain Village Lodge.

Getting there and away Lake Duluti lies about 2km south of the Arusha–Moshi road, and the side roads to Mountain Village Lodge and the Duluti Club, both on the lakeshore, are signposted. On public transport, any vehicle heading from Arusha towards Moshi can drop you at the junction – hop off when you see a large carved wooden giraffe to your left coming from Arusha. The turn-off to Duluti Club is signposted to the right opposite this statue, and the turn-off to Mountain Village Lodge is another 200m or so towards Moshi. It's about 20 minutes' walk from the main road to the campsite. Entrance to the Lake Duluti Forest Reserve, on foot only, is via a manned entrance gate that lies along a rough road 1km east of the Duluti Club and 500m south of Serena Mountain Village Lodge.

Where to stay
Upmarket
🏠 **Serena Mountain Village Lodge** 🕿 027 255 3313/5; e reservations@serenahotels.com; www.serenahotels.com. With expansive green lawns verging on the northern shore of the gorgeous Lake Duluti, & fabulous views across to Mount Meru & Kilimanjaro, Mountain Village Lodge is easily one of the most attractive upmarket lodges in the greater Arusha area. The main building is a converted thatched farmhouse dating to the colonial era, & accommodation is in comfortable self-contained chalets. Subsequent to the lodge being taken over by the excellent Serena chain, the quality of service, meals & décor has been upgraded to match the atmospheric setting. *US$195/245 sgl/dbl B&B, dropping to US$125/185 Apr–May; additional US$30 pp for FB.*

Camping
🏕 **Duluti Club** m 0754 373977. The lovely & surprisingly little-used campsite at the Duluti Club is slightly rundown, but there's an ablution block with hot showers & the lakeshore setting is fabulous. Facilities include a cafeteria serving basic & reasonably priced meals & chilled drinks. *Camping US$6 pp.*

USA RIVER The small and rather amorphous village of Usa River flanks the Moshi road about 20km east of Arusha near the turn-off to Arusha National Park. It is of interest to tourists primarily for a cluster of upmarket hotels, several of which rank as among the most attractive in the Arusha area, as well as being conveniently located for day safaris into the national park. If you're staying in the area, there are several good boutiques and adequate eateries in and around the Usa Mall, which also has an internet café and banking facilities.

Where to stay
Upmarket
🏠 **Dik Dik Hotel** (21 rooms) 🕿 027 255 3499; e dikdik@habari.co.tz; www.dikdik.ch. Owned & managed by the same Swiss family since it opened back in 1990, this attractive small hotel with comfortable, well-equipped en-suite chalets, lies about 1km north of Kilala, a small village on the Arusha–Moshi road a few hundred metres west of Usa River. The thickly wooded 10ha grounds are bisected by an energetic stream, & contain a swimming pool, a small dam, a viewing tower offering clear views to Kilimanjaro, & a restaurant rated as one of the best in the Arusha area. Rooms 19 & 20 are particularly recommended for their view onto a riverine gallery forest inhabited by monkeys & numerous bird species. *US$150/200 sgl/dbl B&B, or US$200/300 FB.*

🏠 **Ngare Sero Lodge** (12 rooms) ☎ 057 250 3638; 📱 0713 560055; e Reservations@Ngare-Sero-Lodge.com; www.Ngare-Sero-Lodge.com. One of the nicest places to stay in the Arusha area is this small, exclusive country-style lodge set on a forested 25ha estate dating to the German colonial era, & accessible along the same dirt road as the Dik Dik Hotel. As is implicit in the name Ngare Sero (Maasai for 'dappled water'), the owner-managed estate is fed by several streams flowing from the higher slopes of Mount Meru, & a crystal clear reservoir below the lodge is stocked with barbel & trout, while also driving the turbine that generates the lodge's electricity. The forest & lake support an incredibly varied selection of birds & butterflies, while blue monkey & black-&-white colobus are both resident on the grounds. A superb range of activities & facilities includes horseback excursions, coffee farm tours, boat rides on the lake, cultural visits to a nearby village, a swimming pool, internet access, yoga & meditation classes, & massages. The rooms, though attractively decorated, are set out in a rather cramped row opposite the main building, but overall this is an excellent option for those who enjoy outdoor pursuits. *US$175/250 pp FB.*

🏠 **Mount Meru Game Sanctuary** (17 rooms) ☎ 027 255 3643; f 027 255 3730; e reservations@intimate-places.com; www.mountmerugamelodge.com. Established in 1959, about 1km east of Usa River immediately before the turn-off to Arusha National Park, this long-serving & highly recommended lodge has something of an *Out of Africa* ambience, consisting of a main stone building & a few semi-detached wooden cabins surrounded by bougainvillaea-draped gardens. A large open enclosure in front of rooms 1 & 2 is stocked with various antelope, while naturally occurring blue monkeys make mischief on the lawn, nicely setting the tone for your safari, & it is also the site of a papyrus heronry where hundreds of cattle egrets roost at dusk, alongside saddle-billed & yellow-billed storks. Rooms are stylishly decorated in classic Edwardian safari style. *US$150/205 sgl/dbl B&B or US$186/277 FB, with huge discount in low season of Apr–Jun.*

🏠 **Rivertrees Country Inn** (12 rooms) ☎ 027 255 3894; 📱 0713 339873; e rivertrees@habari.co.tz; www.rivertrees.com. Situated 300m from the main Moshi road facing the Mount Meru Game Sanctuary, this highly regarded owner-managed lodge is set in magnificently shady green gardens on an old family estate offering great views to Mount Meru & Kilimanjaro, & bounded by a forest-fringed stretch of the Usa River. Centred on a rambling old farmhouse, the inn offers comfortable accommodation in spacious en-suite rooms with large wooden 4-poster beds, as well as a more exclusive river cottage & a stunning river house with 2 dbl bedrooms (the latter used by the German head of state on a recent visit to Tanzania). Facilities include a TV room (with digital satellite TV), internet access, a swimming pool & a highly rated restaurant serving hearty country food, while activities on offer include horseback excursions, village tours & bird walks. *Standard rooms US$155/195 sgl/dbl B&B; river cottage US$280 dbl; river house US$1,280 for up to 4 people.*

🏠 **Arumeru River Lodge** (20 rooms) ☎ 027 255 3573; 📱 0784 459639; e info@arumerulodge.com; www.arumerulodge.com. The newest lodge in the Usa River area, having opened in April 2005, German-owned Arumeru consists of 10 2-room thatch chalets set on a 6ha plot bounded by 2 rivers. A stunning open-sided thatch common area overlooks the heated swimming pool, & the restaurant, complete with French chef, serves top-notch continental cuisine. The gardens currently feel a little underdeveloped, but you won't notice this if you ask for one of the rooms facing the river & associated swampland – home to 3 monkey species & a wide variety of birds – & there is also talk of introducing some antelope into the undeveloped 'bush' part of the property. The en-suite semi-detached rooms have a pleasing airy organic feel, & seem good value. *US$117/174/234 sgl/dbl/trpl B&B or US$160/260/360 FB; discounted Apr & May.*

KILIMANJARO INTERNATIONAL AIRPORT (KIA)

The only international airport serving northern Tanzania lies in almost total isolation roughly midway between Arusha and Moshi, making it a reasonably convenient point of access for both towns but absolutely ideal for neither. All Air Tanzania flights in and out of KIA are connected to both Arusha and Moshi by a free shuttle service, and KLM flights are connected to Arusha by a shuttle run by the Impala Hotel (US$10 pp). Otherwise, arriving at normal hours, you can arrange for your safari operator or hotel to meet you, or catch a taxi. Another option for your first or last night in town is to book into KIA Lodge, 1km from the airport.

Where to stay

🏠 **KIA Lodge** (20 units) 📞 027 255 3243;
📧 reservations@kialodge.com; www.kialodge.com.
Under the same management as Moivaro Lodge, &
similar in feel & quality, the recently opened KIA
Lodge is recommended to visitors with unusual or
inconvenient flight times, as it lies just 1km from
the airport & the staff are used to monitoring
flight arrivals & departures for guests. It's an
attractive set-up, with a good *makuti* restaurant &
hilltop swimming pool, plenty of birdlife in the
surrounding acacia scrub, & great views towards
Kilimanjaro (the mountain, that is), but the noise
from overhead flights makes it less than ideal for
an extended stay. *Self-contained bungalows
US$168/264 sgl/dbl B&B or US$213/489 FB,
dropping to US$143/214 or US$188/414 Mar,
Jun, Sept–Dec & US$114/171 or US$159/358
Apr & May.*

CULTURAL TOURS AROUND ARUSHA

A number of widely praised and increasingly popular cultural tourism programmes
have been implemented around Arusha in recent years with the assistance of the
Dutch agency SNV. Any one of these programmes makes for an excellent half- or
full-day trip out of Arusha, offering tourists the opportunity to experience
something of rural Africa away from the slick lodges and main safari circuit. You
can ask your safari company to tag a visit to one of the cultural programmes onto
your main safari, or can arrange a stand-alone day trip once you arrive in Arusha.
Several of the programmes also offer the opportunity to spend a night locally,
though it should be stressed that accommodation is not up to accepted tourist-class
standards. Of the various programmes, the one at Longido can easily be visited on
public transport, but the rest are only realistically visited in a private vehicle.
Details of recommended safari operators can be found on pages 91–3. The TTB
office on Boma Road and the Cultural Tourism Office in the Old Boma, both in
Arusha (see *Chapter 3*, pages 90–1), stock useful pamphlets about all the cultural
programmes, and can advise you about current costs and accessibility.

MKURU CAMEL SAFARI (📱 0784 724498/472475; 📧 info@mkurucamelsafari.com;
www.mkurucamelsafari.com) This most successful of the cultural tourism
programmes around Arusha is based at Mkuru at the northern base of Mount
Meru. It's a very well organised set-up, offering a selection of facilities and
activities that seems to increase with every passing year, though these days it's
pitched more at the mid-range market than budget travellers. The main attraction
here is organised camelback trips, which range in duration from day outings
(US$45 pp) and overnight trips into the wildlife-rich plains towards Longido
(US$220 pp) to a week-long trek to Ol Doinyo Lengai and Lake Natron (US$995
pp). In addition to camel rides, it offers a variety of day walks – a bird walk on the
plain, a hike to the top of Ol Doinyo Landare, cultural visits to local healers and
women's craft groups – for around US$20 per person. All activities are slightly
cheaper as group sizes increase.

Activities run out of the down-to-earth Mkuru Camel Camp, which is situated
near the pyramidal Ol Doinyo Landare (literally 'Mountain of Goats') and Ngare
Nanyuki (on the northern border of Arusha National Park) and it offers great
views of Kilimanjaro and Meru. This solar-powered camp has comfortable
accommodation in furnished standing tents set on wooden platforms (US$28 pp
bed only or US$45 FB), simple ground tents with beds, sleeping bags, sheets and
towels (US$17 pp bed only or US$35 FB), and you can also pitch your own tent
(US$13 pp bed only or US$31 FB).

LONGIDO (*Longido Cultural Tourism;* 📞 027 250 9209; 📱 0787 855185;
📧 touryman@yahoo.vom) The cultural tourism project run out of the overgrown

4

In 1962, local legend goes, a Maasai cattle herder called Ali Juyawatu was walking through the Mererani Hills after a bush fire, and noticed some unusual blue crystals lying on the ground. Ali picked up the beautiful stones, and took them to the nearby town of Arusha, from where they somehow made their way to the New York gemstone dealer Tiffany & Co, which had never seen anything like them before. In 1967, Tiffany launched the newly discovered gem on the market, naming it tanzanite in honour of its country of origin.

Tanzanite is by any standards a remarkable stone. A copper brown variety of zoisite, it is rather dull in its natural condition, but responds to gentle heating, transforming into a richly saturated dark-blue gem, with purple and violet undertones that have been compared among other things to the, um, eyes of Elizabeth Taylor! The stone is known only from Tanzania's Mererani Hills – rumours of a second deposit in Usangi, 75km from Arusha, have yet to be confirmed – and it is in the order of being a thousand times rarer than diamonds. Despite its upstart status in the jewellery world, tanzanite has rocketed in popularity since its discovery. By 1997, 30 years after its launch, it had become the second most popular gemstone in the North American market, second to sapphires and ahead of rubies and emeralds, generating an annual trade worth US$300 million in the USA alone.

Remarkable, too, is the degree of controversy that the tanzanite trade has attracted in recent years. In the late 1990s, the Tanzanian government, comparing international tanzanite trade figures against their documented exports, realised that as much as 90% of the tanzanite sold in the USA was being smuggled out of Tanzania, resulting in a huge loss of potential government revenue in taxes and royalties. The ease with which the stones were being smuggled was clearly linked to the unregulated nature of the workings at Mererani, which consisted of more than 300 small claims operating in what has been described by more than one observer as a Wild West atmosphere. For the small claim holders, rather than distributing the stones they collected through legitimate sources, it was more profitable – and considerably more straightforward – to sell them for cash to illicit cross-border traders.

The lack of regulations at Mererani, or at least the lack of a body to enforce what regulations do exist, is also largely to blame for a series of tragedies that has dogged the workings in recent years. The greatest single catastrophe occurred during the El Niño rains of 1998, when one of the shafts at Block D flooded and at least 100 miners drowned. But it has been estimated that a similar number of miners died subsequent underground subsequent to this mass tragedy, as a result of suffocation, or of inept dynamite blasting, or of periodic outbreaks of violent fighting over disputed claims. Aside from such accidents, it has long been rumoured that miners who are down on their luck will kidnap and sacrifice children from neighbouring villages, in the hope it will bring them good fortune and prosperity.

village of Longido is one of the most accessible in the region for independent travellers, and it is an excellent place to visit for those who want to spend time among the Maasai. The original programme co-ordinator was a local Maasai who studied abroad as a sociologist before he was paralysed in a serious accident, and his successor can tell you anything you want to know about Maasai culture. Three different walking modules are on offer to tourists. On all modules, you can expect to see a variety of birds (including several colourful finches and barbets), and there is a fair amount of large game left in the area, notably gerenuk, lesser kudu, giraffe, Thomson's gazelle and black-backed jackal. It is worth trying to be in Longido on Wednesday, when a hectic cattle market is held on the outskirts of the village.

In 1999, the Tanzanian government put out to tender a lease on Block C, the largest of the four mining blocks, accounting for about 75% of the known tanzanite deposit. The rights were acquired by a South African company – with a 25% Tanzanian stake – called African Gem Resources (AFGEM), which reputedly pumped US$20 million into establishing the mine with the intention of going online in early 2000. This goal proved to be highly optimistic, as local miners and stakeholders, understandably hostile to the corporate intrusion on their turf, not to mention the threat it posed to the illicit tanzanite trade, attempted to disrupt the new project and persuade AFGEM to withdraw.

The long simmering tensions erupted in April 2001, when a bomb was set off in the new mining plant, killing nobody, but causing large-scale material damage nonetheless. Later in the same month, AFGEM security guards opened fire on a group of 300 irate miners that had invaded the plant, killing one trespasser and causing serious injury to nine. When the Minister for Energy and Minerals visited the scene a few days later, the trespassers claimed to have been protesting against AFGEM's alleged complicity in the alleged death of 20 miners that were buried alive. AFGEM refuted the claims as pure fabrication, part of a smear campaign designed to discredit them and protect the illicit tanzanite trade. The result of the official investigation into the incident has yet to be released.

The tanzanite plot took a new and wholly unexpected twist in late December 2001, when press reports linked four of the men convicted on charges relating to the 1998 US embassy bombings in Nairobi and Dar es Salaam with the illicit tanzanite trade. Amid wild speculation that the underground tanzanite trade was funding Osama bin Laden and his al-Qaeda organisation, three major US jewellery dealers announced a total boycott on the purchase or sale of the gem. Among them, ironically, was the retailer that had first placed it in the spotlight back in 1967. Tiffany & Co publicly conceded a lack of hard evidence supporting the bin Laden link, but announced that it 'troubled' them regardless. By the end of January 2002, the price of tanzanite had fallen from around US$300 per gram to below US$100.

The Tanzanian government elected to suspend operations at Mererani until the claims were fully investigated. At a Tucson trade fair in February 2002, the American Gem Trade Association and the Tanzanian Minister of Energy and Minerals signed a protocol that placed several significant new controls on local access to the tanzanite mines. After the protocol was signed, the US State Department praised Tanzania for having 'done everything in its power to assist us in the war against terrorism' and declared it had 'seen no evidence that ... any terrorist group is currently using tanzanite sales to finance its efforts or launder money'. Sales of the gem have since boomed, and many specialist stores line the streets of Arusha, while the recent opening of a museum called the Tanzanite Experience (see page 109) seems likely to raise the gem's profile even higher.

The first module is a half-day bird walk through the Maasai Plains, which also includes a visit to a rural Maasai *boma* (homestead), and a meal cooked by the local women's group. Then there is a full-day tour which follows the same route as the bird walk, before climbing to the top of the 2,637 Longido Mountain, an ascent of roughly 400m, offering views to Mount Meru and Kilimanjaro on a clear day, as well as over the Maasai Plains to Kenya. The two-day module follows the same route as the one-day walk, but involves camping out overnight in the green Kimokouwa Valley, before visiting a dense rainforest that still harbours a number of buffaloes as well as the usual birds and monkeys.

Longido straddles the main Namanga road roughly 100km from Arusha, so any of the regular minibuses and taxis that run between Arusha and Namanga can drop

Among Germany's more improbable – and less successful – attempts to populate the Arusha area with Europeans was the sponsored settlement of 100 Boer families, mostly of German descent, in the aftermath of South Africa's divisive Anglo–Boer War. In 1904, the Germans arranged for the Boers to be taken by boat to Tanga, from where they travelled to Arusha by ox-wagon. When the oxen all succumbed to tsetse-borne disease, the Germans provided the Boers with teams of local Africans as a substitute. The families were granted large ranches, mainly around Ol Doinyo Sambu on the northern slopes of Mount Meru, but most of them fell out with their benefactors and eventually packed up their ox-wagons to head across the border into Kenya, where several settled in the Eldoret area. A neatly whitewashed stone monument to this latter-day Great Trek still stands in a field near Ol Doinyo Sambu, visible from the road between Arusha and Longido.

you there – these usually leave Arusha from the north end of the bus station opposite the stadium. The tourist project maintains a neat and inexpensive guesthouse about 100m from the main road, or you can arrange to pitch a tent at a Maasai *boma* for a small fee. A limited selection of cheap Tanzanian fare is available from one or two small restaurants that lie along the main road, and a couple of local bars (with pool table) serve cold beers and soft drinks.

NG'IRESI VILLAGE Set on the slopes of Mount Meru some 7km from Arusha town, this cultural tourism programme based in the traditional Wa-Arusha village of Ng'iresi offers many insights into the local culture and agricultural practices. There are also some lovely walks in the surrounding Mount Meru foothills, an area characterised by fast-flowing streams, waterfalls and remnant forest patches. From Ng'iresi, it is possible to walk to Lekimana Hill, from where there are good views over the Maasai Steppes and on a clear day to Kilimanjaro. Another walk takes you to Kivesi Hill, an extinct volcano whose forested slopes support a variety of birds and small mammals.

Three different 'modules' are available at Ng'iresi, all inclusive of meals prepared by the Juhudu Women's Group and guided activities, while the overnight module includes a night's camping in the garden of Mzee Loti. There is no public transport to Ng'iresi, so you must either set up a visit through a safari company or make arrangements with a private vehicle.

MULALA VILLAGE This is another cultural tourism programme situated in a village on the footslopes of Mount Meru. Mulala lies at an altitude of 1,450m, some 30km from Arusha, in a fertile agricultural area, which produces coffee, bananas and other fruit and vegetables. Several short walks can be undertaken in the surrounding hills, including one to the forested Marisha River, home to a variety of birds and primates, and to Mazungu Lake, where it is said that a *mazungu* was once lured to his death by a demon. Another local place of interest is Mama Anna's dairy, which supplies cheese to several upmarket hotels in Arusha. The tourist programme here is run in conjunction with the Agape Women's Group, which provides most of the guides as well as snacks and camping facilities.

MONDULI JUU The settlement of Monduli Juu ('Upper Monduli') is situated some 50km west of Arusha in the Monduli Hills, a forested range that rises from the Rift

Valley floor to an altitude of 2,660m, offering some superb views to other larger mountains such as Kilimanjaro, Meru and Ol Doinyo Lengai. Monduli Juu consists of a cluster of four Maasai villages, namely Emairete, Enguiki, Eluwai and Mfereji, the first of which is set alongside a spectacular crater that betrays the mountains' volcanic origins and is still held sacred by locals.

The cultural programme at Monduli Juu offers several programmes, ranging from a few hours to several days in duration. For nature lovers, a recommended option is the hike to Monduli Peak, passing through patches of montane forest that support a large variety of monkeys, antelope, birds and butterflies as well as relict populations of elephant and buffalo – an armed ranger is mandatory. Other attractions include visits to a traditional healer, Naramatu bead factory and general cultural programmes including a Maasai *boma* visit and a meat market.

A few local families in Monduli Juu offer camping sites, only one of which, Esserian Maasai Camp, has running water. Meals – traditional or Western, as you like – can be prepared with a bit of notice. A useful contact for setting up trips to this area is Tanzania Adventure (see Arusha tour operator listing in *Chapter 3*, pages 91–3).

ARUSHA NATIONAL PARK

Only 45 minutes from Arusha town, this is the most accessible of northern Tanzania's national parks, but – after the remote Rubondo Island and recently created Mkomazi – it is also the one that has been most neglected by the safari industry, largely because it offers limited possibilities to see the so-called Big Five. And yet, this one perceived failing aside, Arusha National Park is a quite extraordinary conservation area, and thoroughly worth a visit. Recently extended from 137km^2 to 542km^2, the park boasts a habitat diversity that spans everything from montane rainforest to moist savanna to alpine moorland, and its prodigious fauna includes some 400 bird and several unusual mammal species.

The most prominent landmark is Mount Meru, Africa's fifth-highest massif and a popular goal for dedicated hikers. The park also has much to offer non-hikers, including a cluster of attractive lakes, a spectacular extinct volcanic crater, and stirring views of Kilimanjaro looming large on the eastern skyline, all of which can be seen in the course of a day trip out of Arusha Town or Usa River. A recently introduced and highly attractive alternative to game drives is the canoe trips run by Green Footprint Adventures (✆ 027 254 4635; m 0784 203000; e info@greenfootprint.co.tz; www.greenfootprint.co.tz).

A detailed booklet, *Arusha National Park*, containing detailed information on every aspect of the park's ecology and wildlife, is widely available in Arusha town, as is Giovanni Tombazzi's excellent map, which has useful details of the ascent of Mount Meru on the flip. The park entrance fee of US$35 per person per 24 hours should be paid by MasterCard or Tanapa Card (issued at any Exim Bank). No other cards are accepted, nor are travellers' cheques, and cash payments attract a 50% penalty.

GETTING THERE AND AWAY From Arusha, follow the surfaced Moshi road for about 20km to Usa River, then take the turn-off to the left signposted for Arusha National Park. After about 8km, this dirt road enters the park boundary, where park entrance fees are paid at the new main gate. The road reaches Hatari! and Momella Lodges after another 15km or so, immediately outside the northern national park boundary. This road is in fair condition and can normally be driven in an ordinary saloon car, though a 4x4 may be necessary after rain.

Any safari company can arrange an overnight trip to the park or a day trip out of Arusha. Most companies can also organise a three-day climb up Meru. If you want

Ngare Nanyuki Village

Momella Lakes

Kinandia Swamp

Lokie Swamp

Momella Lodge

Hatari!

Momella gate

Park HQ

Resthouse

Tululusia Hill

Ngare Nanyuki River

Mirakamba

Little Meru 3820m

Saddle Hut

Ash Cone

Meru Crater

Mount Meru 4565m

Ngongongare Hill

Ngongongare Spring

Ngurdoto Crater

New Ngurdoto gate

Colobus Mountain Lodge

MBT Snake & Reptile Farm

Meru Mbega Lodge

Meru View Lodge

Main Arusha–Moshi Rd (7km)

N

Bradt

5km

3 miles

0

0

© Philip Briggs

to organise your own climb or spend some time exploring the park on foot, you will have to find your own way there. You could hire a taxi in Arusha, but it is cheaper to catch a bus or *dala-dala* along the Moshi road as far as the turn-off, from where 4x4 vehicles serve as *dala-dalas* to the village of Ngare Nanyuki about 3km past the northern boundary of the park, passing through the main entrance gate (where fees must be paid) *en route*.

WHERE TO STAY

Exclusive

⌂ **Hatari! Lodge** (8 rooms) ⟍/f 027 255 3456; e marlies@theafricanembassy.com; www.hatarilodge.com. This characterful owner-managed lodge, situated in a patch of moist yellow fever woodland just outside the Momella Gate, is named after the 1961 film *Hatari!* (danger), & stands on a property formerly owned by Hardy Kruger, one of the film's co-stars. Accommodation is in large en-suite dbl chalets with king-size beds & tall *makuti* ceilings, while the individualistic décor is an imaginative, colourful blend of a classic African

bush feel & a more 'retro' look dating back to the era of the film for which the lodge is named. The common areas – littered with *Hatari!* memorabilia – overlook a swampy area inhabited by buffalo, waterbuck, crowned crane & various other waterbirds. The food is excellent, the service is highly personalised, & there are also stirring views across to nearby Kilimanjaro & Meru. Activities on offer include game drives & walks, canoeing on the Momella Lakes & birdwatching excursions. *Rates on application.*

Upmarket

⌂ **Ngurdoto Mountain Lodge** (188 rooms) ⟍ 027 255 5217/26; f 027 255 5227/8; e Ngurdoto@thengurdotomountainlodge.com; www.thengurdotomountainlodge.com. Situated on a lush 70ha coffee plantation alongside the road between Usa River & Arusha National Park, this impressive new tourist village, affiliated to the Impala Hotel in Arusha, has some of the best facilities of any lodge or hotel in the Arusha area, including a 9-hole golf course, a gym, a 600-seat conference centre, a large swimming pool, 24hr internet access, 2 restaurants & 2 bars. Given the hotel's vast size, the rooms – all en-suite with king-size bed, fireplace & balcony – possess a surprising amount of character, making use of wrought iron & wood to create a feel that is at once contemporary

& ethnic. *Standard rooms US$135/175 sgl/dbl B&B; cottages US$160/200; executive rooms US$200/240, additional meals US$15 pp.*

⌂ **Momella Lodge** (55 rooms) ⟍ 057 250 6423. Set in the shadow of Mount Meru about 3km past Momella Gate, this cosy, low-key & little-used lodge is a world away from its slick, crowded counterparts elsewhere in the northern circuit. It is possessed of a rather alpine atmosphere, reinforced by the log fires in the bar & lounge, while black-&-white movie posters – *Hatari!* of course – decorate the dining area & bar. Though undeniably a bit rundown, the en-suite chalets seem decent value. Facilities include a large swimming pool & satellite TV. *US$80 pp FB.*

Moderate

⌂ **Meru Mbega Lodge** (12 rooms) m 0713 897911; e info@mt-meru.com; www.mt-meru.com. Opened in mid-2008, this latest addition to the chain of affordable lodges run by Mbega has comfortable en-suite accommodation with netted beds in double-storey buildings that offer views over a small pond towards Mount Meru. An attractive *makuti* structure serves as the bar & restaurant. It's a good place to arrange Meru climbs. *US$80/90 sgl/dbl.*

⌂ **Colobus Mountain Lodge** (18 rooms) ⟍ 027 255 3632; e info@colobusmountainlodge.com; www.colobusmountainlodge.com. Clearly signposted 200m from the public road between Usa River &

Ngare Nanyuki, this rustic lodge lies in the shadow of Mount Meru immediately outside the southern boundary of the park. The centrepiece of the site is an open-sided bar & restaurant with a tall *makuti* roof, serving sensibly priced Western & local dishes. *Spacious semi-detached chalet rooms US$75/80 sgl/dbl B&B.*

⌂ **Meru View Lodge** (15 rooms) m 0784 419232/805259; e africanview@habari.co.tz; www.meru-view-lodge.de. This small & very friendly German-owned lodge lies on the eastern side of the road from Usa River, about 1km south of where the road enters the national park. The en-suite rooms,

4

dotted around flowering gardens & a large swimming pool, though very comfortable, aren't quite the

bargain they once were. *US$90/110 sgl/dbl B&B; other meals additional US$10–15 pp.*

Budget and camping

⌂ **National Park Resthouse** Situated 2km from Momella Gate, this self-catering resthouse sleeps up to 5 people. You can book it in advance through the National Parks office outside Arusha. *US$20 pp per night.*

Å **National Park campsites** Three sites lie at the foot of Tululusia Hill, 2km from Momella Gate, & 1

is situated in the forest near Ngurdoto Gate. All are scenically located close to a stream, have drop toilets & firewood. Note, however, that you may not walk between the campsites & the entrance gates without an armed ranger. *US$20 pp.*

Å **Colobus Mountain Lodge** See contacts above. Camping on the large, green lawn. *US$5 pp.*

EXPLORING ARUSHA NATIONAL PARK

Ngurdoto Crater Coming from Arusha, a good first goal is this fully intact 3km-wide, 400m-deep volcanic caldera, which has often been described as a mini-Ngorongoro. Tourists are not permitted to descend into the crater, but the views from the forest-fringed rim over the lush crater floor are fantastic. A large herd of buffalo is resident on the crater floor, and with binoculars it is normally possible to pick up other mammals, such as warthog, baboon and various antelope. Look out, too, for augur buzzard, Verreaux's eagle and other cliff-associated raptors soaring above the crater. The forests around the crater rim harbour many troops of black-and-white colobus and blue monkey, as well as a good variety of birds including several types of hornbill and the gorgeous Hartlaub's turaco and cinnamon-chested bee-eater.

Momella Lakes Another area worth exploring is the Momella Lakes, which lie to the north of Ngurdoto. Underground streams feed this group of shallow alkaline lakes, and each has a different mineral content and is slightly different in colour. In the late evening and early morning, it is often possible to stand at one of the viewpoints over the lakes and see Kilimanjaro on the eastern horizon and Mount Meru to the west. It is on these lakes that Green Footprint Adventures (see page 92) undertakes canoe safaris, a very tranquil way to enjoy the birdlife and scenery.

Momella is one of the best places in Tanzania for waterbirds: flamingo, pelican, little grebe and a variety of herons, ducks and waders are common. Among the more common mammals around the lakes are hippo, buffalo and waterbuck – the waterbuck population evidently intermediate to the Defassa and common waterbuck races. You should also come across a few pairs of Kirk's dik-dik, an attractively marked small antelope that seems to be less skittish here than it is elsewhere in the country. Other large mammals likely to be seen in Arusha National Park include giraffe, zebra and vervet monkey. Elephants are present but seldom seen, since they tend to stick to the forest zone of Mount Meru, while the only large predators are leopard and spotted hyena.

MBT Snake and Reptile Farm Signposted a short distance from the entrance to Arusha National Park, this long-serving private park has a good collection of reptiles and offers an intelligent guided tour. Creatures in residence include Nile crocodile, various chameleon species and other lizards, and a fearsome collection of snakes, including spitting cobras, mambas, puff adders, Gabon viper, water snakes and some hefty pythons. It lies outside the national park so no park fees are payable but an entrance ticket inclusive of guided tour costs Tsh3,000.

Mount Meru Arusha National Park's tallest landmark and most publicised attraction is Mount Meru, whose upper slopes and 4,566m peak lie within its boundaries. The product of the same volcanic activity that formed the Great Rift Valley 15 to 20 million years ago, Mount Meru attained a height similar to that of Kilimanjaro until 250,000 years ago, when a massive eruption tore out its eastern wall. Meru is regarded as a dormant volcano, since lava flowed from it as recently as 100 years ago, but there is no reason to suppose it will do anything dramatic in the foreseeable future. The Arusha and Meru people deify Mount Meru as a rain god, but it is unlikely that any local person actually reached the peak prior to Fritz Jaeger's pioneering ascent in 1904.

Often overlooked by tourists because it is 'only' the fifth-highest mountain in Africa, Meru is no substitute for Kilimanjaro for achievement-orientated travellers. On the other hand, those who climb both mountains invariably enjoy Meru more. Also going in its favour, Meru is less crowded than Kilimanjaro, considerably less expensive, and – although steeper and almost as cold – less likely to engender the health problems associated with Kilimanjaro's greater altitude. Meru is just as interesting as Kilimanjaro from a biological point of view and, because comparatively few people climb it, you are more likely to see forest animals and plains game on the lower slopes.

Meru can technically be climbed in two days, but three days is normal, allowing time to explore Meru Crater and to look at wildlife and plants. Most people arrange a climb through a safari company in Arusha. The going rate for a three-day hike is around US$300 per person. You can make direct arrangements with park officials at the gate, but won't save much money by doing this, and should check hut availability at the Tanapa office in Arusha in advance. The compulsory armed ranger/guide costs US$20 per day (US$10 park fee and US$10 salary), hut fees are US$20 per night, and there is the usual park entrance fee of US$30 per day. A rescue fee of US$20 per person covers the entire climb. The minimum cost for a three-day climb is therefore US$165 per person, with an additional US$60 to be divided between the climbers. Food and transport must be added to this, and porters cost an additional US$5 per day each.

Meru is very cold at night, and you will need to bring clothing adequate for alpine conditions. In the rainy season, mountain boots are necessary. At other times, good walking shoes will probably be adequate. The best time to climb is from October to February.

Day 1 The trail starts at Momella Gate (1,500m). From there it is a relatively gentle three-hour ascent to Miriakamba Hut (2,600m). On the way you pass through well-developed woodland where there is a good chance of seeing large animals such as giraffe. At an altitude of about 2,000m you enter the forest zone. If you leave Momella early, there will be ample time to explore Meru Crater in the afternoon. The 1,500m cliff rising to Meru Peak overlooks the crater. The 3,667m-high ash cone in the crater is an hour from Miriakamba Hut, and can be climbed.

Day 2 It is three hours to Saddle Hut (3,600m), a bit steeper than the previous day's walk. You initially pass through forest, where there is a good chance of seeing black-and-white colobus, then at about 3,000m you will enter a moorland zone similar to that on Kilimanjaro. It is not unusual to see Kilimanjaro peeking above the clouds from Saddle Hut. If you feel energetic, you can climb Little Meru (3,820m) in the afternoon. It takes about an hour each way from Saddle Hut.

Day 3 You will need to rise very early to ascend the 4,566m peak, probably at around 02.00. This ascent takes four to five hours. It is then an eight- to nine-hour walk back down the mountain to Momella Gate.

Some people prefer to climb from Miriakamba Hut to Saddle Hut and do the round trip from Saddle Hut to Meru Peak on the second day (11 hours altogether), leaving only a five-hour walk to Momella on the third. Others climb all the way up to Saddle Hut on the first day (six hours), do the round trip to the peak on the second (eight hours), and return to Momella from the Saddle Hut on the third (five hours).

WEST KILIMANJARO CONSERVATION AREA

Wedged between the northwestern base of Kilimanjaro and Kenya's Amboseli National Park some two to three hours' drive northeast of Arusha, West Kilimanjaro consists of six contiguous blocks of Maasai communal land that are currently in the process of amalgamating as a formal Wildlife Management Area. Although the main attractions here are the superb close-up views of Kilimanjaro and a well-protected elephant population noted for the even temperament and immense tusks of its bulls, this southern extension of Amboseli also retains a genuine wilderness feel, since only one of the six land blocks is currently open to tourists, run as an exclusive concession by Kirurumu Under Canvas.

Much of West Kilimanjaro is composed of very flat land whose fine volcanic soil once formed the bed of Lake Amboseli – then twice as big as present-day Lake Manyara – before it started to dry up some 10,000–15,000 years ago. As the lake dried it left calcareous deposits that were later mined by the Germans in order to make the famous meerschaum tobacco pipes. The abandoned pits left behind by the open-cast mines are now an important part of the ecosystem, since they trap rainwater to provide drinking for the Maasai cattle as well as the wildlife at the driest times of the year.

West Kilimanjaro supports a near-pristine cover of lightly wooded acacia savanna where Maasai herdsmen co-exist with a remarkable variety of wildlife, including wildebeest, zebra, eland, impala, Grant's gazelle, hartebeest and yellow baboon, as well as one of the few Tanzanian populations of the remarkable stretch-necked gerenuk. The area also forms part of a migration corridor used by elephants to cross between Amboseli and the forested slopes of Kilimanjaro. Many impressive bulls are resident throughout the year, but numbers peak in June/July, after the rains, when the smaller family groups merge to form 100-strong herds. This also is when mating takes place, and irascible bulls follow the family herds accompanied by a fanfare of trumpeting.

⌂ WHERE TO STAY

⌂ **Hemingway's Camp** (5 rooms) ☏ 027 250 7011; e info@kirurumu.com; www.kirurumu.com. This upmarket mobile-style camp consists of 5 dbl tents with solar lighting & en-suite showers set out in a stand of mature Acacia tortilis trees at the base of an extinct volcanic cone offering views to Kilimanjaro & Meru, as well as the more distant mountains at Longido & Namanga. In addition to standard game drives, which can offer superb opportunities to track & photograph giant tuskers in the shadow of Kilimanjaro, the camp can arrange night drives & bush walks led by local Maasai guides. It is normally booked out to 1 party at a time, though more than 1 party can share it by arrangement, & a minimum booking of 2 nights is mandatory. US$540/640 sgl/dbl FB or US$810/1020 inc activities, dropping by around 20% in the shoulder season. An additional conservancy fee of US$70 pp per night is levied.

SOUTHERN CROSS SAFARIS
Connoisseur Safaris

www.southerncrosssafaris.com
www.southerncrossscuba.com
www.sataocamp.com
www.sataoelerai.com

EXCELLENCE THROUGH EXPERIENCE

Established in 1957, Southern Cross Safaris is one of Kenya's most experienced and respected tour operators. Our philosophy is simple: we want to create the perfect safari package - having recently won 5 awards for excellence, including the 'Best Tour Operator in Kenya 2005, 2006 and 2007' Travel News & lifestyle Award,we believe we can fulfil our promise and deliver an unforgettable African Experience.

Southern Cross Safaris' extensive operation in East Africa ensure the best safari on offer whether it be in Kenya,Tanzania, Uganda or Rwanda; We also own 3 of our own exclusive camps including Satao Camp in Tsavo East, Satao Elerai at the foot of Mt.Kilimanjaro, bordering Amboseli National Park and Satao Rock Camp in Taita. Our expertise also spreads to the marine world, with Southern Cross Scuba operating 3 watersports bases located at Pinewood Village, Indian Ocean Beach Club and Diani Reef Beach Resort & SPA.

We operate using the most modern four wheel drive vehicles; experienced drivers; qualified, multilingual specialised guides; our own private aircraft; and offer accommodation in a choice of lodges, camps and hotels. Our service is highly personalised and safaris are tailored to suit individual requirements. Our knowledge and experience of Africa is unsurpassed - we will ensure that your dream safari becomes a reality

Southern Cross Centre
P.O. Box 90653, Mombasa, Kenya
Email: sales@southerncrosssafaris.com
Tel: +254 (0) 20 2434600/1/2/3

5

Moshi

Situated at the heart of a major coffee-growing region about 80km east of Arusha, the smaller but not insubstantial town of Moshi – population 250,000 – is a likeable if intrinsically unremarkable commercial centre salvaged from anonymity by its spectacular location. At dusk or dawn, when the great white-helmeted dome of Kilimanjaro is most likely to emerge from its customary blanket of cloud, Moshi can boast a backdrop as imposing and dramatic as any in Africa. And yet, the teasing proximity of that iconic snow-capped silhouette notwithstanding, Moshi is not the cool, breezy highland settlement you might expect it to be. Indeed, situated at an altitude of 810m, it is generally far hotter than Arusha, and not so drizzly, with a hint of stickiness in the air that recalls the coast.

Prior to the arrival of the Germans, Moshi was the capital of the area ruled by Rindi, who came to power in about 1860 and, largely through his diplomatic skills, became one of the most important chiefs in the area. By allying with the Maasai, Rindi extracted large taxes from passing caravans. He made a favourable impression on John Kirk, the British consul in Zanzibar, and signed a treaty with Carl Peters in 1885. When the first German colonial forces arrived at Kilimanjaro in 1891, Rindi assured them he ruled the whole area. At his insistence, they quelled his major rival, Sina of Kibosha.

Moshi is the Swahili word for smoke, but exactly when and why the town acquired that name is something of a mystery. Some sources suggest that it is because Moshi served as the terminus for the steam railway line from Tanga after 1911, but this seems unlikely given that the name pre-dates the arrival of the railway by many years. Equally improbable is the suggestion that the reference to smoke is due to the town lying at the base of a volcano, since Kilimanjaro hadn't displayed any significant activity for thousands of years when its present-day Bantu-speaking inhabitants arrived there.

Stirring views of Kilimanjaro aside, there is little to do or see in Moshi that you couldn't do or see in pretty much any similarly sized African market town. But it's a pleasant enough place to explore on foot, with an interesting central market area, and it comes across as far less tourist-oriented than Arusha, despite the inevitable attention paid to any visiting *mazungu* by a coterie of (mostly very affable) flycatchers offering relatively cheap 'n' dodgy Kilimanjaro climbs.

In terms of facilities, Moshi boasts an immense selection of decent budget to mid-range hotels, as well as several commendable and affordable restaurants. An ever increasing selection of smarter hotels is concentrated in the attractively leafy and somewhat misleadingly named suburb of Shantytown, a short walk north of the town centre and the Arusha Highway. There are also plenty of more upmarket options in the villages of Marangu and Machame on the Kilimanjaro footslopes, and the area can also be explored from the lodges that run along the main road between Arusha and Usa River.

A · Kilemakyaro
   Mountain Lodge

B

C

D

1

Executive ♀   ♀ Jacaranda

Gapco

✚
Kilimanjaro
Christian Medical
Centre
New Nambijo ♀   ♀ Kilimani
                    Garden

2   Sokoine
               Primary School
                              ⌂ Aman's Paradise
        Miami ♀
                              🚐
   El Rancho
     ✕
         Hericote ♀

SHANTY TOWN

        ⌂ Impala

3 Sal Salinero ⌂   Panda
      Villa 🏧 Chinese
   Kilimanjaro   ✕
   Tourist Inn
           ⌂ Ameg
             Lodge

   Glacier Inn ♀   ● Secondary school

              Lutheran Uhuru ⌂
                              Police ●

                       Secondary
                       school ●
         KILIMANJARO Police ●   Green Cottage ⌂
                                 Mr Price
                                 (supermarket
                                 & ATM) ●

4 ← Protea Hotel
   Machame,
   Arusha

            SEKOU TOURE

              UHURU HIGHWAY

                    BOMA

5   Bus station 🚐

                                    Railway station

                           Market

        N
       Bradt

   0 _____ 1000m
   0 _____ 880yds

6   ● Shah   ☆ Club La Liga
                               Enterprises

              ⌂ Safari Resort
              Jaribu Guesthouse ●
                       Rombo Cottage ⌂
                       Suncourt Inn ⌂
                       ● Keys
                       Keys Annex, →
                       Honey Badger Lodge,
                       Dar es Salaam
                       YMCA
                       ⛽ Total

            ARUSHA

            MARKET

            MAWENZI

       see page 133

MOSHI
Orientation

© Philip Briggs

A   B   C   D

Note that passenger trains between Moshi, Tanga and Dar es Salaam were suspended indefinitely several years ago, and are unlikely to resume.

BY AIR Kilimanjaro International Airport (KIA) lies about 40km from Moshi town centre off the Arusha road. The national carrier Air Tanzania flies directly to KIA from some international destinations, and KLM operates a daily direct flight there from Europe. For domestic flights, Air Tanzania, Regional Airlines, Precision Air and several private airlines fly daily between KIA and Dar es Salaam or Zanzibar, while regular Air Tanzania flights also connect KIA to Mwanza and other major urban centres. A potential source of confusion to travellers booking their own flights is that flights to the parks on the northern safari circuit don't leave from KIA, but from Arusha Airport on the outskirts of Arusha town.

If you fly to KIA with Air Tanzania, note that all their flights tie in with a free shuttle service to Moshi, easily located at the airport. When you leave Moshi for the airport, the correct shuttle departure time can be checked in advance at the Air Tanzania office near the Clocktower [133 C3]. For flights operated by other airlines, you'll need to charter a taxi (a none too negotiable US$30 from the airport) or to arrange to be met by a safari company.

BY ROAD The town centre runs southward from the main surfaced road to Dar es Salaam some 80km east of Arusha. The driving time from Arusha in a **private vehicle** is about 60–90 minutes, and from Dar es Salaam at least seven hours. It is possible to drive from Nairobi (Kenya) to Moshi via Namanga and Arusha in about five hours.

Express coaches between Dar es Salaam and Moshi take roughly seven hours, with a 20-minute lunch break in Korogwe or Mombo. Recommended **bus** services include Akamba [133 C6] (*next to the Buffalo Hotel;* ☏ *027 275 3908;* ☎ *0744 057779*), Dar Express [133 C2] (*Old Moshi Rd opposite NBC;* ☎ *0744 286847*), Royal Coach [133 C4] (*Aga Khan Rd;* ☏ *027 275 0940*) and Scandinavia Express [133 C5] (*opposite the Hindu Temple on Nyerere Rd;* ☏ *027 275 1387;* ☎ *0744 295245*). Numerous cheaper and inferior bus services leave from the main bus station [128

A DESCENT INTO HELL...

Moshi Central Bus Station has a justified reputation as one of the most hellish in Africa, and it is certainly the most chaotic and daunting in Tanzania, thanks to gaggles of persistent hustlers who will say anything to get a punter onto any bus, provided they can secure a commission. In my experience, when you've half a dozen hustlers yelling at you, punching each other and trying to grab your bags, the instinct for self-preservation tends to prevail, and you're likely to get onto any bus heading in the right direction before things turn ugly. One traveller who spent several weeks in Moshi wrote of how she was pushed into 'a couple of nightmarish journeys, sitting on a stationary bus for two hours after it was scheduled to leave, then stopping for half an hour at practically every settlement it passed'. This isn't such a problem for short trips, for instance to Arusha or Marangu, but for long trips you should use your judgement in boarding the first 'express bus' that is pointed out to you, and be aware that overcharging *wazungu* (white people) is commonplace. Bearing all this in mind, it's a good idea to visit the bus station the day before you're due to travel and book a seat in advance – that way, you don't have to deflect the hustlers while also protecting your luggage. Better still, use one of the (generally superior) companies whose booking offices lie outside the main bus station.

Moshi GETTING THERE AND AWAY

5

C4 & 133 C4], mostly in the morning. There are also plenty of direct buses between Moshi and Tanga, which can drop you off at Same, Mombo, Muheza and other junction towns *en route*.

A steady flow of buses and *dala-dalas* connects Arusha to Moshi, taking up to two hours, and to a lesser extent between Moshi and Marangu. There is no need to book ahead for these routes, as vehicles will leave when they fill up, but be warned that there is a high incidence of accidents, particularly with minibuses.

Most shuttle bus services between Nairobi and Arusha continue on to Moshi, or start there. The Impala Shuttle (027 275 1786; m 0754 293119; e impala@kilinet.co.tz), based in an office on Kibo Road next to Chrisburgers [133 C2], runs two services daily, as does the Riverside Shuttle (027 275 0093) in the THB building on Boma Road [133 C3], and the Bobby Shuttle [133 C5] (027 250 3490; e shuttle@bobbytours.com; www.bobbytours.com), which is represented by Duma Expeditions next to the Coffee Shop on Hill Street. These coaches generally leave Moshi at 06.30 and 12.00 and Nairobi at 08.00 and 14.00 daily, and take about six hours in either direction, but timings may change to fit in with departure and arrival times for Arusha.

TOURIST INFORMATION

There's no tourist information office as such in Moshi, but if you are spending some time there it's worth getting hold of the *Moshi Guide*, compiled and sold by the people who run the Coffee Shop on Hill Street [133 B5]. Most of the tour operators in town can provide – not necessarily impartial – local travel information. Also worth a look is the website www.kiliweb.com.

WHERE TO STAY

UPMARKET

Protea Hotel Machame [128 A4] (30 rooms) 027 275 6941/8; f 027 275 6821; e proteaaishareservations@satconet.com; www.proteahotels.com. Situated along the surfaced Machame rd about 12km from Moshi & 27km from KIA, this smart rural hotel, managed by the South Africa Protea Hotels group, is easily the most upmarket option in the vicinity of Moshi. The recently refurbished motel-style en-suite rooms aren't exactly bursting with character, but the property itself is lovely, with a large thatched dining room & bar area facing a patch of indigenous forest on the footslopes of the great mountain. The hotel specialises in Kilimanjaro climbs, & has good equipment, but it also offers a variety of excursions to more sedentary guests, ranging from local cultural tours & horseback trips to day visits to Lake Chala, Arusha National Park & a short walk to the 30m-high Makoa Waterfall & bat-infested Matangalima Cave. The swimming pool is solar heated. *US$115/145 sgl/dbl B&B.*

Ameg Lodge [128 A3] (20 rooms) 027 275 0175/0185; m 0744 058268; f 027 275 0196; e info@ameglodge.com; www.ameglodge.com. This modern new lodge, set in a 2ha plot in the leafy northern suburbs of Shantytown, is probably now the smartest hotel within the city limits, & certainly the best-value option in the mid to upper price range. The large, airy en-suite rooms are unusually stylish, combining an ethnic feel with a contemporary touch, & they all come with digital satellite TV, fan & private balcony. Other facilities include a swimming pool with views of Kilimanjaro, a gym, a business centre with 24hr internet access, & a good restaurant serving Indian & continental cuisine. The only negative is that the gardens are still rather bare & undeveloped, but this is bound to change with time. *US$79 B&B for standard dbl; US$94 for larger dbl with walk-in dressing area; US$110 for suite with AC & unlimited internet use.*

Kilemakyaro Mountain Lodge [128 B1] (20 rooms) 027 275 4925; m 0744 264845; e info@kilimanjarosafari.com; www.kilimanjarosafari.com. Wonderfully sited, on a hilltop 9km north of the town centre, this smart new hotel was formerly part of the Kifumbu Tea Estate, & the gracious reception & dining areas are housed in the restored 1880s homestead of the estate owner. The attractive landscaped gardens, complete with swimmimg pool, offer wonderful views to the forested slopes & peak of Kilimanjaro. The accommodation, in newly built self-contained chalets with digital satellite TV, is nothing special & is a touch overpriced, but still a good choice for atmosphere & location. *US$85/145 sgl/dbl B&B or US$110/190 FB.*

🏠 **Impala Hotel** [128 A3] (18 rooms) ✆ 027 275 3443/4; f 027 275 3440; e impala@kilinet.co.tz; www.impalahotel.com. Related to the eponymous hotel in Arusha, but smaller & plusher, the recently opened Impala Hotel lies on Lema Rd in the leafy suburbia of Shantytown about 2km from the town centre. The large wood-panelled rooms with fan, hot bath & satellite TV are fair value. Although the Impala Hotel lacks the fine location of the Kilemakyaro, the rooms are better & there are more facilities, notably a swimming pool, internet café & forex bureau, & a good restaurant specialising in Indian dishes. *US$80/100 sgl/dbl B&B; vast suites US$140 dbl.*

MODERATE

🏠 **Bristol Cottages** [133 B3] (17 rooms) ✆ 027 275 5083; f 027 275 3745; e info@bristolcottages.com; www.bristolcottages.com. Located behind the Standard Chartered Bank close to the bus station, this neat lodge set in small, secure & peaceful manicured gardens is probably the pick in this range, as well as being very central. Accommodation is in spacious suites & cottages with AC & hot shower, satellite TV, nets, 2 beds & attractive modern décor. Facilities include secure parking, internet, email, fax & secretarial services. The clean open-sided restaurant serves a variety of Asian & continental dishes in the Tsh6,000–8,000 range. *Rooms in the new wing US$45/60 sgl/dbl B&B; suites & cottages US$66–140.*

🏠 **Kilimanjaro Crane Hotel** [133 C2] (40 rooms) ✆ 027 275 1114; f 027 275 4876; e kilicrane@kilionline.com; www.kilimanjarocranehotels.com. The smartest place in the town centre is this modern high-rise hotel, with its en-suite rooms with large beds, digital satellite TV, private balcony, netting, fan & hot bath. Situated on Kaunda St, a block east of the Clocktower, the hotel has a compact but green garden, a welcome swimming pool, & the rooftop bar is a great spot for sundowners facing Kilimanjaro. A good restaurant serves pizzas, as well as Chinese & Indian cuisine. The ground-floor souvenir shop stocks probably the most comprehensive selection of books in Moshi. Excellent value. *US$40/45 sgl/dbl B&B with fan; US$50 dbl with AC; US$90 suite.*

🏠 **Moshi Leopard Hotel** [133 B7] (47 rooms) ✆ 027 275 0884/5134; f 027 275 1261;

🏠 **Sal Salinero Hotel** [128 A3] (7 rooms, more scheduled for 2009) ✆ 027 275 2240; m 0784 683605; f 027 275 2240; e salinerohotel@yahoo.com; www.salinerohotel.com. This reasonably priced but rather pretentious new hotel in Shantytown has large smart rooms with tiled floors, king-size beds, wooden ceilings, huge changing rooms, & excellent facilities, including satellite TV, tea/coffee-making facilities & a large en-suite bathroom with separate tub & shower. Unfortunately, the otherwise high quality of the accommodation is let down by the rather bombastic décor. The gloomy public areas are similarly schizoid, with classy finishes set alongside some decidedly tacky touches. Far nicer are the restaurant & bar, with outdoor seating in a green garden. *Standard rooms US$75/95 sgl/dbl B&B; suites US$130.*

e leopardhotel@eoltz.com; www.leopardhotel.com. Among the most commodious options in the town centre, the recently extended multi-storey Leopard Hotel is clean, comfortable & thoroughly adequate without approaching the Kilimanjaro Crane Hotel in terms of quality or amenities. The smart tiled en-suite rooms have AC, fan, TV, dbl or twin bed with netting, & a hot shower. *US$40/50 sgl/dbl B&B.*

🏠 **Keys Hotel** [128 D4] (30 rooms) ✆ 027 275 2250/1875; f 027 275 0073; e info@keys-hotel-tours.com; www.keys-hotel-tours.com. Situated in attractive suburban grounds about 1km from the Clocktower, the Keys Hotel has offered good value for several years, & it remains, with justification, one of the most popular hotels within its price range. Visitors have the choice of a room in the double-storey main building or a *makuti*-roofed cottage in the gardens behind it. All rooms are en suite & have hot water, satellite TV & nets. There is a swimming pool & decent restaurant serving typical Tanzania hotel fare. Keys is also one of the more reliable places to organise climbs of Kilimanjaro, & while rates are a little higher than at some other places, they do include 1 night's HB accommodation at the hotel on either side of the climb. *Self-contained rooms US$55/65 sgl/dbl B&B, discounted by roughly 50% for Tanzanian residents. Camping US$5 pp.*

🏠 **Keys Annex** [128 D4] (48 rooms) Contact details as for Keys Hotel. Tucked away in an unsignposted location on Mbokomu Rd, off the main Dar es Salaam Highway, this larger annexe to the well-known Keys Hotel is smarter & more modern than its elder sibling, but comparatively lacking in character. Smart tiled rooms, in a large double-storey building, have 2 beds & large bathrooms with combined tub/shower. Facilities include a restaurant, bar & swimming pool. *US$55/65 sgl/dbl B&B, discounted by roughly 50% for Tanzanian residents.*

⌂ **Kilimanjaro Tourist Inn** [128 A3] (8 rooms) ↖ 027 275 3252; f 027 275 2748; e kkkmarealle@yahoo.com; www.kiliweb.com/kti This converted colonial house set in a large suburban garden on Lema Rd has a friendly, homely atmosphere that will appeal to travellers who avoid more institutionalised hotels. It's good value, too, & all rooms come with large beds, net, fan & en-suite shower. *Tsh10,000/20,000 sgl/dbl.*

⌂ **Lutheran Uhuru Hostel** [128 B4] (60 rooms) ↖ 027 275 4084; m 0753 037216; f 027 275 3518; e uhuru@elct.com; www.uhuruhostel.org. Set in vast & pretty suburban gardens about 1.5km from the town centre on Shantytown's Sekou Toure Rd, this hostel used to be popular with tourists, but the recent boom in hotel construction in & around

Moshi seems to have reduced its custom, & it feels somewhat overpriced for non-residents. It offers a variety of rooms, some self-contained with running hot water & private balconies, & some with TV. The attached Bamboo Restaurant serves decent meals, but smoking & drinking are strictly prohibited. The hostel is about 3km out of town. *US$30/40 sgl/dbl using common shower, US$40/50 en-suite sgl/dbl, US$45/55 en-suite with TV (about 30% cheaper for residents).*

⌂ **Aman's Paradise Hotel** [128 C2] m 0754 919127; e liliantanz@hotmail.com. Situated in a rambling green compound on a quiet back road in the Shantytown area, this cosy private house, run by a Swedish–Tanzanian family, is well suited to those seeking a more down-to-earth experience than is offered by any formal tourist hotel. It's a friendly set-up, orientated mainly towards long stays, & 5% of the room rates go towards local NGOs. Facilities include satellite TV & internet access, with a proper restaurant likely to be added following pending renovations. *En-suite rooms US$35–60, with substantial discounts offered for longer stays.*

BUDGET

⌂ **Honey Badger Lodge** [128 D4] (8 rooms) m/f 0754 309980; e honeybadger@africamail.com; www.hbcc-campsites.com. Situated 6km out of town along the Dar es Salaam road, this rustic, friendly lodge forms a refreshingly low-key alternative to the budget hotels in town. Basically a converted house set within a fenced green compound, the lodge consists of 4 large en-suite dbl rooms in the main house, & 4 newer luxury rooms, all with hot showers. Camping is also available in individual campsites, & a common hot shower is available. Local dishes are available by advance order, & there is a self-catering kitchen & well-stocked outdoor *makuti* bar. Traditional drumming performances & lessons can be arranged. They also arrange performances of traditional Chagga *ngoma* (drums) with songs & acting depicting stories about marriage, harvesting time & initiation rites. Other cultural activities include traditional face painting, traditional fashion shows & culinary lessons, & they also arrange day hikes on the Kilimanjaro foothills. Internet is available at US$2 per hour in the high season (Jun–Oct) & a swimming pool will be ready by late 2009. *US$30–50 pp B&B; camping US$5 pp.*

⌂ **Kindoroko Hotel** [133 C6] (30 rooms) ↖ 027 275 4054; m 0787 037263; f 027 275 4062; e info@kindorokohotels.com; www.kindorokohotels.com. For some years the smartest

of the cluster of popular budget hotels situated on & around Nyerere Rd a couple of blocks south of the bus station, the four-storey Kindoroko has maintained high standards & reasonable prices. Following a complete refurbishment, the small but very clean rooms come with hot shower, fan, netting & digital satellite TV. Facilities include a lively courtyard bar, popular with travellers & locals alike, a restaurant serving adequate meals, an onsite internet café & a massage centre. The hotel also arranges reliable Kilimanjaro climbs. *US$15/30/45 sgl/dbl/trpl B&B.*

⌂ **Zebra Hotel** [133 C6] (72 rooms) ↖ 027 275 0611; f 027 275 0611; e zebhoteltz@yahoo.com; www.zebrahotelstz.com. This smart 7-storey hotel, which opened around the corner from the Kindoroko in 2005, is exceptional value for money, partly because the lack of elevator access to the upper stories has made it difficult to market in the mid-range category where it would otherwise belong. The rooms are clean & spacious, & come with AC, fan, satellite TV & en-suite hot shower. A ground-floor restaurant is attached. *US$30 sgl, US$ 35 dbl (king-size bed) or twin (2 x ³/₄ beds).*

⌂ **Buffalo Hotel** [133 C6] (31 rooms) ↖ 027 275 0270; m 0754 018302; e buffalohotel2000@yahoo.com. This clean & perennially popular budget hotel situated behind the Kindoroko underwent major renovations in 2007, & the spacious rooms are now

MOSHI
Town Centre

YMCA

HIGHWAY

Marangu,
Dar es Salaam

UHURU

Total

China Garden

Kilimanjaro International
Airport, Arusha

KIBO

OLD MOSHI

BATH

Regional library
Corina supermarket
Impala shuttle
Chrisburgers
Pub Alberto
Coffee Tree

Gapco
Akaro tours
Ice-cream parlour
Precision
Air

Kilimanjaro Crane
Horombo Lodge
Dar Express

Malindi Club
Corner Café
Nat Bank of Commerce
Philip
Moshi Pharmacy
Air Tanzania
Oryx
Liberty

RENGUA

Vodacom shop
Clocktower
Forex Bureau
Kilimanjaro

Stanbic
(& ATM)
Immigration
Hot Bread Shop

BOMA

Telecomms
Easycom internet &
Davanu shuttle

Green Palm
Café
Aleem's
supermarket
Exim

Riverside shuttle

RINDI

Central Garden Café

AGA KHAN

First Health
Standard Chartered

MTEI Coach

Bristol Cottages

Lutheran church

Gapco

Bus
station

BP

Royal Coach

MARKET

NYERERE

KAUNDA

Railway
station

GHALLA

0   150m
0   150yds

Police
station

ARUSHA

BENBELLA

BP

Mawenzi

Sikh
temple

HILL

Climbers
Deli Chez

Mawenzi

Coffee
Shop

Police
Bobby shuttle
Fahari Cyber Centre
Hill Street
Accommodation

Scandinavia Express

East African Pub Inn

MAKINGA

Second-hand
book stall

Gapco
National
Microfinance

FLORIDA

Dhruti's

SCHOOL

Zebra

Kilimanjaro
supermarket

Akamba bus

KENYATTA

Salzburger
Café
Siesta Inn
Big Mountain Inn

KIASU

Dreamers

Camel

GUINEA

Moshi Leopard
Grenada
Tanzania Coffee Lounge

Arawa

Newcastle
Buffalo
Kindoroko

Barclays
Haria

Indo Italiano

One Heritage
Craft Shop

CHAGGA

Club La Liga,
Shah Enterprise

Serengeti
Villa

Market
Trust
Bureau de Change
Kilimanjaro
Backpackers

Motel Silva

RIADHA

Moshi View
(100m)

Safari
supermarket

Riadha Mosque

© Philip Briggs

N
Bradt

brightly tiled, with en-suite hot showers throughout. The attached restaurant serves tasty & inexpensive Indian & Chinese meals. *Tsh15,000/20,000 sgl without/with fan, Tsh25,000 dbl with fan & TV, or Tsh30,000 dbl with AC, fridge & TV; suites Tsh50,000.*

⌂ **Hotel Newcastle** [133 C6] (40 rooms) ☎ 027 275 0853. A couple of doors down from the Kindoroko, this used to be similar in feel & standard but these days it's a lot more frayed at the edges. The rundown self-contained rooms have hot shower, fan & nets. The ground-floor restaurant/bar is sometimes very lively. Overpriced. *Tsh15,000/20,000 sgl/dbl.*

⌂ **Camel Hotel** [133 C6] (6 rooms) ☎ 027 275 2029; m 0784 879050. Opened in 2007, this small central hotel seems very friendly & reasonably priced, & the clean rooms all have tiled floors, satellite TV, & large bathrooms with hot shower. *Tsh18,000/23,000 sgl/dbl with fan, or 23,000/25,000 with AC.*

⌂ **Big Mountain Inn** [133 A6] (10 rooms) ☎ 027 275 1862; m 0754 376921; e pmtitos@

hotmail.com. This new hotel on Kiusa St has large clean rooms with tiled floor, TV, fan & en-suite hot shower. The pleasant courtyard restaurant serves a good selection of mostly Indian dishes in the Tsh5,000–7,000 range. Fair value. *Tsh25,000/30,000 sgl/dbl.*

⌂ **Motel Silva** [133 A7] (11 rooms) ☎ 027 275 3122. Situated close to the market, this 3-storey hotel has been one of the better budget options in Moshi for longer than a decade. The small but clean & brightly painted en-suite rooms have fans, nets & hot showers, & there is an agreeable rooftop garden. *Tsh15,000/20,000 for an en-suite sgl/dbl, or Tsh10,000 for a sgl using common showers.*

⌂ **Horombo Lodge** [133 C2] (29 rooms) ☎ 027 275 0134; e horomboldge_2005@yahoo.co.uk. With a central location on Old Moshi Rd immediately north of the Clocktower, this neat new hotel is a good compromise between quality & cost, with compact but clean en-suite rooms with TV, fan, net, phone & hot water. *From US$20/30 sgl/dbl.*

SHOESTRING

⌂ **Kilimanjaro Backpackers Hotel** [133 B7] (16 rooms) ☎ 027 275 5189; e info@ kilimanjarobackpacker.com; www.kilimanjarobackpacker.com. Situated 1 block south of the affiliated Kindoroko, the former Hotel Da Costa is deservedly the most popular cheapie in Moshi, offering accommodation in clean but no-frills tiled rooms & dormitories with net, fan & access to a common shower with a 24hr hot-water supply. Good value. *US$7/12 sgl/dbl B&B, or US$5 per dorm bed, with lunch & dinner an additional US$4 pp.*

⌂ **Haria Hotel** [133 B7] (8 rooms) m 0754 305453. Formerly a downmarket annexe to the Kindoroko Hotel opposite, this remains one of the best-value cheapies in Moshi, offering secure accommodation in large, clean rooms with tiled floors & nets. *Tsh8,000 for a twin using common showers, or Tsh 10,000 for an en-suite twin with hot shower.*

⌂ **Hill Street Accommodation** [133 C5] (12 rooms) ☎ 027 275 3455. This friendly hotel on Hill St has a convenient location close to the bus station & several good eateries, & the recently renovated rooms all have tiled floors & en-suite hot showers, but no fan or netting. *Tsh15,000/20,000/30,000 sgl/dbl/trpl.*

⌂ **Climbers Hotel** [133 B5] (8 rooms) ☎ 027 275 8025. Another decent & convenient cheapie situated along Hill St. *Tsh 8,000 small clean dbl using common shower, or Tsh10,000 for similar en-suite room.*

⌂ **Siesta Inn** [133 A6] (10 rooms) ☎ 027 275 0158. Alongside the Big Mountain Inn, this is another new hotel with large, clean but rather tatty rooms with en-suite hot showers & king-size beds. It's a friendly set-up, & reasonably priced. *Tsh18,000 dbl.*

⌂ **Coffee Tree Hotel** [133 C2] (57 rooms) ☎ 027 275 1382. This long-standing cheapie really couldn't be more centrally located, & the spacious rooms, though admittedly a bit rundown, are very good value. The restaurant isn't up to much, but it affords good views towards Kilimanjaro. *Tsh8,000/12,000 self-contained sgl/dbl with net, fan & cold water.*

⌂ **YMCA Hostel** [128 D4 & 133 C1] (42 rooms) ☎ 027 275 1754/4240; f 027 275 1734. On the opposite side of town to the above hotels, the YMCA is a perennial favourite with travellers, offering clean secure accommodation in green grounds with a large swimming pool. *US$13/17 small sgl/dbl B&B using communal showers.*

CAMPING Camping is permitted at the **Keys Hotel** [128 D4] for US$5 per person. Further out of town, the campsite at the **Honey Badger Lodge** [128 D4] is a far more homely option for campers.

Many of the places listed under *Where to stay*, above, have restaurants. Of the costlier places, the one most likely to attract passing custom to its restaurant is the **Kilimanjaro Crane Hotel** [133 C2], which has a central location, good Indian food at around Tsh5,000–6,000, pizzas, and a great view of Kilimanjaro from the rooftop bar. The restaurant at the **Kindoroko Hotel** [133 C6] is popular with budget travellers, and there's a lively bar attached. The majority of stand-alone restaurants are in the town centre but there are also several smarter options in the suburb of Shantytown to the north. The Shantytown restaurants are not accessible by public transport, so travellers staying more centrally will need to walk there and back (probably not a clever idea after dark) or to arrange to be collected by taxi.

✕ **El Rancho** [128 A2] ↘ 027 275 5115; ⊕ lunch & dinner Tue–Sun. Top-notch Indian restaurant & bar in a converted old house & green garden close to the Impala Hotel in Shantytown. A broad selection of vegetarian meals is available at around Tsh4,000, while meat dishes are slightly more expensive. Highly recommended.

✕ **Panda Chinese Restaurant** [128 A3] m 0754 838193/0784 875725; ⊕ lunch & dinner daily. This friendly & reliable Chinese eatery lies in pretty gardens just around the corner from the Ameg Lodge in Shantytown. It has the usual lengthy menu of meat, fish, chicken & vegetarian dishes, most at around Tsh7,000–8,000, though prawns are more expensive. Take-away available.

✕ **Salzburger Café** [133 A6] ↘ 027 275 0681; ⊕ 11.00–22.00 daily. Owned by a Tanzanian formerly resident in Austria, this unique restaurant on Kenyatta Rd is a real gem, decorated with mementoes of the old European city to create an atmosphere of full-on kitsch. If the décor doesn't do it for you, then the food certainly should — Tsh5,000–6,000 for a variety of very good steak, chicken & spaghetti dishes, with the unusual (for Tanzania) accompaniment of mashed potato & salads in addition to the conventional chips & rice.

✕ **Indo-Italiano Restaurant** [133 C6] ↘ 027 275 2195; ⊕ 09.00–22.00 daily. This popular restaurant has a convenient location opposite the Buffalo Hotel & it serves a wide range of Indian & Italian dishes — tandoori grills & pizzas particularly recommended — in the Tsh5,000–6,000 range. Meals can be served indoors or on the wide veranda.

✕ **Tanzania Coffee Lounge** [133 B7] ↘ 027 275 1006; www.toku-tanzania.com; ⊕ 08.00–20.00 daily. Indisputably the tastiest caffeine fix in Moshi, with filter, espresso, latte & cappuccino all available, this trendy little place on Chagga Rd also serves great

waffles, variable cakes & pastries, & the tasty lunchtime salads will satisfy those desperate for some fresh greens. A bona fide 50s jukebox beats out a selection of songs you probably haven't heard in years, & there's a high-speed internet café at the back.

✕ **The Coffee Shop** [133 B5] ↘ 027 275 2707; ⊕ 08.00–17.00 Mon–Sat. Tucked away on Hill St between the bus station & market, this church-run institution used to be *the* place for a fix of real coffee. It has been superseded in this role by the newer Tanzania Coffee Lounge, but it's still worth visiting for the irresistible selection of homemade cakes, burgers, sandwiches, pies, snacks & light lunches, mostly at around Tsh2,000–3,000, served indoors or in a tranquil courtyard garden. It's also a good spot for b/fast.

✕ **Deli Chez Restaurant** [133 B5] ↘ 027 275 1144; m 0784 786241; ⊕ lunch & dinner Wed–Mon. This new deli on the corner of Hill & Market St serves a great selection of Indian dishes, as well as a more limited selection of Chinese meals & fast food, & a sumptuous selection of milkshakes, sundaes & other desserts. No alcohol served.

✕ **Corner Café** [133 B2]. Centrally located on Rengua Rd, a block west of the Clocktower, this small café serves good toasted & cold sandwiches for around Tsh2,000, as well as salads, local dishes & coffee. Seating is inside or outdoors.

✕ **Central Garden Café** [133 C3] Located opposite the Clocktower & close to the bus station, this is a convenient spot for a quick alfresco cold drink or greasy local meal. Meals & 'bitings' are in the Tsh1,000–3,000 range.

✕ **Chrisburgers** [133 C2] ⊕ 08.00–15.00 Mon–Sat. Cheap daytime snacks such as hamburgers, samosas & excellent fruit juice, opposite the Clocktower.

NIGHTLIFE

♀ **Glacier Inn** [128 A4] ⌖ 0737 022764. Set in large jacaranda-shaded gardens on the corner of Lema & Kilimanjaro Rd, this is a great spot for a few outdoor drinks in suburban Shantytown. It also serves a varied selection of grills, Indian & Italian dishes in the Tsh4,000–6,000 range, & a selection of cheaper pub grub. A satellite TV ensures its popularity during major international sporting events.
☆ **Club La Liga** [128 D6] ⌖ 0767 770022/0715 750076; ⊕ 18.00–late Tue–Sun; entrance Tsh5,000 Fri & Tsh3,000 other nights; free for women on Sun. Moshi's premier nightclub lies about 500m from the town centre, among a row of old warehouses that can be reached by following Chagga Rd eastward across the railway tracks, where it becomes Viwanda Rd. It usually has live music on Thu, while DJs play a selection of bongo flava (Tanzanian hip-hop) & other dance music on other nights.
♀ **East African Pub Inn** [133 C5] Situated on Nyerere Rd, 2 blocks north of the Kindoroko Hotel, this lively 2-storey bar has a wooden roof, TV & loud music, with cheap 'n' cheerful drink prices aimed at a predominantly local clientele.
☆ **Pub Alberto** [133 C2] ⊕ 18.00–04.00 Tue–Sun. Brightly decorated nightclub next to Chrisburgers. Good place for a last round.

SHOPPING

SUPERMARKETS Aleem's supermarket on Boma Road (behind the post office) [133 B3] stocks a good range of imported goods and foods. The Carina supermarket next to Chrisburgers [133 C2] is also very well stocked. Opposite Aleem's, the Hot Bread Shop [133 B3] sells freshly baked bread as well as a selection of cakes and pies. There are also several good supermarkets on Nyerere Road between the bus station and central market.

BOOKS A good second-hand bookstall can be found on Nyerere Road, between the bus station and the Newcastle Hotel. For new books, particularly material relating specifically to Tanzania, the bookshop on the ground floor of the Kilimanjaro Crane Hotel [133 C2] is the best stocked in town.

CRAFTS AND SOUVENIRS Although Moshi doesn't boast quite the proliferation of curio stalls and shops associated with Arusha, there are still plenty around, and prices tend to be a bit lower, as does the pushiness factor. The main concentration of craft shops in the town centre lies along Chagga Road close to the main cluster of budget hotels, and there's no better starting point here than the vast and hassle-free One Heritage Craft Shop [133 C7], which stocks a good selection of books and postcards alongside the usual carvings, paintings and other local crafts. Follow Chagga Road east across the railway tracks towards Club La Liga to visit Shah Enterprises [128 C6] (✆ 027 275 2414), an excellent craft workshop specialising in leatherwork and staffed mainly by disabled Tanzanians. For paintings, the best selection is a cluster of perhaps a dozen stalls situated about 200m east of the main traffic circle along the Arusha–Dar es Salaam highway.

OTHER PRACTICALITIES

FOREIGN EXCHANGE AND BANKS The National Bank of Commerce opposite the Clocktower [133 C2] changes cash and travellers' cheques at the usual rate and commission. Several forex bureaux are dotted around town, but while exchange rates are fairly good, you will generally get better in Arusha or Dar es Salaam. One exception, Trust Bureau de Change, on Chagga Road [133 B7] (⊕ 09.00–18.00 Mon–Sat, 09.00–14.00 Sun) diagonally opposite the Kindoroko Hotel, offers good rates on US dollar travellers' cheques or cash and charges no commission.

There are now several 24-hour ATMs where up to Tsh200,000 cash can be drawn daily with certain credit or debit cards. The ATMs at the Standard

Chartered Bank [133 B3], National Bank of Commerce [133 C2] and Barclays Bank [133 B7] accept Visa, the one at the Exim Bank [133 B3] accepts MasterCard, while the one at Stanbic [133 B3] accepts both Visa and MasterCard, as well as Maestro and Cirrus. Other cards such as American Express are not accepted anywhere in Moshi.

HOSPITALS AND CLINICS The best place to head for in the case of a medical emergency is the Kilimanjaro Christian Medical Centre (KCMC) in Shantytown [128 B2] (❧ *027 275 4377/83; www.kcmc.ac.tz*) about 5km north of the town centre. More central options include the First Health Hospital on Rindi Road [133 B3] (❧ *027 275 4051*) alongside the Standard Chartered Bank, and Mawenzi Hospital next to the Hindu Temple on the junction of Hill and Benbella [133 B5].

IMMIGRATION Situated in Kibo House on Boma Road a few doors east of the Stanbic Bank, the immigration office in Moshi [133 B3] can process visa extensions on the spot during office hours (08.00–15.00 Mon–Fri).

MEDIA AND COMMUNICATIONS

Internet and email Numerous internet cafés are dotted around town. Most charge around Tsh500 per 15 or 30 minutes – the more expensive cafés generally provide a faster service – and stay open from around 08.00–20.00 daily, though some close on Sundays. In the Clocktower area, IBC Internet and Twiga Communications, set alongside each other on the Old Moshi Road near the Coffee Tree Hotel [133 C2], are both speedy and helpful, as is Easycom in Twiga House on the main traffic circle [133 C3]. South of the bus station, Fahari Cyber Centre of Hill Street [133 C5] and the Tanzania Coffee Lounge on Chagga Road [133 B7] are both recommended, though the latter is a little pricier than average.

Telephone Phone cards can be bought and used at the Tanzania Telecommunications Centre next to the post office near the Clocktower [133 C3]. This is also the best place to make international phone calls, and to send and receive faxes.

SWIMMING Use of the swimming pool at the YMCA [128 D4 & 133 C1] is free to hostel residents, but visitors must pay a daily entrance fee of Tsh3,000. The Keys Hotel [128 D4] a similar price to casual swimmers, but the pool is smaller and it is further out of town. You could also try the pool at the Kilimanjaro Crane Hotel [133 C2].

AROUND MOSHI

The most popular tourist destination in the vicinity of Moshi is of course Mount Kilimanjaro, the upper slopes and ascent of which are detailed in *Chapter 6, Mount Kilimanjaro National Park*. Other lesser attractions in the region, such as the villages of Marangu and Machame on the Kilimanjaro foothills, or the spectacular lakes Chala and Jipe and remote Mkomazi Game Reserve are covered below, together with a selection of ecotourist projects relating to Chagga culture.

MARANGU The village of Marangu, whose name derives from the local Chagga word meaning 'spring water', is situated on the lower slopes of Kilimanjaro about 40km from Moshi and 5km south of the main entrance gate to Mount Kilimanjaro National Park. Unlike lower-lying Moshi, Marangu has an appropriately alpine feel, surrounded as it is by lush vegetation and bisected by a babbling mountain stream, and it remains a popular springboard for Kilimanjaro ascents using the Marangu Route. For those who lack the time, inclination or money to climb Kilimanjaro, Marangu is a pleasant place to spend a night or a few days exploring the lower slopes of the great mountain, with several attractive waterfalls situated within easy striking distance.

Getting there and away The 40km drive from Moshi shouldn't take much longer than 30 minutes in a private vehicle. To get there, first head out along the Dar es Salaam road, bearing left after 23km as if heading towards Taveta, then turning left again after another 4km at the junction village of Himo. Buses and *dala-dalas* between Moshi and Marangu leave in either direction when they are full, normally at least once an hour, and generally take 45–60 minutes.

Where to stay and eat
Upmarket

Nakara Hotel (18 rooms) ☎ 027 275 6599/0744; e nakaratz@africaonline.co.tz; www.nakara-hotels.com. Probably the smartest option in Marangu these days, this soulless but efficiently staffed high-rise hotel lies about 3km past Marangu & around 2km before the eponymous entrance gate to Mount Kilimanjaro National Park. The compact but comfortable self-contained twin rooms might lack for character, but they are in far better shape than those at several rivals. Unfortunately, the rather cramped grounds lack the greenery & character of other options in this price range. *US$100/160 sgl/dbl B&B, an additional $25 pp for FB.*

Kibo Hotel (35 rooms) ☎/f 027 275 1308; e info@kibohotel.com or kibohotel@yahoo.com; www.kibohotel.com. The venerable Kibo Hotel stands in attractive flowering gardens roughly 1km from the village centre towards the park entrance gate. Formerly on a par with the Marangu Hotel, the Kibo has emphatically seen better days – incredibly, lest it escape your attention, former US president Jimmy Carter stayed here in 1988 – but it has retained a winning air of faded dignity epitomised by the liberal wood panelling & creaky old verandas. If nothing else, following a recent change of management & sensible cut in rates, the large, self-contained rooms are good value. Facilities include a swimming pool, internet access, gift shop & a decent restaurant bursting with character, & the hotel makes a great base for casual rambling in the Kilimanjaro foothills. It has been arranging reliable Kilimanjaro climbs for decades. *US$45/69/99 sgl/dbl/trpl B&B or US$71/117/160 FB; camping US$5 pp per night.*

Marangu Hotel (26 rooms) ☎ 027 275 6591; f 027 275 6594; e info@maranguhotel.com; www.maranguhotel.com. This comfortable, family-run hotel, situated back along the Moshi road 5km before Marangu, has an unpretentiously rustic feel, all ivy-draped walls & neat hedges that might have been transported straight from the English countryside. It also has a long-standing reputation for organising reliable Kilimanjaro climbs, whether you're looking at the standard all-inclusive package or the 'hard way' package aimed at budget travellers. Accommodation is in self-contained rooms. The large green campsite behind the main hotel buildings has a hot shower & is probably the best value for campers in the Marangu area. *US$85/120 sgl/dbl FB; camping US$3 pp.*

Capricorn Hotel (70 rooms) ☎ 027 275 1309; m 0754 841981; f 027 275 2442; e capricorn@africaonline.co.tz; www.capricornhotel.com. Straggling over a steep hillside some 2km from Marangu along the road towards Kilimanjaro National Park's Marangu entrance gate, this is one of the newer hotels in the Marangu area, but the en-suite rooms with satellite TV & minibar are rather variable in quality & the older ones are starting to look quite frayed at the edges. Situated within the forest zone, the lushly wooded 2.5ha garden is teeming with birds. The restaurant has a mediocre reputation, but Kilimanjaro climbs arranged through the hotel are as reliable as it gets. *US$60/80 B&B for sgl/dbl cottages in the old wing, or US$95/130 in the new wing; FB an additional US$27 pp.*

Moderate

Babylon Lodge (22 rooms) ☎ 027 275 6355 f 027 275 6597; e babylon@africaonline.co.tz. Situated 500m from Marangu Post Office along the

Mwika road, this former budget hotel has undergone a series of facelifts over the past decade, the most recent of which is scheduled for completion in early

2009. The en-suite rooms with combination tub/shower & attractive ethnic décor are immaculately kept, but a touch on the cramped side. Overall, it's one of the best-value lodges in the Marangu area, especially when it comes to cleanliness & quality of service. An onsite internet café should be operational in 2009. *US$30/50 sgl/dbl B&B, another US$10 pp for lunch or dinner.*

Budget and camping

⚑ Coffee Tree Campsite ✆ 027 275 6604; e kilimanjaro@iwayafrica.com. Situated along the road to the park entrance gate, alongside the Nakara Hotel, this neatly laid-out site is also a good place to arrange budget Kilimanjaro climbs. Accommodation in dbl chalets costs US$15 pp, while a bed in a rondavel costs US$12 pp — not exactly great value, but you won't find cheaper in Marangu. The camping seems a bit dear at US$8 pp, & even allowing for the above-average facilities — fridge, bar, BBQ, sauna & hot shower — the campsite at the Marangu or Kibo hotels (see *Upmarket* above) seem infinitely better value. Tents & gas stoves are available for hire, various cultural tours can be arranged & there are onsite email & internet facilities. If you don't fancy self-catering, you could eat at the adjacent Nakara Hotel.

⚑ Gilman's Camping Site ✆ 027 275 6490; m 0744 299486; e gilmanscamp@yahoo.com. Situated near the Moonjo Waterfall about 1km past the Kibo Hotel, where it is reached by a rather less perilous 200m dirt track, this campsite charges US$10 pp to pitch a tent, a rather hefty price only partially justified by its superior facilities, namely a clean ablution block with hot showers & access to a kitchen & comfortable lounge. The tall, conical traditional Chagga house behind the campsite is one of the last in existence & well worth a look.

Excursions from Marangu

Kinukamori Waterfall The most central tourist attraction in Marangu is the Kinukamori – 'Little Moon' – Waterfall. Situated about 20 minutes' walk from the town centre, from where it is signposted, this approximately 15m-high waterfall lies in a small park maintained by the district council (entrance US$1) as an ecotourism project in collaboration with two nearby villages. It's pretty enough without being an essential side trip, though the wooded banks of the Unna River above the waterfall harbour a variety of forest birds, and regularly attract troops of black-and-white colobus in the rainy season. A legend associated with Kinukamori relates to an unmarried girl called Makinuka, who discovered she was pregnant, a crime punishable by death in strict Chagga society, and decided to take her own life by jumping over the waterfall. When Makinuka arrived at the waterfall and looked over the edge, she changed her mind and turned to go home to plead for mercy. As she did so, however, she came face to face with a leopard and ran back screaming in fear, forgetting about the gorge behind her, to plunge to an accidental death. A statue of Makinuka and her nemesis stands above the waterfall. The waterfall can be visited independently, or by arrangement with your hotel as part of a longer sightseeing tour.

Kilasia Waterfall (m *0755 011040/252893;* e *kilasiawaterfalls@yahoo.com*) Clearly signposted to the left of the dirt road connecting the Kibo Hotel and Kilimanjaro Mountain Resort lies the rather spectacular Kilasia Waterfall, the centrepiece of a new ecotourist community that charges US$3 for a guided nature walk. Approximately 30m high, the waterfall tumbles into the base of a sheer-sided gorge before running through a set of violent rapids into a lovely pool that's said to be safe for swimming. The waterfall is at its most powerful during the rains, but it flows solidly throughout the year – the name Kilasia derives from a Chagga word meaning 'without end', reputedly a reference to its reliable flow. The path to the base of the falls, though no more than 500m long, is very steep and potentially dangerous when wet. The rocky gorge below the waterfall is lined with ferns and evergreen trees, and a troop of blue monkeys often passes through in the early morning and late afternoon. For further details, contact the community project manager.

LAKE CHALA Straddling the Kenyan border some 30km east of Moshi as the crow flies, this roughly circular crater lake, a full 3km wide yet invisible until you virtually topple over the rim, is one of northern Tanzania's true off-the-beaten-track scenic gems. The brilliant turquoise water, hemmed in by sheer cliffs draped in tropical greenery, is an arresting sight at any time, and utterly fantastic when Kilimanjaro emerges from the clouds to the immediate west. Not for the faint-hearted, a very steep footpath leads from the rim to the edge of the lake, its translucent waters plunging near-vertically to an undetermined depth from the rocky shore. Abundant birdlife aside, wildlife is in short supply, though Chala, in common with many other African crater lakes, is said locally to harbour its due quota of mysterious and malignant Nessie-like beasties. A more demonstrable cause for concern should you be nurturing any thoughts of dipping a toe in the water, however, is the presence of crocodiles, one of which savaged and drowned a British volunteer off the Kenyan shore in March 2002.

Recent attempts to attract tourism to Chala could hardly be deemed an unqualified success. A tourist lodge established in 1999 on the Kenyan rim closed down several years ago, and the Kilimanjaro Chala Lodge and Campsite on the Tanzanian side has been under construction since 2002 and looks unlikely to be completed any time soon.

Getting there For the time being, the only practical way to reach Chala is as an organised day or overnight trip out of Moshi, or in a private 4x4 vehicle. If you're driving, follow the Dar es Salaam road out of Moshi for 25km until you reach the junction at Himo, where a left turn leads to the Kenyan border at Taveta. About 7km along the Taveta road, turn left on to the rough road signposted for Kilimanjaro Mountain Lodge, which you must follow for about 40 minutes to reach the lake.

LAKE JIPE Shallow, narrow and enclosed by dense beds of tall papyrus, Lake Jipe runs for 10km along a natural sump on the Kenyan border between Kilimanjaro, the main source of its water, and the Mkomazi Game Reserve. It's an atmospheric body of water, with a fabulous setting: the Pare Mountains to the south, Chala crater rising from the flat plain to the east, and – when the clouds clear – Kilimanjaro hulking over the northeast skyline. Lake Jipe is seldom visited, and almost never from the Tanzanian side, but it is reasonably accessible, and there's quite a bit of wildlife around, since part of the northern shore is protected within Kenya's unfenced Tsavo National Park. Gazelle and other antelope are likely to be seen in the arid country approaching the lake, and cheetah and lion are occasionally observed darting across the road. The lake itself is teeming with hippopotami and crocodiles, and the papyrus beds harbour several localised birds, such as lesser jacana, African water rail, pygmy goose and black egret. Elephants regularly come to drink and bathe along the northern shore, especially during the dry season. Look out, too, for the lovely impala lily – this shrub-sized succulent, known for its bright pink and white flowers, is common in the dry acacia plains approaching the lake.

Although the papyrus that encloses Lake Jipe gives the lake much of its character, the rapid expansion of the plant over some 50% of the water in the last few decades is possibly symptomatic of a dying lake. Certainly, local fishermen, who now have to reach the open water along shallow canals cut through the crocodile-infested reeds, claim that the fish yield decreases every year along with the amount of open water. The probable explanation for the recent proliferation of papyrus – which can only grow at depths where it can take root in soil – is that the lake has gradually become shallower, due to increased silt levels in the water that flows down from Kilimanjaro. In a chain of cause and effect, the infestation of papyrus on Jipe would thus appear to be a result of the extensive deforestation and a corresponding increase in erosion on Kilimanjaro's lower slopes over the last 50 years.

Whether or not this process will result in the lake drying up entirely is a matter of conjecture, but researchers have expressed serious concerns for its future. The loss of Jipe would be immense, not only to the thousands of villagers for whom the lake has traditionally formed a source of fresh water and protein, but also to the wildlife that is drawn to its water during the dry season. Measures that would contribute to the lake's future – and which are in any case ecologically sound – include an extensive reforestation programme on the Kilimanjaro footslopes, and an attempt to modernise traditional farming methods that tend to cause soil erosion as land pressure intensifies and the earth is worked harder.

Getting there The junction town for Lake Jipe, called Kifaru, straddles the B1 some 40km south of Moshi. At Kifaru, turn to the east along a reasonable dirt road towards Kiwakuku. After about 15km, turn onto a track running to the left, distinguished by a blue signpost reading 'Jipe' and, up ahead, a hill with a prominent bald boulder on top. Follow this track for about 2km, and you'll be in Makayuni on the lakeshore. In a private vehicle, the drive from Kifaru takes 30–45 minutes, depending on the condition of the road, so it would be feasible to visit Jipe as a day trip from Moshi. The only public transport from Kifaru is the daily bus to Kiwakuku. This generally leaves Kiwakuku at 04.00, passes the Makayuni junction at around 06.30 and arrives in Kifaru at 09.00 to start the return trip at around 14.00. One Moshi-based safari company that regularly arranges day or overnight trips to Lake Jipe is Akaro Tours.

Once at Makayuni, it's straightforward enough to arrange to be poled onto the lake in a local dugout canoe, whether you want to fish, watch birds or just enjoy the lovely scenery and hope for glimpses of big game on the nearby Kenyan shore. Expect to pay around Tsh5,000 for a short excursion or Tsh15,000 for a full day on the lake. The best time to head onto the lake is in the early morning or late afternoon, when it's not too hot, game is more active and Kilimanjaro is most likely to be visible. Getting out onto the open water first involves a long pole through shallow papyrus marsh, with brightly coloured kingfishers darting in front of the boat and hippos grunting invisibly in the nearby reeds. This stretch can be quite difficult with two passengers weighing down the dugout, so it's best to take one per person. There is no accommodation near Lake Jipe (at least not along the Tanzanian shore) but it is permitted to pitch a tent in Makayuni for a nominal fee. Aside from fish, no food is available locally, and you'll need to bring all drinking water with you too. Mosquitoes (and occasionally lake flies) are prolific on the shore, so do cover up at dusk. Away from the lake, a few basic guesthouses can be found in Kifaru.

MKOMAZI NATIONAL PARK (*www.mkomazi.com; entrance US$20 pp per 24hr period*) Gazetted as a game reserve in 1951 and upgraded to national park status in 2008, Mkomazi is effectively a southern extension of Kenya's vast Tsavo National Park, covering an area of 3,234km² to the east of Kilimanjaro and immediately north of the Pare Mountains. Together with Tsavo, it forms part of one of east Africa's most important savanna ecosystems, characterised by the semi-arid climatic conditions of the Sahel Arc, and housing a great many dry-country species rare or absent elsewhere in Tanzania.

Several cultural tourism projects operate in the Kilimanjaro foothills in association with local communities. In addition to offering insights into Chagga culture and the opportunity to limber up the limbs before a full-on ascent of Kilimanjaro, these cultural tours allow non-climbers to get a good look at the scenic Kilimanjaro foothills, with a chance of catching a glimpse of the snow-capped peak itself. In addition to the local telephone contacts given below, full details of the programmes can be obtained through the central website www.tourismtanzania.org (e info@tourismtanzania.org). One operator in Moshi that specialises in setting up budget-friendly day trips to the cultural programmes, as well as running its own day hike in the Kilimanjaro foothills, is Akaro Tours (see box, *Kilimanjaro recommended tour operators*, in *Chapter 6*, page 155, for contact details).

MACHAME CULTURAL TOURISM PROGRAMME (☎ 027 275 7033) This programme is based at the village of Kyalia, close to the Machame Gate of Kilimanjaro National Park. A good day tour for those with a strong interest in scenery is the five-hour Sieny-Ngira Trail, which passes through the lush montane forest to a group of large sacred caves, a natural rock bridge over the Marire and Namwi rivers, and a nearby waterfall. For those with a greater interest in culture, the five-hour Nronga Tour, which visits a milk purification and processing co-operative run by women, is best done on Monday, market day in Kyalia village. Of similar duration, the Nkuu Tour focuses instead on agriculture, in particular coffee production. Longer excursions include the two-day Ng'uni Hike and three-day Lyamungo Tour. In a private vehicle, Kyalia can be reached by following the Arusha road out of Moshi for 12km, then following the turn-off signposted for Machame Gate and driving for another 14km. The road to Kyalia is surfaced in its entirety, and regular *dala-dalas* run to Kyalia from the junction on the Moshi–Arusha road.

In 1992, the Tanzanian government invited the Royal Geographical Society (RGS) to undertake a detailed ecological study of Mkomazi. Although mammal populations were very low, it was determined that most large mammal species present in Tsavo are either resident in Mkomazi or regularly migrate there from Kenya, including lion, cheetah, elephant, giraffe, buffalo, zebra, impala and Tanzania's most significant gerenuk population. African wild dogs were re-introduced into Mkomazi in the 1990s, as was a herd of black rhinos from South Africa, though neither is likely to be seen on an ordinary safari.

Mkomazi is listed as an Important Bird Area, with more than 400 species recorded, including several northern dry-country endemics that were newly added to the Tanzania list by the RGS – for instance three-streaked tchagra, Shelley's starling, Somali long-billed crombec, yellow-vented eremomella and the extremely localised Friedmann's lark. It is the only place in Tanzania where the lovely vulturine guineafowl, notable for its bright cobalt chest, is likely to be seen. Other conspicuous large ground birds include common ostrich, secretary bird, southern ground hornbill and various francolins and bustards.

Until recently, Mkomazi was practically undeveloped for tourism. It had also been subject to considerable pressure as the human population around its peripheries grew in number. As a result, wildlife is thinly distributed and skittish. This is likely to change, however, as animal populations benefit from the higher level of protection Mkomazi will be accorded as part of the national park system. It is also likely that the wildlife will become more habituated to safari vehicles following the recent construction of an exclusive tented camp within the park's boundaries.

MARANGU CULTURAL TOURISM PROGRAMME Geared primarily towards travellers staying in Marangu prior to a Kilimanjaro climb, this programme offers a variety of half-day trips taking in various natural and cultural sites in the surrounding slopes. Popular goals include any of three waterfalls, as well as the first coffee tree planted in Tanzania more than a century ago, and a traditional conical Chagga homestead. Few prospective climbers will be unmoved by the grave of the legendary Yohanu Lauwo, who guided Hans Meyer to the summit of Kilimanjaro back in 1889, continued working as a guide into his 70s, and lived to the remarkable age of 124! Other walks lead to nearby Mamba and Makundi, known for their traditional Chagga blacksmiths and woodcarvers, and for the Laka Caves, where women and children were hidden during the frequent 19th-century clashes with the Maasai of the surrounding plains. Guided tours can be arranged through any of the hotels in and around Marangu.

MATERUNI AND KURINGE WATERFALL TOUR Operated exclusively by Akaro Tours, whose founder grew up in a nearby shamba, this rewarding half- or full-day tour starts at the village of Materuni on the foothills of Kilimanjaro some 14km from Moshi. The walk follows sloping roads and footpaths through the surrounding mountainside to the Kuringe Waterfall, a 70m-high 'bridal veil' fall set at the head of a steep wooded gorge. One of the loveliest waterfalls I've seen anywhere in Africa, Kuringe is genuinely worth making an effort to visit, something I don't say lightly after having regularly hiked for miles in the line of duty to check out what, it transpired, was yet another unmemorable small cataract. On the full day, you continue from the waterfall, climbing steep cultivated slopes, to a Chagga homestead, where lunch and home-grown coffee are provided. From here, you can continue on to the Rua Forest, which harbours black-and-white colobus monkeys as well as most of the montane forest birds associated with Kilimanjaro. The full-day version can also incorporate a visit to a typical Chagga coffee and banana subsistence farm.

Although Mkomazi doesn't offer game viewing to compare to other reserves in northern Tanzania, this is compensated for by the wild scenery – mountains rise in all direction, with Kilimanjaro often visible to the northwest at dawn and dusk – and the near certainty of not seeing another tourist. The best game-viewing circuit runs for about 20km between Zange Entrance Gate and Dindera Dam, where topi, eland, giraffe, common zebra and gazelles are all quite likely to be seen. The thicker bush further east is a good place to see lesser kudu and gerenuk.

Getting there and away Mkomazi is among the most accessible of Tanzania national parks. The gateway town is Same, a small but busy trading centre that straddles the main Dar es Salaam Highway about 105km southeast of Moshi. The drive from Moshi to Same shouldn't take longer than 90 minutes in a private vehicle, and any public transport heading from Moshi to places further south can drop you off there. From Same, a good 5km dirt road runs to the Zange Entrance Gate, where you need to pay the entrance fee.

Although Mkomazi is not often included on northern Tanzania safari itineraries, this is likely to change as wildlife viewing improves and its tented camp gains greater publicity, and there is no reason why any established safari operator couldn't append it to a longer safari. For budget travellers, the park could easily be visited as a day trip out of Same, where 4x4 and other vehicles are usually available for hire at a negotiable rate. Mkomazi is best avoided in the rainy season, due to the poor roads.

Where to stay and eat
Upmarket

Babu's Camp (5 rooms) ↘ 027 250 3094;
e babuscamp@bol.co.tz; www.babuscamp.com.
Established in 2006, this exclusive tented camp, some
13km inside the park coming from Zange Entrance
Gate, is spaciously laid out within a grove of
gigantic baobabs & acacias, & it offers great views
across the plains to the Pare Mountains & lower
hills within the park. The spacious walk-in tents all
have their own balcony & a private open roof
shower & toilet out the back, offering fabulous views
of the sparkling African night sky. It is usefully
based for game drives, about 45 mins' drive from
Dindera Dam. The birdlife around camp can be
fabulous, & African wild dogs & other predators
occasionally pass through. *US$288/520 sgl/dbl B&B.*

Budget

Elephant Motel (20 rooms) ↘ 027 275 8193;
m 0754 839545; e manager@elephantmotel.com;
www.elephantmotel.com. The smartest accommodation
in the vicinity of Same is this recently refurbished
motel, set in large green grounds about 1.5km south
of the town centre along the B1 to Dar es Salaam.
It offers clean en-suite rooms with netting, TV & hot
running water, & good Indian, Tanzanian & Western
meals in the restaurant or garden cost around
Tsh5,000–6,000. *US$20/28 sgl/dbl, booking highly
recommended.*

Shoestring

Amani Lutheran Centre (c12 rooms) Situated on
the main tar road through Same, about 200m uphill
from the bus station, this clean & long-serving hostel
consists of around a dozen rooms enclosing a small
green courtyard. It's a friendly set-up, & facilities
include an internet cafe, canteen & safe parking.
*Tsh7,000/10,000 en-suite sgl/dbl B&B, or Tsh
15,000 suite.*

Mount Kilimanjaro National Park

Reaching an altitude of 5,895m (19,340ft), Kilimanjaro is the highest mountain in Africa, and on the rare occasions when it is not veiled in clouds, its distinctive silhouette and snow-capped peak form one of the most breathtaking sights on the continent. There are, of course, higher peaks on other continents, but Kilimanjaro is effectively the world's largest single mountain, a free-standing entity that towers an incredible 5km above the surrounding plains. It is also the highest mountain anywhere that can be ascended by somebody without specialised mountaineering experience or equipment.

Kilimanjaro straddles the border with Kenya, but the peaks all fall within Tanzania and can only be climbed from within the country. There are several places on the lower slopes from where the mountain can be ascended, but most people use the Marangu Route (which begins at the eponymous village) because it is the cheapest option and has the best facilities. The less heavily trampled Machame Route, starting from the village of the same name, has grown in popularity in recent years. A number of more obscure routes can be used, though they are generally only available through specialist trekking companies. Most prospective climbers arrange their ascent of 'Kili' – as it is popularly called – well in advance, through an overseas tour operator or online with a local operator, but you can also shop around on the spot using specialist trekking companies based in Moshi, Marangu or even Arusha. Kilimanjaro can be climbed at any time of year, but the hike is more difficult in the rainy months, especially between March and May.

GEOLOGY

In geological terms, Kilimanjaro is a relatively young mountain. Like most other large mountains near the Rift Valley, it was formed by volcanic activity, first erupting about one million years ago. The 3,962m-high Shira Peak collapsed around half a million years ago, but the 5,895m-high Uhuru Peak on Mount Kibo

WHAT'S IN A NAME?

Nobody is sure about the meaning of the name Kilimanjaro, or even whether it is Swahili, Maasai or Chagga in origin. That the term 'kilima' is Swahili for little mountain (a joke?) is not in doubt. But 'njaro' could derive from the Chagga word for caravan (the mountain was an important landmark on the northern caravan route), or from the Maasai word 'ngare' meaning water (it is the source of most of the region's rivers), or the name of a Swahili demon of cold. Another unrelated version of the name's origin is that it's a bastardisation of the phrase 'kilema kyaro' (impossible journey), the initial Chagga response to European queries about trekking to the peak!

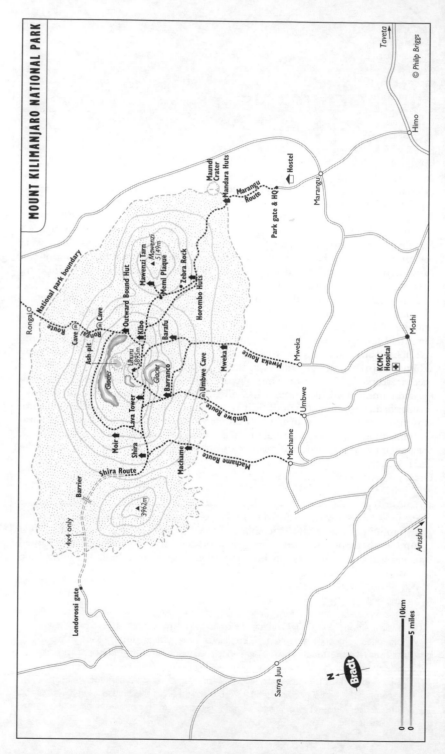

MOUNT KILIMANJARO NATIONAL PARK

© Philip Briggs

National park boundary

Rongai
Rongai Route

Londorossi gate

4x4 only

Barrier

Shira Route

Moir

Shira

Lava Tower

Cave
Cave
Ash pit
Glacier
Uhuru 5895m
Glacier
Barranco

3962m

Machame

Umbwe Cave

Outward Bound Hut
Kibo
Barafu

Mawenzi Tarn
Mawenzi 5149m
Meml Plaque
Zebra Rock
Horombo Huts

Maundi Crater
Mandara Huts
Marangu Route

Park gate & HQ

Hostel

Mweka
Mweka Route

Umbwe
Umbwe Route

Machame
Machame Route

KCMC Hospital

Moshi

Marangu

Himo

Taveta

Sanya Juu

Arusha

0   10km
0   5 miles

N
Bradt

146

and 5,149m-high Mawenzi Peak continued to grow until more recently. Shira plateau formed 360,000 years ago, when the caldera was filled by lava from Kibo after a particularly violent eruption. Kibo is now dormant, and nobody knows when it last displayed any serious volcanic activity. The Kilimanjaro National Park, gazetted in 1977, protects the entire Tanzanian part of the mountain above the 2,700m contour, an area of 756km².

HISTORY

Blessed by fertile volcanic soil and reliable rainfall, Kilimanjaro has probably always been a magnet for human settlement. Ancient stone tools of indeterminate age have been found on the lower slopes, as have the remains of pottery artefacts thought to be at least 2,000 years old. Archaeological evidence suggests that, between 1,000 and 1,500 years ago, Kilimanjaro was the centre of an Iron Age culture spreading out to the coastal belt between Pangani and Mombasa. Before that, it's anybody's guess really, but references in Ptolemy's *Geography* and the *Periplus of the Erythraean Sea* suggest that the mountain was known to the early coastal traders, and might even have served as the terminus of a trade route starting at modern-day Pangani and following the eponymous river inland. Kilimanjaro is also alluded to in an account written by a 12th-century Chinese trader, and by the 16th-century Spanish geographer, Fernandes de Encisco.

These ancient allusions fired the curiosity of 19th-century geographers, who outdid each other in publishing wild speculations about the African interior. In 1848, locals told Johan Rebmann, a German missionary working in the Taita Hills, about a very large silver-capped mountain known to the Maasai as Ol Doinyo Naibor – White Mountain – and reputedly protected by evil spirits that froze anybody who tried to ascend it. When Rebmann visited the mountain, he immediately recognised the spirit-infested silver cap to be snow, but this observation, first published in 1849, was derided by European experts, who thought it ludicrous to claim there was snow so near the Equator. Only in 1861, when an experienced geologist, Von der Decken, saw and surveyed Kilimanjaro, was its existence and that of its snow-capped peaks accepted internationally. Oral tradition suggests that no local person had successfully climbed Kilimanjaro – or at least returned to tell the tale – before Hans Meyer and Ludwig Purtscheller reached the summit in 1889.

Kilimanjaro is home to the Chagga people, a group of Bantu-speaking agriculturists whose ancestors are said to have arrived in the area in the 15th

A ROYAL VISIT

An unsubstantiated legend holds that Emperor Menelik I of Ethiopia, the illegitimate son of King Solomon and the Queen of Sheba, visited Kilimanjaro about 3,000 years ago while returning from a successful military campaign in east Africa. The emperor camped on the saddle for a night, and then ascended Kibo, where he suddenly fell ill and died, possibly from exposure and/or altitude-related causes. Menelik's slaves buried the imperial corpse in the snowy crater, where it remains to this day, so the story goes, together with a royal cache of jewels, religious scrolls and other treasures. An extension of this legend prophesies that a descendant of Menelik I will one day ascend Kibo, find the frozen body and claim the seal ring of Solomon worn by it, endowing him with the wisdom of Solomon and heroic spirit of Menelik. Pure apocrypha, so far as I can ascertain, is the story that the ancient Ethiopian emperor's 19th-century successor and namesake Menelik II once climbed Kilimanjaro in an unsuccessful bid to fulfil this centuries-old prophecy.

The names of Kilimanjaro's two main peaks, Kibo and Mawenzi, derive from local Chagga words respectively meaning 'cold' and 'jagged'. According to Chagga legend, the peaks are sisters, and both were once as smoothly shaped as the perfect dome of Kibo is today. But the younger sister Mawenzi was habitually too lazy to collect her own firewood and kept borrowing from Kibo until one day the elder sister instructed her to go out and gather her own. When Mawenzi refused, the enraged Kibo reached into her woodpile, grabbed the largest log there, and started beating her over the head, resulting in the jagged shape of the younger sister today.

century. This dating is contradicted by an intriguing local legend relating to an eruption of Kilimanjaro, which doesn't tally with the geological evidence for the past 500 years, so it's probable that the story was handed down by earlier inhabitants. The Chagga have no tradition of central leadership, and an estimated 100 small chieftaincies existed in the region in the mid 19th century. Today, the Chagga have a reputation for industriousness, and are generally relatively well educated, for which reason you'll find that a high proportion of salaried workers and safari guides come from Kilimanjaro region.

VEGETATION AND BIOLOGY

There are five vegetation zones on Kilimanjaro: the cultivated lower slopes; the forest; heath and moorland; alpine; and the barren arctic summit zone. Vegetation is sparse higher up due to lower temperatures and rainfall.

The **lower slopes** of the mountain were probably once forested, but are now mainly covered in cultivation. The volcanic soils make them highly fertile and they support a dense human population. The most biologically interesting aspect of the lower slopes is the abundance of wild flowers, seen between Marangu and the park entrance gate.

The **montane forest zone** of the southern slopes lies between the altitudes of 1,800m and 3,000m. Receiving up to 2,000mm of rainfall annually, this zone displays a high biological diversity, and still supports a fair amount of wildlife. The most frequently seen mammals are the black-and-white colobus and blue monkeys, while typical forest antelope include three duiker species and the beautifully marked bushbuck. Leopard, bushpig and porcupine are fairly common but seldom encountered by hikers, while eland, buffalo and elephant are present in small numbers. The forest is home to many varieties of butterfly, including four endemic species. The forests of Kilimanjaro are less rich in birds (particularly endemics) than the more ancient forests of the Eastern Arc Mountains, but some 40 species peculiar to Afro-montane forest have been recorded. Most forest birds are quite difficult to observe, but trekkers should at least hear the raucous silvery-cheeked hornbill and beautiful Hartlaub's turaco.

The semi-alpine **moorland zone**, which lies between 3,000m and 4,000m, is characterised by heath-like vegetation and abundant wild flowers. As you climb into the moorland, two distinctive plants become common. These are *Lobelia deckenii*, which grows to 3m high, and the groundsel *Senecio kilimanjarin*, which grows up to 5m high and can be distinguished by a spike of yellow flowers. The moorland zone supports a low density of mammals, but pairs of klipspringer are quite common on rocky outcrops and several other species are recorded from time to time. Hill chat and scarlet-tufted malachite sunbird are two birds whose range is restricted to the moorland of large east African mountains. Other localised birds are lammergeyer and alpine swift. Because it is so open, the views from the moorland are stunning.

The **alpine zone** between 4,000m and 5,000m is classified as a semi-desert because it receives an annual rainfall of less than 250mm. The ground often freezes at night, but ground temperatures may soar to above 30°C by day. Few plants survive in these conditions; only 55 species are present, many of them lichens and grasses. Six species of moss are endemic to the higher reaches of Kilimanjaro. Large mammals have been recorded at this altitude, most commonly eland, but none is resident.

Approaching the summit, the **arctic zone** starts at an altitude of around 5,000m. This area receives virtually no rainfall, and supports little permanent life other than the odd lichen. Two remarkable records concern a frozen leopard discovered here in 1926, and a family of hunting dogs seen in 1962. The most notable natural features at the summit are the inner and outer craters of Kibo, surrounding a 120m-deep ash pit, and the Great Northern Glacier, which has retreated markedly since Hans Meyer first saw it in 1889.

CLIMBING KILIMANJARO

As Africa's highest peak and most identifiable landmark, Kilimanjaro offers an irresistible challenge to many tourists. Dozens of visitors to Tanzania set off for Uhuru Peak every day, ranging from teenagers to pensioners (a seven-year-old boy recently became the youngest person to reach the summit), and those who make it generally regard the achievement to be the highlight of their time in the country. A major part of Kilimanjaro's attraction is that any reasonably fit person stands a fair chance of reaching the top. The ascent requires no special climbing skills or experience; on the contrary, it basically amounts to a long uphill slog over four days, followed by a more rapid descent.

The relative ease of climbing Kilimanjaro should not lull travellers into thinking of the ascent as some sort of prolonged Sunday stroll. It is a seriously tough hike, with potentially fatal penalties for those who are inadequately prepared or who belittle the health risks attached to being at an altitude of above 4,000m. It should also be recognised that there is no such thing as a cheap Kilimanjaro climb. Indeed, following the fee increases of 2006 (when the main entrance fee rose from US$40 to US$60 per day), the full set of park fees (entrance, camping, guide, porter and

CHAGGA HOME GARDENS

Emma Thomson

For decades the Chagga have been making use of the fertile soil that lies at the foot of Kilimanjaro. Originally, the land was divided into family allotments or *shamba* (usually 0.68ha) and passed from father to son. Later on land was seized by the state, and re-allocated depending on the size of the family. These lush plots are used to grow coffee, plantain, bananas and medicinal herbs, allowing the Chagga to be self-sufficient. This cropping system remained stable for at least a century, and only recently has it come under pressure from rapid population growth, diminishing land resources, changes in dietary habits and economic pressures for improved housing and schooling. These pressing needs have forced the younger generations to travel into the towns in search of paid work. However, this migration of youngsters to urban areas not only leads to labour shortages on the farms but also disrupts the traditional transmission from one generation to the next of the knowledge and experience required for the successful management of the farms.

These guidelines are produced by the Kilimanjaro Porters Assistance Project (KPAP) (*below the Kilimanjaro Backpackers Hotel, Nyerere Rd, Moshi;* m *0754 817615;* e *info@kiliporters.org; www.kiliporters.org*), an initiative of the International Mountain Explorers Connection, a non-profit organisation based in the United States. Visit the website for further information, or drop into the office in Moshi to attend a 'Porter Briefing', obtain a free Swahili–English language card, purchase discounted maps, arrange for off-the-beaten-path trips and homestays which directly support the local people, report any instances of porter abuse, or make a donation of clothing, money or volunteer help.

1 Ensure your porters are adequately clothed with suitable footwear, socks, waterproof jackets and trousers, gloves, hats, sunglasses, etc. Clothing for loan is available at the KPAP office in Moshi.
2 Fair wages should be paid. Kilimanjaro National Park recommends Tsh6,000 daily on Marangu Route and Tsh8,000 on other routes. Ask your company how much your porters are paid (and whether it includes food) to encourage fair treatment from operators and guides.
3 Porters should eat at least two meals a day and have access to water.
4 Check the weights of the loads. The recommended maximum of 25kg includes the porter's personal gear (assumed to be 5kg), so the load for the company should not exceed 20kg. If additional porters need to be hired make sure that the tour company is paying each porter their full wage when you return.
5 Count the number of porters every day: you are paying and tipping for them. Porters should not be sent down early as they will not receive their tips, and the other porters are then overloaded.
6 Make sure your porters are provided with proper shelter. Where no shelter is available, porters need proper sleeping accommodation that includes tents and sleeping bags. Sleeping in the mess tent means that the porters have to wait outside for climbers to finish their meals.
7 Ensure that each porter receives the intended tip. If you give tips to one individual you run the risk that they may not distribute the proper amount to the crew.
8 Take care of sick or injured porters. Porters deserve the same standard of treatment, care and rescue as their clients. Sick or injured porters need to be sent down with someone who speaks their language and understands the problem. If available, porters should also be provided insurance.
9 Get to know your porters. Some porters speak English and will appreciate any effort to speak with them. Free Swahili-language cards are available at the KPAP office in Moshi. The word *pole* (which translates loosely as 'sorry') shows respect for porters after a long day carrying your bags. *Asante* means 'thank you'.
10 After your climb, report any instances of abuse or neglect by email or by visiting the office.

rescue) amounts to US$525 per person for a five-day hike (the minimum length) and an additional US$110 per person for every extra day. Realistically, it would be difficult for the most corner-cutting of local operators to put together a five-day Marangu climb at much under US$900 per person, and the majority of budget operators now mostly charge more than US$1,000 for the same route, depending to some extent on group size. People using high-quality operators and/or the more obscure route should be prepared to pay considerably more!

MARANGU ROUTE Starting at the Marangu Gate some 5km from the village of the same name, the so-called 'tourist route' is the most popular way to the top of Kilimanjaro, largely because it is less arduous than most of the alternatives, as well as having better facilities and being cheaper to climb. Marangu is also probably the safest route, due to the volume of other climbers and good rescue facilities relative to more obscure routes, and it offers a better chance of seeing some wildlife. It is the only route where you can sleep in proper huts throughout, with bathing water and bottled drinks normally available too. The main drawback of the Marangu route is that it is heavily trampled by comparison with other routes, for which reason many people complain that it can feel overcrowded.

Day 1: Marangu to Mandara Hut (12km, 4hrs) On an organised climb you will be dropped at the park entrance gate a few kilometres past Marangu. There is a high chance of rain in the afternoon, so it is wise to set off on this four-hour hike as early in the day as you can. Foot traffic is heavy along this stretch, which means that although you pass through thick forest, the shy animals that inhabit the forest are not likely to be seen. If your guide will go that way, use the parallel trail which meets the main trail halfway between the gate and the hut. Mandara Hut (2,700m) is an attractive collection of buildings with room for 200 people.

Day 2: Mandara Hut to Horombo Hut (15km, 6hrs) You continue through forest for a short time before reaching the heather and moorland zone, from where there are good views of the peaks and Moshi. The walk takes up to six hours. Horombo Hut (3,720m) sleeps up to 120 people. It is in a valley and surrounded by giant lobelia and groundsel. If you do a six-day hike, you will spend a day at Horombo to acclimatise.

Day 3: Horombo Hut to Kibo Hut (15km, 6–7hrs) The vegetation thins out as you enter the desert-like alpine zone, and when you cross the saddle Kibo Peak comes into view. This six- to seven-hour walk should be done slowly: many people start to feel the effects of altitude. Kibo Hut (4,703m) is a stone construction that sleeps up to 120 people. Water must be carried there from a stream above Horombo. You may find it difficult to sleep at this altitude, and as you will have to rise at around 01.00 the next morning, many people feel it is better not to bother trying.

Days 4 and 5: Kibo Hut to the summit to Marangu The best time to climb is during the night, as it is marginally easier to climb the scree slope to Gillman's Point on the crater rim when it is frozen. This 5km ascent typically takes about six hours, so you need to get going between midnight and 01.00 to stand a chance of reaching the summit in time to catch the sunrise. From Gillman's Point it is a further two-hour round trip along the crater's edge to Uhuru Peak, the highest point in Africa. From the summit, it's a roughly seven-hour descent with a break at Kibo Hut to Horombo Hut, where you will spend your last night on the mountain. The final day's descent from Horombo to Marangu generally takes 7–8 hours, so you should arrive in Marangu in the mid-afternoon.

OTHER ROUTES Although the vast majority of trekkers stick to the Marangu Route, some prefer to ascend Kilimanjaro using one of five relatively off-the-beaten-track alternatives. While the merits and demerits of avoiding the Marangu Route are hotly debated, there is no doubt about two things: firstly that you'll see few other tourists on the more obscure routes, and secondly that you'll pay considerably more for this privilege. Aesthetic and financial considerations aside, two unambiguous logistical disadvantages of the less-used routes are that they are generally tougher going (though only the Umbwe is markedly so), and that the huts – where they exist – are virtually derelict, which enforces camping.

Machame Route In recent years, the Machame Route has grown greatly in popularity. It is widely regarded to be the most scenic viable ascent route, with great views across to Mount Meru, and as a whole it is relatively gradual, requiring at least six days for the full ascent and descent. Short sections are steeper and slightly more difficult than any part of the Marangu Route, but this is compensated for by the longer period for acclimatisation.

The route is named after the village of Machame, from where it is a two-hour walk to the park gate (1,950m). Most companies will provide transport as far as the gate (at least when the road is passable), and then it's a six- to eight-hour trek through thick forest to Machame Hut, which lies on the edge of the moorland zone at 2,890m. The Machame Hut is now a ruin, so camping is necessary, but water is available. The second day of this trail consists of a 9km, four- to six-hour hike through the moorland zone of Shira Plateau to Shira Hut (3,840m), which is near a stream. Once again, this hut has fallen into disuse, so the options are camping or sleeping in a nearby cave.

From Shira, a number of options exist: you could spend your third night at Lava Tower Hut (4,630m), four hours from Shira, but the ascent to the summit from there is tricky and only advisable if you are experienced and have good equipment. A less arduous option is to spend your third night at Barranco Campsite (3,950m), a tough 12km, six-hour hike from Shira, then to go on to Barafu Hut (4,600m) on the fourth day, a walk of approximately seven hours. From Barafu, it is normal to begin the steep seven- to eight-hour clamber to Stella Point (5,735m) at midnight, so that you arrive at sunrise, with the option of continuing on to Uhuru Peak, a two-hour round trip, before hiking back down to Mweka Hut via Barafu in the afternoon. This day can involve up to 16 hours of walking altogether. After spending your fifth night at Mweka Hut (3,100m), you will descend the mountain on the sixth day via the Mweka Route, a four- to six-hour walk.

Although the huts along this route are practically unusable, you still get to pay the US$40 'hut fee'. Any reliable operator will provide you with camping equipment and employ enough porters to carry the camp and set it up.

Mweka Route This is the steepest and fastest route to the summit. There are two huts along it – Mweka (3,100m) and Barafu (4,600m), uniports that sleep up to 16 people – though neither is reputedly habitable at the time of writing. There is water at Mweka but not at Barafu. This route starts at the Mweka Wildlife College, 12km from Moshi. From there it takes about eight hours to get to Mweka Hut, then a further eight hours to Barafu, from where it replicates the Machame Route. The Mweka Route is not recommended for ascending the mountain, since it is too short for proper acclimatisation, but is often used as a descent route by people climbing the Machame or Shira routes.

Shira Route Although this route could technically be covered in five days by driving to the high-altitude trailhead, this would allow one very little time to acclimatise, and greatly decrease the odds of reaching the summit. A minimum of six days is recommended, but better seven so that you can spend a full day at Shira Hut to acclimatise. The route starts at Londorossi Gate on the western side of the mountain, from where a 19km track leads to the trailhead at around 3,500m. It is

top left **Adult male serval**
Felis serval (NG)
page 264

top right **Cheetah**
Acynonix jubatus (AVZ)
page 264

above right **Lioness**
Panthera leo (AVZ)
page 263

above left **Young male leopard**
Panthera pardus (NG)
page 263

right **Large spotted genet**
Genetta tigrina (AVZ)
page 266

above left **Hippopotamus**
Hippopotamus amphibius (AVZ)
page 272

above right **Warthog**
Phacochoerus africanus (AVZ)
page 273

below left **Giraffe**
Giraffa camelopardis (AVZ)
page 273

below right **Burchell's zebra**
Equus burchelli (AVZ)
page 273

above left **Female impala**
Aepeceros melampus (AVZ)
page 271

above centre **Male impala**
Aepeceros melampus (AVZ)
page 271

above right **Oribi**
Ourebia ourebi (AVZ)
page 271

left **Kirk's dik dik**
Madoqua kirki (AVZ)
page 271

below left **Thomson's gazelle**
Gazella thomsoni (AVZ)
page 270

above left **Topi**
Damaliscus lunatus jimela (AVZ)
page 269

above right **Defassa waterbuck**
Kobus ellipsiprymnus defassa
(AVZ) page 269

right **Common eland**
Taurotragus oryx (AVZ)
page 269

below left **Grant's gazelle**
Gazella granti (AVZ)
page 271

below right **Jackson's hartebeest**
Alcelaphus buselaphus (AVZ)
page 269

top left **Nile crocodile** *Crocodylus niloticus* (AVZ) page 33

above **Flat-headed rock agama lizard** *Agama mwanzae* (AVZ) page 34

top right **Chimpanzee** *Pan troglodytes* (AVZ) page 266

centre right **Dwarf mongoose** *Helogale parvula* (AVZ) page 266

bottom right **Greater galago (bushbaby)** *Galago crassicaudatus* (AVZ) page 268

clockwise from top left

Greater flamingoes
Phoenicopterus ruber (AVZ)

Fischer's lovebird
Agapornis fischeri (AVZ)

Pearl-spotted owlet
Glaucidium perlatum (AVZ)

Lilac-breasted roller
Coracias caudata (AVZ)

White-fronted bee-eater
Merops bullockoides (AVZ)

Kori bustard
Ardeotis kori (AVZ)

Crowned crane
Balearica pavonina (AVZ)

D'Arnaud's barbet
Glaucidium perlatum (AVZ)

Karama Lodge & Spa is an eco-friendly lodge providing a touch of the country within eas reach of Arusha Town.

Twenty-two stilted cabins have been constructed from local materials in a manner sensit to our fragile environment. The cabins are uniquely decorated with attention to detail, providing rustic, yet comfortable accommodation. Butterflies flit amongst the lushly landscaped gardens and surrounding forest all within view of Mts Kilimanjaro and Meru.

Our highly qualified chef and friendly staff will make your stay at Karama a real delight.

Karama
LODGE & SPA

Tel: +255(0)754-475188 or +255(0)73-2971823
www.karama-lodge.com info@karama-lodge.com

Visit Tanzania with

KIBO SOUTH CIRC
BARRANCO & BARAFU

ROY SAFARIS LIMITED
ARUSHA TANZANIA

"We go thru' every measure
to give you Wild pleasure"

Roysafaris@intafrica.com   www.roysafaris.com

Do not attempt to climb Kilimanjaro unless you are reasonably fit, or if you have heart or lung problems (although asthma sufferers should be all right). Bear in mind, however, that very fit people are more prone to altitude sickness because they ascend too fast.

Above 3,000m you may not feel hungry, but you should try to eat. Carbohydrates and fruit are recommended, whereas rich or fatty foods are harder to digest. You should drink plenty of liquids, at least three litres of water daily, and will need enough water bottles to carry this. Dehydration is one of the most common reasons for failing to complete the climb. If you dress in layers, you can take off clothes before you sweat too much, thereby reducing water loss.

Few people climb Kilimanjaro without feeling some of the symptoms of altitude sickness: headaches, nausea, fatigue, breathlessness, sleeplessness and swelling of the hands and feet. You can reduce these by allowing yourself time to acclimatise by taking an extra day over the ascent, eating and drinking properly, and trying not to push yourself. If you walk slowly and steadily, you will tire less quickly than if you try to rush each day's walk. Acetazolamide (Diamox) helps speed acclimatisation and many people find it useful; take 250mg twice a day for five days, starting two or three days before reaching 3,500m. However, the side effects from this drug may resemble altitude sickness and therefore it is advisable to try the medication for a couple of days about two weeks before the trip to see if it suits you.

Should symptoms become severe, and especially if they are clearly getting worse, then descend immediately. Even going down 500m is enough to start recovery. Sleeping high with significant symptoms is dangerous; if in doubt descend to sleep low.

Pulmonary and cerebral oedemas are altitude-related problems that can be rapidly fatal if you do not descend. Symptoms of the former include shortness of breath when at rest, coughing up frothy spit or even blood, and undue breathlessness compared with accompanying friends. Symptoms of high altitude cerebral oedema are headaches, poor co-ordination, staggering like a drunk, disorientation, poor judgement and even hallucinations. The danger is that the sufferer usually doesn't realise how sick he/she is and may argue against descending. The only treatment for altitude sickness is descent.

Hypothermia is a lowering of body temperature usually caused by a combination of cold and wet. Mild cases usually manifest themselves as uncontrollable shivering. Put on dry, warm clothes and get into a sleeping bag; this will normally raise your body temperature sufficiently. Severe hypothermia is potentially fatal: symptoms include disorientation, lethargy, mental confusion (including an inappropriate feeling of well-being and warmth!) and coma. In severe cases the rescue team should be summoned.

A US$20 rescue fee is paid by all climbers upon entering the national park. The rescue team ordinarily covers the Marangu Route only; if you use another route their services must be organised in advance.

possible to motor to the trailhead in a 4x4, but for reasons already mentioned it would be advisable to walk, with an overnight stop to camp outside Simba Cave, which lies in an area of moorland where elephants and buffalo are regularly encountered. From the trailhead, it's a straightforward 4km to the campsite at the disused Shira Hut. If you opt to spend two nights at Shira in order to acclimatise, there are some worthwhile day walks in the vicinity. From Shira Hut, the route is identical to the Machame Route, and it is normal to return along the Mweka Route.

Rongai Route The only route ascending Kilimanjaro from the northeast, the recently reopened Rongai Route starts close to the Kenyan border and was closed for several years due to border sensitivity. In terms of gradients, it is probably less physically demanding than the Marangu Route, and the scenery, with views over the Tsavo Plains, is regarded to be as beautiful. The Rongai Route can be covered over five days, with equally good if not better conditions for acclimatisation than the Marangu Route, though as with Marangu the odds of reaching the summit improve if you opt for an additional day.

The route starts at the village of Nale Moru (2,000m) near the Kenyan border, from where a footpath leads through cultivated fields and plantation forest before entering the montane forest zone, where black-and-white colobus monkeys are frequently encountered. The first campsite is reached after three to five hours, and lies at about 2,700m on the frontier of the forest and moorland zones. On the five-day hike, the second day involves a gentle five- to six-hour ascent, through an area of moorland where elephants are sometimes seen, to Third Cave Campsite (3,500m). On the third day, it's a four- to five-hour walk to School Campsite (4,750m) at the base of Kibo, with the option of camping here or else continuing to the nearby Kibo Hut, which is more crowded but more commodious. The ascent from here is identical to the Marangu Route. A six-day variation on the above route involves spending the second night at Kikelewa Caves (3,600m, 6–7hr walk), a night at Mawenzi Tarn near the synonymous peak (4,330m, 4hr walk), then crossing the saddle between Mawenzi and Kibo to rejoin the five-day route at School Campsite.

Umbwe Route This short, steep route, possibly the most scenic of the lot, is not recommended as an ascent route as it is very steep in parts and involves one short stretch of genuine rock climbing. It is occasionally used as a descent route, and can be tied in with almost any of the ascent routes, though many operators understandably prefer not to take the risk, or charge a premium for using it. Umbwe Route descends from Barranco Hut, and comes out at the village of Umbwe. It is possible to sleep in two caves on the lower slopes along this route.

ARRANGING A CLIMB The only sensible way to go about climbing Kilimanjaro is through a reliable operator that specialises in Kili climbs. Readers who pre-book a climb through a known tour operator in their own country can be confident that they will be going with a reputable ground operator in Tanzania. For readers who want to make their arrangements online or after they arrive in Tanzania, several trekking companies operate out of Moshi, Arusha and Marangu, and you should be able to negotiate a far better price by cutting out the middleman, but do be very circumspect about dealing with any company without a verifiable pedigree. A list of respected operators is included in the box below, and while such a list can never

KILIMANJARO: RECOMMENDED TOUR OPERATORS

The most popular base for organising a Kilimanjaro climb on the spot is Moshi, but most of the hotels at Marangu arrange reliable climbs, and many tourists who pre-book a climb prefer to work through a company based in Arusha. The following companies are all recommended.

MOSHI
Zara Tours ☎ 027 275 0233; m 0784 451000; e zara@zaratours.com; www.zaratours.com. Situated on Rindi Lane diagonally opposite the Stanbic Bank, Zara Tours has been one of the most prominent & reliable operators of Kili climbs for more than 20 years. Marangu Route ascents cost US$1,172 while 6-day climbs using the other routes cost US$1,447 pp.
Keys Hotel ☎ 027 275 2250/1870; f 027 275 0073; e keys-hotel@africaonline.co.tz; www.keys-hotels.com. Excellent & experienced operator based at one of the town's best hotels, & very reasonably priced.
Akaro Tours ☎ 027 275 2986; m 0744 272124; f 027 275 2249; e safaris@akarotours.com; www.akarotours.com. Founded by a dynamic former Kilimanjaro guide with vast hands-on experience of the mountain, this small operator offers reliable no-frills climbs at a good price for Kili climbs, as well as a great range of cultural day tours out of Moshi.

MARANGU The family-run Marangu Hotel has been taking people up Kilimanjaro for decades, and they have an impeccable reputation. The standard packages aren't the cheapest available, but they are pretty good value, and the standard of service and equipment is very high. The self-catering 'hard-way' climbs organised by the Marangu Hotel are probably the cheapest reliable deals you'll find, working out at US$720 per person for five days, and US$135 per person each day thereafter, inclusive of park fees. Also reliable are the Capricorn and Kibo hotels and Babylon Lodge. Contact details for these hotels are found in *Chapter 5* under *Where to stay* in Marangu, pages 138–9.

ARUSHA Most safari companies in Arusha arrange Kilimanjaro climbs, but will generally work through a ground operator in Moshi or Marangu, which means that they have to charge slightly higher rates. Any of the Arusha-based safari companies listed in that section can be recommended, and short-stay visitors who are already going on safari with one of these companies will probably find that the ease and efficiency of arranging a Kilimanjaro climb through that company outweighs the minor additional expenditure.

There are a few companies that arrange their own Kili climbs out of Arusha. Hoopoe Adventure Tours has a long track record of organising ascents along the lesser-known routes, and is well worth contacting should you want to do that sort of thing and you're prepared to pay a premium for top guides and equipment. So too is Nature Discovery, a highly regarded company that specialises in the more obscure routes up the mountain, and routinely sets up camp in the crater of Kibo, allowing you to explore the peaks area and ash cone at relative leisure. Tropical Trails, based at Maasai Camp on the outskirts of Arusha, has an excellent reputation for Kili climbs. Roy Safaris also arranges its own trekking and climbing on Kilimanjaro, Mount Meru and elsewhere. Contact details of all these companies are on pages 91–3, *Chapter 3*.

be comprehensive, it is reasonable to assume that anybody who can offer you a significantly cheaper package than the more budget-friendly companies on this list is not to be trusted.

In 2009, five-day Marangu climbs with a reliable operator start at an all-inclusive price of around US$1,000 per person for two people. You may be able to negotiate the starting price down slightly, especially for a larger group, but when you are paying this sort of money, it strikes me as sensible to shop around for the best quality of service rather than a fractional saving. A reputable operator will provide good food, experienced guides and porters, and reliable equipment – all of which go a long way to ensuring not only that you reach the top, but also that you come back down alive. You can assume that the cost of any package with a reputable operator will include a registered guide, two porters per person, park fees, food, and transport to and from the gate. It is, however, advisable to check exactly what you are paying for, and (especially for larger parties) to ensure that one porter is also registered as a guide, so that if somebody has to turn back, the rest of the group can still continue their climb. It might also be worth pointing out the potential risk attached to forming an impromptu group with strangers merely to cut 5% or so off the price. If you hike on your own or with people you know well, you can dictate your own pace and there is less danger of personality clashes developing mid-climb.

The standard duration of a climb on the Marangu Route is five days. Many people with repeated experience of Kilimanjaro recommend adding a sixth day to acclimatise at Horombo Hut. It is often said that this will improve the odds of reaching the summit by as much as 20%. Others feel that the extra day makes little difference except that it adds a similar figure to the cost of the climb. One person who owns a climbing company in Arusha kept records for three years and noted only a slightly increased success rate in people who take the extra day, and which he attributes to their extra determination to reach the top after having paid more money.

In this context, it is worth noting that the exhaustion felt by almost all hikers as they approach the peak is not merely a function of altitude. On the Marangu Route, for instance, most people hike for six to eight hours on day three, and then after a minimal dose of sleep (if any at all) rise at around midnight to start the final five- to six-hour ascent to the peak. In other words, when you reach the peak

ABBOTT'S DUIKER

An antelope occasionally encountered by hikers on Kilimanjaro is Abbott's duiker *Cephalophus spadix*, a montane forest species that was formerly quite widespread in suitable east African habitats, but is today endemic to eastern Tanzania due to environmental loss and poaching elsewhere in its natural range. After Ader's duiker, a lowland species of the east African coastal belt, Abbott's is the most threatened of African duikers, categorised as vulnerable in the International Union for Conservation of Nature (IUCN) Red Data list for 2000, but based on present trends likely to decline to a status of critically endangered in the foreseeable future. Abbott's duiker is today confined to five forested montane 'islands' in eastern Tanzania, namely Kilimanjaro, Usambara, Udzungwa, Uluguru and Rungwe. The total population is unknown – a 1998 estimate of 2,500 based on limited data is not implausible – but Udzungwa probably harbours the most substantial and secure single population, followed by Kilimanjaro. Should you be lucky enough to stumble across this rare antelope, it has a glossy, unmarked off-black torso, a paler head and a distinctive red forehead tuft. Its size alone should, however, be diagnostic: the shoulder height of up to 75cm is the third largest of any duiker species, and far exceeds that of other more diminutive duikers that occur in Tanzania.

following the conventional five-day hike, you will have been walking for up to 14 of the last 20-odd hours, without any significant sleep – something that would tire out most people even if they weren't facing an altitudinal climb of around 2,000m. On that basis alone, an extra night along the way would have some value in pure recuperative terms. And certainly, my firm impression is that travellers who spend six days on the mountain enjoy the climb far more than those who take five days, whether or not they reach the peak. The choice is yours.

Of the less popular routes up Kilimanjaro, the one most frequently used by tourists, the Machame Route, requires a minimum of six days. Most operators will charge at least 25% more for this route, because it requires far more outlay on their part. The huts along the Machame Route are in such poor condition that tents and camping equipment must be provided, along with a coterie of porters to carry and set up the makeshift camp. The same problem exists on all routes except Marangu, so that any off-the-beaten-track climb will be considerably more costly than the standard one. Should you decide to use a route other than Marangu, it is critical that you work through an operator with experience of that route.

The dubious alternative to using a reputable company is to take your chances with a small operator or private individual who approaches you in the street. These guys will offer climbs for around US$100 cheaper than an established operator, but the risks are greater and because they generally have no office there is little accountability on their side. Many of these guides are genuine and reliable, but it's difficult to be certain unless you have a recommendation from somebody who has used the same person. A crucial point when comparing this situation with the similar one that surrounds arranging a safari out of Arusha is that you're not merely talking about losing a day through breakdown or something like that. With Kilimanjaro, you could literally die on the mountain. I've heard several stories of climbers being supplied with inadequate equipment and food, even of travellers being abandoned by their guide mid-climb. The very least you can do, if you make arrangements of this sort, is to verify that your guide is registered; he should have a small wallet-like document to prove it, though even this can be faked.

The reason why climbing Kilimanjaro is so expensive boils down to the high park fees. The daily entrance fee is US$60 per person, then there's a hut or camping fee of US$40 per person per night, and a one-off rescue fee of US$20 per person per climb. An additional daily entrance fee of US$10 is charged for the guide, along with a separate one-off rescue fee of US$20. To this must be added the cost of transport, food and cooking fuel, and the guide's and porters' salaries. Hikers are expected to tip their guides and porters. The company you go with can give you an idea of the going rate, but around US$5 per day per guide/porter per climbing party is fair.

OTHER PREPARATIONS Two climatic factors must be considered when preparing to climb Kilimanjaro. The obvious one is the cold. Bring plenty of warm clothes, a windproof jacket, a pair of gloves, a balaclava, a warm sleeping bag and an insulation mat. During the rainy season, a waterproof jacket and trousers will come in useful. A less obvious factor is the sun, which is fierce at high altitudes. Bring sunglasses, sunscreen and a hat.

Other essentials are water bottles, and solid shoes or preferably boots that have already been worn in. Most of these items can be hired in Moshi or at the park gate, or from the company you arrange to climb with. I've heard varying reports about the condition of locally hired items, but standards seem to be far higher than they were only a few years back.

A good medical kit is essential, especially if you are climbing with a cheap company. You'll go through plenty of plasters if you acquire a few blisters (assume that you will), and can also expect to want headache tablets.

You might want to buy biscuits, chocolate, sweets, glucose powder and other energy-rich snacks to take with you up the mountain. No companies supply this sort of thing, and although they are sometimes available at the huts, you'll pay through your nose for them.

MAPS AND FURTHER READING Trekkers are not permitted on the mountain without a registered guide, and all sensible trekkers will make arrangements through a reliable operator, which means that there is no real need for detailed route descriptions once you're on the mountain. Nevertheless, many trekkers will benefit from the detailed practical advice and overview of route possibilities provided in a few specialist Kilimanjaro guidebooks. The pick of these is undoubtedly the 336-page *Kilimanjaro: The Trekking Guide to Africa's Highest Mountain* by Henry Stedman (Trailblazer Guides), which can be bought locally or ordered in advance through online bookshops such as amazon.co.uk and amazon.com. Also recommended, *Kilimanjaro & East Africa: A Climbing and Trekking Guide* by Cameron M Burns, published in 2006 by Mountaineers Books is especially useful for anybody planning to do serious rock climbing or to hike away from the main routes, or for those who also want to hike on Mount Kenya and the Rwenzori.

More concerned with the overall geology and natural history of Kilimanjaro, making it a more useful companion to trekkers on organised hikes, *Kilimanjaro: Africa's Beacon* is one of a series of glossy and informative pocket-sized guides published by the Zimbabwe-based African Publishing Group in association with Tanapa. It is widely available in Arusha and Moshi for around US$8. Its predecessor, the 60-page national park handbook *Kilimanjaro National Park*, is arguably more informative but less attractively put together, and is still widely available in Arusha and Moshi for around US$5.

Giovanni Tombazzi's *New Map of Kilimanjaro National Park*, sold in Arusha and Moshi, is arguably the best map available, and certainly the most visually attractive. Current climbing tips are printed on the back of this map, along with a close-scale map of the final ascent to Kibo, and day-by-day contour 'graphs' for the Machame and Marangu routes.

Before you leave home – or as a memento when you get back – try to get hold of *Kilimanjaro* by John Reader (Elm Tree Books, London, 1982), which is long out of print but easily bought second-hand through the likes of Amazon. Although it is superficially a coffee-table book, it offers a well-written and absorbing overview of the mountain's history and various ecosystems. The photographs are good too.

7

Tarangire and the Central Rift Valley

The least celebrated of the quartet of wildlife sanctuaries that comprise northern Tanzania's established safari circuit, Tarangire National Park is nevertheless highly rewarding, especially during the latter half of the year, when it is a recommended inclusion on any safari itinerary of longer than a week in duration. The park is best known for its density of baobab trees and year-round proliferation of elephants, but predators are also well represented, the birdlife is excellent, and from July until November large herds of migrant grazers are drawn to the perennial water of the Tarangire River.

Tarangire lies in the floor of the Central Rift Valley, a semi-arid region that's still inhabited by various traditional pastoralists, most famously the Maasai, who live in the immediate vicinity of the national park, but also the Barabaig and other subgroups of the Datoga further southwest. And although most tourists confine their exploration of this area to the national park, there is plenty else to see in the area, ranging from the underrated rock art of the Maasai Escarpment to the pretty Lake Babati and the little-known Mount Hanang, an isolated volcanic relict that rises from the Rift Valley floor to the impressive altitude of 3,417m.

As with the other game reserves along the northern circuit, Tarangire is serviced by a range of lodges to suit most tastes, and is most easily explored as part of a road safari out of Arusha, though fly-in packages are available. At a push, the rock art of the Maasai Escarpment could be visited as a day trip out of Tarangire, but it's more sensible perhaps to make an overnight excursion of it, either camping at Kolo near the paintings or bedding down at one of the basic lodges in the small town of Kondoa further south. Babati and Mount Hanang are rather more accessible by public transport, and an excellent cultural tourism project in Babati can arrange mountain hikes as well as trips on the lake.

TARANGIRE NATIONAL PARK

The 2,850km² Tarangire National Park lies at the core of a much more expansive ecosystem, one that also comprises the 585km² Tarangire Conservation Area (TCA) and some 5,000km² of unprotected land extending across the Maasai Steppes. In general, the Tarangire region is drier than the Serengeti, but also more densely vegetated, covered primarily in a tangle of semi-arid acacia and mixed woodland. The park's dominant geographic feature is the Tarangire River, which is flanked by a cover of dense elephant grass and a sporadic ribbon of riparian woodland dotted with the occasional palm tree. A memorable feature of the park is its immense baobab trees, which are abundant throughout.

As with the Serengeti, there is a great deal of migratory movement within the greater Tarangire ecosystem. During the wet season, most of the wildlife disperses from the park onto the Maasai Steppes, while the wildebeest and zebra move northwest to the Rift Valley floor between lakes Natron and Manyara. In

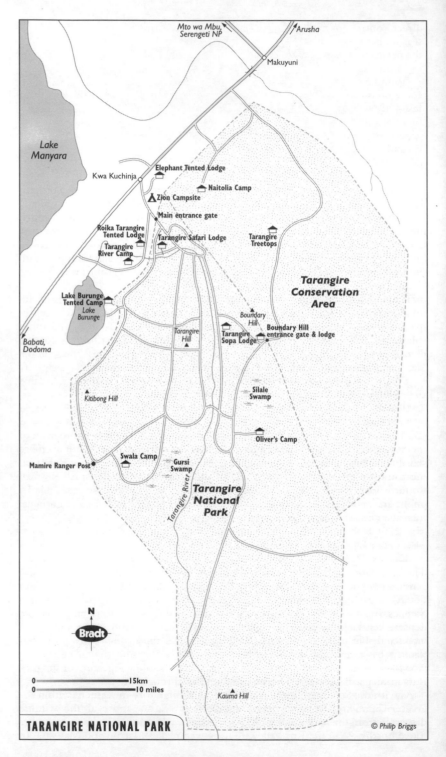

Mto wa Mbu,
Serengeti NP

Arusha

Makuyuni

Lake
Manyara

Elephant Tented Lodge

Kwa Kuchinja

Naitolia Camp

Zion Campsite

Main entrance gate

Roika Tarangire
Tented Lodge

Tarangire Safari Lodge

Tarangire
Treetops

Tarangire
River Camp

Tarangire
Conservation
Area

Lake Burunge
Tented Camp

Lake
Burunge

Boundary
Hill

Tarangire
Hill

Tarangire
Sopa Lodge

Boundary Hill
entrance gate & lodge

Babati,
Dodoma

Kitibong Hill

Silale
Swamp

Oliver's Camp

Swala Camp

Mamire Ranger Post

Gursi
Swamp

Tarangire
National
Park

N

Bradt

0   15km
0   10 miles

Kauma Hill

TARANGIRE NATIONAL PARK

© Philip Briggs

direct contrast to the Serengeti, Tarangire comes into its own during the dry season, between July and November, when the large herds of game attracted to the permanent waters of the Tarangire River make this reserve as alluring as any in Tanzania.

Abutting the northeastern border of the national park, the TCA consists of four contiguous tracts of land that were used for trophy hunting until ownership was restored to their traditional Maasai inhabitants in the late 1990s. The TCA now functions as a buffer conservation area to the national park, encompassing the main watershed for the Tarangire River, the wetlands around Gosuwa Swamp, and the migration routes used by wildebeest and zebra to reach their breeding grounds near Lolkisale Mountain. The Maasai communities in the area earn revenue from levies raised by tourist lodges such as Tarangire Treetops, Boundary Hill and Naitolia. An important difference between these lodges and their counterparts within the national park is that game walks and night drives are permitted.

A detailed booklet, *Tarangire National Park*, is available from the National Parks office in Arusha. The park entrance fee of US$35 per person per 24 hours should ideally be paid by MasterCard or Tanapa Card (issued at any Exim Bank). No other cards are accepted, nor are travellers' cheques, and cash payments attract a 50% penalty.

GETTING THERE AND AWAY Tarangire lies about 7km off the main Arusha–Dodoma road. Coming from Arusha, this road is tarred as far as the turn-off to the park, which is clearly signposted about 100km south of Arusha and 20km past Makuyuni (the junction for Manyara and the Serengeti). Most people tag a visit to Tarangire onto a longer safari, but if your time or money is limited, a one- or two-day stand-alone safari would be a viable option.

WHERE TO STAY
Exclusive

Swala Camp (9 rooms) ↘ 027 250 9817; f 027 250 8273; e tanzania@sanctuarylodges.com; www.sanctuarylodges.com. Situated in the southern half of the park, this classic luxury tented camp stands in a grove of tall acacia trees overlooking the remote Gurusi Swamp, where it is wonderfully isolated from any other lodge or the more popular game-viewing circuits. The camp itself is something of a magnet for wildlife: the *swala* (antelope) for which it is named are much in evidence, especially a resident herd of impala, accompanied by a noisy entourage of vervet monkeys, guineafowl & various plovers, buffalo-weavers & starlings. The small waterhole in front of the camp attracts elephants in Jul & Aug, while a near-resident lion pride & the occasional leopard pass through with surprising regularity. The food is excellent, especially the bush dinners held in a grove of baobabs about 5 mins' drive from camp, & the quality of tented accommodation is in line with the best lodges of this type in southern Africa. *US$470/640 FB inc drinks, or US$575/850 full game package; substantial discount Nov–mid-Dec & Jan–Mar. Closed Apr & May.*

Tarangire Treetops Lodge (20 rooms) ↘ 027 254 0630/9; f 027 254 8245; e info@elewana.com; www.elewana.com. Situated to the northeast of the national park within the Tarangire Conservation Area, this architecturally innovative lodge consists of 20 spacious & luxurious en-suite tree houses, each with a floor area of 65m², perched up in the branches of a stand of massive baobab trees – so atmospheric & comfortable it almost seems a shame to leave them to go on a game drive! Because the lodge lies on private land, activities such as game walks, birding walks along a nearby watercourse, night drives & mountain-biking excursions supplement the usual diurnal game drives. The quality of game viewing in the immediate vicinity varies seasonally, but it's only 45 mins by road to Boundary Hill Gate, the main road circuit in northern Tarangire. Ideal for honeymooners, this lodge is also a wonderful place to recover from jetlag at the start of a safari, or to stretch your legs at the end of one. A portion of the room rate funds community projects such as the construction of schools & bore holes. *US$1,118/1,490 sgl/dbl FB, inc most drinks, laundry, transfer to/from Kuro airstrip, dropping to*

US$1,020/1,360 in Mar, Nov & early Dec, & US$945 11,260 Apr & May. Full game package inc drives an additional US$100 pp.

⌂ **Oliver's Camp** (5 rooms) ☎ 027 250 4118; m 0784 763338; e info@asilialodges.com; www.asilialodges.com. This excellent bush camp is located near the Silale Swamp within the park boundaries, but far away from the busy northern section of the park so that activities can usually be undertaken without seeing other tourists. It caters both for 2-night stays incorporated into more wide-ranging safaris as well as for extended stays of 3 days or more, in which visitors explore the area on foot (it is the only location where walking safaris can be undertaken inside Tarangire) & by vehicle, as well as spending 1 or more nights at a mobile fly-camp. The lodge itself is unpretentious & comfortable rather than opulently luxurious, the guides are unusually personable & knowledgeable, & a superb library of natural history books underscores the emphasis on substance over style – strongly recommended to anybody seeking a genuinely holistic bush experience. US$620/890 sgl/dbl FB, or US$730/1110 full game package, with low-season discount of c20%.

⌂ **Boundary Hill Lodge** (8 suites) m 0787 293727; e simon@eastafricansafari.info; www.tarangireconservation.com. Situated on a hilltop in the private Lolkisale concession, outside the Boundary Hill entrance gate, this new lodge is the first in Tanzania to have a local community shareholding, with the Maasai village of Lolkisale

owning 50%. The 8 spacious suites, set among the rocky cliffs, are individually designed & lavishly decorated, & have private sitting areas & wide balconies offering spectacular views over the Silale & Gosuwa swamps, where elephant & buffalo are resident, & en-suite facilities include cast-iron baths. In addition to daytime game drives into the national park, the lodge offers guided game walks with the local Maasai & night drives. The concession lies on a migration route & is particularly busy with wildlife over Nov–Mar. US$390/480 sgl/dbl FB, or US$550 pp full game package.

⌂ **Naitolia Camp** (5 rooms) m 0787 293727; e simon@eastafricansafari.info; www.tarangireconservation.com. Under the same management as Boundary Hill, this excellent bush camp is set in an exclusive 55km² tract of Maasailand on the northern border of the park. The main camp consists of attractively furnished huts made entirely of canvas & local materials such as stone, wood & thatch, each with a king-size bed with walk-in netting & a private balcony, shower & toilet with a view. Because the camp lies on communal land, guided game walks can be undertaken, with a good chance of spotting giraffe, elephant, zebra & a variety of antelope & birds, & it is possible to be taken to Maasai *bomas* that don't normally receive tourists. Also on offer are overnight walking safaris within the community area, using fly-camps. *It is leased out to a private operator at the time of writing, but expect rates to be comparable to Boundary Hill.*

Upmarket

⌂ **Lake Burunge Tented Camp** (16 rooms) ☎ 027 254 4556; m 0784 207727; f 027 250 8937; e twc-reservations@habari.co.tz; www.tanganyikawildernesscamps.com. Overlooking the seasonal Lake Burunge, this intimate new lodge lies some 10 mins drive outside from the park boundary, some distance south of the main Tarangire tourist circuit, in an area of dense bush known for its populations of dry-country antelope such as lesser kudu & gerenuk. Accommodation is in spacious & attractively rustic en-suite twin & dbl tents built on stilted platforms & shaded by *makuti* roofs. The camp is well positioned for game drives, & it also offers guided nature walks, along with canoe trips when the lake holds water. Comparable in feel & style to several places in the exclusive category, this under-utilised camp is good value. US$300/400 sgl/dbl FB.

⌂ **Tarangire Safari Lodge** (40 rooms) ☎ 027 253 1447; m 0784 202777; f 027 254 4752;

e bookings@tarangiresafarilodge.com; www.tarangiresafarilodge.com. This owner-managed lodge is the oldest in the park, with a sublime location on a tall bluff overlooking the Tarangire River. Game viewing from the veranda can be excellent, with large herds of hippo, giraffe & other animals coming down to the river to drink. The grounds are also highly attractive to birders, not only for the remarkably habituated hornbills, buffalo-weavers & starlings that parade around the common areas, but also for the host of smaller birds that are resident in the acacia scrub. Facilities include a swimming pool. This comfortable, unpretentious & well-managed lodge ranks as one of my favourites anywhere on the northern circuit. The accommodation in standing tents with en-suite toilets is outstanding value. US$109/188 sgl/dbl B&B. Lunch US$16, dinner US$20, limited selection of snacks available at around US$5 pp.

⌂ **Tarangire Sopa Lodge** (75 rooms) ⦨ 027 250 0630/9; f 027 250 8245; e info@sopalodges.com; www.sopalodges.com. Set in the heart of the national park, the Tarangire Sopa is the largest & most conventionally luxurious – & least 'bush' – of the lodges around Tarangire. The facilities & accommodation match the customary high standards of this chain, with smart self-contained suites & excellent food. The indifferent location, alongside a small & normally dry watercourse below a baobab-studded slope, is compensated for by the superb game viewing in the surrounding area – the roads between here & Tarangire Safari Lodge are far & away the most rewarding in the park. *US$ 320/550 sgl/dbl FB; US$265/450 in Mar, Nov & early Dec, & US$100/200 over Apr–May.*

⌂ **Tarangire River Camp** (20 rooms) ⦨ 027 254 7007; m 0787 532785; e zina@mbalimbali.com; www.mbalimbali.com. Situated just 3.5km outside the main gate as the crow flies (but more like 15km by road) this relatively new tented camp lies within a 250km² concession, set aside for conservation by the Maasai community of Minjingu, along the northwest boundary of the national park. The camp is set below a massive old baobab on a cliff overlooking

the (normally dry) Minjingu River, a tributary of the Tarangire, & wildlife can be quite prolific in the vicinity seasonally, even though it is not in the park. The lodge is centred on a vast stilted thatch & timber structure composed of a main lounge, a small library, & a dining & cocktail area, offering sweeping views across the riverbed to the Maasai Steppes. The large en-suite tents with private balcony, 2 x ³/₄ beds & 24hr solar power are good value. *US$250/350 sgl/dbl FB.*

⌂ **Roika Tarangire Tented Lodge** (21 rooms) ⦨ 027 250 9994; e info@roikatours.com; www.roikatours.com. Situated in a stand of tangled acacia scrub about 5km from the park entrance gate *en route* to Tarangire River Lodge, this recent addition to Tarangire's burgeoning selection of lodges offers accommodation in large en-suite standing tents set on stilted wooden platforms. Shaded by *makuti* roofs, the tents are very comfortable, with 2 dbl beds each, & decorated simply in safari style, though the rustic mood is undermined somewhat by the tackily sculpted animal-shaped baths. The main building is thatched with open sides & overlooks a large swimming pool. Good value. *US$125 pp FB.*

Budget and camping

Ⴟ Zion Campsite This small private camp, formerly known as Kigongoni, lies a few kilometres outside the park entrance gate, & is used by many budget camping safaris to Tarangire. To get there, turn off from the main Arusha–Dodoma road as if heading towards the entrance gate to Tarangire. After about 2km, you'll see the campsite immediately to your left. *Tsh10,000 pp.*

For those on camping safaris, there are a couple of campsites within Tarangire. These are strong on bush atmosphere, but short on facilities, and rather costly at the customary US$20 per person.

EXPLORING TARANGIRE NATIONAL PARK Most people spend only one day in Tarangire and thus concentrate on the game-viewing roads along its well-developed northern circuit, which follows the river between the Tarangire Safari Lodge and Tarangire Sopa Lodge. And this is unambiguously the best game-viewing area, especially in the dry season when many of the greater Tarangire ecosystem's 25,000 wildebeest, 30,000 zebra, 6,000 buffalo, 2,700 giraffe, 5,500 eland, 30,000 impala and 2,000 warthog congregate along the river, the only source of water for many miles around.

Tarangire is justifiably famous for the prolific elephant herds that congregate along the river during the dry season. According to the most recent census, now several years old, the region supports a total population of around 3,000 elephant, but it's likely the population has grown significantly in the interim. Indeed, in peak times, it is no exaggeration to say that you might see 500 elephants over the course of a day here. Tarangire's elephants used to be a lot more skittish than their counterparts in Manyara and Ngorongoro, but these days they are quite relaxed.

The full range of large predators is present on the main tourist road circuit too, but the dense vegetation can make it relatively difficult to pick up the likes of lion and leopard, even though they are quite common. Two localised antelope that occur in Tarangire are the fringe-eared oryx and gerenuk, though neither is seen with great regularity. Of the smaller mammals, the colonial dwarf mongoose is characteristic of the park, and often seen on the termite hills where it breeds.

Tarangire is a great birdwatching site, with around 500 species recorded to date. A wide range of resident raptors includes bateleur, fish eagle and palmnut vulture, while the river supports saddle-billed and yellow-billed storks and several other waterbirds. Characteristic acacia birds are yellow-necked spurfowl, orange-bellied parrot, barefaced go-away bird, red-fronted barbet, and silverbird. A personal favourite is the red-and-yellow barbet, with its quaintly comical clockwork duet, typically performed on termite mounds.

Tarangire's location at the western limit of the Somali-Maasai biome means it harbours several dry-country bird species at the extremity of their range, among them vulturine guineafowl, Donaldson-Smith's nightjar, pink-breasted lark, northern pied babbler and mouse-coloured penduline tit. It is also the easiest place to observe a pair of bird species endemic to the dry heartland of central Tanzania: the lovely yellow-collared lovebird, and the somewhat drabber ashy starling, both of which are common locally.

For those with sufficient time to explore beyond the main tourist circuit, the Lake Burunge area offers the best chance of seeing bushbuck and lesser kudu, while the Kitibong Hill area is home to large herds of buffalo, and Lamarkau Swamp supports hippo and numerous waterbirds during the wet season. Further south, cheetahs favour the southern plains, while Mkungero Pools is a good place to look for buffalo, waterbuck and gerenuk.

KONDOA ROCK ART SITES

Inscribed as a UNESCO World Heritage Site in 2006, the prodigious prehistoric rock art that adorns the Maasai Escarpment south of Tarangire is the most intriguing and extensive outdoor gallery of its sort in east Africa, and among the most ancient and stylistically varied anywhere on the African continent. Although it extends over an area of 2,350km^2, the best-known panels are centred around Kolo, a village situated about 20km north of Kondoa and 50km south of Babati on the Great North Road. About three hours' drive from Tarangire, the site also makes for a reasonably straightforward addition to a safari, even though it has thus far received greater attention from academics and archaeologists than from tourists.

At least 150 painted panels are documented in Kondoa region, the largest concentration north of the Zambezi and south of the Sahel. The major rock art sites around Kolo are situated within small caves or beneath solid overhangs aligned to an east–west axis, a propensity that might reflect the preferences of the artists, or might simply have provided conditions favourable to preservation from the elements. The paintings are tentatively placed at between 200 and 4,000 years old, and the identity and intent of the artists is a matter of speculation.

The proposal to enshrine this rock art as a UNESCO World Heritage Site stated that 'in terms of conservation, most of the sites are stable and relatively well preserved although there are a variety of problems including salt encrustation, erosion, water damage, and fading caused by sunlight'. The rock art has been left undisturbed by locals in the past because it is regarded as sacred or taboo, but the erosion of traditional beliefs in recent years places the art at greater threat, and a few sites have already been partially defaced by graffiti or scratching. Unofficial guides have also been recorded splashing the paintings with water to bring out the colours for snap-happy visitors, and many tourists photograph the paintings using a flash, which can cause great damage to sensitive organic pigments over repeated

© Philip Briggs

Babati,
Arusha

KONDOA ROCK ART SITES

Bubu River

Bereku

Kisese

(A1–4)

Itololo
(A6)

(A7–8) Kandaga

N

Bradt

0 ——————————— 10km
0 ——————————— 6 miles

(A12) Masange

Cheke
(A17)

Fenga Hill
(D1–3)

Itundwe

Tlawi Hill
(D4–15,
15–20)

Lusangi/Pahi

Mnenya   (B4–13)

Kolo

(B1–3)

Kundusi
(B15–19)

Bubu River

Lake Haubi

Singida

Lake Serya   Kondoa

Dodoma

KEY
Rock-Art sites indicated by code   (B1–3)

There is a strangely eerie sensation attached to emerging from a remote and nondescript tract of bush to be confronted by an isolated panel of primitive paintings executed by an artist or artists unknown, hundreds or maybe thousands of years before the time of Christ. Faded as many of the panels are, and lacking the perspective to which modern eyes are accustomed, one can still hardly fail to be impressed by the fine detail of many of the animal portraits, or to wonder at the surrealistic distortion of form that characterises the human figures. And, almost invariably, first exposure to these charismatic works of ancient art prompts three questions: how old are they, who were the artists and what was their intent?

When, who and why? The simple answers are that nobody really knows. The broadest time frame, induced from the absence of any representations of extinct species in the rock galleries of Kondoa, places the paintings at less than 20,000 years old. The absence of a plausible tradition of attribution among the existing inhabitants of the area – a Gogo claim that the paintings were the work of the Portuguese can safely be discounted – makes it unlikely that even the most modern paintings are less than 200 years old. Furthermore, experts have noted a clear progression from the simplest early styles to more complex, expressive works of art, and a subsequent regression to the clumsy graffiti-like finger painting of the 'late white' phase, indicating that the paintings were created over a substantial period of time.

Early attempts at dating the Kondoa rock art concentrated on categorising it chronologically based on the sequence of superimposition of different styles on busy panels. The results were inconclusive, even contradictory, probably because the superimposition of images was an integral part of the art, so that a foreground image might be roughly contemporaneous with an image underneath it. It is also difficult to know the extent to which regional style, or even individual style, might be of greater significance than chronological variation. The most useful clue to the age of the paintings is the stratified organic debris deposited alongside red ochre 'pencils' at several sites. Carbon dating of a handful of sites where such deposits have been found suggests that the artists were most active about 3,000 years ago, though many individual paintings are undoubtedly much older. The crude 'late white' paintings, on the other hand, are widely agreed to be hundreds rather than thousands of years old, and there is evidence to suggest that some underwent ritual restoration by local people who held them sacred into historical times.

The identity of the artists is another imponderable. In the first half of the 20th century, the rock art of southern Africa was solely attributed to 'Bushmen' hunter-gatherers, a people whose click-based Khoisan tongue is unrelated to Bantu and who are of vastly different ethnic stock from any Bantu speakers. True, the Bushmen are the only people who practised the craft in historical times, but much of the rock art of southern Africa (like that of eastern Africa) dates back thousands of years. Coincidentally, two of east Africa's few remaining click-tongued hunter-gatherers, the Sandawe and the Hadzabe, both live in close proximity to the main concentration of Tanzanian rock art, but neither has a tradition relating to the paintings.

Given that the archaeological record indicates east-southern Africa was populated entirely by hunter-gatherers when the paintings were probably executed, furthermore that a succession of human migrations has subsequently passed through the region, postulating an

exposure. More bizarrely, a local legend that the Germans buried a hoard of gold near one of the rock art sites during World War I has resulted in fortune-seekers manually excavating and dynamiting close to several rock sites.

The pigments for the paintings were made with leaf extracts (yellow and green), powdered ochre and manganese (red and black) and possibly bird ancestral link between the artists of Kondoa and modern hunter-gatherers would be tenuous in the extreme. If anything, the probable chronology of the rock art points in the opposite direction. Assuming that creative activity peaked some 3,000 years ago, it preceded the single most important known migration into east Africa, the mass invasion of the Bantu-speakers who today comprise the vast majority of Tanzania's population. Most probable, then, that a Bantu- or perhaps Nilotic-speaking group, or another group forced to migrate locally as a ripple effect of the Bantu invasion, moved into the Kondoa region and conquered or assimilated the culture responsible for the rock art, resulting in the gradual stylistic regression noted by archaeologists. All that can be said about the artists with reasonable certainty is they were hunter-gatherers whose culture, were it not for the painted testament left behind on the granite faces of Kondoa, would have vanished without trace.

The most haunting of the questions surrounding the rock art of Kondoa is the intent of its creators. In determining the answer to this, one obstacle is that nobody knows just how representative the surviving legacy might be. Most extant rock art in Kondoa is located in caves or overhangs, but the small number of faded paintings that survive on more open sites must be a random subset of similarly exposed panels that have been wiped clean by the elements. We have no record, either, of whether the artists dabbled on canvases less durable than rock, but unless one assumes that posterity was a conscious goal, it seems wholly presumptuous to think otherwise. The long and short of it, then, is that the extant galleries might indeed represent a sufficiently complete record to form a reliable basis for any hypothesis, but they might just as easily represent a fraction of a percentage of the art executed at the time. Furthermore, there is no way of telling whether rocks were only painted in specific circumstances – it is conceivable that the rock art would maker greater sense viewed in conjunction with other types of painting that have not survived.

Two broad schools of thought surround the interpretation of Africa's ancient rock art. The first has it that the paintings were essentially recreational, documentary and/or expressive in intent – art for art's sake, if you like – while the second regards them to be mystical works of ritual significance. It is quite possible that the truth of the matter lies between these poles of opinion. A striking feature of the rock art of Kondoa is the almost uniform discrepancy in the styles used to depict human and non-human subjects. Animals are sometimes painted in stencil form, sometimes filled with bold white or red paint, but – allowing for varying degrees of artistic competence – the presentation is always naturalistic. The people, by contrast, are almost invariably heavily stylised in form, with elongated stick-like bodies and disproportionately round heads topped by a forest of unkempt hair. Some such paintings are so downright bizarre that they might more reasonably described as humanoid than human (a phenomenon that has not gone unnoticed by UFO theorists searching for prehistoric evidence of extraterrestrial visits).

The discrepancy between the naturalistic style favoured for animals and highly stylised presentation of humans has attracted numerous theoretical explanations. Most crumble under detailed examination of the evidence, but all incline towards supporting the mystical or ritualistic school of interpretation. Ultimately, however, for every tentative answer we can provide, these enigmatic ancient works pose a dozen more questions. It is an integral part of their charisma that we can speculate to our heart's content, but will never know the whole truth!

excrement (white), and were bound together by animal fat. The subjects and styles vary greatly. Most common are various animals, with giraffe and eland probably the most widely depicted creatures. A large number of panels also contain human figures, generally highly stylised and often apparently engaged in ritual dances or ceremonies. At some sites, identifiable subjects are vastly outnumbered by abstract or geometric figures, the significance of which can only be guessed at.

GETTING THERE AND AWAY Although few people do so, it is perfectly feasible to tag Kolo onto a standard northern circuit safari. Some safari companies will visit the

THE BARABAIG

The Barabaig are the most populous of a dozen closely related tribes, collectively known as the Datoga or Tatoga. At around 100,000, the Datoga are one of Tanzania's smaller ethno-linguistic groupings, but their territory, centred on Mount Hanang, extends into large semi-arid tracts within Arusha, Dodoma and Singida.

Superficially similar to, and frequently confused with, their Maasai neighbours by outsiders, the Barabaig are dedicated cattle-herders, speaking a Nilotic tongue, who have steadfastly resisted external pressure to forsake their semi-nomadic pastoralist ways. Unlike the Maasai, however, the Barabaig are representatives of the earliest known Nilotic migration into east Africa from southwest Ethiopia. Their forebears probably settled in western Kenya during the middle of the first millennium AD, splitting into two groups. One – the Kalenjin – stayed put. The other, the proto-Datoga, migrated south of Lake Natron 500 to 1,000 years ago to the highlands of Ngorongoro and Mbulu, and Rift Valley plains south towards Dodoma.

Datoga territory was greatest before 1600, thereafter being eroded by migrations of various Bantu-speaking peoples into northern and central Tanzania. The most significant incursion came in the early 19th century, with the arrival of the Maasai. Oral traditions indicate that several fierce territorial battles were fought between the two pastoralist groups, resulting in the Maasai taking over the Crater Highlands and Serengeti Plains, and the Datoga retreating to their modern homeland near Mount Hanang. The Lerai Forest in Ngorongoro Crater is said to mark the grave of a Datoga leader who fell in battle in about 1840, and the site is still visited by Datoga elders from the Lake Eyasi area. The Maasai call the Barabaig the 'Mangati' (feared enemies), and the Barabaig territory around Mount Hanang is sometimes referred to as the Mangati Plains.

The Barabaig used to move around the plains according to the feeding and watering requirements of their herds. They tend a variety of livestock, including goats, donkeys and chickens, but their culture and economy revolve around cattle, which are perceived to be a measure of wealth and prestige, and every part and product of the animal, including the dung, is ingested, or worn or used in rituals. In recent years, agriculture has played an increasingly significant support role in the subsistence of the Barabaig, which together with increased population pressures has more or less put paid to the nomadic lifestyle.

Barabaig territory receives an average annual rainfall of less than 500mm, which means that water is often in short supply. Although the area is dotted with numerous lakes, most are brackish and unsuitable to drink from. Barabaig women often walk miles every day to collect gourds of drinking water, much of which comes from boreholes dug with foreign aid. The cattle cannot drink from the lakes directly when water levels are low and salinity is high, but the Barabaig get around this by digging wells on the lakes' edges and allowing the water to filter through the soil. Even so, the herders won't let their cattle drink from these wells on successive days for fear that it will make them ill.

Barabaig social structure is not dissimilar to that of the Maasai, although it lacks the rigid division into hierarchical age-sets pivotal to Maasai and other east African pastoralist societies. The Barabaig do not recognise one centralised leader, but are divided into several hereditary clans, each answering to a chosen elder who sits on a tribal council. The central unit of society is the family homestead or *gheida*, dwelt in by one man, his wives and their unwed offspring. This consists of a tall outer protective rock art sites as a day trip from Tarangire National Park, a slightly pressured but by no means impossible foray. Equally, you could spend a night in the region, either pitching tent at the campsite at Kolo or sleeping in a guesthouse in the small town of Kondoa 20km further south. Whatever you choose to do, all visitors must report to the Department of Antiquities office at the main junction in Kolo, to pay the

wall, built of thorny acacia branches and shaped like a figure eight, with one outer gate entered through a narrow passage. Within this wall stand several small rectangular houses – low, thick-roofed constructions of wooden poles plastered with mud – and the all-important cattle stockade. Different huts are reserved for young men, young women, wives and elders. A number of *gheida* may be grouped together to create an informal community, and decisions are made communally rather than by a chief.

Patrilineal polygamy is actively encouraged. Elders accumulate four or more wives, up to three of which might share one hut, but marriage within any given clan is regarded to be incestuous. The concept of divorce is not recognised, but a woman may separate from her husband and return to her parents' home under some circumstances. The Barabaig openly regard extramarital sex to be normal, even desirable, although a great many taboos and conventions dictate just who may have intercourse with whom, and where they can perform the act. Traditionally, should a married woman bear a child whose biological father is other than her husband, the child remains the property of the husband – even when husband and wife are separated.

The appearance of the Barabaig is striking. The women wear heavy ochre-dyed goatskin or cowhide dresses, tasselled below the waist, and decorated with colourful yellow and orange beads. They adorn themselves with brass bracelets and neck-coils, tattoo circular patterns around their eyes, and some practise facial scarification. Men are less ornate, with a dyed cotton cloth draped over the shoulders and another around the waist. Traditionally, young men would prove themselves by killing a person (other than a Datoga) or an elephant, lion or buffalo, which might be used as the base of a ceremonial headdress along with the pelts of other animals they had killed.

The Barabaig are monotheists who believe in a universal creator whom they call Aseeta. The sun – which they give the same name – is the all-seeing eye of Aseeta, who lives far away and has little involvement in their lives. Barabaig legend has it that they are descended from Aseeta's brother Salohog, whose eldest son Gumbandaing was the first true Datoga. Traditionally, most Barabaig elders can trace their lineage back over tens of generations to this founding father, and ancestral worship plays a greater role in their spiritual life than direct worship of God. Oddly, given the arid nature of their homeland, the Barabaig have a reputation as powerful rainmakers. It is said that only 1% of the Barabaig have abandoned their traditional beliefs in favour of exotic religions – a scenario which, judging by the number of internet sites devoted to the state of the Barabaig's souls, has spun quite a few evangelical types into a giddy froth.

The above statistic is indicative of the Barabaig's stubborn adherence to a traditional way of life. In the colonial era, the Barabaig refused to be co-opted into the migrant labour system, on the not unreasonable basis that they could sell one good bullock for more than the typical labourer would earn in a year. Other Tanzanians tend to view the Barabaig as embarrassingly primitive and ignorant – when the Nyerere government outlawed the wearing of traditional togas in favour of Westernised clothing, the Barabaig resolutely ignored them. Even today, few have much formal education or speak a word of English – it would, for that matter, be pretty unusual to meet a Barabaig who could hold a sustained conversation in Swahili.

nominal entrance fee and collect a guide. A recommended specialist guide based on Kondoa is Moshi Changai (m *0784 948858;* e *moshi@tanzaniaculturaltours.com; www.tanzaniaculturaltours.com*).

WHERE TO STAY Accommodation options in the immediate vicinity of Kolo are restricted to an attractive campsite run by the Department of Antiquities in Kolo on the banks of the seasonal Kolo River about 3km east of town towards Mungomi wa Kolo and Mnenya. Water and toilet facilities are available at the campsite, but food and other drinks must be brought from Kolo. There is no accommodation in Kolo, but basic local guesthouses can be found in Pahi and Masange, both of which lie below the Maasai Escarpment within walking distance of several good sites. Far better, though not exactly luxurious, are the **New Planet Hotel** (✆ *026 236 1957*) and **Sunset Beach Hotel** (m *0784 948858*) in the town of Kondoa, both of which charge around Tsh10,000–12,000 for a no-frills en-suite room with net, fan and running water.

SOME KEY SITES The region's recognised showpiece is the cluster of three sites situated about 10km from Kolo on Ichoi Hill and prosaically labelled B1–3 but more evocatively known as Mungomi wa Kolo (Dancers of Kolo). This cluster of panels provides a good overview of the region's rock art, and – aside from the last, very steep, foot ascent to the actual panels – is easily reached in a 4x4 vehicle. Probably the most intriguing of the panels is B1, which includes several fine but very faded paintings of animals (giraffe, leopard, zebra and rhino), as well as some abstract designs and numerous humanoid forms. One striking scene, dubbed The Abduction, depicts five humanoid forms with stick bodies, spindly limbs and distended heads. The two figures on the right have elongated heads, while the two on the left have round heads, as does the central figure, which also appears to have breasts and whose arms are being held by the flanking figures. Leakey interpreted the painting as a depiction of an attempted abduction, but it could as easily depict a ritual dance or similar. And one website makes an oddly compelling case for this haunting scene providing evidence of extraterrestrial visits – according to this interpretation, a separate scene to the right shows another alien standing in a hot-air balloon!

Panels B4–13 all lie close to the base of the escarpment near the twin villages of Lusangi and Pahi, about 12km from Kolo. The art here is not as impressive as B1–3, but it is a more suitable goal to those unwilling or unable to climb steep footpaths. Several figures here stand out, the most notable being a 70cm-high outlined giraffe superimposed on a very old painting of a rhino. Below this, a red-and-yellow figure of an eland with a disproportionately small head is regarded to be one of the oldest paintings in the region. From Pahi, it's possible to drive another 12km to Kinyasi, where sites B14–19 are situated in a valley below Kome Mountain. The most interesting of these sites is a 1m² panel of small, finely executed antelopes, which also includes one of the few known examples of a painting depicting a homestead.

Those with more time could explore the Bubu River sites, clustered to the west of the Great North Road about 12km from Kolo. Here you'll find several well-preserved panels in close proximity. Don't miss panel D3 on Fenga Hill, sometimes referred to as the Trapped Elephants after the central painting of two elephants surrounded by a stencilled oblong line. Some experts believe that this depicts an elephant trap, a theory supported by three fronds below the elephants that might well represent branches used to camouflage a pit. Others believe that it might have a more mystical purpose, placing the elephants in a kind of magic circle. A trickle of circles dripping from the left base of the picture could be blood, or the elephants' spoor.

About 3km south of Fenga Hill, the immediate vicinity around Tlawi Hill hosts at least ten panels, numbered D4–5 and D15–22. A dedicated enthusiast could easily devote half a day to this cluster of very different sites – D19 is notable for an almost life-size and unusually naturalistic attempt to paint a human figure in a crouched or seated position, D20 depicts several seated human figures, D22 is also known as the Red Lion for the striking painting of a lion that dominates the shelter, and D17 has a rare action painting of a hunter killing a large antelope with bow and arrow. Several other interesting human figures are found on these twin shelters.

BABATI AND HANANG

The small but bustling market town of Babati, which lies on the Great North Road some 70km north of Kondoa and 170km south of Arusha, is known for the eponymous lake on its outskirts, which supports a good selection of egrets, waders, pelicans, storks and other waterbirds, as well as several pods of hippo. Babati is also the springboard for a visit to Mount Hanang, an extinct volcano which towers to an altitude of 3,418m – the fourth-highest point in Kilimanjaro, Meru and Lolmalasin – above the surrounding plains and is visible from hundreds of kilometres away on a clear day.

Seldom visited by tourists, Hanang is nevertheless eminently climbable, and – because it lies outside the national park system – it forms a very affordable prospect by comparison with Kilimanjaro or Meru. The slopes support the usual range of montane forest and grassland habitats, and offer excellent views over a stretch of the Rift Valley studded with smaller volcanic cones and shallow lakes. The normal springboard for climbing Hanang is the dusty and rather amorphous small town of Katesh, which straddles the Singida road 75km west of Babati at the southern base of the mountain.

The attractions of the Hanang area are not restricted to the mountain. Several substantial lakes also lie in the vicinity of Katesh, including the shallow and highly saline Lake Balangida, which is set at the base of the Rift Valley scarp immediately north of Mount Hanang. Katesh also forms the starting point for an obscure but not unrewarding back route to Karatu and the Ngorongoro Crater Highlands via Basotu, Dongobesh and Mbulu. And one could scarcely spend time in the area without being conscious of the Barabaig, charismatic pastoralists who have consciously retained their traditional way of life.

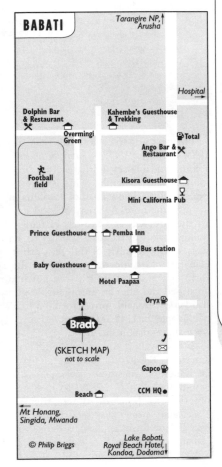

BABATI

Tarangire NP,↑ Arusha

Hospital

Dolphin Bar & Restaurant
Overmingi Green
Kahembe's Guesthouse & Trekking
Total
Ango Bar & Restaurant
Football field
Kisora Guesthouse
Mini California Pub

Prince Guesthouse — Pemba Inn
Bus station
Baby Guesthouse
Motel Paapaa
N
Oryx
Bradt
(SKETCH MAP)
not to scale
Gapco
Beach — CCM HQ
←Mt Honang, Singida, Mwanda
© Philip Briggs
Lake Babati, Royal Beach Hotel, Kondoa, Dodoma↓

LEGEND OF THE CAT

Emma Thomson

To maintain the balance of power between the sexes the Rangi people have devised an ingenious plan. From sunrise to sunset the men are in charge, but come sunset the rule of power shifts to the women, allowing them to reign supreme until daybreak.

This female empowerment was established following the legend of the cat, told to me by a village member one starry night near Kelema:

The cat was looking for a hero. While walking through the jungle one day he befriended a cheetah. 'This cheetah is surely the strongest and fastest animal in the forest – he will be my hero,' exclaimed the cat.

The next day, while walking with the cat through the undergrowth, the cheetah encountered a lion. They fought until the cheetah fell to the ground dead. 'The lion then must be the strongest and fiercest animal in the forest – he will be my new hero,' decided the cat.

The following day the two felines encountered an elephant foraging in the trees. Startled, the elephant charged, killing the lion. Bemused, the cat approached the elephant; 'You truly are the king of the jungle – will you be my hero?'

One day the elephant and cat were surprised by a man hunting. In fear the man killed the elephant and after cutting the meat from the body he turned for home. The cat decided to follow this beast that could defeat an animal without even touching it.

On arriving home the man approached his wife who took the elephant meat from him and set to work in the kitchen. The cat gasped: 'This woman surely must be the queen of all beasts – an animal that can take from another without fighting! She will forever be my hero.' From that day on, the cat is always to be found in the kitchen admiring its heroine.

The best way to explore this region is with the Kahembe Trekking (✆ 027 253 1088; m 0784 397477; e *kahembeculture@yahoo.com; www.kahembeculturalsafaris.com*) a commendable set-up that started life in the mid 1990s and is still managed by founder Jaos Kahembe. This is an excellent contact for anybody who wants to explore a little-known part of Tanzania in an organised manner, but without paying through the nose. A variety of local tours are offered, of which the most popular are the three-day and two-day Hanang climbs. Other trips range from a three-day walking safari in Barabaig country to a 16-day expedition that includes overnight stays with a number of different ethnic groups, as well as an ascent of Mount Hanang, and game walks around Lake Burunge (bordering Tarangire National Park). These overnight trips are not luxurious by any standard, but they are well organised and offer an unforgettable glimpse into an ancient way of life. They are also very reasonably priced, at US$40 all-inclusive per person per day for one or two people, or US$30 for larger groups. For further details, check out the website www.authenticculture.org.

Alternatively, if you prefer the DIY approach, plenty of buses connect Arusha to Katesh via Babati and there are plenty of affordable guesthouses in both towns – the Kahembe Guesthouse (*same contact details as Kahembe's above*) in Babati and Colt Guesthouse (✆ 027 253 0030) in Katesh are recommended budget options. Far superior to both of these, the Royal Beach Hotel (m 0784 395814; e *meshakingomuo@yahoo.com*) boasts an idyllic situation on a small peninsula on Lake Babati, forms an ideal base for visiting the Kondoa Rock Art, trekking Mount Hanang or cruising Lake Babati, and charges Tsh 30,000 for a double with large beds, net, TV and en-suite toilet and shower.

8

Lake Manyara and the Northern Rift Valley

Before it ascends to the Ngorongoro Highlands and Serengeti, the main road heading westward from Arusha runs through a dramatic stretch of the Rift Valley whose semi-arid, acacia-studded floor, hemmed in by a sheer western escarpment, supports a chain of shallow mineral-rich lakes. The largest of these lakes, Eyasi, Manyara and Natron, are prone to substantial cyclic fluctuations in their water level, dependent to some extent on local rainfall patterns, but each one of them reaches a length of 50km or greater when full.

The most accessible and popular tourist attraction in this area is Lake Manyara, the northwestern shores of which are protected within an eponymous national park known for its dense elephant population, tree-climbing lions and prodigious birdlife. Only two hours' drive from Arusha on a good asphalt road, Lake Manyara makes for an obvious first port of call on any northern Tanzanian safari. It is serviced by several upmarket lodges, most of which run along the escarpment above the lake, while a selection of cheaper lodgings and campsites is centred on the village of Mto wa Mbu near the entrance gate.

Considerably more remote, Lake Natron is the site of a legendary but practically inaccessible flamingo breeding ground, as well as the majestic (and, if you're up to it, climbable) volcano known to the Maasai as Ol Doinyo Lengai (God's Mountain). Relatively few tourists pass through the Natron area, but it makes for a worthy off-the-beaten-track addition to any safari, especially as it can be used as an alternative route between the northern Serengeti and Mto Wa Mbu, meaning that you don't need to retrace your steps by driving through Ngorongoro Conservation Area in both directions. One mid-range lodge and a few more basic campsites service Lake Natron.

More remote still, Eyasi is the largest of these Rift Valley lakes, and of interest primarily for the Hadzabe hunter-gatherers who inhabit its semi-arid hinterland. The lake is also something of a travel cul-de-sac, since it is connected to the outside world by just one rough road running southwest from the small town of Karatu. A basic campsite and one recently opened lodge can be found in the vicinity of Eyasi; both can arrange visits to Hadzabe encampments.

LAKE MANYARA NATIONAL PARK

Lake Manyara is a shallow, alkaline lake set at the base of a sheer stretch of the Western Rift Valley escarpment. The northwestern part of the lake and its immediate hinterland are protected in a scenic 330km² national park whose diversity of terrestrial habitats – grassy floodplain, rocky escarpment, acacia woodland and lush groundwater forest – seems all the more remarkable given that up to two-thirds of the surface area comprises water. And this habitat diversity is reflected in Manyara's varied mammalian fauna, with buffalo, giraffe, olive baboon, blue monkey and various antelopes likely to be seen in the course of any game drive.

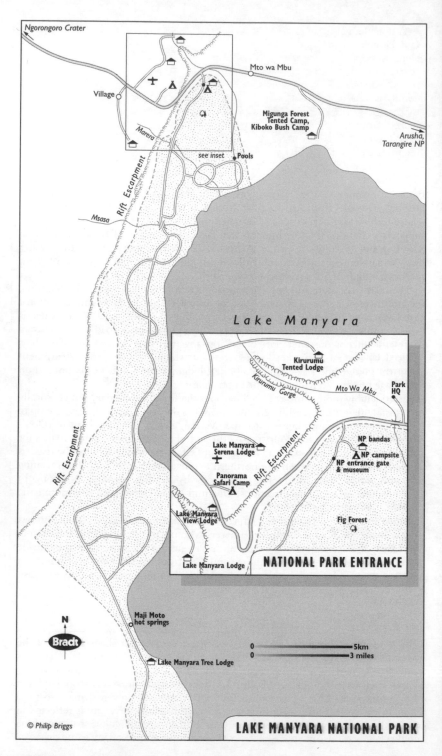

Ngorongoro Crater

Mto wa Mbu

Village

Migunga Forest
Tented Camp,
Kiboko Bush Camp

Arusha,
Tarangire NP

Marera

see inset

Pools

Msasa

Rift Escarpment

Rift Escarpment

Lake Manyara

Kirurumu
Tented Lodge

Kirurumu Gorge

Mto Wa Mbu

Park
HQ

Lake Manyara
Serena Lodge

NP bandas

NP campsite

NP entrance gate
& museum

Panorama
Safari Camp

Rift Escarpment

Lake Manyara
View Lodge

Fig Forest

Lake Manyara Lodge

NATIONAL PARK ENTRANCE

N

Bradt

Maji Moto
hot springs

0   5km
0   3 miles

Lake Manyara Tree Lodge

© Philip Briggs

LAKE MANYARA NATIONAL PARK

A notable feature of Lake Manyara is its prolific elephants, as immortalised by Iain Douglas-Hamilton in his 1970s book *Amongst the Elephants*. Although the elephant population suffered a subsequent decline due to poaching, this was not as severe as in many larger parks in southern Tanzania and numbers are now fully recovered. The elephants in Manyara are generally very relaxed around vehicles by comparison with their counterparts in Tarangire and the southern reserves, which makes for great elephant watching – especially as there are still some serious tuskers around.

Manyara, despite its small size, is a great birding reserve, with almost 400 species recorded. As Duncan Butchart, writing in the CCAfrica *Ecological Journal*, noted, 'If a first-time birdwatcher to Africa had the time to visit only a single reserve in Tanzania, then Manyara must surely be it.' It's perfectly feasible for a casual birder to see 100 species here in a day, ranging from a variety of colourful bee-eaters, barbets, kingfishers and rollers to the gigantic ground hornbill and white-backed pelican. Substantial flocks of flamingo are also present when the water level is suitable. A remarkable 51 diurnal raptor species are known from the park, of which 28 are resident or regular. In addition, six species of owl are regularly recorded.

Manyara's well-defined game-viewing circuit kicks off a high proportion of safaris through northern Tanzania. And the park is a valuable addition to a safari of several days' duration, offering the opportunity to see several species that are less common or shyer elsewhere on the northern circuit. Those on shorter safaris, however, might reasonably elect to forsake Manyara's more subtle attractions for an additional day on the predator-rich plains of the Serengeti.

The booklet *Lake Manyara National Park*, published by Tanzania National Parks, gives detailed coverage of the park's flora and fauna, as does the newer booklet *Lake Manyara* published by the African Publishing House in association with Tanapa. The park entrance fee of US$35 per person per 24 hours should ideally be paid by MasterCard or Tanapa Card (issued at any Exim Bank). No other cards are accepted, nor are travellers' cheques, and cash payments attract a 50% penalty.

GETTING THERE AND AWAY The only entrance gate to Lake Manyara lies at the northern end of the park on the outskirts of the village of Mto wa Mbu. The 120km drive from Arusha takes less than two hours following the completion of the new surfaced road from Makuyuni.

WHERE TO STAY AND EAT There is only one lodge situated within the park boundaries, the new Lake Manyara Tree Lodge. There is, however, plenty of accommodation bordering the park. Most of the tourist-class lodges are situated on the Rift Valley escarpment overlooking Lake Manyara, while the budget accommodation and campsites are dotted around the small village of Mto wa Mbu outside the main entrance gate.

Exclusive

⌂ **Lake Manyara Tree Lodge** (10 rooms) ⟍ 027 254 8549/8038 or (South Africa) +27 (0)11 809 4447; e inboundsales@andbeyond.com; www.andbeyond.com. Opened in 2003 as a replacement for the defunct Maji Moto Lodge, Lake Manyara Tree Camp is a small, luxurious tented camp operated by &Beyond (formerly CCAfrica) deep in a mahogany forest about 20 mins' drive south of the hot springs at Maji Moto. Like other &Beyond lodges, Lake Manyara Tree Lodge offers the ultimate in exclusive bush luxury, consisting of 10 stilted en-suite tree houses built with wood & makuti, & with private decks offering great views of the escarpment. Exciting walking routes run from the lodge to the lakeshore through the forest, while other facilities include a swimming pool & personal butler service. FB rates of US$950, dropping to US$625 pp over Mar, May, Nov & early Dec, inc all meals, drinks & activities. Closed during Apr.

Upmarket

🏠 **Lake Manyara Serena Lodge** (54 rooms) 📞 028 262 1507; f 028 262 1520; e reservations@serena.co.tz; www.serenahotels.com. This smart & popular upmarket lodge is situated on the edge of the escarpment overlooking the lake & its environs. Like other lodges in the Serena chain, it is a very appealing set-up, run through by a small wooded stream that attracts a wide range of birds including chattering flocks of breeding weavers. Adventure activities such as abseiling & mountain biking are offered by Serena Active, a company based in the lodge. Accommodation is in attractively furnished ethnic-looking rondavels with private balconies. The buffet food is generally very good. *US$375/550 sgl/dbl FB; US$225/335 Apr–Jun.*

🏠 **Lake Manyara Lodge** (100 rooms) 📞 027 254 4595; f 027 254 8633; e res@hotelsandlodges-tanzania.com; www.hotelsandlodges-tanzania.com. The oldest & most spectacularly located of the lodges that line the escarpment above Lake Manyara, this former government property fell into a terribly rundown state in the 1990s, & it remains somewhat architecturally confrontational. That said, the new private management embarked on an ambitious facelift over the course of 2008, & the renovated & redecorated common areas & en-suite rooms are now in line with other similarly priced lodges on the northern safari circuit. A definite attraction of this lodge is the attractively wooded grounds centred upon a large swimming pool, but its single best feature remains the peerless view over Manyara's groundwater forest & lake, with the Rift Valley hills fading to the horizon. With binoculars, you should be able to pick out elephants, giraffes & buffaloes on the Rift Valley floor; closer to home, there is good birding within the lodge grounds. *Rates on application.*

🏠 **Kirurumu Tented Lodge** (20 rooms) 📞 027 250 7011/7541; f 027 254 8226; e info@kirirumu.net; www.kirurumu.net. Owned & managed by Hoopoe Adventure Tours, this popular tented lodge is perched on the rift escarpment to the north of the Serena, from where it offers a grand view across the plains of the Rift Valley to the north of Lake Manyara. The unpretentious rustic bush atmosphere that characterises Kirurumu contrasts strongly with that of the other more built-up lodges on the Rift escarpment, & it will be far more attractive to people who want to feel like they are sleeping in the bush rather than in a large hotel. There's plenty of small wildlife around too, ranging from bush squirrels to foot-long yellow-speckled plated lizards by day to hedgehogs & bushbabies by night – plus a wide variety of birds. The food is good & the service friendly & efficient. Accommodation is in comfortable & secluded en-suite dbl tents, each of which has a private veranda. *US$176/249 sgl/dbl B&B, or US$238/386 FB in high season, US$105 pp FB low season.*

MTO WA MBU

This village, which lies close to the Lake Manyara entrance gate, sees a large volume of tourist traffic and is said locally to be the only place in Tanzania where representatives of 120 Tanzanian tribes are resident. Mto wa Mbu is the normal base for budget safaris visiting Lake Manyara, and even if you aren't staying in the village or visiting Lake Manyara, your safari driver will probably stop at the huge curio market in the hope of picking up a commission. Mto wa Mbu (pronounced as one word, mtowambu) means River of Mosquitoes, and if you do spend the night here, then you'll be in no doubt about how it got its name. By day, the curio dealers who will swarm around you the moment you leave your vehicle might draw an obvious analogy.

A clutch of inexpensive walking tours out of Mto wa Mbu have been set up as part of a cultural tourism programme with the assistance of SNV (Stichting Nederlandse Vrijwilligers (Foundation of Netherlands Volunteers)). One of the most interesting of these walks is the papyrus lake tour, which takes you to the Miwaleni waterfall, as well as to a papyrus lake where Rangi people collect basket- and mat-weaving material, and to the homesteads of Sandawe hunter-gatherers. Other tours take you to Balaa Hill, which boasts excellent views over the village and lake, and to Chagga farms and Maasai bomas. The tourism programme is run out of the Red Banana Restaurant in the centre of the village, where you must pay your fees, arrange a guide and (if you like) rent a bicycle, as well as paying the mandatory village development fee.

Moderate

🏠 **Migunga Forest Camp** (19 rooms) ☎ 027 255 3243/250 6315; e migunga@moivaro.com; www.moivaro.com. This well-established but little-known tented camp, recently taken over by Moivaro Lodge, shares many assets with Kirurumu, but it is considerably more downmarket in feel, & priced accordingly. Migunga has a winning location in a yellow fever forest about 2km by road from Mto wa Mbu. When the lake is high, the camp lies close to the northeast & can be reached by a short walking trail, but at the time of writing the distance to the lake is around 5km. Reedbuck, bushbuck & buffalo sometimes pass through, while a troop of vervet monkeys is more or less resident & the lesser bushbaby is often seen at night. Roughly 70 acacia-associated bird species have been recorded within the camp. Accommodation is in comfortable dbl standing tents with en-suite hot showers. Price-wise, it's an excellent compromise between the smarter but more expensive lodges & the relatively utilitarian accommodation in Mto wa Mbu. *US$206/257 sgl/dbl FB, with low-season discount in Apr & May.*

🏠 **Kiboko Bush Camp** (12 rooms) ☎ 027 253 9152; e kibokotz@yahoo.co.uk;

Budget and camping

🏠 **Njake Jambo Lodge & Campsite** (16 rooms) ☎ 027 250 1329; e info@njake.com; www.njake.com. Following extensive renovations over recent years, this once rather low-key campsite in the heart of Mto wa Mbu is now a top quality budget lodge, offering accommodation in 4 double-storey blocks each containing 4 smart en-suite rooms with 2 four-poster beds with netting, satellite TV, fridge, phone & tiled bathroom with hot shower. The large green gardens also host a restaurant, bar & large swimming pool area, as well as a shady campsite. It lacks the bush atmosphere of pricier lodges, but still seems excellent value. *US$60/90 sgl/dbl B&B, US$50/60 in low season; camping US$7.*

🏠 **Twiga Campsite & Lodge** m 0754 288430; e twigacampsite@yahoo.com; www.twigacampsite.com. Once the pick of several locally run lodges in Mto wa Mbu, Twiga lies in neatly cropped gardens in the heart of town. It consists of a spacious campsite, popular with budget safari operators, & a block of large self-contained dbl rooms with hot water & nets. There is a 'wild video show' in the lounge every evening, a good restaurant, & a recently constructed swimming pool to flop around in by day. It remains a likeable set-up, but it's not as smart or well managed as Njake

www.equatorialsafaris.com. Situated a few hundred metres away from Migunga, & similar in price & standard, though with a more nondescript setting, this new camp provides comfortable accommodation in en-suite standing tents, each with 2 x ¾ beds, & set on a stilted wooden platform with a small private veranda. Once again, it's good value. *US$100 pp FB. Camping US$5 pp.*

🏠 **Lake Manyara View Lodge** (70 rooms) ☎ 027 250 1329; m 0732 978474; e reservations@lakemanyaraview.com; www.lakemanyaraview.com. This recently constructed lodge rises above the Rift Valley escarpment alongside the main asphalt road between Mto wa Mbu & Karatu. In common with other lodges along the escarpment, it offers stunning views over Lake Manyara & Rift Valley floor, but its enormous potential is totally undermined by the unfinished look of the common areas (including an empty swimming pool) & general aura of operating with all lights dimmed. Nothing wrong with the en-suite rooms, however, & the ambience & service must surely improve once the lodge becomes more settled. *US$60/100–150/170 sgl/dbl B&B, depending on season & room type, FB another US$30 pp.*

Jambo, & overall it seems like poor value by comparison. *Camping US$10 pp; dbl rooms US$70 (old wing), US$110 (new wing).*

🏠 **National Park Bandas & Campsite** ☎ 027 250 3471/4082; f 027 250 8216; e info@tanzaniaparks.com; www.tanzaniaparks.com. Situated in a lovely forest glade immediately outside the national park entrance gate, this is easily the most inherently attractive place to stay in this price category, & comparatively good value too. Clean self-contained brick bandas have hot water but no net — the latter a serious omission in Mto wa Mbu. Facilities include a kitchen & dining area, & an elevated tree house looking into the forest canopy. *Camping US$30 pp; US$20 pp banda accommodation for non-residents.*

🏕 **Migunga Campsite** ☎ 027 255 3243/250 6315; e migunga@moivaro.com; www.moivaro.com. Situated alongside the eponymous tented camp & under the same management, this campsite boasts a stunning setting amid the yellow fever trees, & facilities include hot showers — highly recommended. *US$5 pp.*

🏕 **Panorama Safari Camp** m 0755 118514. Boasting a prime location on the escarpment overlooking the lake, this relatively new campsite set only 500m from the main asphalt road towards Karatu forms

Lake Manyara National Park is famous for its tree-climbing lions, which, unlike conventional lions, habitually rest up in the branches for most of the day, to the excitement of those lucky tourists who chance upon them. But while the tree-climbing phenomenon is well documented, the explanation behind it remains largely a matter of conjecture.

In the 1960s, Stephen Makacha undertook research into lion behaviour at Manyara to compare with similar studies being conducted by George Schaller in the Serengeti. In Schaller's book, *The Serengeti Lion: A Study of Predator–Prey Relations*, he noted that:

> The lions in the Lake Manyara National Park climbed trees far more often than those in the Serengeti. They were resting in trees on two-thirds of the occasions on which we encountered them during the day. The reason why Manyara lions rest in trees so often is unknown. Fosbrooke noted that lions in the Ngorongoro Crater ascended trees during an epidemic of biting flies, but this is an unusual situation … and the vegetation in the various parks is in many respects so similar that no correlation between it and tree climbing is evident. The Manyara lions sometimes escaped from buffalo and elephant by climbing trees, but there would seem to be no reason for lions to remain in them all day because of the remote chance that they might have to climb one. I think that the behaviour represents a habit, one that may have been initiated by for example, a prolonged fly epidemic, and has since been transmitted culturally.

Schaller's suggestion that the lions were climbing trees to avoid flies made the most sense to me, but I had also heard that the lions climbed to enjoy the cool breezes that came off the lake, and to keep a lookout for prey and threats. So I decided to make notes whenever I saw the lions in order to explore these theories. For every sighting I noted whether flies were present on the ground or in the trees; the temperature and breeze conditions; whether buffalo or elephant were in the vicinity; how high up the tree the lions were and the view it afforded; and the species of tree.

In the 1960s, Iain Douglas-Hamilton noted that on 80% of the occasions when tree-climbing lions were observed, they were in one of just 17 individual trees. These favoured trees were so well known to park guides at the time that they were given

an attractively located alternative to the more mundane cheapies in town. There's a clean shower & toilet block with running hot water, & other facilities include a bar & restaurant, though the swimming pool that was due to be constructed a few years back has yet to materialise. *Large standing tent with bedding & towel provided Tsh7,000 pp; camping in own tent Tsh4,000.*

EXPLORING LAKE MANYARA

Game drives For logistical reasons, most safari operators visit the national park in the afternoon. But there's much to be said for doing an additional morning game drive, starting as soon as possible after the entrance gate opens at 06.30. Manyara is wonderfully and unexpectedly peaceful in the morning, and you'll probably see fewer other vehicles over two or three hours than you would in five minutes in the late afternoon. By being the first car through the gate, you also stand a chance of disturbing one of the park's profuse but skittish leopards before it vanishes into the thickets for the day.

All game drives start at the entrance gate, which lies on the northern boundary near Mto wa Mbu. From the entrance gate, the main road winds for several kilometres through a cool, lush, mature groundwater forest dominated by large ficus trees and a tangle of green epiphytes. With appropriate jungle noises supplied by outsized silvery-cheeked hornbills, this is one part of the northern safari circuit particular names and – to protect them from debarking and destruction by elephants – wrapped in coils of wire mesh. My observations indicated a similar pattern. Lions were found to be resting in trees on about half of the times they were sighted, and although six different tree species were used, three – *Acacia tortilis*, *Kigelia africana* and *Balanites aegyptiaca* – accounted for 90% of sightings. Specific trees were usually favoured, and the lions often moved a considerable distance to reach them.

In most cases the lions were seen to be resting during the heat of the day, and they would usually come down at dusk. Only 5% of sightings coincided with hot weather and breezy conditions, and at most sightings there was no significant breeze, so it seems unlikely that the lions climb to escape the heat. Although buffalo have been documented killing lions at Manyara, there was never any sign of the lions taking to trees to avoid harassment. Most of the time the lions were found to be resting approximately 5–6m above the ground, which afforded them a better view of their surroundings, but since the trees were normally in densely vegetated areas, it would have been difficult for them to observe any potential prey or threat.

My conclusions were similar to those of Makacha and Schaller. Although lions that I found resting on the ground were apparently not greatly concerned by biting flies, lions observed in trees were surrounded by flies in only 10% of cases, when flies were present on the ground below them about 60% of the time. Because the lions generally rested above 5m and flies were seldom encountered at this height, it seems likely that the behaviour was originally initiated during a fly epidemic, and it has since been passed on culturally. I observed the cubs of the Maji pride begin their attempts to climb up to the adults when they were about seven or eight months old. It seemed definitely to be a case of 'lion see, lion do', as there was no apparent reason as to why they should have climbed. Once they had mastered climbing, they too spent a lot of time playing and climbing up and down the trees. More thorough research would be required to fully understand the reasons for this unusual and fascinating behaviour.

Edited from Notes on Tree-climbing Lions of Manyara *by Kevin Pretorius, a former manager of Maji Moto Lodge, as originally published in the* CC Africa Ecological Journal, *volume 2:79–81 (2000). The journal can be ordered online at www.wildwatch.com.*

that might conjure up images of Tarzan swinging into view. It's a good place to see olive baboons (Manyara supports a density of 2,500 baboons in 100km^2), which plonk themselves down alongside the road, sometimes in the company of the smaller and more beautiful blue monkey. The shy bushbuck might also be encountered here, but otherwise the main point of faunal interest is the diversity of birds and butterflies.

The road emerges from the forest onto the northern floodplain, where a series of small pools on the Mto wa Mbu River supports a wide variety of birds, notably giant kingfisher and African and painted snipe. This is a lovely spot, too, with the Rift Valley escarpment rising to the west, and the sparsely vegetated floodplain of Lake Manyara stretching to the south. Giraffes are common in this area, many of them so dark in colour that they appear to be almost melanistic. The nearby hippo pool was submerged for several years following the El Niño floods of 1997/98, causing the hippos to relocate to the main lake, but it has since re-emerged and harbours several dozen soaking, yawning hippos, as well as an impressive selection of waterbirds. An ongoing relic of the El Niño floods is the ghost forest of dead tree stumps lining the floodplain between the fig forest and the lakeshore.

For large mammals, the best road runs inland of the lake to the Maji Moto (literally 'Hot Water') springs in the south. The tangled acacia woodland here offers views across the floodplain, where you should see large herds of zebra and wildebeest, and the occasional warthog, impala, Kirk's dik-dik and giraffe. The acacia woodland is the place to look out for the famous tree-climbing lions of Manyara (see box, pages 180–1) – though on an afternoon game drive, the safari driver grapevine is bound to ensure that you know about any arboreal lions long before you encounter them. The marshy area around the hot springs reliably harbours waterbuck and plenty of buffaloes, while several pairs of klipspringer are resident on the rocky escarpment base towards the southern end of the park.

Other activities An exciting aspect of Lake Manyara is a varied selection of mild adventure activities operated exclusively by Green Footprint Adventures for Serena Active, which is based out of the Manyara Serena Lodge, but takes on guests staying at other lodges in the area. These activities offer safari-goers tired of bouncing around dusty roads within the confines of a vehicle the opportunity to stretch their legs or arms in natural surrounds. No experience is required for any of the activities, and all equipment is supplied at no extra cost. On-the-spot enquiries are welcomed, but bookings can be made through any safari operator or directly through Serena Active (❧ *027 254 4635;* m *0784 203 0000;* e *info@greenfootprint.co.tz; www.serenahotels.com/serena-active.htm or www.greenfootprint.co.tz*).

The most popular of these activities is mountain biking down the Rift Valley escarpment, with a variety of different itineraries available. Also offered are an afternoon walk through the groundwater forest in the Kirurumu Gorge outside the national park entrance, and a village walk with a local guide through agricultural areas around Mto wa Mbu. For more hardcore adventurers, there is the option of abseiling down the rift escarpment above the lake with a qualified instructor, and canoeing on Lake Manyara may one day be resumed if the water level is sufficiently high. Most of these activities cost around US$50–70 per person, and a more recent – and costly – addition to the programme is a microlight flight over the lake or (if you like) as far north as Natron.

KARATU

This small, dusty town straddling the main road between Manyara and Ngorongoro may not look like much when you pass through coming from Arusha, but it is probably the most populous settlement anywhere along the 400km length of the B142 between Arusha and Mwanza. Tourists on a lodge-based safari typically pass through Karatu in the blink of an eye *en route* to Ngorongoro or the Serengeti, but the town does boast a fair selection of tourist facilities, including several restaurants, guesthouses, filling stations and shops. The Ngorongoro Camp & Lodge in the town centre has the most affordable internet connection in the region, and the nearby National Bank of Commerce offers good foreign exchange facilities and an ATM where local currency can be drawn against Visa cards.

Nicknamed 'safari junction', Karatu and environs forms a popular stopover for budget camping safaris, since camping is a lot cheaper here than in the Ngorongoro Conservation Area (NCA), but it's a useful base for day trips into Ngorongoro Crater. The farmland west of Karatu also hosts an ever growing number of more exclusive lodges built to supplement the limited bed space in the NCA, and these too are routinely used as bases for crater game drives. Note, however, that sleeping outside the NCA precludes the sort of very early start that allows you to get the most from a trip into Ngorongoro Crater. Another worthwhile overnight trip (or, at a push, day trip) out of Karatu is to Lake Eyasi and one of the Hadzabe settlements in the surrounding area (see box, *The last hunter-gatherers,* pages 184–5).

GETTING THERE AND AWAY Karatu is now connected to Mto wa Mbu and Arusha by a good asphalt road and the drive from Mto wa Mbu takes about one hour. Regular buses connect Karatu to Arusha via Mto wa Mbu, and the Ngorongoro Camp & Lodge in Karatu rents 4x4 vehicles for day safaris to Ngorongoro and Manyara.

WHERE TO STAY
Exclusive

🏠 **Gibb's Farm** (18 rooms) ☏ 027 250 8930; f 027 250 8930; e reservations@gibbsfarm.net; www.gibbsfarm.net. This small boutique hotel, once a rather low-key & idiosyncratic farm retreat on the eastern border of the NCA, has blossomed into one of the most sumptuously exclusive lodges anywhere in northern Tanzania following radical renovations in 2008. It lies 6km from Karatu along a rough dirt road, on an active coffee estate bordering an extensive patch of indigenous forest on the Ngorongoro footslopes. The main building, a converted 1920s farmhouse, retains a strong period feel with its red polished cement floor, tall bay windows, hearty home-style 4-course meals, & leather & wood furnishing, & its colonial ambience is far removed from the relative uniformity that characterises so many upmarket lodges in northern Tanzania. The exquisite suites combine a more contemporary feel with farmhouse rusticity, & are seriously spacious, with 2 dbl beds in each bedroom, varnished wood floors, comfy armchairs, lovely views from the balcony, & the choice of indoor or outdoor shower. The lodge is a popular base for day trips into the Ngorongoro Crater (though it does have the disadvantage of lying away from the spectacular crater rim) & other activities include bird walks with the resident naturalist, cultural & farm excursions, a 2hr hike to a waterfall & cave made by elephants on the forested slopes of the crater, & a spa & massage room. There is no TV or swimming pool. US$514/744 sgl/dbl FB.

Upmarket

🏠 **Ngorongoro Farm House** (50 rooms) ☏ 027 254 4556; m 0784 207727; f 027 250 8937; e twc-reservations@habari.co.tz; www.tanganyikawildernesscamps.com. Situated on a large coffee farm about halfway between Karatu & the NCA, this stylish new lodge offers luxurious en-suite accommodation in 3 separate camps of large semi-detached thatched cottages with views across what will eventually be a 9-hole golf course to the forested slopes of Ngorongoro. There's a very pleasant swimming pool area & the restaurant serves good country-style cooking. In terms of location, it doesn't quite match up to the lodges on the crater rim, but it's much smaller & has a less packaged feel than most lodges set within the NCA. Guided nature walks, mountain biking & other leg-stretching activities are on offer too. US$300/400 sgl/dbl FB.

🏠 **Tloma Mountain Lodge** (20 rooms) ☏ 027 254 4556; m 0784 207727; f 027 250 8937; e twc-reservations@habari.co.tz; www.tanganyikawildernesscamps.com. Situated about 1km from Gibbs Farm & sharing a similarly lovely view over the forested Ngorongoro footslopes, this attractive new lodge is set in spacious grounds that lead down to a wooden deck enclosing a large swimming pool. Accommodation is in large, cosy earth-coloured cottages with colonial-style green corrugated iron roofs, screed floors, wood ceilings, fireplaces, 4-poster king-size or twin beds, & a large bathroom with shower. The food here is excellent, & facilities include birdwatching tours, massage, village walks, internet, coffee plantation demonstrations & the obligatory day tours to Ngorongoro Crater. US$300/400 sgl/dbl FB.

🏠 **Plantation Lodge** (16 rooms) ☏ 027 253 4364/5; m 0744 393180; e info@plantation-lodge.com; www.plantation-lodge.com. This popular German-owned lodge is set in flowering grounds only 2km from the Ngorongoro road a few kilometres out of Karatu. It has a classic whitewash & thatch exterior, complemented by the stylish décor of the spacious self-contained rooms, making for a refreshingly individualistic contrast to the chain lodges that characterise the northern circuit, while also forming a good base for day trips to Ngorongoro Crater. US$270/390 sgl/dbl FB.

Moderate

🏠 **Bougainvillea Lodge** (24 rooms) ☏ 027 253 4063; f 027 253 4600; e bougainvillea@habari.co.tz; www.bougainvillealodge.net. Owned & managed by the highly regarded Tanzanian chef Reggie Bayo, this comfortable new lodge lies in large but characterless gardens about 300m from the main road towards NCA just outside Karatu. For budget-conscious tourists it's a decent compromise

The Hadza (or Hadzabe) of the Lake Eyasi hinterland, which lies to the east of Karatu, represent a unique – and increasingly fragile – link between modern east Africa and the most ancient of the region's human lifestyles and languages. Numbering at most 2,000 individuals, the Hadza are Tanzania's only remaining tribe of true hunter-gatherers, and their Hadzame language is one of only two in the country to be classified in the Khoisan family, a group of click-based tongues that also includes the San (Bushmen) of southern Africa.

The Hadza live in nomadic family bands, typically numbering about 20 adults and a coterie of children. Their rudimentary encampments of light grass shelters are erected in the space of a couple of hours, and might be used as a base for anything from ten days to one month before the inhabitants move on. These movements, though often rather whimsical, might be influenced by changes in the weather or local game distribution, and a band will also often relocate close to a fresh kill that is sufficiently large to sustain them for several days. The Hadza are fairly indiscriminate about what meat they eat – anything from mice to giraffe are fair game, and we once saw a family roasting a feral cat, fur and all, on their campfire – but baboons are regarded to be the ultimate delicacy and reptiles are generally avoided. Hunting with poisoned arrows and honey gathering are generally male activities, while women and children collect roots, seeds, tubers and fruit – vegetarian fodder actually accounts for about 80% of the food intake.

The Hadza have a reputation for living for the present and they care little for conserving food resources, probably because their lifestyle inherently places very little stress on the environment. This philosophy is epitomised in a popular game of chance, which Hadza men will often play – and gamble valuable possessions on – to while away a quiet afternoon. A large master disc is made from baobab bark, and each participant makes a smaller personal disc, with all discs possessing distinct rough and smooth faces. The discs are stacked and thrown in the air, an action that is repeated until only one of the small discs lands with the same face up as the large disc, deciding the winner.

Many Hadza people still dress in the traditional attire of animal skins – women favour impala hide, men the furry coat of a small predator or baboon – which are often decorated with shells and beads. Hadza social groupings are neither permanent nor strongly hierarchical: individuals and couples are free to move between bands, and there is no concept of territorial possession. In order to be eligible for marriage, a Hadza man must kill five baboons to prove his worth. Once married, a couple might stay together for several decades or a lifetime, but there is no taboo against separation and either partner can terminate the union at any time by physically abandoning the other partner.

---

betwen quality & cost, offering unpretentious accommodation in neat & comfortably decorated tiled cottages set in a circle around the swimming pool area. All cottages have twin or king-size beds with netting, a fan, a fireplace, a sitting area with cane furniture & a private balcony facing the pool.

Budget and camping

🏠 **Ngorongoro Safari Resort** (32 rooms) 📞 025 253 4287/90; **f** 025 253 4288; **e** info@ ngorongorocampandlodge.net; www.ngorongorocampandlodge.net. This smart & modern complex in Karatu offers accommodation in clean, comfortable self-contained rooms, as well as

The lodge serves good meals & has a gift shop specialising in local Iraqw beadwork, & it's a useful base for excursions to Eyasi & Ngorongoro. Good value. *US$109/201 sgl/dbl FB.*

camping in a neat well-maintained site. The attached supermarket, though not cheap, is the best in Karatu, & the restaurant serves a good range of tasty Indian & continental dishes at around Tsh8,000 per main course. Other facilities include an internet café (Tsh1,000 per 15 mins), a filling station, a large

The Hadza might reasonably be regarded as a sociological and anthropological equivalent of a living fossil, since they are one of the very few remaining adherents to the hunter-gatherer lifestyle that sustained the entire human population of the planet for 98% of its history. In both the colonial and post-independence eras, the Hadza have resolutely refused to allow the government to coerce them into following a more settled agricultural or pastoral way of life. The last concerted attempt to modernise Hadza society took place in the 1960s, under the Nyerere government, when a settlement of brick houses with piped water, schools and a clinic was constructed for them alongside an agricultural scheme. Within ten years, the model settlement had been all but abandoned as the Hadza returned to their preferred lifestyle of hunting and gathering. The government, admirably, has since tacitly accepted the right of the Hadza to lead the life of their choice; a large tract of communal land fringing Lake Eyasi has been set aside for their use and they remain the only people in Tanzania automatically exempt from taxes!

The Khoisan language spoken by the Hadza is also something of a relic, belonging to a linguistic family that would almost certainly have dominated eastern and southern Africa until perhaps 3,000 years ago. As Bantu-speaking agriculturists and pastoralists swept into the region from the northwest, however, the Khoisan-speaking hunter-gatherer communities were killed or assimilated into Bantu-speaking communities or forced to retreat into arid and montane territories ill-suited to herding and cultivation. This slow but steady marginalising process has continued into historical times: it has been estimated that of around 100 documented Khoisan languages only 30 are still in use today, and that the total Khoisan-speaking population of Africa now stands at less than 200,000.

That most Khoisan languages, if not already extinct, are headed that way, takes on an added poignancy if, as a minority of linguists suggested throughout the 20th century, the unique click sounds are a preserved element of the very earliest human language. In order to investigate this possibility, the anthropological geneticists Alec Knight and Joanna Mountain recently analysed the chromosome content of samples taken from the geographically diverse San and Hadza, and concluded that they 'are as genetically distant from one another as two populations could be'. Discounting the somewhat improbable scenario that the clicking noises of the Hadza and San languages arose independently, this wide genetic gulf would imply a very ancient common linguistic root indeed. Several linguists dispute Knight and Mountain's conclusion, but if it is correct, then Hadzame, along with Africa's other dying Khoisan languages, might represent one last fading echo of the first human voices to have carried across the African savanna.

To learn more about the Hadzabe visit www.hadzabe.com.

bar with satellite TV, & 4x4 rental. US$79/128 sgl/dbl B&B; camping US$5 pp.

🏠 **Kudu Lodge & Campsite** (15 rooms) ✆ 025 253 4055; m 0744 474792; f 025 453 4268; e kuducamp-lodge@kuducamp.com; www.kuducamp.com. The best of a few campsites in the Karatu area catering primarily to budget camping safaris, Kudu Lodge lies on a small farm just outside town in the direction of Ngorongoro. It offers a good selection of activities ranging from day trips to the crater to local village walks. In addition to camping on a neat lawn, it also now offers a range of en-suite rooms catering more to the mid-range market than budget safari-goers. *Camping US$15 pp; different room types US$150/158–US$237/274 sgl/dbl B&B.*

LAKE EYASI AND SURROUNDS

The vast Lake Eyasi verges on the remote southern border of the Ngorongoro Conservation Area, and lies at the base of the 800m Eyasi Escarpment, part of the Western Rift Valley wall. In years of plentiful rain, this shallow soda lake can extend for 80km from north to south, but in drier periods it sometimes dries out altogether to form an expansive white crust. Most of the time, it falls somewhere between the two extremes: an eerily bleak and windswept body of water surrounded by a white muddy crust and tangled dry acacia scrub. When we visited in the middle of the day, the lake had a rather desolate appearance, but I imagine that it might be very beautiful in the early morning or late afternoon. There is little resident wildlife in the area, aside from dik-dik and baboons, but depending on the water level, the lake is an important source of fish for Arusha and it often supports hundreds of thousands of flamingos as well as a variety of other waterbirds.

Lake Eyasi is primarily of interest to tourists as the home of the Hadza (see box *The last hunter-gatherers*), and it is now reasonably straightforward to visit a Hadza encampment and go hunting with its male inhabitants. These visits must be arranged through one of three appointed guides based in the largest village in the region, which is called Mang'ola but sometimes referred to as Lake Eyasi (misleadingly, since it actually lies about 10km from the lakeshore). In addition to the entrance fee of US$2 per person charged by the Council of Mang'ola, fees of around US$10 and US$15 per party must be paid respectively to the guide and to the Hadza encampment visited.

We felt our visit to a Hadza encampment highly worthwhile. The people struck us as being very warm and unaffected, and going on an actual hunt was a primal and exciting experience – even if the waiting wives were mildly disappointed when their men returned to camp with only two mice and one bird to show for their efforts. Other travellers we've spoken to were luckier, though do be warned that a temporary conversion to vegetarianism might be in order should you come back from the hunt with a baboon or another large mammal – as a guest, you'll be offered the greatest delicacy, which is the raw liver. It could be argued that regular exposure to tourists might erode the traditional lifestyle of certain Hadza bands, but I saw no sign of this, and it should be borne in mind that the Hadza have chosen their nomadic lifestyle despite repeated attempts to settle them by successive governments. So far as I can ascertain, the guides ensure that no one band is visited more than once or twice a week, and the fee paid to the community is used to buy metal for spears and beads for decoration, but not food. And, incidentally, if you're the sort of daft person who wanders around African villages armed with piles of sweets or pens or whatever to hand out, then either don't visit the Hadza, or if you do, please leave the bag of goodies in Karatu.

GETTING THERE AND AWAY Mang'ola lies about one hour's drive from Karatu, and can be reached by following the Ngorongoro road out of town for about 5km, then taking a left turn towards the lake. Once at Mang'ola, it's easy enough to locate the guides and arrange a visit to a Hadza encampment. The full excursion can be completed as a half-day trip out of Karatu with private transport, and can easily be appended to a standard northern circuit safari.

WHERE TO STAY
Upmarket
⌂ **Kisima Ngeda** (6 rooms) ☎ 027 254 8715; m 0782 101150; f 027 250 2283; e reservations@kisimangeda.com; www.kisimangeda.com. This remote owner-managed tented camp is set in a shady grove of doum palms near the eastern shore of Lake Eyasi, with magnificent views across to the kilometre-tall western Rift Valley escarpment, the Ngorongoro Highlands & the Oldeani Mountains. It makes an excellent base for visiting a Hadzabe encampment or exploring the arid lake hinterland. The accommodation is comfortable but simple, rather than luxurious, & the structures around the en-suite tents are made entirely from organic local materials. The excellent food includes fresh tilapia caught from the lake. *US$287/540 sgl/dbl FB.*

Camping

A Council Campsite Mang'ola Council operates a lovely but basic campsite, set about 4km from the town on the road towards the lake, in a glade of acacias surrounding a hot spring. There are no facilities to speak of.

NORTH OF MANYARA

The vast majority of Serengeti safaris head directly west from Manyara along the new asphalt road that climbs the Rift Valley escarpment into the Ngorongoro Highlands, and then return to Arusha exactly the same way. An offbeat alternative to this well-trodden route, one that will transform your safari itinerary into a genuine loop, is the spine-jarring 265km road that connects Mto wa Mbu to the northern Serengeti via the parched stretch of the Rift Valley abutting the border with Kenya. This is not, it should be stressed, a route that should instil any great enthusiasm in anybody who nurses a dodgy back or chronic agoraphobia, or who has limited tolerance for simple travel conditions. But equally this half-forgotten corner of northern Tanzania also possesses some genuinely alluring off-the-beaten-track landmarks in the form of the ruined city of Engaruka, the malevolent Lake Natron, and above all perhaps the fiery volcanic majesty of Ol Doinyo Lengai.

Most experienced safari operators can arrange trips to the northern Rift Valley, taking Lake Natron as their focal point, but many will also discourage you from visiting the area as it is rough on vehicles and has been prone to outbursts of banditry in the past. Technically, it is possible to travel between Mto wa Mbu and the northern Serengeti via Natron in nine to ten hours of flat driving, but it would make for a very long day and would rather defeat the point of the exercise. More realistic is to split the drive over two days, stopping for a night at the lakeshore village of Ngare Sero, or two nights if you intend to climb Ol Doinyo Lengai or undertake any other exploration of the region. It is common practice to tag this area onto the end of a safari, but there is a strong case for slotting it in between the Tarangire/Manyara and Ngorongoro/Serengeti legs of your itinerary, if for no other reason than it would break up the vehicle-bound regime of game drives with a decent leg-stretch – whether you opt for a gentle stroll around the Engaruka ruins or the southern shore of Natron, the slightly more demanding hike to the Ngare Sero Waterfall in the escarpment west of Natron, or the decidedly challenging nocturnal ascent of Ol Doinyo Lengai.

If you visit this area in your own vehicle, treat it as you would any wilderness trip: carry adequate supplies of food, water and fuel. If you go with a safari company, avoid those at the lower end of the price scale, or you risk getting stuck in the middle of nowhere in a battered vehicle. Note that the scenic 160km road between Natron and Klein's Gate suffered a spate of unrest in 1998–99, instigated by Somali exiles from Kenya. The insurgents killed at least one police officer and several local Maasai, and a tourist vehicle was attacked near Loliondo, fortunately without any fatalities. The situation has been stable for a few years now, but still you are advised to make enquiries with a specialised operator.

ENGARUKA RUINS Situated below the Rift Valley escarpment about 65km north of Manyara, Engaruka is the Maasai name for the extensive ruins of a mysterious terraced city and irrigation system constructed at least 500 years ago by a late Iron Age culture in the eastern foothills of Mount Empakaai. Nobody knows for sure who built the city: some say it was the Mbulu, who inhabited the area immediately before the Maasai arrived there; others that it was built by Datoga settlers from the north. Locally, the city is said to have been home to forebears of the Sukuma, whose greeting 'Mwanga lukwa' was later bastardised to Engaruka by the Maasai –

more likely, however, is that the name of this well-watered spot has roots in the Maasai word 'ngare' (water).

The discovery of the ruins by outsiders is generally credited to Dr Fischer, who followed the base of the Rift Valley through Maasailand in 1883, and wrote how 'peculiar masses of stone became suddenly apparent, rising from the plain to heights up to ten feet. Partly they looked like mouldering tree trunks, partly like the tumbled down walls of ancient castles.' An older reference to Engaruka can be found on the so-called Slug Map drawn up by the missionaries Krapf and Erhardt in 1855. The first person to excavate the site was Hans Reck in the early 20th century, followed by the legendary Louis Leakey, who reckoned it consisted of seven large villages containing roughly 1,000 homes apiece and thought the total population must have exceeded 30,000.

The ruined villages overlook a complex stone-block irrigation system that extends over some 25km^2 and is fed by the perennial Engaruka River. This highly specialised and integrated agricultural community was abandoned in the 18th century, probably due to a combination of changes in the local hydrology and the immigration of more militaristic pastoralist tribes from the north. Yet Engaruka is unique only in scale, since a number of smaller deserted sites in the vicinity form part of the same cultural and agricultural complex, and recent radiocarbon dating suggests it might be older than has been assumed in the past – possibly as old as the 4th century AD, which would make it a likely precursor to the great centralised empires that thrived in pre-colonial Uganda and Rwanda.

Guided tours of the ruins can be arranged easily in Engaruka village – the Engaruka Ruins Campsite is as good a place to ask around as any. Without a local guide, it's debatable whether the ruins would convey anything much to the average passing tourist. The floor plan of the main village is still quite clear, and a few of the circular stone houses remain more or less intact to around waist level, their floors strewn with shards of broken earthenware. Substantial sections of the irrigation canal are still in place, as are some old burial mounds that might or might not be related to the war with the Maasai that caused the village to be abandoned.

Getting there and away The ruins can be reached by forking westward at the modern village of Engaruka, which is almost exactly halfway along the 120km road between Mto wa Mbu and Ngare Sero, and takes about 90 minutes to reach coming in either direction. From the junction, continue through the semi-urban sprawl of Engaruka for about 5km until you reach the Jerusalem Campsite, from where it is a ten-minute walk to the nearest ruined village. No entrance fee is charged, but the local guides will expect to be paid around US$5 per party to show you around. At least one bus daily connects Arusha to Engaruka, leaving Arusha from opposite the Shoprite at 10.00 and passing through Mto wa Mbu at around 14.00 before dropping passengers at the station next to the Engaruka Ruins Campsite at around 18.00.

Where to stay

Å Engaruka Ruins Campsite ↘ 027 253 9103; m 0455 507939; e engaruka@yahoo.com. Set in compact green grounds next to the bus station, this friendly campsite has the best facilities in town, including hot running water, electricity, flush toilets, a bar & a restaurant. The staff can arrange guided tours of the ruins for a nominal fee, as well as visits to local Maasai bomas & traditional dancing displays. Guided ascents of Ol Doinyo Lengai

arranged through the campsite work out at around US$50 pp, & the camp can also lay on 4x4 transport to/from the base of the mountain for US$120 1-way for up to 4 or 5 people. US$7 pp.

Å Jerusalem Campsite Set in a pretty grove close to the ruins, this site has no facilities other than toilets, making it more suitable for groups than for independent travellers. US$5 pp.

LAKE NATRON There are but a handful of places where the Rift Valley evokes its geologically violent origins with graphic immediacy. Ethiopia's Danakil Desert is one such spot; the volcanic Virunga Range in the Albertine Rift is another. And so too is the most northerly landmark in the Tanzanian Rift Valley, the low-lying Lake Natron, a shallow sliver of exceptionally alkaline water that extends southward from the Kenya border near Mount Shompole for 58km. The Natron skyline is dominated by the textbook volcanic silhouette of Ol Doinyo Lengai, which rises more than 2,000m above the Rift Valley floor, its harsh black contours softened by an icing of white ash that glistens brightly below the sun, as if in parody of Kilimanjaro's snows. Then there is the lake itself, a thrillingly primordial phenomenon whose caustic waters are enclosed by a crust of sodden grey volcanic ash and desiccated salt, punctuated by isolated patches of steamy, reed-lined swamp where the hot springs that sustain the lake bubble to the surface.

Thought to be about 1.5 million years old, Natron is a product of the same tectonic activity that formed the Ngorongoro Highlands and Mount Gelai, the latter being an extinct volcano that rises from the eastern lakeshore. Nowhere more than 50cm deep, it has changed shape significantly since that time, largely as a result of volcanic activity associated with the creation of Ol Doinyo Lengai to its immediate south. It lies at an altitude of 610m in an unusually arid stretch of the rift floor, receiving an average of 400mm of rainfall annually, and it would have probably dried out centuries ago were it not also fed by the freshwater Ewaso Ngiro River, which has its catchment in the central Kenyan Highlands, and the hot springs that rise below its floor. The alkaline level has also increased drastically over the millennia, partially because of the high salinity of ash and lava deposits from Lengai, partially because the lake's only known outlet is evaporation. Today, depending on recent rainfall, the viscous water has an average pH of 9–11, making it almost as caustic as ammonia when the level is very low, and it can reach a temperature of up to 60°C in extreme circumstances.

Natron's hyper-salinity makes it incapable of sustaining any but the most specialised life forms. The only resident vertebrate is the endemic white-lipped tilapia *Oreochromis alcalica*, a 10cm-long fish that congregates near hot spring inlets where the water temperature is around 36–40°C. The microbiology of the lake is dominated by halophytic (salt-loving) organisms such as spirulina, a form of blue-green algae whose red pigments make the salt-encrusted flats in the centre of the lake look bright red when seen from the air. Natron is also the only known breeding ground for east Africa's 2.5 million lesser flamingos, which usually congregate there between August and October, feeding on the abundant algae (whose pigments are responsible for the birds' trademark pink hue). The breeding ground's inhospitality to potential predators makes it an ideal flamingo nursery, but it also makes it difficult of access to human visitors – situated in the centre of the lake, it was discovered as recently as the 1950s and it can only be seen from the air today. In addition to the flamingos, Natron attracts up to 100,000 migrant waterbirds during the European winter, and its hinterland supports a thin population of large mammals typical of the Rift Valley, including wildebeest, zebra, fringe-eared oryx, Grant's and Thomson's gazelle, and even the odd lion and cheetah.

Getting there and away The centre of tourist activity on Natron is the small lakeshore village of Ngare Sero, bisected by the wooded freshwater stream from which its Maasai name is derived ('black water', 'clear water', 'dappled water' or 'forest of water', depending on who's doing the translating). The village lies about 120km north of Mto wa Mbu along a very rough road – bank on a four-hour drive, though this might improve if and when bridges are built across the larger

A common cause of friction on safaris is the matter of photographing Maasai people, something that invariably involves a payment, leading many tourists to conclude that the Maasai are 'too commercialised'. This misguided allegation has become something of a personal bugbear, not least because it strikes me as reflecting Western misconceptions and prejudices far more than it does any aspect of modern Maasai culture.

To diverge slightly, I expect that many visitors find it difficult to come to terms with the cocktail of traditionalism and exotic Western influences that informs modern African culture. To give one clearly identifiable example, you'll find that most Africans today are devout Christians or Muslims, yet many also simultaneously adhere to an apparently conflicting traditional belief system. Then look around the streets of Arusha, where cellphone-bearing businessmen and trendy safari guides brush past traditional Maasai street hawkers, and it's clear modernity and traditionalism co-exist here in a manner that seems contradictory to outsiders but is unremarkable to the country's inhabitants. And less immediately apparent is that the slick businessmen or casually dressed safari guide, should he happen to be Maasai, will probably return home for special occasions dressed in traditional attire, to all outward purposes indistinguishable from relatives who might always dress that way.

The point being that, as outsiders, it is all too easy to perceive an absolute cultural division between those Tanzanians who are outwardly modern and those who are outwardly traditional in their appearance. Just as many modern Tanzanian professionals might still visit traditional healers on occasion, or return home for important tribal ceremonies, it is absurd to attribute any modern influence in a Maasai pastoralist to a lack of cultural integrity. The Maasai, like us, are living in the 21st century, and a variety of external factors – among them, population growth, the gazetting of traditional grazing land as national parks, exposure to other Tanzanian cultures and exotic religions, the creation of a cash economy – all ensure that Maasai culture is not a static museum piece, but a dynamic, modern entity.

For most visitors to Tanzania, direct exposure to Maasai culture will take place in one of a number of bomas (family enclosures) that operate as tourist 'cultural villages' in the vicinity of Tarangire, Lake Manyara and Ngorongoro. Visiting such bomas is straightforward enough – ask your driver to arrange it – and the standard practice is to agree a price for the whole group, which will allow you to wander around as you please and photograph whomever you like. While I see absolutely nothing wrong with these cultural villages, and much that is commendable about them, any visitor should approach them with realistic expectations. The village you visit is basically operating as a cottage industry, and its inhabitants probably derive a substantial part of their living from tourist visits, so it stands to reason that there will be an element of contrivance to the experience they offer. And accept, too, that it is we, the tourists, who are the distorting factor in what

watercourses north of Engaruka. The village is about 160km from Klein's Gate in the northern Serengeti, a drive that takes five to six hours without stops, and involves a spectacular ascent (or descent) of the rift escarpment to the west of the lake. There is no public transport to Ngare Sero, but buses do run twice daily as far as Engaruka, where you can hire a 4x4 to Natron and/or Lengai from the Engaruka Ruins Campsite.

Where to stay

Lake Natron Camp (9 rooms) 027 255 3243 or 250 6315; e reservations@moivaro.com; www.moivaro.com. Established in Ngare Sero in 1989, this low-key camp has a spectacular setting alongside a stream some 4km from the southern lakeshore, & offers great views across the floodplain to Mt Gerai, is otherwise a genuine working Maasai settlement, one that probably existed long before we came along and whose inhabitants are absolutely traditional in all but this one respect. In my view, to conclude that the Maasai are 'too commercialised' on the basis of an isolated visit to what is an inherently commercial enterprise is as daft as walking into a London shop and concluding that the English are 'too commercialised' because the assistant expects you to pay for the items you select.

If you want to photograph the Maasai, the only realistic alternative to visiting a cultural village would be to snap one of the individuals who hang around strategic spots along the northern safari circuit for the express purpose of selling their beadwork or image to tourists. If you do this, a payment will be demanded, and quite rightly so because you will be photographing a person who derives their income from passing tourist traffic. But, make no mistake: were you to wander off into a Maasai boma that doesn't routinely deal with tourists, the odds are that its inhabitants will simply refuse to be photographed no matter what payment you offer. What's more, you might well find a spear dangling from the end of your lens if you don't respect their wishes!

There is a deeper irony to this whole debate. Here we have well-off visitors from media-obsessed, materialistic Europe or North America twiddling their video cameras, straightening their custom-bought safari outfits, and planning the diet they'll go on back home to compensate for the endless lodge buffets. They are confronted by a culture as resilient, non-materialistic and ascetic as that of the Maasai, and they accuse it with a straight face of being 'too commercialised'. This genuinely concerns me: are we so culture bound, so riddled with romantic expectations about how the Maasai should behave, that any slight deviation from these preconceptions prevents us from seeing things for what they are?

So let's start again. The Maasai are proud and dramatically attired pastoralists who adhere almost entirely to the traditions of their forefathers. They fascinate us, but being the bunch of gadget-obsessed *wazungu* we are, our response is not to absorb their presence or to try to communicate with them, but to run around thrusting cameras in their faces. And this, I would imagine, irritates the hell out of those Maasai who happen to live along main tourist circuits, so they decide not to let tourists photograph them except for a fee or in the context of an organised tourist village. In theory, everybody should be happy. In practice, we somehow construe this reasonable attempt by relatively poor people to make a bit of honest money as rampant commercialism. Okay, I recognise this is a bit simplistic, but we create the demand, the Maasai satisfy it, and if we pay to do so, that's just good capitalism, something the West has always been keen to encourage in Africa. If you don't like it, save your film and buy a postcard – in all honesty, you'll probably get a lot more from meeting these charismatic people if you leave your camera behind and enjoy the moment!

an extinct volcano less impressive in outline but actually marginally taller than nearby Lengai. Though it has a decidedly no-frills feel in keeping with the austere surrounds, the camp does have a welcoming swimming pool, & there's a pleasant restaurant & bar area. Accommodation is in en-suite tents with hot water. Inexpensive organised guided climbs of nearby Ol Doinyo Lengai are offered too. *US$240/300 sgl/dbl FB; low-season discount Apr & May, premium charged over Christmas period.*

🏠 **Riverside Campsite** (5 rooms) 📞 027 250 7145; f 027 250 8035; e info@sunnysafaris.com or sunny@arusha.com. This new campsite is run by a local Maasai elder & set alongside the river running through Ngare Sero. *US$50 pp FB for a bed in a basic en-suite twin standing tent with netting; US$10 pp to pitch a tent on the green lawn.*

⚠ **Waterfall Campsite** Situated 1–2km out of town close to the starting point for the walk to Ngare Sero Waterfall, this basic campsite has a great location but it seems very overpriced. *US$10 pp to pitch a tent.*

Exploring Lake Natron

Southern lakeshore To reach the southern lakeshore from Ngare Sero, you need to drive for around 5km to an unofficial parking spot about 1km from the water's edge, then walk for about ten minutes across salt-encrusted flats to a series of pockmarked black volcanic protrusions that serve as vantage points over the water. It's a lovely spot, with Lengai looming in the background, and it hosts a profusion of waterbirds, most visibly large flocks of the pink-tinged lesser flamingo, but also various pelicans, egrets, herons and waders. Wildebeest and zebra are also often seen in the area. If your driver doesn't know the way to the lakeshore – it's a rather obscure track – then ask for a local guide at one of the campsites. Whatever else you do, don't let the driver take the vehicle beyond the tracks left behind by his predecessors, or you run a serious risk of getting stuck in the treacherously narrow saline crust that surrounds the lake.

Ngare Sero Waterfall The Ngare Sero River forms a series of pretty waterfalls as it descends from the Nguruman Escarpment west of Lake Natron. The lowest two falls can be reached by driving out to Waterfall Campsite, then following the river upstream on foot for 45–60 minutes, through the gorge it has carved into the escarpment wall. If you are not already sufficiently doused by the time you reach the second waterfall, there's a chilly natural swimming pool below it. There is no clear footpath through the gorge: you will need to wade across the river several times (potentially dangerous after heavy rain) and can also expect to do a fair bit of clambering along ledges and rocks. This walk can only be recommended to reasonably fit and agile travellers, and it's advisable to take somebody who knows the way to help you navigate a couple of tricky stretches – a guide can be arranged at any of the camps listed above.

Ol Doinyo Lengai Estimated to be around 350,000–400,000 years old, Ol Doinyo Lengai – the Maasai 'Mountain of God' – is one of the youngest volcanoes in east Africa and possibly the most active. Its crater is known to have experienced almost continuous low-key activity since 1883, when Dr Fischer, the first European to pass through this part of Maasailand, observed smoke rising from the summit and was told second-hand that the mountain regularly emitted rumbling noises. At least a dozen minor or major eruptions have occurred since then. An interesting feature of Lengai is that it is the only active volcano known to emit carbonate lava, a form of molten rock that contains almost no silicon, is about 50% cooler than other forms of lava at around 500°C, and is also exceptionally fluid, with a viscosity comparable to water.

During an eruption in 2004, plumes in the crater could be seen from as far away as Ngare Sero and many local Maasai herdsmen moved their livestock out of the area. The mountain once again experienced a high level of volcanic activity between July 2007 and June 2008. On 18 July 2007, tremors emanating from the mountain measured 6.0 on the Richter scale and were felt as far away as Nairobi city. It erupted spectacularly on 4 September, emanating an ashen steamy plume almost 20km downwind and sending fresh lava flows along the north and west flanks. Eruptions continued intermittently into mid 2008, with further eruptions occurring in March and April. It has quietened down since then, but further eruptions during the lifespan of this edition are more than likely.

An increasingly popular option with adventurous travellers is the ascent of Lengai, which passes through some magnificently arid scenery and offers spectacular views back towards the Rift Valley, before leading to the bleakly visceral lunar landscape of the crater, studded with ash cones, lava pools, steam vents and other evidence of volcanic activity. Suitable only for reasonably fit and agile travellers, the track to the top of Lengai is very steep, climbing in altitude from

The most impressive eruption of Ol Doinyo Lengai in recorded history occurred in the latter part of 1966, when ash fall was reported as far away as Seronera, more than 100km to the west, as well as at Loliondo and Shombole, both some 70km further north. It is believed that the otherwise inexplicable death of large numbers of game around Empakaai Crater in that year was a result of an ash fall that coated the grass up to 2cm deep, though it is unclear whether the animals starved to death or they succumbed to a toxin within the ash. The effect on Maasai livestock was also devastating, according to Tepilit Ole Saitoti, who recalled the incident as follows in his excellent book *Worlds of a Maasai Warrior*:

In the year 1966, God, who my people believe dwells in this holy mountain, unleashed Her fury unsparingly. The mountain thunder shook the earth, and the volcanic flame, which came from deep down in the earth's crust, was like a continuous flash of lightning. During days when the eruption was most powerful, clouds of smoke and steam appeared. Many cattle died and still more would die. Poisonous volcanic ash spewed all over the land as far as a hundred miles away, completely covering the pastures and the leaves of trees. Cattle swallowed ash each time they tried to graze and were weakened. They could not wake up without human assistance. We had to carry long wooden staffs to put under the fallen animals to lift them up. There must have been more than enough reason for God to have unleashed Her anger on us, and all we could do was pray for mercy. My pastoral people stubbornly braved the gusting warm winds as they approached the flaming mountain to pray. Women and men dressed in their best walked in stately lines towards God, singing. The mountain was unappeased and cattle died in the thousands. Just before the people started dying too, my father decided to move; as he put it: 'We must move while we still have children, or else we will all lose them.'

around 800m to over 2,878m, while the descent can be very tough on knees and ankles. The climb normally takes five to six hours along slopes practically bereft of shade, for which reason many locals recommend leaving at midnight to avoid the intense heat and to reach the crater rim in time for sunrise. If you ascend by day, a 05.00 start is advised, and precautions should be taken against dehydration and sunstroke. Either way, the descent takes about two hours.

Most adventure safari operators in Arusha offer guided Lengai climbs, but it is also possible to arrange a one-day climb locally for around US$50 per person. The best place to pick up a reliable guide is either at Engaruka Ruins Campsite or at one of the camps dotted around Ngare Sero. The mountain lies outside any conservation area, so no park fees are charged, but you may be required to pay a daily fee of around US$20 per person. If you are thinking of sleeping on the mountain, then it is strongly recommended that you set up camp in the inactive south crater rather than the active north crater – not only is it far more pleasant to camp in the south crater, but you also don't run the risk of your camp being engulfed by an unexpected lava flow or bombarded by eruptive rocks. All hikers should be aware that the cones on the crater floor can easily collapse under pressure and they often cover deadly lava lakes. Under no circumstances should you climb on a cone, or walk inside a partially collapsed cone. It is inadvisable to climb the mountain altogether during periods of high activity.

For further information on the Ol Doinyo Lengai, check out the excellent websites www.mtsu.edu/~fbelton/lengai.html (good practical information) or http://it.stlawu.edu/~cnya/ (with detailed geological background).

Lake Manyara and the Northern Rift Valley   NORTH OF MANYARA

NGORONGORO CONSERVATION AREA

KEY
- Boma •
- Ranger post ←
- Airstrip ✈
- Emergency airstrip ✈
- Vehicle road ——
- Hiking trail ·····

© Philip Briggs

20km
10 miles

N

Bradt

Ol Doinyo Lengai (active volcano)
Lake Natron
Engaruka
Selela
Rift Valley
Rift Wall
Upper Kitete
Mto Wa Mbu
Arusha
Naiyobi
Kapenjiro
Mt Kerimasi
Empakaai Crater
Bulati
Mt Lolomalasin 3600m
Olturorowas
Northern Highlands Forest Reserve
Nainokanoka
Robian Glade
Forest Walks
Endoro River
Karatu
Tloma Aawak
Njiapanda
Irkeepus
Lemala
Olmoti Crater
Makeseni
Alayanai
Olbalbal
Lodoare gate
Oldeani
Ngorongoro Crater
Ngorongoro
Eyasi Basin
Seneto
Loongoku
Loongoku
Ilmisigiyo
Mt Oldeani 3216m
Olduvai Gorge
Mt Lemagrut 3135m
Mokilal
Mti Moja
Intake
Gol Mtns & Eastern Plain
Olkarien Gorge
Nasera Rock
Lemuta Hill
Esirwa Embaruwai
Endulen
Olpiro
Endamaghay
Lake Eyasi
Eyasi Basin
Serengeti Plain
Laetoli
Ndonyomati
Orbili
Osinoni
Eyasi Escarpment
Irkisate
Kakesio
Naibartat
Park boundary
Serengeti National Park
Naabi Gate
Ndutu Woodlands
Ndutu
Park boundary

9

Ngorongoro Conservation Area

An eastern annex to Serengeti National Park, the 8,292km² Ngorongoro Conservation Area (NCA) is named after Ngorongoro Crater, the world's largest intact volcanic caldera, and a shoo-in contender for any global shortlist of natural wonders – not only for its inherent geological magnificence, but also because its verdant floor serves as a quite extraordinary natural sanctuary for some of Africa's densest large mammal populations. The rest of the NCA can be divided into two broad ecological zones. In the east lie the Crater Highlands, a sprawling volcanic massif studded with craggy peaks (notably the 3,648m-high Lolmalasin, the third-highest mountain in Tanzania after Kilimanjaro and Meru) and more than a dozen calderas, among them Ngorongoro itself. By contrast, the sparsely wooded western plains of the NCA are essentially a continuation of the Serengeti ecosystem, supporting a cover of short grass that attracts immense concentrations of grazers during the rainy season.

Coming from the direction of Arusha, the approach road to the Ngorongoro Crater rim is a sensational scene setter, winding up the extinct volcano's densely forested outer slopes to Heroes Point, where most visitors will catch their first breathtaking view over the 260km² crater floor lying 600m below. Even at this distance, it is possible to pick out ant-like formations chomping their way across the crater floor – in fact, thousand-strong herds of wildebeest, zebra and buffalo – and with binoculars you might even see a few of the elephants that haunt the fringes of Lerai Forest. The drive along the crater rim to your lodge will be equally riveting: patches of forest interspersed with sweeping views back across to the Rift Valley, and the possibility of encountering buffalo, zebra, bushbuck, elephant and even the occasional leopard.

The Ngorongoro Crater is the main focal point of tourist activity in the NCA. But those who have the time can explore any number of less publicised natural features further afield. Olduvai Gorge, for instance, is the site of some of Africa's most important hominid fossil finds, and can easily be visited *en route* from the crater rim to the Serengeti. Other highlights include the Empakaai and, to a lesser extent, Olmoti crater in the northern NCA, while the crater rim is highly rewarding for montane forest birds.

An excellent 84-page booklet, *Ngorongoro Conservation Area*, similar in style to the national park booklets, is readily available in Arusha and has good information on the crater and Olduvai Gorge. It is especially worth buying if you plan to visit some of the off-the-beaten-track parts of the conservation area. For a more detailed overview of the national park, Veronica Roodt's excellent *Tourist Travel & Field Guide to the Ngorongoro Conservation Area* is widely available at hotel gift shops and craft shops in Arusha and elsewhere in northern Tanzania.

The NCA entrance fee of US$50 per person per 24 hours is payable by all, even those in quick transit to or from Serengeti National Park. An additional Crater Fee of US$200 per vehicle is levied for each and every visit to the crater floor during the course of a stay in the NCA. In order to curb congestion, the fee is now valid for half a day only. Unlike the surrounding national parks, all fees for the NCA are payable in hard currency cash or travellers' cheques (ideally US dollars); no credit card of any form is accepted, nor is local currency. Note, too, that the crater rim gets very cold at night, and is often blanketed in mist in the early morning, so you will need a jumper or two, and possibly a windbreaker if you are camping.

GETTING THERE AND AWAY

The road from Arusha to the eastern entrance gate of the NCA via Makuyuni, Mto wa Mbu and Karatu is now surfaced in its entirely and it can be covered comfortably

GEOLOGY AND HISTORY

With an altitudinal range of 1,230–3,648m above sea level, the NCA is among the most geologically spectacular reserves anywhere in Africa, comprising flat short-grass plains in the southwest and low rocky mountains in the northwest, while the west is dominated by the so-called Crater Highlands, a tall breezy plateau studded with stand-alone mountains. The mountains of the NCA date from two periods. The Gol Range, to the north of the main road to the Serengeti, is an exposed granite block that formed some 500 million years ago. Somewhat less antiquated, at least in geological terms, the Crater Highlands and associated free-standing mountains of the eastern NCA are volcanic in origin, their formation linked to the same fracturing process that created the Rift Valley 15–20 million years ago.

Ngorongoro Crater itself is the relic of an immense volcanic mountain that attained a similar height to that of Kilimanjaro before it imploded violently some two to three million years ago. It is the world's sixth-largest caldera, and the largest with an unbroken wall. Eight smaller craters in the NCA, most notably Olmoti and Empakaai, are the product of similar eruptions. The Crater Highlands are no longer volcanically active, but the free-standing Ol Doinyo Lengai immediately northeast of the main highland block is among the world's most active volcanoes, having last erupted over 2007/08.

Based on fossil evidence unearthed at Olduvai Gorge in the western NCA, it is known that various species of hominid have occupied this area for at least three million years. It was the domain of hunter-gatherers until a few thousand years ago, when pastoralists moved in. The fate of these early pastoralists is unknown, because a succession of immigrants replaced them: the ancestors of the Cushitic-speaking Mbulu some 2,000 years ago and those of the Nilotic-speaking Datoga about 300 years ago. A century later the militaristic Maasai drove both of these groups out of what is now the NCA: the Datoga to the Eyasi Basin and the Mbulu to the highlands near Manyara. Most place names in the area are Maasai, and although several explanations for the name Ngorongoro are floating around, the most credible is that it is named after a type of Maasai bowl.

Europeans settled in the NCA around the turn of the 20th century. Two German brothers farmed on the crater floor until the outbreak of World War I. One of their old farmhouses is still used by researchers, and a few sisal plants dating to this time can be seen in the northeast of the crater. Tourism began in the 1930s when the original Ngorongoro Crater Lodge was built on the crater rim. The NCA formed part of the original Serengeti National Park as gazetted in 1951, but Maasai protests at being denied access to such a huge tract of their grazing land led to it being split off from the national park in 1959 and downgraded to a multi-use conservation area. The NCA was inscribed as a UNESCO World Heritage Site in 1979, and two years later it was declared an International Biosphere Reserve, together with the neighbouring Serengeti.

in less than three hours, with another 30–60 minutes required to get to any of the lodges on the crater rim. All roads within the NCA are unsurfaced, and a decent 4x4 is required to reach the crater floor. Most tourists visit Ngorongoro as part of a longer safari, but those with time or budgetary restrictions could think about visiting the crater as a self-contained one-night safari out of Arusha.

WHERE TO STAY AND EAT

No accommodation or camping facilities exist within Ngorongoro Crater, but four upmarket lodges are perched on the rim, all offering superb views to the crater floor, as does the public campsite there. The crater can be (and often is) visited as a day trip from one of the mid-range to upmarket lodges that lie along the road between the NCA and Karatu, while budget-conscious travellers have a choice of more basic accommodation in Karatu itself (see *Chapter 8*, pages 183–5 for details of lodges in and around Karatu), though this does mean missing out on the dusk view over the crater and dawn game drives on the crater floor. The anomalous Ndutu Lodge, which lies just within the western border of the NCA, is not a realistic base from which to explore the Ngorongoro Highlands and ecologically it really feels like part of the Serengeti, so it is covered in that chapter.

EXCLUSIVE

Ngorongoro Crater Lodge (40 rooms) ℡ 027 254 8549/8038 or (South Africa) +27 (0)11 809 4447; e inboundsales@andbeyond.com; www.andbeyond.com. This top-of-the-range lodge was originally built in 1934 as a private hunting lodge with a commanding view over the crater, & was converted to a hotel shortly after independence in 1961. The property was bought by &Beyond (formerly CCAfrica) in 1995 & rebuilt from scratch with the stated aim of creating 'the finest safari lodge in Africa'. Architecturally, the lodge is literally fantastic. Each individual suite consists of 2 adjoining round structures, similar to African huts but distorted in an almost Dadaist style. The large interiors boast a décor as ostentatious as it is eclectic, combining elements of Baroque, Classical, African, colonial & much more besides in a manner the management describes as 'Maasai meets Versailles'. The entire lodge has been designed in such a way that the crater is almost constantly in sight (even the baths & the toilets have a view), & the food, service & ambience are all world class. Whether or not CCAfrica/&Beyond has succeeded in creating Africa's finest safari lodge is a matter of taste & opinion – certainly, the decidedly non-'bush' atmosphere might offend some purists – but it is difficult to fault in terms of

ambition & originality. The fact that it was commended in *Condé Nast Traveller's* prestigious 1998 end-of-year listings says enough. *US$1,280 pp, US$1,450 Jul–Aug, dropping to US$655 Mar–May, Nov & early Dec; rate inc all meals, most drinks & game drives. No sgl supplement.*

Lemala Camp (9 tents) ℡ 027 254 8966; f 027 254 8937; e info@lemalacamp.com; www.lemalacamp.com. Opened in Dec 2007, this is the only semi-permanent luxury tented camp on the crater rim, situated in a wonderful stand of lichen-stained flat-topped red-thorn acacias immediately inside the Lemala Gate (the start of the same road used to descend into & ascend from the crater rim from Ngorongoro Sopa Lodge). The views from the camp are great, it has an outdoor atmosphere lacking from all other camps on the rim, & it also has a peerless location for early-morning game drives into the crater itself. The tents are very spacious & decorated in classic safari style, with a wooden floor & canvas top, & all have twin or king-size beds, solar powered lighting & hot water. It's not cheap, but must rank as the 1st choice of accommodation for anybody seeking to experience Ngorongoro in a real bush atmosphere. Closed Oct–Nov, Apr–May. *US$710/960 sgl/dbl FB.*

UPMARKET

Ngorongoro Serena Lodge (75 rooms) ℡ 027 253 7050/2/3/5; f 027 253 7056; e reservations@serena.co.tz; www.serenahotels.com.

Meeting the usual high Serena standards, this is arguably the pick of the more conventional lodges on the crater rim, receiving consistent praise from tourists & from within the safari industry. It lies on the western crater rim along the road towards Seronera, several kilometres past the park headquarters & Crater Lodge. It is the closest of the lodges to the main descent road into the crater, a decided advantage for those who want to get to the crater floor as early as possible. The setting is a secluded wooded valley rustling with birdlife & offering a good view over the crater. Serena Active, which operates out of the lodge, offers a good range of afternoon & full-day walks ranging from a gentle stroll through the grassy highlands to a rather more challenging ascent of Olmoti Crater. The facilities, food & service are all of a high standard, & rooms are centrally heated. *US$375/550 sgl/dbl FB; US$225/335 Apr–Jun.*

🏠 **Ngorongoro Sopa Lodge** (96 rooms) ☎ 027 250 0630/9; f 027 250 8245; e info@sopalodges.com; www.sopalodges.com. Situated on the forested eastern edge of the crater rim some 20km distant from the

THE MAASAI

The northern safari circuit is the homeland of the Nilotic-speaking Maasai, whose reputation as fearsome warriors ensured that the 19th-century slave caravans studiously avoided their territory, which was one of the last parts of east Africa ventured into by Europeans. The Maasai today remain the most familiar of African people to outsiders, a reputation that rests as much on their continued adherence to a traditional lifestyle as on past exploits. Instantly identifiable, Maasai men drape themselves in toga-like red blankets, carry long wooden poles, and often dye their hair with red ochre and style it in a manner that has been compared to a Roman helmet. And while the women dress similarly to many other Tanzanian women, their extensive use of beaded jewellery is highly distinctive too.

The Maasai are often regarded to be the archetypal east African pastoralists, but are in fact relatively recent arrivals to the area. Their language Maa (Maasai literally means 'Maa-speakers') is affiliated to those spoken by the Nuer of southwest Ethiopia and the Bari of southern Sudan, and oral traditions suggest that the proto-Maasai started to migrate southward from the lower Nile area in the 15th century. They arrived in their present territory in the 17th or 18th century, forcefully displacing earlier inhabitants such as the Datoga and Chagga, who respectively migrated south to the Hanang area and east to the Kilimanjaro foothills. The Maasai territory reached its greatest extent in the mid 19th century, when it covered most of the Rift Valley from Marsabit (Kenya) south to Dodoma. Over the 1880s/90s, the Maasai were hit by a series of disasters linked to the arrival of Europeans – rinderpest and smallpox epidemics exacerbated by a severe drought and a bloody secession dispute – and much of their former territory was re-colonised by tribes whom they had displaced a century earlier. During the colonial era, a further 50% of their land was lost to game reserves and settler farms. These territorial incursions notwithstanding, the Maasai today have one of the most extensive territories of any Tanzanian tribe, ranging across the vast Maasai Steppes to the Ngorongoro Highlands and Serengeti Plains.

The Maasai are monotheists whose belief in a single deity with a dualistic nature – the benevolent Engai Narok (Black God) and vengeful Engai Nanyokie (Red God) – has some overtones of the Judaic faith. They believe that Engai, who resides in the volcano Ol Doinyo Lengai, made them the rightful owners of all the cattle in the world, a view that has occasionally made life difficult for neighbouring herders. Traditionally, this arrogance does not merely extend to cattle: agriculturist and fish-eating peoples are scorned, while Europeans' uptight style of clothing earned them the Maasai name Iloredaa Enjekat – Fart Smotherers! Today, the Maasai co-exist peacefully with their non-Maasai compatriots, but while their tolerance for their neighbours' idiosyncrasies has increased in recent decades, they show little interest in changing their own lifestyle.

The Maasai measure a man's wealth in terms of cattle and children rather than money – a herd of about 50 cattle is respectable, the more children the better, and a man who headquarters & main cluster of lodges, this attractive modern hotel is similar in standard to the Serena & arguably nudges ahead of it on the basis of location. Accommodation is in vast semi-detached suites, each with 2 dbl beds, a heater, a large bathroom, a fridge, & a wide bay window facing the crater & Ol Mokarot Mountain. There is a swimming pool in front of the bar, & the food & service are excellent. One thing that stands out about this lodge is the large, forested grounds, a good place to look for

characteristic montane forest birds, with sunbirds (tacazze, golden-winged & eastern double-collared) well represented & a variety of weavers, seedeaters & robins present. Another is that it lies close to what, in effect, is a private road that can be used both to ascend from & descend into the crater, which greatly reduces the driving time either side of game drives – particularly useful for an early morning start. *US$ 320/550 sgl/dbl FB; US$265/450 in Mar, Nov & early Dec; US$100/200 Apr/May.*

has plenty of one but not the other is regarded as poor. Traditionally, the Maasai will not hunt or eat vegetable matter or fish, but feed almost exclusively off their cattle. The main diet is a blend of cow's milk and blood, the latter drained – it is said painlessly – from a strategic nick in the animal's jugular vein. Because the cows are more valuable to them alive than dead, they are generally slaughtered only on special occasions. Meat and milk are never eaten on the same day, because it is insulting to the cattle to feed off the living and the dead at the same time. Despite the apparent hardship of their chosen lifestyle, many Maasai are wealthy by any standards. On one safari, our driver pointed out a not unusually large herd of cattle that would fetch the market equivalent of three new Land Rovers.

The central unit of Maasai society is the age-set. Every 15 years or so, a new and individually named generation of warriors or Ilmoran will be initiated, consisting of all the young men who have reached puberty and are not part of a previous age-set – most boys aged between 12 and 25. Every boy must undergo the Emorata (circumcision ceremony) before he is accepted as a warrior. If he cries out during the five-minute operation, which is performed without any anaesthetic, the post-circumcision ceremony will be cancelled, the parents are spat on for raising a coward, and the initiate will be taunted by his peers for several years before he is forgiven. When a new generation of warriors is initiated, the existing Ilmoran will graduate to become junior elders, who are responsible for all political and legislative decisions until they in turn graduate to become senior elders. All political decisions are made democratically, and the role of the chief elder or Laibon is essentially that of a spiritual and moral leader.

Maasai girls are permitted to marry as soon as they have been initiated, but warriors must wait until their age-set has graduated to elder status, which will be 15 years later, when a fresh warrior age-set has been initiated. This arrangement ties in with the polygamous nature of Maasai society: in days past, most elders would typically have acquired between three and ten wives by the time they reached old age. Marriages are generally arranged, sometimes even before the female party is born, as a man may 'book' the next daughter produced by a friend to be his son's wife. Marriage is evidently viewed as a straightforward child-producing business arrangement: it is normal for married men and women to have sleeping partners other than their spouse, provided that those partners are of an appropriate age-set. Should a woman become pregnant by another lover, the prestige attached to having many children outweighs any minor concerns about infidelity, and the husband will still bring up the child as his own. By contrast, although sex before marriage is condoned, an unmarried girl who falls pregnant brings disgrace on her family, and in former times would have been fed to the hyenas.

For further details about Maasai society and beliefs, get hold of the coffee-table book *Maasai*, by the photographer Carol Beckwith and Maasai historian Tepilit Ole Saitoti (Harry N Abrams, New York, reprinted 1993).

♔ **Ngorongoro Wildlife Lodge** (72 rooms) ℡ 027 254 4595; f 027 254 8633; e res@hotelsandlodges-tanzania.com; www.hotelsandlodges-tanzania.com. Situated roughly 2km away from Ngorongoro Crater Lodge, this former government hotel is one of the oldest on the crater rim & it shows its antiquity in the rather monolithic architecture. Until recently, fittings & furnishings also carried a rather timeworn sheen, but as with other hotels in this chain, it received a real facelift in 2008, though service & food remain a little substandard. This is compensated for by the finest location of all the crater rim lodges, directly above the yellow fevers of Lerai Forest — it truly defies superlatives. Following renovations, the rooms are comfortable & pleasantly furnished, with piping hot baths & windows facing the crater. You can pick out animals on the crater floor, using a telescope fixed on the patio, & the grounds support a fair range of forest birds. *Rates on application.*

♔ **Ngorongoro Wilderness Camp** (10 rooms) ℡ 027 250 2668; e serecamp.wildfrontiers@habari.co.tz; www.wildfrontiers.com. This comfortable mobile camp provides a more down-to-earth bush alternative to the large bland lodges that otherwise occupy the crater rim. It moves location every 3–6 months in line with NCA policy, but locations usually offer great views over the crater floor & the camp offers a varied programme of game drives into the crater & guided walks elsewhere in the NCA. The en-suite tents have solar lighting, eco-friendly toilets, & warm duvets & hot water bottles to protect against chilly highland nights. Closes mid-Apr–May. *US$450/680 sgl/dbl FB.*

MODERATE

♔ **Rhino Lodge** (24 rooms) m 0762 359055; e rhino@ngorongoro.cc; www.ngorongoro.cc. Formerly the home of the first conservator of NCA & later managed as a guesthouse by the conservation authorities, this modest low-rise lodge had been closed for the best part of a decade prior to being leased to the Dar es Salaam-based operator Coastal Aviation, who undertook extensive renovations prior to reopening it in 2007. It is far & away the most affordable lodge on the crater rim, & though it lacks a direct crater view, the surrounding mist-swathed forest has a charm of its own, & the location is very convenient for game drives. Accommodation is in simple but comfortable ground-floor rooms with twin or dbl beds & en-suite hot shower, & rates include good buffet meals in the cosy dining room, which comes complete with log fire. Superb value. *US$125/220 sgl/dbl FB.*

BUDGET AND CAMPING

Å **Simba Campsite** Situated about 2km from the park headquarters, this is the only place where you can pitch a tent on the crater rim, & it's hardly great value at US$30 pp, given that facilities are limited to basic latrines, cold shower & rubbish pit. Still, the wonderful view makes it a preferable option to camping in Karatu, assuming you place a greater priority on the experience than creature comforts. The village near the headquarters has a few basic bars & shops, & there is nothing preventing you from dropping into nearby Ngorongoro Wildlife Lodge for a drink or snack.

EXPLORING NGORONGORO CONSERVATION AREA

NGORONGORO CRATER FLOOR The opportunity of spending a day on the crater floor is simply not to be missed. There are few places where you can so reliably see such large concentrations of wildlife all year round, and your game viewing (and photography) will only be enhanced by the striking backdrop of the 600m-high crater wall. The crater is also excellent Big Five territory: lion, elephant and buffalo are all but guaranteed, rhino are regularly seen, and a leopard is chanced upon from time to time. The official road down to the crater descends from Malanja Depression to the western shore of Lake Magadi, while the official road up starts near Lerai Forest and reaches the rim on the stretch of road between Wildlife and Crater lodges. There is a third road into the crater, which starts near the Sopa Lodge, and this can be used either to ascend or to descend.

There are several notable physical features within the crater. Lerai Forest consists almost entirely of yellow fever trees, large acacias noted for their jaundiced bark (it was once thought that this tree, which is often associated with marsh and

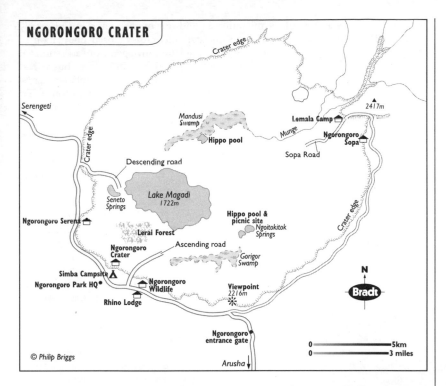

lake fringes, the breeding ground for mosquitoes, was the cause of yellow fever and malaria). To the north of this forest, Lake Magadi is a shallow soda lake that varies greatly in extent depending on the season. Standing close to the lakeshore is a cluster of burial cairns that show some similarities with the tombs at the Engaruka ruins further east, and are presumably a relic of the Datoga occupation of the crater prior to the arrival of the Maasai. To the south and east of this, the Gorigor Swamp also varies in extent seasonally, but it generally supports some water. There is a permanent hippo pool at the Ngoitokitok Springs at the eastern end of the swamp. The northern half of the crater is generally drier, though it is bisected by the Munge River, which is lined by thickets and forms a seasonally substantial area of swamp to the immediate north of Lake Magadi.

The open grassland that covers most of the crater floor supports large concentrations of wildebeest and zebra (the population of these species is estimated at 10,000 and 5,000 respectively), and smaller numbers of buffalo, tsessebe, and Thomson's and Grant's gazelle. The vicinity of Lerai Forest is the best area in which to see waterbuck, bushbuck and eland. The forest and adjoining Gorigor Swamp are the main haunt of the crater's elephant population, which typically stands at around 70. All the elephants resident in the crater are old males (though females and families sometimes pass through the area), and you stand a good chance of seeing big tuskers of the sort that have been poached away elsewhere in east Africa. Two curious absentees from the crater floor are impala and giraffe, both of which are common in the surrounding plains. Some researchers attribute the absence of giraffe to a lack of suitable browsing fodder, others to their presumed inability to descend the steep crater walls. Quite why there are no impala in the crater is a mystery.

The crater floor reputedly supports the densest concentration of predators in Africa. The resident lion population has fluctuated greatly ever since records were maintained, partly as a result of migration in and out of the crater, but primarily because of the vulnerability of the concentrated and rather closed population to epidemics. Over the course of 1962, the lion population dropped from an estimated 90 to about 15 due to an outbreak of disease spread by biting flies, but it had recovered to about 70 within a decade. In recent years, the pattern of fluctuation saw the population estimated at 80 in 1995, 35 in 1998, and 55 divided into four main prides and a few nomadic males in 2000. The crater's lions might be encountered just about anywhere, and are generally very relaxed around vehicles.

The most populous large predator is the spotted hyena, the population of which is estimated at around 400. You won't spend long in the crater without seeing a hyena: they often rest up on the eastern shore of Lake Magadi during the day, sometimes trying – and mostly failing – to sneak up on the flamingos in the hope of a quick snack. Until recently, no cheetahs were resident within the crater, which might seem surprising given that the open grassland is textbook cheetah habitat, but is probably due to the high rate of competition from other predators. At least two female cheetahs recently colonised the crater floor – one of which had four cubs in late 2001 – and sightings are now fairly regular. Leopards are resident,

NOT A BLOODY ZOO

A regular criticism of the Ngorongoro Crater, one that in my opinion is desperately misguided, is that it is 'like a zoo'. Aside from being yawningly unoriginal – I must hear this phrase two dozen times in the course of researching any given edition of this book – this allegation is as facile as it is nonsensical. The wildlife in the crater is not caged, nor is it artificially fed, surely the defining qualities of a zoo, but is instead free to come and go as it pleases. Yes, the crater's animals are generally very relaxed around vehicles, but that doesn't make them tame, merely habituated – no different, really, to the mountain gorillas of Rwanda or the chimps at Mahale.

The point that many visitors to Ngorongoro miss is that, for all the elitism attached to Africa's more remote game reserves, it is only in places where the wildlife is almost totally habituated that casual visitors can watch the animals behave much as they would were no human observers present. And, trust me, this is an infinitely more satisfying experience than travelling through a reserve where the wildlife is so skittish that most sightings amount to little more than a rump disappearing into the bush.

I suspect that the notion of Ngorongoro as a glorified zoo stems from something else entirely. This is the high volume of tourist traffic, which admittedly robs the crater floor of some of its atmosphere, and has some potential to cause environmental degradation, but is of questionable impact on the animals. On the contrary, the wildlife of Ngorongoro is apparently far less affected by the presence of vehicles than, say, the elephants and giraffes in the Selous, which regularly display clear signs of distress at the approach of a vehicle.

The problem, basically, is that the high volume of other tourists in the relatively small and open confines of the crater jars against our sense of aesthetics – especially when game spotting entails looking for a group of vehicles clustered together in the distance rather than looking for an actual animal! Personally, I feel that the scenery and abundance of animals more than makes up for the mild congestion, but if crowds put you off, then there are other places to visit in Tanzania. Instead of adding to the tourist traffic, then moaning about it, why not give the crater a miss? Or, better still, make the effort to be in the crater first thing in the morning, when, for a brief hour or two before the post-breakfast crowds descend, it really does live up to every expectation of untrammelled beauty.

particularly in swampy areas, but they are not often seen. Other common predators are the golden and black-backed jackals, with the former being more frequently encountered due to its relatively diurnal habits.

The crater floor offers some great birding. Lake Magadi normally harbours large flocks of flamingo, giving its edges a pinkish tinge when seen from a distance. The pools at the Mandusi Swamp can be excellent for waterbirds, with all manner of waders, storks, ducks and herons present. The grassland is a good place to see a number of striking ground birds. One very common resident is the kori bustard, reputedly the world's heaviest flying bird, and spectacular if you catch it during a mating dance. Ostrich are also common, along with the gorgeously garish crowned crane, and (in the rainy season) huge flocks of migrant storks. Less prominent, but common, and of great interest to more dedicated birders, is the lovely rosy-throated longclaw. Two of the most striking and visible birds of prey are the augur buzzard, sometimes seen here in its unusual melanistic form, and the foppish long-crested eagle. The localised Egyptian vulture – whose ability to crack open ostrich eggs by holding a stone in its beak makes it the only bird that arguably uses tools – is sometimes seen in the vicinity of Mungu Stream.

There are a few hippo pools in the crater, but the one most often visited is Ngoitokitok Springs, a popular picnic spot where lunch is enlivened by a flock of black kites which have become adept at swooping down on tourists and snatching the food from their hands.

The authorities rigidly forbid tourists from entering the crater before 07.00, and they must be out of the crater before 18.00. This is a frustrating ruling for photographers, since it means that you miss out on the best light of the day, and it has encouraged a situation where most safari drivers suggest that their clients take breakfast before going on a game drive, and carry a picnic lunch. This programme is difficult to avoid if you are on a group safari, but for those on a private safari, it is well worth getting down to the crater as early as permitted. Photography aside, this is the one time in the day when you might have the crater to yourself, the one time, in other words, when you can really experience the Ngorongoro Crater of television documentary land. Note that it is forbidden to descend to the base of the crater after 16.00, and that a 'crater service fee' of US$200 per vehicle for a half-day visit is payable every time you enter the crater.

EMPAKAAI AND OLMOTI CRATERS The NCA also protects two other major craters, both relics of the volcanic activity that shaped the breezy Crater Highlands over the past ten million years or so. Both are worth a visit, despite being dwarfed in size and reputation by the peerless Ngorongoro, as they offer welcome opportunity to break the regime of twice-daily game drives with a stiff steep walk in lovely mountain scenery. And the view from the rim of Empakaai Crater is among the most spectacular in east Africa.

The most alluring of the two craters is Empakaai, which is around 540m deep and has a diameter of almost 8km. The crater floor, enclosed by sheer forested cliffs, supports a sparkling soda lake that covers about half of its area and has a depth of around 60m. The emerald lake's shallows are frequently tinged pink with thousands of flamingos, and a variety of other aquatic birds are common too. As for mammals, elephant and leopard are still present in the area, but bushbuck, buffalo and blue monkey are more likely to be seen, especially on the crater rim.

The drive from Ngorongoro to Empakaai takes around 90 minutes, leaving from the Ngorongoro Crater rim close to the Sopa Lodge. A 4x4 is required, and if you want to hike to the crater floor you need to stop *en route* at Nainokanoka village to pick up the mandatory armed ranger. Past Nainokanoka, the road descends to the

9

Ngorongoro Crater has always been noted for its density of black rhinos. Back in 1892, Dr Oscar Baumann, the first European to visit the area, remarked on the large numbers of rhino, particularly around Lerai Forest – and he shot seven of the unfortunate beasts to prove his point. More recently, the biologist John Goddard estimated the resident population at greater than 100 in 1964. By 1992, poaching had reduced the crater's rhino population to no more than ten individuals, although this number had increased to 18 by 1998, including a mother and calf relocated from South Africa's Addo National Park to boost the local genetic pool. Sadly, five of these rhinos died in the early part of the present decade, one taken by a lion and the remainder thought to be victims of a tick-borne disease linked to the low rainfall of 2000/01. Since then, numbers have gradually recovered and the population resident in the crater stood at around 20 individuals in 2008. The crater's rhinos all have a tracking device implanted in their horns, to discourage poachers and to enable the rangers to monitor movements.

Despite the overall decline in numbers over recent decades, Ngorongoro is today the only accessible part of the northern safari circuit where these endangered animals are seen with any regularity. For many visitors to the crater, therefore, rhino sightings are a very high priority, and fortunately the chances are pretty good. In the wet season, the rhinos are often seen in the vicinity of the Ngoitokitok Springs and the Sopa road. For most of the year, however, they range between the Lerai Forest by night and Lake Magadi by day. Early risers are very likely to encounter a pair on the road fringing the forest, since they tend to move towards the lake shortly after dawn.

The crater's rhinos display a couple of local quirks. The black rhino (unlike its 'white' cousin) is normally a diurnal browser, which makes it rather odd to see them spending most of the day in open grassland, but the story is that they mostly feed by night while they are in the forest. Baumann noted that the crater's rhinos were unusually pale in colour, a phenomenon that is still observed today, due to their predilection for bathing and rolling in the saline lake and fringing salt flats.

open grassy expanses of the Embulbul Depression (lowest point 2,325m), which lies at the base of the 3,260m Mount Losirua and 3,648m Lolmalasin, the latter being the highest point in the Crater Highlands (and third-highest in Tanzania). The road then climbs Empakaai's outer slopes, passing through alpine moorland and lush Afro-montane forest, before reaching the rim and its fantastic views over the crater to Ol Doinyo Lengai and, on very clear days, Kilimanjaro and Lake Natron.

A road circles part of the forested rim, which reaches an elevation of 3,200m in the east. An excellent footpath to the crater floor was constructed in 2008 – a steep but wonderful walk that takes around 45 minutes each away and requires decent walking shoes. There is a campsite with rustic ablution facilities on the crater rim a few metres from the start of the footpath, but no other accommodation in the area.

If that walk hasn't sapped your energy, the smaller and less dramatic Olmoti Crater, a sunken caldera situated close to Nainokanoka, is worth a stop on the way back to Ngorongoro. A motorable track leads from Nainokanoka to a ranger post further west, from where the crater rim can only be reached on foot, following a recently upgraded footpath through montane forest that takes about 30 minutes up and 20 minutes back down. From the ranger post it is a half-hour walk to the rim. This is a shallow crater, covered in grass and bisected by a river valley, and it offers good grazing for Maasai cattle and also sometimes supports a few antelope. From the viewpoint at the rim, you're bound to see pairs of augur buzzard cartwheeling high in the sky, and might also catch a glimpse of the mighty cliff-loving Verreaux's eagle. On a clear day, the viewpoint also offers glimpses of the distant southern wall of Ngorongoro Crater, and you can follow a short footpath to the seasonal Munge Waterfall, where the eponymous river leaves the crater.

OLDUVAI GORGE It's difficult to believe today perhaps, but for much of the past two million years the seasonally parched plains around Olduvai – or more correctly *oldupai*, the Maasai name for sisal – were submerged beneath a lake that formed an important watering hole for local animals and our hominid ancestors. This was a fluctuating body of water, at times expansive, at other times drying up altogether, creating a high level of stratification accentuated by sporadic deposits of fine ash from the volcanoes that surrounded it. Then, tens of thousands of years ago, volcanic activity associated with the rifting process caused the land to tilt, and a new lake formed to the east. The river that flowed out of this new lake gradually incised a gorge through the former lakebed, exposing layers of stratification up to 100m deep. Olduvai Gorge thus cuts through a chronological sequence of rock beds preserving a practically continuous archaeological and fossil record of life on the plains over the past two million years.

The significance of Olduvai Gorge was first recognised by the German entomologist Professor Katwinkle, who stumbled across it in 1911 while searching for insect specimens. Two years later, Katwinkle led an archaeological expedition to the gorge, and unearthed a number of animal fossils before the excavations were abandoned at the outbreak of World War I. In 1931, the palaeontologist Louis Leakey visited the long-abandoned diggings and realised that the site provided ideal conditions for following the hominid fossil record back to its beginnings. Leakey found ample evidence demonstrating that ancient hominids had occupied the site, but lacking for financial backing, his investigations went slowly and frustratingly refused to yield any truly ancient fossilised hominid remains.

The pay-off for the long years of searching came in 1959 when Mary Leakey – Louis's wife, and a more than accomplished archaeologist in her own right – discovered a heavy fossilised jawbone that displayed unambiguous human affinities but was also clearly unlike any other hominid fossil documented at the time. Christened 'Nutcracker man' by the Leakeys in reference to its bulk, this jawbone proved to be that of an Australopithecine (now designated as *Australopithecus boisei*) that had lived and died on the ancient lakeshore some 1.75 million years ago. Subsequently superseded by more ancient fossils unearthed elsewhere in east Africa, this was nevertheless a critical landmark in the history of palaeontology: the first conclusive evidence that hominid evolution stretched back over more than a million years and had been enacted on the plains of east Africa.

This important breakthrough shot the Leakeys' work to international prominence, and with proper funding at their disposal, a series of exciting new discoveries followed, including the first fossilised remains of *Homo habilis*, a direct ancestor of modern man that would have dwelt on the lakeshore contemporaneously with *Australopithecus boisei*. After Louis's death in 1972, Mary Leakey continued working in the area until she retired in 1984. In 1976, at the nearby site of Laetoli, she discovered footprints created more than three million years ago by a party of early hominids which had walked through a bed of freshly deposited volcanic ash – still the most ancient hominid footprints ever found.

Olduvai Gorge lies within the conservation area about 3km north of the main road between Ngorongoro Crater and the Serengeti, and is a popular and worthwhile place to stop for a picnic lunch. The actual diggings may only be explored with a guide, and – since all fossils are immediately removed – they are probably of greater immediate interest for the geology than for the archaeology.

Because the NCA lies outside the national park system, it is permissible to walk and hike along a number of trails covering most main points of interest (but not the crater floor) in the company of an authorised guide. For those seeking a short morning or afternoon walk on the crater rim appended to a standard road safari, the best option is to take one of three short guided hikes offered by Serena Active, based in the Ngorongoro Serena Lodge. These walks can be pre-booked, but it's also fine just to pitch up at their booking desk spontaneously on the day, whether you're staying at the Serena (✆ 027 253 9160/1/2; f 027 253 9163; e serenaactive@serena.co.tz) or at another lodge on the crater rim.

You could in theory spend a fortnight exploring the NCA along a network of longer trails that connects Lake Eyasi in the south to Lake Natron in the north, as well as running west across the plains towards Laetoli and Lake Ndutu and northwest to Olduvai Gorge. Other possible targets for hikers include the Olmoti and Empakaai craters, the 3,600m Mount Lolmalasin (the third-highest in Tanzania), and the remote Gol Mountains. In theory, any safari operator can advise you about routes and arrange hikes with the NCA authorities, but I would strongly advise the traveller thinking of doing this to work through an operator with specialist trekking experience (see the Safari operators listings in Chapter 3, *Arusha*, pages 91–3).

It would also be possible to set up a trekking trip directly with the NCA, bussing to the crater rim from Arusha. Were you to attempt something like this, you would have to organise food yourself, to clarify arrangements for a tent, sleeping bag and other equipment, and to take warm clothes since parts of the NCA are very chilly at night. The best place to make initial enquiries and arrangements for a DIY trekking trip would be the NCA Information Centre on Boma Road in Arusha (✆ 027 254 4625; f 027 250 2603; www.ngorongorocrater.org). At least five different one-day hiking trails from the crater rim can be arranged at very short notice. Some of the longer hikes and trekking routes require 30 days' notice to set up, so you will need to make advance contact.

Not so the excellent site museum, which displays replicas of some of the more interesting hominid fossils unearthed at the site as well as the Laetoli footprints. Also on display are genuine fossils of some of the extinct animals that used to roam the plains: pygmy and short-necked giraffes, giant swine, river elephant, various equines and a bizarre antelope with long de-curved horns. Outside the museum, evolutionary diversity is represented by the variety of colourful – and very alive – dry-country birds that hop around the picnic area: red-and-yellow barbet, slaty-coloured boubou, rufous chatterer, speckle-fronted weaver and purple grenadier are practically guaranteed.

LAKE NDUTU This alkaline lake lies south of the B142 on the Ngorongoro–Serengeti border. When it is full, Maasai use it to water their cattle. In the rainy season it supports large numbers of animals, so Ndutu Lodge (see page 216) is a good base for game drives. The acacia woodland around the lake supports different birds from those in surrounding areas. The campsite on the lakeshore costs US$40 per person.

10

Serengeti National Park

There is little to say about the Serengeti that hasn't been said already. It is Africa's most famous wildlife sanctuary, renowned for its dense predator population and annual wildebeest migration, and the sort of place that's been hyped so heavily you might reasonably brace yourself for disappointment when you actually get to visit it. But the Serengeti is all it is cracked up to be – arguably the finest game reserve anywhere in Africa, as notable for the sheer volume of wildlife that inhabits its vast plains as for the liberating sense of space attached to exploring them.

Serengeti National Park covers an area of almost 15,000km², but the Serengeti ecosystem – which includes a number of game reserves bordering the national park as well as Kenya's Maasai Mara National Reserve – is more than double that size. Most of the national park is open and grassy, broken by isolated granite hillocks or koppies (a Dutch or Afrikaans word literally meaning 'little heads') and patches of acacia woodland. There is little permanent water, so animal migration in the area is strongly linked to rainfall patterns.

Several guides to the park are available locally. They include the official 72-page booklet *Serengeti National Park*, with good maps and introductory information, and the newer and glossier *Serengeti* published by African Publishing House. Far more detailed is Veronica Roodt's *Tourist Travel & Field Guide to the Serengeti*, which is strong on maps, photographs and information.

Entrance costs US$50 per 24 hours and there is speculation it will increase in the not too distant future. The fee should ideally be paid by MasterCard or Tanapa Card (issued at any Exim Bank). No other cards are accepted, nor are travellers' cheques, and cash payments attract a 50% penalty.

HISTORY

Prior to becoming a national park, the Serengeti was inhabited by the Maasai, who migrated into the area in the 17th century, when they forcefully displaced the Datoga pastoralists. The name Serengeti derives from the Maa word *serengit*, meaning 'Endless Plain', and it most properly refers to the short-grass plains of the southeast rather than the whole park. Partly because it lay within the territory of the then inhospitable Maasai, the Serengeti area was little known to outsiders until after World War I, when the first European hunters moved in to bag its plentiful wildlife.

Serengeti National Park was gazetted in 1951 and originally covered the present-day national park along with what is now the Ngorongoro Conservation Area (NCA). The park's Maasai residents were threatened with forceful eviction, leading to widespread protests and eventually a compromise wherein the NCA was split off from the park and the Maasai were allowed to stay there. The Maasai are no longer allowed to graze their cattle in the national park, but evidence of their previous occupation can be seen in the form of well-preserved rock paintings at Moru Koppies. The Serengeti became famous through the work of Professor

SERENGETI NATIONAL PARK

Lake Victoria

Tarime

Mara River

Musoma

Bunda

Kibara

Speke Gulf

Kijirewshi Tented Camp

Ndabaka gate

Grumeti River Camp

Sabora

Serengeti Stop Over

Kirawira Tented Camp

Grumeti

Speke Bay Lodge

Dutwa Plain

Mbalageti Serengeti

Mbalageti

Mwanza

Ndoha Plain

Serengeti

SERONERA

Lobo,
Ndabaka gate

Nyaraswiga Plain

Seronera River

Songore River

Olakira Camp
(June–Oct)

Ngore Namuki River

Turner Springs

Seronera Wildlife Lodge

Maswa
Game Reserve

Seronera

Wandhu River

Seronera River

Maasai Koppes

Serengeti Sopa Lodge

Naabi Hill gate

208

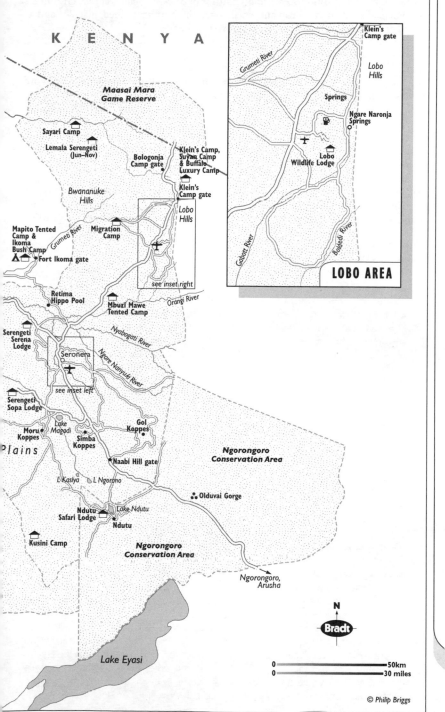

K E N Y A

Maasai Mara
Game Reserve

Sayari Camp

Lemala Serengeti
(Jun–Nov)

Bologonja
Camp gate

Klein's Camp,
Suyan Camp
& Buffalo
Luxury Camp

Klein's
Camp gate

Bwananuke
Hills

Lobo
Hills

Mapito Tented
Camp &
Ikoma
Bush Camp

Grumeti River

Migration
Camp

Fort Ikoma gate

see inset right

Retima
Hippo Pool

Mbuzi Mawe
Tented Camp

Orangi River

Nyabogati River

Serengeti
Serena
Lodge

Seronera

Ngare Nanyuki River

see inset left

Serengeti
Sopa Lodge

Moru
Koppes

Lake
Magadi

Gol
Koppes

Simba
Koppes

Naabi Hill gate

Plains

L Kasiya

L Ngorono

Ngorongoro
Conservation Area

Olduvai Gorge

Ndutu
Safari Lodge

Lake Ndutu

Ndutu

Kusini Camp

Ngorongoro
Conservation Area

Ngorongoro,
Arusha

N

Bradt

0 ——————— 50km
0 ——————— 30 miles

Lake Eyasi

© Philip Briggs

Klein's
Camp gate

Grumeti River

Lobo
Hills

Springs

Ngare Naronja
Springs

Lobo
Wildlife Lodge

Gabati River

Boldedi River

LOBO AREA

Bernard Grzimek (pronounced Jimek), author of *Serengeti Shall Not Die*. Grzimek's son Michael died in an aeroplane crash over the Serengeti aged just 24, and is buried at Heroes Point on the Ngorongoro Crater rim.

WILDLIFE

The most recent census figures indicate that the commonest large herbivore species in the Serengeti ecosystem are wildebeest (1,300,000), Thomson's gazelle (250,000), Burchell's zebra (200,000), impala (70,000), topi (50,000), Grant's gazelle (30,000), kongoni (15,000) and eland (10,000), and anecdotal sources indicate that these figures are now on the low side. The current population of wildebeest may well be as high as two million, while the total number of zebra probably stands at around 500,000, with the two species often encountered together in immense mixed herds.

Other antelope species include Kirk's dik-dik, klipspringer, and small numbers of roan, oryx, oribi and waterbuck. There are significant numbers of buffalo, giraffe and warthog. Elephant are relatively scarce on the open plains, but can be

THE GREAT MIGRATION

The annual migration of at least two million ungulates – predominantly wildebeest but also large concentrations of zebra and lesser numbers of Thomson's gazelle, Grant's gazelle and eland – through the greater Serengeti ecosystem is indubitably the greatest extant spectacle of its type in Africa. Dictated by local rainfall patterns, the Serengeti migration does follow a reasonably predictable annual cycle, though there is also fair amount of variation from one year to the next, dependent mainly on the precise timing of the rainy seasons. The cycle breaks up into the following main periods.

DECEMBER–APRIL The plains that stretch southeast from Seronera into the Ngorongoro Conservation Area form the Serengeti's main wildebeest calving grounds, centred on the Ndutu area of the NCA–Serengeti border. The wildebeest typically disperse into this area during the short rains, which fall in late November or early December, and stay put until the end of the long rains, generally in early May. These southeastern plains are the most accessible part of the park, particularly for those on a budget safari, and this is a fantastic time to be on safari in the Serengeti. True, you won't see the big herds on the move, but it's not uncommon to see herds of 10,000 animals, and the scenery is lush and green. The optimum time to visit this area is the peak calving season (late January into February) when hundreds, even thousands, of calves are dropped daily, and predator concentrations are also at their peak.

MAY–JULY Usually towards the end of April, the wildebeest and their entourage start to congregate on the southern plains in preparation for the 800km northward migration. The actual migration, regularly delayed in recent years due to late rain, might start any time from late April into early June, with a herd of more than a million migrating animals marching in a braying column of up to 40km long, one of the most impressive spectacles in the world. The major obstacle faced by the wildebeest on this migration is the crossing of the Grumeti River through the Western Corridor, which typically occurs from June into early July. A great many animals die in the crossing, many of them taken by the Grumeti's ravenous and prolific population of outsized crocodiles, and the first herds to cross are generally at the greatest risk. For this reason, it can take up to two weeks from when the first wildebeest arrive at the southern bank of the river for the actual crossing to begin, by which time thousands upon thousands of wildebeest are congregated in the Western Corridor.

very common in the north and west. The park's last resident herd of black rhinoceros – a mere seven individuals, as opposed to an estimated 700 in the mid-1970s – is restricted to the vicinity of the Moru Koppies in the far southeast, while another small population evidently ranges between Kenya's Maasai Mara National Reserve and the small wedge of the Serengeti that lies to the northwest of the Mara River. The most common and widespread diurnal primates are the olive baboon and vervet monkey, but an isolated and seldom seen population of patas monkey is resident in the west, and a few troops of black-and-white colobus haunt the riparian woodland along the Grumeti River through the Western Corridor.

Ultimately, the success of any safari lies in the number and quality of encounters with big cats. There is something infinitely compelling about these animals, a fascination that seems to affect even the most jaded of safari drivers – many of whom are leopard obsessive, content to drive up and down the Seronera Valley all day in the search for a telltale tail dangling from a tree. And when it comes to big cats, the Serengeti rarely disappoints. Lions are a practical certainty: the Tanzania side of the greater Serengeti ecosystem supports an estimated 2,500–3,000 individuals, which is probably the largest single population anywhere in Africa, and

AUGUST–NOVEMBER Following the great northward sweep across the Grumeti, the ungulates usually cross the Mara River in August, before dispersing across the plains of the northwest. Conventional wisdom has it that August–October is a bad time to visit the Serengeti, because the wildebeest have crossed the Kenya border into the Maasai Mara National Reserve. In reality, however, about half of the wildebeest stay in the northwest Serengeti over these months, and game viewing can be excellent, assuming that you can afford to base yourself at one of the exclusive tented camps in the Mara River area. Here, relatively small herds of wildebeest – typically between 500 and a few thousand – frequently travel back and forth between the northern and southern banks of the Mara River in response to changes in the local rainfall pattern, a truly spectacular event. In October, sometimes earlier, the animals generally cross the Mara River one last time and start to plod back southward to the short-grass plains of the southeast, and there is a good chance of catching the southward migration in the Lobo area between late October and mid-November. The wildebeest usually reach the short-grass plains around Ndutu in late November, when the cycle starts all over again.

Whether it is worth planning your safari dates around the migration is a matter of choice. With the best will in the world, it would be practically impossible to ensure that a few days in the Serengeti will coincide with the exact date of a river crossing, which is the most spectacular event in the migration calendar. On the other hand, if you choose the right part of the Serengeti – the southeast from December–May, the Western Corridor over May–July, the Mara River area from July–October, and the Lobo area over October–November – large herds of grazers should be easy enough to locate and there's a fair chance of witnessing a more spectacular migrational movement or river crossing.

On the other hand, bearing in mind that most predators and ungulate species other than zebra and wildebeest are strongly territorial and do not stray far from their core territory over the course of any given year, there is a lot to be said for avoiding the migration. Most of the lodges now charge considerably lower rates over April and May, with a knock-on effect on the rates offered by safari companies that suddenly become hungry for business. Furthermore, the safari circuit as a whole is far less crowded outside of peak seasons, and in our experience the Serengeti, irrespective of season, will still offer game viewing to equal that of any game reserve in Africa.

Many visitors whose experience of the Serengeti is limited to the Seronera area complain that the park is uncomfortably crowded, and that any worthwhile sighting attracts a gaggle of safari vehicles within a few minutes. To some extent, this reputation is justified: Seronera is the most accessible part of the park, coming from the direction of Arusha, and it boasts the highest concentration of camping and lodge facilities, so that game-viewing roads within a 5–10km radius tend to carry an uncharacteristically high level of vehicular traffic.

This situation is exacerbated by the tendency of the budget safari companies that favour Seronera to impose heavy budgetary restrictions on drivers, discouraging them from burning excess fuel to explore further afield. Furthermore, the safari industry's obsession with the 'Big Five' and large predators has created a mindset where drivers tend to rely heavily on radio messages from other drivers to locate the animals they think their clients most want to see. As a result, all vehicles within radio earshot tend to congregate on any such sighting within minutes. Sadly, this all goes to create the common misperception that one of Africa's wildest and most wonderful parks is far more crowded with tourists than is actually the case.

What can you do about this? Well, for one, assuming that you can afford it, arrange your safari through a company that specialises in more offbeat areas of the park and whose budget incorporates unlimited mileage – see pages 91–3 for recommendations. If you work with a cheaper company, try to avoid being based at Seronera. True, this area does usually offer the best wildlife viewing in the park, but many other parts of the Serengeti are almost as good, whilst carrying a significantly lower tourist volume. Failing that, should your itinerary include Seronera, speak to the safari company about what if any fuel restrictions they impose on drivers, and try to reach an understanding in advance.

It's also worth bearing in mind that roads around Seronera tend to be busiest during peak game viewing hours of 07.30–10.00 and 14.00–16.30. So it's well worth asking for a packed breakfast and heading out as early as possible – game drives are permitted from 06.00 onwards, and even if you ignore the crowding issue, that first hour of daylight is the best time to see predators on the move. Bearing in mind that drivers tend to place emphasis on seeking out big cats because they think it's what their clients want, travellers with different priorities should talk them through with the driver – more radically, ask him to switch off his radio, stop worrying about what everybody else might be seeing, and just enjoy what animals you happen to chance upon.

hundreds of resident lions stalk the plains around Seronera, with the main concentration centred on Simba, Moru and Gol koppies close to the main Ngorongoro road. Here, it's normal to see two or three prides in the course of one game drive. Sociable, languid and deceptively pussycat-like, lions are most often seen lying low in the grass or basking on rocks. The challenge is to see a lion exert itself beyond a half-interested movement of the head when a vehicle stops nearby. Cheetahs, too, are very common: the park's estimated population of 500–600 is densest in the open grasslands around Seronera and further east towards Ndutu. In direct contrast to their more languid cousins, these streamlined, solitary creatures are most normally seen pacing the plains with the air of an agitated greyhound.

Of the other predators which can be seen in the Serengeti, spotted hyenas are very common, perhaps more numerous than lions. Golden jackals and bat-eared foxes appear to be the most abundant canid species on the plains around Seronera, while black-backed jackals are reasonably common in the thicker vegetation towards Lobo. Driving at dusk or dawn, you stand the best chance of seeing nocturnal predators such as civet, serval, genet and African wildcat. The real rarity among the larger predators is the African wild dog, which was very common in the area until the 1970s, before the population dwindled to local extinction as a result of canid-borne diseases and persecution by farmers living on the park's periphery. Fortunately, wild dogs are very mobile and wide-ranging animals, and sightings have been reported with increased frequency over recent years, particularly in the far north and the adjacent Longido concessions.

SERONERA AND THE SOUTHERN PLAINS

The short-grass plains stretching southeast from Seronera into the NCA might be termed the 'classic' Serengeti: a vast open expanse teeming with all manner of wild creatures ranging from the endearing bat-eared fox to the imperious lion, from flocks of habitually panicked ostrich to strutting pairs of secretary birds, and from the gigantic eland antelope to the diminutive mongooses. Densely populated with wildlife all year through, these southern plains are especially rewarding between December and May, when the rains act as a magnet to the migrant herds of wildebeest and zebra.

The main focal point of the region – indeed of the entire national park – is the park headquarters at Seronera, which is also the site of the oldest lodge in the Serengeti, as well as a cluster of public and special campsites, the staff village and various research projects. The recently opened visitors information centre at Seronera is well worth a visit: facilities include a small site museum, as well as a picnic area and coffee shop, while an elevated wooden walkway leads through an informative open-air display.

The southern plains are interspersed with several clusters of rocky hills known as koppies, each of which forms a microhabitat inhabited by non-plains wildlife such as klipspringer, rock hyrax, leopard, rock agama, rock thrushes, mocking chat and various cliff-nesting raptors. As the name suggests, Simba Koppies, which straddles the main road between the NCA and Seronera, is particularly good for lion, while the grassland around the more easterly Gol Koppies is excellent for cheetah and lion. About 25km south of Seronera, the Moru Koppies area can also provide good lion and cheetah sightings, and it's home to the park's last resident black rhino, a herd of seven that evidently migrated across from the NCA in the mid 1990s.

A striking feature of this part of the Serengeti is the paucity of trees, which flourish only at the sides of koppies and along the riparian belts that follow the Mbalageti and Seronera rivers. The most likely explanation for this quirk is that the soil, which consists of volcanic deposits from an ancient eruption of Ngorongoro, is too hard for most roots to penetrate, except where it has been eroded by flowing water. Paradoxically, one consequence of this is that the thin strip of sausage trees and camelthorn acacias that follows the course of the Seronera River Valley ranks among the best places in Africa to search for leopards – there are simply too few tall trees for these normally elusive creatures to be as well hidden as they tend to be in dense woodland.

Aside from the two perennial rivers, both of which might be described as streams in another context, there is little permanent standing water in this part of the Serengeti. One exception is the small, saline Lake Magadi, which is fed by the Mbalageti River immediately northeast of Moru Koppies and supports large numbers of aquatic birds, including thousands of flamingos when the water level is suitable. A small hippo pool lies on the Seronera River about 5km south of Seronera along the road back towards the NCA. Far more impressive, however, is the Retima Hippo Pool, where up to a hundred of these aquatic animals can be

MAASAI ROCK ART

An unusual relict of the Serengeti's former Maasai inhabitants is to be found at Moru Koppies in the form of some well-preserved rock paintings of animals, shields and other traditional military regalia near the base of a small koppie. This is one of the few such sites associated with the Maasai, and the paintings, which are mostly red, black and white, may well have been inspired by the more ancient and more accomplished rock art of the Kondoa area – though it's anybody's guess whether they possess some sort of ritual significance, or are purely decorative. On another koppie not far from the rock paintings is an ancient rock gong thought to have been used by the Datoga predecessors of the Maasai – a short but steep scramble up a large boulder leads to the rock gong, which also makes for a good picnic spot.

seen basking near the confluence of the Seronera and Grumeti rivers about 15km north of the park headquarters.

The most central base for exploring this region is Seronera Wildlife Lodge, or one of the nearby campsites at the park headquarters. Two of the other three large lodges in the Serengeti – respectively part of the Serena and Sopa chains – are also well positioned for exploring the southern plains, and have far better facilities. Many safari companies also set up seasonal or semi-permanent tented camps at one or another of the myriad special campsites in the vicinity of Seronera. Of the smaller lodges in the national park, the underrated Ndutu Safari Lodge (which actually lies within the NCA) and the wonderfully remote Kusini Camp are both well sited for exploring the southern plains, and remote from the perennially busy road circuit in the immediate vicinity of Seronera.

WHERE TO STAY
Exclusive

Kusini Camp (14 rooms) 🕾 027 250 9817; f 027 250 8273; e tanzania@sanctuarylodges.com; www.sanctuarylodges.com. With its fantastic location among a set of tall black boulders some 40km south of the Moru Koppies, this spaciously laid-out camp is the most remote & exclusive place to stay in the southern Serengeti, especially in Mar when the area hosts immense herds of wildebeest & zebra. At other times of the year, elephant, giraffe & buffalo are quite common in the surrounding acacia woodland – indeed, some impressively hefty buffalo bulls are resident in camp – & lion & leopard are seen with some frequency. The best goal for game drives out of Kusini is Moru Koppies, where lion are plentiful & rhino present but seldom seen, & there are plenty of birds around, including the striking secretary bird for which the camp is named. *US$470/640 FB inc drinks, or US$575/850 full game package; substantial discount Nov–mid-Dec & Jan–Mar. Closed Apr & May.*

Olakira Camp (6 tents) 🕾 027 250 4118/9; m 0784 763338; e info@asilialodges.com; www.asilialodges.com. This wonderful mobile camp

moves seasonally between 2 different locations in the southern Serengeti to complement its more northerly sister camp Sayari. It is based at Ndutu for the wildebeest calving season, usually from Nov through Mar. It closes over Apr–May, then moves up to Turner Springs, a private special campsite 20 mins' drive from Seronera, in an area notable for its dense (& nocturnally vociferous) population of spotted hyena. The Turner Springs site is well placed to catch the migration as it passes through the area in Jun/Jul, & for balloon flights from Seronera Wildlife Lodge. It has a classic safari ambience & décor, consisting of attractively furnished standing tents with king-size or twin beds, private veranda & en-suite flush toilet & hot shower. *US$670/990 sgl/dbl FB or US$730/1110 full game package; low-season discount around 20%.*

Lemala Serengeti (10 tents) This mobile tented camp, described on page 219, is set up about 5km from Ndutu Airstrip from Dec–Apr, when it is well positioned to catch the migration as is disperses in the southeast & during calving season. *US$745/990 sgl/dbl FB.*

Upmarket

Seronera Wildlife Lodge (100 rooms) ☎ 027 254 4595; f 027 254 8633; e res@ hotelsandlodges-tanzania.com; www.hotelsandlodges-tanzania.com. The most central lodge in the Serengeti, situated only a couple of kilometres from the park HQ at Seronera, has an unbeatable location for game drives. It was built around a granite koppie in the early 1970s, & utilises the natural features to create an individual & unmistakably African character. The bar, frequented by bats & rock hyraxes, is reached through a narrow corridor between 2 boulders, while the natural rock walls of the cavernous restaurant are decorated with traditionally styled paintings. In common with other former government lodges, the service, food & facilities have long lagged behind those of most newer lodges, & the outmoded fittings just feel rather tacky after 3 decades of service, but this should have changed following an extensive renovation &

refurbishing programme initiated by the new private management in 2008. Rooms are compact but comfortable, with en-suite bathrooms & large windows facing the surrounding bush. The best reason to select this lodge is simply its brilliant location for game drives, at the heart of the superlative (but sometimes rather overcrowded – see page 212) Seronera game-viewing circuit. *Rates on application.*

Serengeti Serena Lodge (66 rooms) ☎ 028 262 1507; f 028 262 1520, e reservations@ serena.co.tz; www.serenahotels.com. Situated on a hilltop roughly 20km west of Seronera, this is probably the most comfortable of the larger lodges in this part of the Serengeti. Accommodation is in a village-like cluster of Maasai-style double-storey rondavels (round African-style huts), built with slate, wood & thatch to create a pleasing organic feel. The spacious self-contained rooms each have I sgl & I king-size bed, nets & fans & hot showers. There is a

---

SERENGETI BALLOON SAFARIS

Serengeti Balloon Safaris is – no prizes for guessing – the name of the company that runs balloon safaris from a launch site close to Seronera Lodge at 06.00 every morning. Although not cheap, a balloon safari is definitely worth the expense if you can afford it. Gliding serenely above the trees as the sun rises allows you to see the expansive plains from a new and quite thrilling angle. It also offers the chance to see secretive species such as bushbuck and reedbuck, and, because you leave so early in the morning, you are likely to spot a few nocturnal predators (we saw hyenas in abundance, civet twice and had a rare glimpse of an African wild cat). That said, any images you have of sweeping above innumerable wildebeest and zebra may prove a little removed from reality; you can only be confident of seeing large herds of ungulates if you're fortunate enough to be around during the exact week or two when animals concentrate immediately around Seronera.

The safari culminates with a champagne breakfast in the bush, set up at a different site every day, depending on which way the balloons are blown. The meal is presented with some flourish: the immaculately uniformed waiters in particular conjure up images of the safaris of old. Our particular mad-hatters' breakfast party was enlivened by the arrival of three male lions, who strolled less than 100m from the table apparently oblivious to the unusual apparition of 24 people eating scrambled eggs and sausages at a starched tablecloth in the bush. Presumably, this sort of thing doesn't happen every day, whether you're a lion or a human!

The package, which costs US$479 per person, includes the transfer to the balloon site, a balloon trip of roughly one hour's duration and the champagne breakfast. There is a booking desk at the Seronera Wildlife Lodge, as well as at the Serengeti Sopa and Serena lodges. The other Serengeti lodges are too far from the launching site to get there in time (as things stand the transfer from Seronera leaves at 05.30 and from the other lodges at around 04.30!). If you want to be certain of a place, however, it is advisable to book in advance, particularly during high season. Reservations can be made through any safari company, or directly through Serengeti Balloon Safaris (☎ 027 254 8967; e info@balloonsafaris.com; www.info@balloonsafaris.com)

Emma Thomson

Maasai jewellery beads are composed of nine main colours. It's a common misconception that the colours are blended to create complex messages. In fact, while the colours carry meaning, the combinations are randomly selected, mainly for beauty. It's often possible to tell the age of some necklaces according to the fashionable arrangement of colours that vary from year to year. Tendons extracted from the meat consumed originally served as string to hold these intricate designs together. However, these have now been replaced by shredded plastic bags. The meanings for each colour vary from area to area but in general they mean the following:

black	God/rain	orange	rainbow
blue	water	red	warrior/blood/bravery
dark blue	God in the sky	white	milk/peace
gold	ground water	yellow	sun
green	life/spring (rainy season)		

swimming pool, & the buffet meals are far superior to those in most east African safari lodges. The one negative is that game viewing in the thick scrub around the lodge is poor except for when the migration passes through, & it's a good half-hour drive before you reach the main game-viewing circuit east of Seronera Lodge. *US$375/550 sgl/dbl FB; US$225/335 Apr–Jun.*

⌂ **Serengeti Sopa Lodge** (73 rooms) ➋ 027 250 0630/9; f 027 250 8245; e info@sopalodges.com; www.sopalodges.com. This large ostentatious lodge lies about 30 mins' drive south of Seronera, on the side of a hill near the Moru Koppies. The rooms here are practically suites: each has 2 dbl beds, a small sitting room, a large bathroom, a private balcony & a large window giving a grandstand view over the plains below, perfectly appointed to catch the sunset. Following extensive renovations over 2005/06, the formerly rather ostentatious & jarring interior has been supplanted by a more attractive & distinctively African look. The food is excellent & facilities include a swimming pool & internet café. Game viewing in the surrounding area is generally very good, with a high chance of encountering tree-climbing lions on the road north to Seronera, & there's much less traffic in the immediate vicinity than there is around the park HQ. *US$320/550 sgl/dbl FB; US$265/450 in Mar, Nov & early Dec, US$100/200 Apr/May.*

⌂ **Ndutu Safari Lodge** (35 rooms) ➋ 027 250 2829/6702; f 027 250 8310; e bookings@ ndutu.com; www.ndutu.com. Although it is actually situated just within the Ngorongoro Conservation

Area on the southeast border with the Serengeti, Ndutu is most logically bracketed with the Seronera lodges, since the western plains of the conservation area essentially belong to the same seasonal ecosystem. A low-key & underrated retreat, Ndutu Safari Lodge is set in thick acacia woodland overlooking the seasonal Lake Ndutu, & it has a distinct 'bush' atmosphere lacking from other comparably priced lodges in the Serengeti ecosystem. The rooms are in small, unfussy stone chalets & have netting & hot water. The bar & restaurant are open-sided stone & thatch structures frequented by a legion of genets by night. This is an excellent place to stay if you want to avoid the crowds, & the surrounding plains offer good general game viewing, particularly during the wet season when they are teeming with wildebeest. Despite lying within the NCA, Ndutu isn't well positioned for visiting Ngorongoro Crater. It should also be noted that crossing into the Serengeti while staying at Ndutu would attract a separate national park entrance fee. *Self-contained bungalows US$249/385 sgl/dbl FB; US$199/302 May–Nov.*

⌂ **Serengeti Savannah Camps** (12 rooms) ➋ 027 254 7066; e bookings@ serengetisavannahcamps.com; www.serengetisavannahcamps.com. This small, mobile tented camp, one of the few in northern Tanzania that's not part of a chain, aims to offer safari-goers a genuine bush experience at a reasonable price. It moves between 2 locations, 1 in the Seronera area from Jun–Nov & 1 near Ndutu between Dec & Mar to catch the calving season. The tents are simply but comfortably furnished & all have a private veranda, chemical toilet & starlight shower. US$280/460 sgl/dbl FB, hefty discounts for east African residents.

🏠 **Simiyu Mobile Camp** (9 rooms) ➘ 027 254 4556; m 0784 207727; f 027 250 8937; e twc-reservations@habari.co.tz; www.tanganyikawildernesscamps.com. This highly rated luxury mobile camp moves between 4 locations over the course of the year in order to stick close to the migration. Dates might change from one year to the next depending on the movement of the wildebeest, but usually it would be around Ndutu from Dec–Mar, split between the Seronera area & the Western Corridor from May–Aug & somewhere further north from Aug–Nov. All tents are en-suite &

comfortably furnished with king-size or twin bed, flush toilet & bucket shower inside. Dinner is usually served outside, weather permitting. Good value. US$300/400 sgl/dbl FB.

🏠 **Serengeti Wilderness Camp** (10 rooms) ➘ 027 250 2668; e serecamp.wildfrontiers@habari.co.tz; www.wildfrontiers.com. This down-to-earth mobile tented camp, run by the highly regarded operator Wild Frontiers, moves location every few months as dictated by the movements of the wildebeest migration. The en-suite tents have solar lighting, eco-friendly toilets & comfortable but unpretentious furnishings. It generally spends the period Nov–Apr in the southern plains, relocating to the Western Corridor over Jun–Jul & moving further north Aug–Oct. Closed mid-Apr–May. US$ 450/680 FB.

MODERN-DAY MAASAI

Emma Thomson

The future of the Maasai seems an uncertain one. The Tanzanian government regards them as primitive and criticises them for 'holding the country back'. They are banned from wearing their distinctive rubega/shuka (robes) on public transport and in order to attend primary or secondary school the children are forced to remove their elaborate bead jewellery, and dress in Western-style clothes, while boys must shave off their long hair. All this follows a scheme launched by the government in the 1960s named the 'official national ideology of development', whose unspoken aims were to integrate the Maasai forcibly into mainstream society and settle them so the government could implement taxation.

Originally transhumant pastoralists, alternating the movement of their cattle between established wet- and dry-season pastures, the Maasai have now lost these latter areas to commercial farmers and wildlife conservation. Increasingly unpredictable rains leave grass and cattle dehydrated, and freak outbreaks of rinderpest and east coast fever (brought by explorers in the early 19th century) combine to often wipe out herds all together.

Squeezed into this bottleneck of depleted herds and land, the Maasai have had to overcome one of their greatest taboos – the ban on 'breaking the ground' and destroying grass, believed to have been sent by the Creator as sacred food for the cattle – in order to grow crops. Skills were acquired from nearby neighbours, the Chagga and Meru, and the latest studies show that now 40–45% of Maasai in east Africa trade meat for beans and maize, with only 50% living purely on the traditional diet of milk, blood and meat.

Unfortunately, when farming fails as a result of nutrient-poor soil, members of the family come back into the towns in search of paid work to supplement the unavoidable financial needs of providing for their families in the modern world. Men often find employment as nightwatchmen, while the women may have to resort to petty trading, beer brewing and, increasingly, prostitution.

However, the Maasai are both resourceful and resilient and the developing tourist industry brings new opportunities. Gemma EnoLengila, co-founder of the NGO, Serian UK, stresses that 'the real challenge lies in creating sustainable projects that are developed in partnership with (traditional) communities, in a way that empowers rather than oppresses them'.

10

Budget and camping There is a simple resthouse at the Seronera park headquarters charging US$30 per person per night bed and breakfast, as well as a hostel with bunk accommodation at US$20 per person per night bed and breakfast. A cluster of seven campsites lies about 5km from Seronera Lodge. Camping costs the usual US$30 per person. Facilities are limited to long-drop toilets and a rubbish pit. You may be able to organise a shower and fill up water containers for a small fee at the lodge. There is a good chance of seeing nocturnal scavengers such as hyena and genet – even, rather disconcertingly, the occasional lion pride – pass through the campsites after dark.

LOBO AND THE NORTHERN SERENGETI

Wildly beautiful, and refreshingly untrammelled coming after Seronera, the northern third of the Serengeti is characterised by green, rolling hills that undulate gently towards the Kenyan border, capped by some spectacular granite outcrops, particularly in the vicinity of Lobo. A cover of dense acacia woodland is interspersed with tracts of more open grassland, bisected by the ribbons of lush riparian woodland that enclose the Grumeti and Mara rivers and their various tributaries. Partially due to the relatively dense foliage, the northern Serengeti doesn't generally match up to the south in terms of game viewing, but then nor is it anything like as overrun with tourist traffic as the road circuits around Seronera – it's still possible to do an entire game drive without seeing another vehicle in this part of the Serengeti.

If it is sheer volumes of wildlife you're after, Lobo and surrounds generally comes into its own during September and October, when the wildebeest pass through on the southward migration from Kenya to the Serengeti Plains. But even at other times of year, there is plenty to hold your interest. The area supports most of the park's elephant population, and the base of the Lobo Hills in particular is noted for large prides of lions, as well as providing refuge to cheetah, leopard, spotted hyena, bat-eared fox and several pairs of the exquisite serval, a small spotted cat most often seen darting through open grassland shortly after sunrise.

The one part of the northern Serengeti to match the southern plains for general game viewing is the wedge of sloping grassland that divides the Mara River from the Kenyan border. Sometimes referred to as the Mara Triangle, this southern extension of the legendary Maasai Mara National Reserve supports prodigious herds of eland, topi, gazelle, zebra, wildebeest, buffalo et al throughout the year, and it can be little short of mind-boggling when the migration moves in over July to September. During this time of year, large herds of wildebeest frequently gather on one or other side of the river, sometimes milling around for hours, even days, before one brave or foolish individual initiates a sudden river crossing, often for no apparent reason – indeed, it's not unusual for the same group of wildebeest to cross back in the opposite direction within hours of the initial crossing, suggesting these ostensibly slow-witted beasts adhere firmly to the maxim that the grass is always greener on the other side.

Prior to 2005, the Mara Triangle had been effectively closed to casual tourism for decades, partly due to its remoteness from any lodge, and partly due to problems with banditry and poaching. Today, the few visitors who make it up this far are still unlikely to meet much other tourist traffic, but the area can be readily accessed from two seasonal tented camps, Sayari and Lemala Serengeti, both of which lie to the south of the Mara River near Kogatende Rangers Post, where a concrete causeway crosses the river.

🏠 **WHERE TO STAY**
Exclusive
🏠 **Sayari Camp** (6 rooms) ☎ 027 250 2799; m 0784 763338; e info@asilialodges.com; www.asilialodges.com. Established in 2005, this wonderful, remote tented camp lies close to the

south bank of the Mara River, offering ready access to what is arguably the best-kept game-viewing secret in all of northern Tanzania: the superb Mara Triangle. This untrammelled wedge of open grassland supports some of the densest grazer populations in east Africa, as well as all the Big 5 (rhino sometimes cross from Kenya's Maasai Mara) & a great many birds. The accommodation is as upmarket as you might hope for in a semi-permanent camp, consisting of stylishly decorated walk-in tents with private balconies & en-suite toilets & hot showers, & the food is both imaginative & classy. But the main attraction of Sayari is the genuine wilderness atmosphere & remoteness from other lodges. *US$775/1,160 sgl/dbl FB, or US$830/1,290 full game package, with low-season discount of around 20%.*

⌂ **Lemala Serengeti** (10 tents) ⤨ 027 254 8966; f 027 254 8937; e info@lemalacamp.com; www.lemalacamp.com. Established in 2007, this semi-permanent luxury tented camp spends the period Dec–Apr in the Ndutu area, then relocates to the north from early Jun–mid-Nov. The northern location lies on a boulder-strewn slope close to the main Lobo road about 25km south of the Kogatende Rangers Post & causeway offering access to the Mara Triangle. The impressive koppies between Lemala & Kogatende have long hosted a resident pride of large lions, which are often seen sprawled out on the rocks. The tents are very spacious & decorated in classic safari style, with a wooden floor & canvas top, & all have twin or king-size beds, solar powered lighting & hot water. *US$775/1150 sgl/dbl FB, with substantial discount Jun & Nov.*

⌂ **Migration Camp** (20 rooms) ⤨ 027 254 0630/9; f 027 254 8245; e info@elewana.com; www.elewana.com. Set in the Ndasiata Hills about 20km from Lobo, this formerly rather rundown camp has undergone 2 major makeovers, most recently after being acquired by Elewana in 2004. It now ranks as one of the most exclusive lodges within the Serengeti National Park. Accommodation is in spacious en-suite luxury 'tents' made of canvas & wood, complemented by stylish wooden décor evoking the Edwardian era, & with large balconies facing the perennial Grumeti River. The lushly wooded grounds are rustling with birds & lizards, & there is a hippo pool on the river, with larger mammals often passing through camp. The surrounding area supports resident populations of lion, leopard, elephant & buffalo, & is fantastic when the migration passes through. Facilities include a swimming pool, jacuzzi, cocktail bar, library & lounge. An unusual feature of

the camp is that short, guided game walks can be undertaken along several trails leading out from it. *US$1,118/1,490 sgl/dbl FB, inc most drinks, laundry, transfer to/from Lobo airstrip; US$1,020/1,360 in Mar, Nov & early Dec, & US$945/1,260 Apr & May. Full game package including drives an additional US$100 pp.*

⌂ **Klein's Camp** (10 bandas) ⤨ 027 254 8549/8038 or (South Africa) +27 (0)11 809 4447; e inboundsales@andbeyond.com; www.andbeyond.com. This excellent &Beyond lodge lies just outside the eastern border of the national park, on a private conservancy leased from the local Maasai, & it effectively functions as an exclusive private game reserve, since camp residents have sole use of the concession. Because Klein's Camp lies outside the national park, there are no restrictions prohibiting night drives & guided game walks, both of which add an extra dimension to a safari. The camp has a stunning location on the side of a hill offering panoramic views in all directions, & game viewing in the region is generally good, particularly along the Grumeti River, with a similar range of species as found in the Lobo area. The camp consists of self-contained bandas, all with hot shower, nets & a private balcony with a view. *US$950 FB, US$625 pp over Mar, May, Nov & early Dec, inc all meals, drinks & activities. Closed Apr.*

⌂ **Suyan Camp** (6 rooms) ⤨ 027 250 2799; m 0784 763338; e info@asilialodges.com; www.asilialodges.com. Situated about 2km outside Klein's Gate, this wonderful luxury tented camp lies along a stretch of lush riverine forest in the vast Loliondo Game Controlled Area, which is bounded by Serengeti National Park to the west, Lake Natron to the east & the NCA to the south. A good base for game drives in the Lobo area or Serengeti National Park, & within day-tripping distance of the Mara River, the camp also offer guided game walks with a Maasai guide, & night drives in the concession, which supports a similar range of species to the neighbouring national park. A significant portion of proceeds is paid to the local Maasai community that leases the land. *US$730/1,110 full game package, with low-season discount of around 20%.*

⌂ **Buffalo Luxury Camp** (20 rooms) ⤨ 027 255 3858; e info@buffaloluxurycamp.com; www.buffaloluxurycamp.com. Situated within the Loliondo Game Controlled Area, on a 30ha titled plot near Klein's Gate, this promising new luxury tented camp offers the opportunity to undertake game drives in the game-rich Lobo Hills of the northern Serengeti as well as other activities such as

The Serengeti National Park, though popularly associated with grassland and open savanna, is in fact a reasonably ecologically varied entity. The western part of the national park consists of broken savanna, interspersed with impenetrable stands of whistling thorns and other acacias, and run through by the perennial Grumeti River and an attendant ribbon of riparian forest. The north, abutting Kenya's Maasai Mara National Reserve, is unexpectedly hilly, particularly around Lobo, and it supports a variety of more or less wooded savanna habitats. So, while the actual Serengeti Plains in the southeast of the park do support the relatively limited avifauna one tends to associate with open grassland, the national park ranks with the best of them in terms of avian variety. A working Serengeti checklist compiled by Schmidt in the 1980s tallied 505 species, and a further 30 species have been added since 1990.

The Serengeti-Mara ecosystem is one of Africa's Endemic Bird Areas, hosting five bird species found nowhere else, some of which are confined to the Tanzanian portion of the ecosystem. These 'Serengeti specials' are easy to locate and identify within their restricted range. The grey-throated spurfowl, a common roadside bird around the park headquarters at Seronera, is easily distinguished from the similar red-throated spurfowl by the white stripe below its red mask. In areas of woodland, parties of exquisite Fischer's lovebird draw attention to themselves by their incessant screeching and squawking as they flap energetically between trees. If the endemic spurfowl and lovebird are essentially local variations on a more widespread generic type, not so the rufous-tailed weaver, a fascinating bird placed in its own genus, but with nesting habits that indicate an affiliation to the sparrow-weavers. The rufous-tailed weaver is significantly larger and more sturdily built than most African ploceids, and its scaly feathering, pale eyes and habit of bouncing around boisterously in small flocks could lead to it being mistaken for a type of babbler – albeit one with an unusually large bill!

Of the two other Serengeti-Mara EBA endemics, the most visible and widespread is the Usambiro barbet, a close relative of the slightly smaller D'Arnaud's barbet, with which it is sometimes considered conspecific. Altogether more elusive is the grey-crested helmet-shrike, which strongly resembles the white helmet-shrike but is larger, has a more upright grey crest, and lacks an eye wattle. Although this striking bird indulges in typically conspicuous helmet-shrike behaviour, with small parties streaming noisily from one tree to the next, it is absent from the southern Serengeti, and thinly distributed in the north, where it is often associated with stands of whistling thorns.

Endemic chasing will be a priority of any serious birding visit to the Serengeti, but the mixed woodland and grassland of the north and west produce consistently good birdwatching, including many species that will delight non-birders. The massive ostrich is common, as are other primarily terrestrial giants such as the kori bustard, secretary bird and southern ground hornbill. Perhaps the most distinctive of the smaller birds is the lilac-breasted roller, an exquisitely coloured gem often seen perched on trees alongside the road. Highlights are inevitably subjective, but recent memorable sightings included a breeding colony of Jackson's golden-backed weaver at Grumeti River Camp, a magnificent black eagle soaring above the cliffs at Lobo, and six different vulture species squabbling over a kill in the Western Corridor. And there is always the chance of an exciting 'first'. Recent additions to the Tanzanian bird list from Serengeti include European turtledove (1997), short-eared owl (1998), long-tailed nightjar, black-backed cisticola and swallow-tailed kite (2000). In 2001, close to Grumeti River Camp, we were fortunate enough to see (and photograph) the first golden pipit ever recorded in the national park.

Adapted from an article by the author that originally appeared in the April/May 2002 issue of Africa Birds & Birding.

guided walks & night drives. Large en-suite standing tents have an elevated sleeping area, a sitting room, electricity, running water & flush toilets. *US$625 FB,* *US$560 Apr–May, inc unlimited day & night game drives, walking safaris, Maasai cultural excursions, drinks & laundry.*

Upmarket

🏠 **Lobo Wildlife Lodge** (75 rooms) ☎ 027 254 4595; f 027 254 8633; e sales@ hotelsandlodges-tanzania.com; www.sales@hotelsandlodges-tanzania.com. As with the other former government hotels in this chain, Lobo boasts an inalienable asset in the form of a stunning location, but one that was long let down by the poor standard of service & maintenance, though is soon to change following the initiation of an extensive programme of renovations in late 2008. The lodge was built over 1968–70, at which time most tourism to the Serengeti came directly from Kenya, & it has waned in popularity now that visitors to the Serengeti come through Arusha. This is a shame, because it is an amazing construction. Like Seronera, it's built around a koppie, but the design is even more impressive & imaginative than that of the more southerly lodge, spanning 4 floors & with a fantastic view over the surrounding plains. The surrounding hills can offer some wonderful game viewing (a pride of 20 lions is resident in the immediate vicinity of the lodge) & the grounds are crawling with hyraxes & colourful agama lizards. Lobo is relatively good value. *Rates on application.*

🏠 **Mbuzi Mawe Tented Camp** (16 rooms) ☎ 027 250 4058; f 027 250 8282; e reservations@ serena.co.tz; www.serenahotels.com. This new tented camp is set among a group of ancient granite koppies overlooking the Tagora Plains roughly 45km northeast of Seronera & 30km southwest of Lobo. The lodge's central location makes it a useful base from which to explore most of the key game-viewing areas in the Serengeti, & there is quite a bit of wildlife resident in the immediate vicinity (including the rock-dwelling klipspringer for which it is named), supplemented by the migration as it heads southwards in Nov or Dec. Accommodation is in large, earthily decorated en-suite standing tents, each of which contains 2 dbl beds & has a private stone patio with a view towards the rocks. A swimming pool is planned. *US$375/550 sgl/dbl FB; US$225/335 Apr–Jun.*

Camping The campsite immediately outside of the Lobo Wildlife Lodge is little used by comparison with those at Seronera. It also costs US$30 per person. Facilities are limited to a toilet and rubbish pit. You can pop into the neighbouring lodge for a drink or meal if you like.

THE WESTERN CORRIDOR

The relatively narrow arm of the Serengeti that stretches westward from Seronera almost as far as the shore of Lake Victoria is generally flatter than the more northerly parts of the park, but moister and more densely vegetated than the southern plains. Aside from a few small isolated mountain ranges, the dominant geographic feature of the Western Corridor is a pair of rivers, the Grumeti and Mbalageti, whose near-parallel west-flowing courses, which run less than 20km apart, support tall ribbons of riparian forest before eventually they exit the national park to empty into Lake Victoria. The characteristic vegetation of the Western Corridor is park-like woodland, interspersed with areas of open grassland and dense stands of the ghostly grey 'whistling thorn' *Acacia drepanolobrium.*

Tourist traffic in this part of the park is relatively low: few camping safaris make it this far south, and accommodation is limited to a handful of smallish camps. Game viewing is pretty good throughout the year: the broken savanna to the south of the Grumeti River supports substantial resident populations of lion, giraffe, wildebeest, zebra and most other typical plains animals, while the riverine forest harbours a few troops of the exquisite black-and-white colobus monkey, and the little-visited vistas of open grassland north of the river are especially good for cheetah. Between May and July, the migration usually passes through the Western Corridor, though it may stick further east in years of heavy rain. The crossing of

10

the Grumeti, usually in June or July, is one of the most dramatic sequences in the annual wildebeest migration, and a positive bonanza for a dense population of gargantuan crocodiles.

🏠 WHERE TO STAY
Exclusive

🏠 **Singita Grumeti Reserves** (24 rooms across 3 lodges) ❯ (South Africa) +27 (0)21 683 3424; e singita@singita.com; www.singita.com. The legendary South African lodge operator Singita recently acquired exclusive traversing rights across the 1,400km² Grumeti Game Reserve, a northern extension of the Western Corridor, where it now operates a trio of luxury upmarket lodges aimed at seriously affluent travellers seeking an exclusive safari experience. The flagship Sasakwa Lodge on the eponymous hill offers dramatic elevated views across the verdant plains of the western corridor, while Faru Faru Lodge lies in a wooded area noted for its high mammal & bird diversity, & the more earthy Sabora Camp is a tented camp set in the open plains. The wildlife in this formerly undeveloped corner of the greater Serengeti is similar to other parts of the vast ecosystem, but notable population increases have been recorded since 2003, & plans to translocate 48 black rhino from South Africa are underway. The enterprise employs 600 people, mostly from surrounding communities, & it offers cultural visits to nearby villages. Although wildlife viewing is good all year through, it peaks during Jul–Sep, when the migration is in the area. *US$1,250/1,990 sgl/dbl for Sabora or Faru Faru, or US$2,000/3,200 sgl/dbl for Sasakwa. Rates inc all meals, drinks & activities.*

🏠 **Grumeti River Camp** (10 rooms) ❯ 027 254 8549/8038 or (South Africa) +27 (0)11 809 4447; e inboundsales@andbeyond.com; www.andbeyond.com. Overlooking a small pool near the Grumeti River, this archetypal bush camp easily ranks as our favourite lodge anywhere in the Serengeti. The mood here is pure in-your-face Africa: the pool in front of the bar supports a resident pod of hippos & attracts a steady stream of other large mammals coming to drink, while birdlife is prolific both at the water's edge & in the surrounding thickets. At night, the place comes alive with a steady chorus of insects & frogs, & hippos & buffaloes grazing noisily around the tents. This place isn't for the faint-hearted, & you shouldn't even think about walking around at night without an armed escort, as the buffaloes have been known to charge. Facilities include an outdoor *boma*, where evening meals are served (except when it rains), & a small circular swimming pool from where you can watch hippos bathing while you do the same thing. Accommodation consists of 10 stylish tents, each of which has a netted king-size bed & en-suite toilet & showers. The atmosphere is very informal, & the service is excellent without ever becoming impersonal. *US$950 FB, dropping to US$625 pp Mar, May, Nov & early Dec, inc meals, drinks & activities. Closed Apr.*

🏠 **Kirawira Tented Camp** (25 rooms) ❯ 027 250 4058; f 027 250 8282; e reservations@serena.co.tz; www.serenahotels.com. Part of the Serena chain, this is another very upmarket tented camp, set on a small acacia-covered hill offering sweeping views over the Western Corridor. The Edwardian décor of the communal areas creates something of an *Out of Africa* feel, & while the atmosphere is neither as intimate nor as 'bush' as at Grumeti, Kirawira does have a definite charm — & it will probably appeal more to safari-goers who don't find the thought of having hippo & buffalo chomping around their tent a major draw. Accommodation consists of 25 standing tents, each of which is set on its own raised platform, & is comfortably decorated with a netted king-size bed & en-suite shower & toilet. There is a large swimming pool, the service is immaculate & the food is probably the best in the Serengeti. *US$950/1,450 sgl/dbl, US$435/755 Apr–May, inc meals, drinks, game drives & walks.*

Upmarket

🏠 **Mbalageti Serengeti** (40 rooms) ❯ 255 27 2548632; e mbalageti@bol.co.tz. www.mbalageti.com. Located in the Western Corridor, Mbalageti is perched on the northwestern slopes of Mwamnevi Hill, which lies 16km south of the main road through the Western Corridor, crossing the game-rich seasonal Dutwa floodplain & the Mbalageti River en route. Accommodation is in stunning thatch, wood, stone & canvas cottages, all of which are secluded in the evergreen woodland running along the ridge of the hill, & come with large wooden decks offering a superb view over the river to the Dutwa Plains from the outdoor bath. The dining area & bar are centred on a swimming pool, also offering panoramic views, & the food – different theme buffets every night – is excellent. Overall, it's a very comfortable & relatively affordable alternative to the more established lodges in the Western Corridor.

Moderate

🏠 **Ikoma Bush Camp** (17 rooms) \ 027 255 3243/250 6315; e reservations@moivaro.com; www.moivaro.com. This refreshingly unpretentious camp is situated on a concession immediately outside of the national park, roughly 3km from Ikoma Gate by road, & about 40km northwest of Seronera. The concession has been granted to the lodge by the nearby village of Robanda, which is paid a fee (used to fund the local school, water pump & clinic) in exchange for use of the land & assistance with anti-poaching patrols. Set in a glade of acacias, accommodation is in old-style no-frills dbl & twin tents with en-suite showers & small verandas facing out towards the bush. Because it lies outside the park, guided game walks are on offer, as are night drives, which come with a chance of encountering the likes of leopard, genet & more occasionally the secretive aardvark. It's a great base at any time of year, but especially in Jun when the migration passes through, & still quite reasonably priced. *US$286/357 sgl/dbl FB, US$251/314 Mar, Jun, Sep–mid-Dec & US$176/220 Apr/May.*

Budget and camping

🏠 **Serengeti Stop Over** (10 rooms) \ 028 262 273; m 0784 406996/422359; f 028 250 0388; e info@serengetistopover.com; www.serengetistopover.com. This excellent budget lodge lies along the eastern side of the main

US$340/420 standard sgl/dbl, US$350/645 tented chalet, dropping to US$260/395 & US$330/585 over most of Dec–Mar & Sep/Oct, & US$200/290 & US$250/370 in Apr/May, inc meals & most drinks.

🏠 **Mapito Tented Camp** (10 rooms) m 0732 975210; f 0784 864626; e info@mapito-tented-camp.com; www.mapito-tented-camp.com. Similar in style & feel to Ikoma Bush Camp & situated outside the same entrance gate, this is a very likeable & reasonably priced tented camp with a real bush feel, plenty of avian & mammal activity in the immediate vicinity, & a variety of activities on offer, including guided walks & night drives. Set on stone platforms, the standing tents come with twin or king-size beds, & are furnished with a strong African touch, & have a private veranda & en-suite toilets & showers. The solar-lit mess tent serves hearty home-style meals. *US$259/428 sgl/dbl FB, US$248/408 Sep–mid-Dec. Closed Apr/May.*

🏠 **Kijireshi Tented Camp** \ 028 262 1231; e tilapia@mwanza.com; www.kijireshi.com. Under the same ownership as the Tilapia Hotel in Mwanza, this little-known camp lies close to Bunda on the western border of the Serengeti. It offers comfortable accommodation in furnished tents, & has a bar & restaurant. *US$100/150 FB self-contained dbl.*

Mwanza–Musoma road, in an area where quite a bit of game can be present, about 1km south of the Ndaraka Entrance Gate to Serengeti National Park & 18km south of Bunda. The lodge consists of 10 bandas & a campsite with hot showers & cooking

---

OLOIBONI

Emma Thomson

The oloiboni acts as a spiritual psychiatrist within Maasai communities, using stones to divine past, present and future events. Members of the homestead are able to consult him about family or mental and physical health problems, the answers to which come to the oloiboni in dreams. A reading involves the patient sitting cross-legged before him, spitting on the stones to infuse them with his/her spirit, and waiting for the results.

The skills are only passed on through the patrilineal line, and even then sons are not permitted to practise their powers of mediation until their 20th birthday.

Intriguingly, two oloibonis are forbidden to meet each other, so if a neighbouring spiritual leader appears to be stealing business or enjoying good trade, villagers will claim that their oloiboni will send lions to attack the offending culprit.

shades. A great advantage of staying here for motorised travellers coming from Kenya or Mwanza is that park fees are only payable once you enter the park. The lodge can arrange safaris to Serengeti National Park, which will work out more cheaply than a safari out of Arusha, if only because the lodge is a mere 1km from the entrance gate & 135km from Seronera, so that an overnight or day trip is a realistic possibility. The cost of a vehicle to carry up to 5 people for a day trip into the park costs US$130. Other activities on offer include a walking safari to Lake Victoria at US$18 per trip, traditional & game fishing trips, a visit to the Nyerere Museum, & dancing & other cultural activities. *Camping US$10 tent hire plus US$5 pp; banda US$30/55 sgl/dbl B&B.*

| |

Lake Victoria

The world's second-largest freshwater body (after Lake Superior in North America), Lake Victoria extends over almost 70,000km^2 – an area comparable to Ireland – of which some 51% falls within Tanzania, with the remainder being split between Kenya and Uganda. The lake, which fills an elevated depression situated between the two major forks of the Great Rift Valley, is nowhere more than 75m deep and it contains numerous islands, of which four (including Ukerewe and Rubondo in Tanzania) rank among the 20 largest freshwater islands in the world. The level of Lake Victoria has remained more or less unchanged in historical times, but it probably dried up entirely as recently as 10,000–15,000 years ago. The lake's major affluent is the Kagera River, whose sources in the highlands of Burundi and Rwanda are also the most remote sources of the Nile River, which flows out of Lake Victoria near Jinja in Uganda.

Lake Victoria has never featured prominently on Tanzania's tourist circuit, even though it practically borders the Serengeti and its eastern shore is easy enough to visit from any of the lodges in the Western Corridor. The closest port coming from the Serengeti is Musoma, on the border with Kenya, but the larger and more southerly port of Mwanza is also accessible from the Serengeti. A more rewarding extension to a standard safari, however, is the lake's one nascent upmarket tourist attraction, the underrated and pedestrian-friendly Rubondo Island National Park, now accessible on scheduled daily flights from Arusha via the Serengeti and Mwanza.

MWANZA

The fourth-largest city in Tanzania, with a population of 220,000, Mwanza sprawls across the undulating and rocky southeastern shore of Lake Victoria, below the small hill where Speke reputedly first arrived at the lake back in 1858. The town (whose name is a European bastardisation of the Sukuma word *nyanza*, meaning lake) was founded as a German administrative outpost in 1890, and rose to local prominence in the 1920s following the discovery of gold in the region and the completion of the northern extension of the Central Railway from Dar es Salaam.

Today, central Mwanza exudes a likeable cocktail of economic vigour and tropical languor, given physical manifestation by the mismatch of new modern buildings and mildly decrepit colonial-era landmarks that line the streets, but it boasts few tourist attractions. The best-known local landmark is Bismarck Rock, a precariously balanced granite formation that lies within the main harbour, but several similarly impressive outcrops can be seen by wandering along Station Road on the peninsula to the south of the city centre. More alluring out-of-town attractions include the proposed Saanane National Park and the excellent Bujora Sukuma Museum.

TOURIST INFORMATION There is no tourist information office in Mwanza. An informative website (*www.mwanza-guide.com*) is well worth checking out and the webmaster is very helpful when it comes to answering queries.

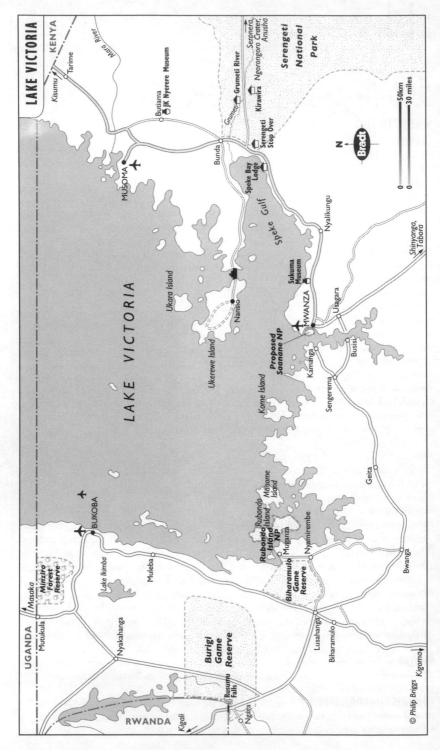

TOUR OPERATORS For flights and other bookings, the best bet is Fourways Travel on the main roundabout on Station Road (↘ *028 250 2273/2620;* e *fourways@ fourwaystravel.net; www.fourwaystravel.net*). For budget travellers, a day or overnight safari to the Serengeti National Park from the Mwanza side will be far cheaper than a full northern circuit safari out of Arusha. A good contact for affordable Serengeti excursions is Serengeti Stop Over near the national park's Ndaraka Entrance Gate (see page 223).

WHERE TO STAY
Exclusive

🏠 **Wag Hill Lodge** (3 rooms) ↘ 028 250 2445; m 0754 917974/777086; e info@waghill.com; www.waghill.com. Situated on a 17ha stand on a forested stretch of lakeshore a few mins by boat from central Mwanza, this small & exclusive new lodge is particularly suited to keen anglers & birdwatchers, or anybody else who just wants to get away from it all. *US$275 pp inc meals, drinks & a 10.00 pick-up by boat from the Mwanza Yacht Club.*

Upmarket

🏠 **Hotel Tilapia** (40 rooms) ↘ 028 250 0517/617; f 028 250 0141; e tilapia@ mwanza-online.com or info@tilapiahotel.com; www.tilapiahotel.com. This comfortable hotel, situated about 1km from the town centre along Station Rd, has an attractive lakeshore position adjacent to the jetty for Saanane Island. Facilities include a swimming pool, car hire, business centre, Japanese, Thai & Indian restaurants, satellite flat screen TV & AC in all rooms, & an attractive wooden bar & patio overlooking the lake. *Dbl chalets US$85 B&B; luxury dbl berth on the docked African Queen US$110; suites US$120 upwards; substantial discounts offered to residents.*

🏠 **New Mwanza Hotel** (55 rooms) ↘ 028 250 1070/1; f 028 250 3202; e nmh@raha.com or nmh@mwanza-online.com. Recently privatised & renovated, this former government hotel on Post Rd in central Mwanza is similar in standard to the Hotel Tilapia, with the advantages of a more central location & cheaper rates for non-residents, & disadvantages of a blander atmosphere & the absence of a lake view. A business centre, coffee shop, restaurant, casino & shopping arcade are all located within the hotel building. *Standard dbls with AC & satellite TV US$50 B&B; suites US$80, ostentatious presidential suite US$250.*

🏠 **Isamilo Lodge** (25 rooms) ↘ 028 254 1627/8; f 028 254 1628; e isamilolodge@isamilo.com; www.isamilo-lodge.com. This impressive new lodge is carved into the hillside overlooking Mwanza at the reputed spot where Speke first saw Lake Victoria in 1858. Catering to local business travellers, its rooms all have AC, wireless internet, satellite TV, phone & tiled en-suite bathrooms. 2 restaurants serve a mix of continental, Indian & Asian dishes, & the pleasant terrace bar offers panoramic views of the lake. It's in the Isamilo area 3km from central Mwanza & 8km from the airport. *US$60/70/80/120 sgl/dbl/twin/suite.*

Moderate

🏠 **The Treehouse** (5 rooms) ↘ 028 254 1160; e treehouse@streetwise-africa.org; www.streetwise-africa.org This homely B&B, located 600m from Isamilo Lodge, is perfect for travellers interested in contributing to the community. Run by the charity group Streetwise Africa, all profits go directly to a programme supporting street kids in Mwanza. All rooms have 24hr internet access & a delicious homemade b/fast is included. *2 comfy sgls with shared bath US$30 each; 2 en-suite dbls US$45/50 sgl/dbl; 1 family banda US$70. Discounts for backpackers & volunteers.*

Budget

🏠 **Lake Hotel** ↘ 028 254 2030. Mwanza's long-serving Lake Hotel is conveniently situated off Kenyatta Rd between the railway station & town centre, & despite looking a bit rundown it remains a reliable fallback in the budget range. The restaurant has been closed for years, but the outdoor bar remains one of the better drinking holes in Mwanza. *Large self-contained rooms with hot water, nets & fan Tsh15,000/20,000 sgl/dbl, inc derisory b/fast.*

Lake Victoria MWANZA

11

✗ WHERE TO EAT

✗ **Yun Long Chinese Restaurant** m 0784 821723;
⊕ lunch & dinner daily. About 5 mins' walk from the town centre, this lovely outdoor bar & restaurant is pretty much unique for Mwanza in that it actually has a view over the lake & Bismarck Rock. It's a great spot for sundowners, but the restaurant also serves

LAKE VICTORIA AND THE RIDDLE OF THE NILE

The first European to see Lake Victoria was John Hanning Speke, who marched from Tabora to the site of present-day Mwanza in 1858 following his joint 'discovery' of Lake Tanganyika with Richard Burton the previous year. Speke named the lake for Queen Victoria, but prior to that Arab slave traders called it Ukerewe (still the name of its largest island). It is unclear what name was in local use, since the only one used by Speke is Nyanza, which simply means lake.

A major goal of the Burton–Speke expedition had been to solve the great geographical enigma of the age, the source of the White Nile. Speke, based on his brief glimpse of the southeast corner of Lake Victoria, somewhat whimsically proclaimed his 'discovery' to be the answer to that riddle. Burton, with a comparable lack of compelling evidence, was convinced that the great river flowed out of Lake Tanganyika. The dispute between the former travelling companions erupted bitterly on their return to Britain, where Burton – the more persuasive writer and respected traveller – gained the backing of the scientific establishment.

Over 1862–63, Speke and Captain James Grant returned to Lake Victoria, hoping to prove Speke's theory correct. They looped inland around the western shore of the lake, arriving at the court of King Mutesa of Buganda, then continued east to the site of present-day Jinja, where a substantial river flowed out of the lake after tumbling over the cataract that Speke named Ripon Falls. From here, the two explorers headed north, sporadically crossing paths with the river throughout what is today Uganda, before following the Nile to Khartoum and Cairo.

Speke's declaration that 'The Nile is settled' met with mixed support back home. Burton and other sceptics pointed out that Speke had bypassed the entire western shore of his purported great lake, had visited only a couple of points on the northern shore, and had not attempted to explore the east. Nor, for that matter, had he followed the course of the Nile in its entirety. Speke, claimed his detractors, had seen several different lakes and different stretches of river, connected only in Speke's deluded mind. The sceptics had a point, but Speke had nevertheless gathered sufficient geographical evidence to render his claim highly plausible, and his notion of one great lake, far from being mere whimsy, was backed by anecdotal information gathered from local sources along the way.

Matters were scheduled to reach a head on 16 September 1864, when an eagerly awaited debate between Burton and Speke – in the words of the former, 'what silly tongues called the "Nile Duel"' – was due to take place at the Royal Geographical Society (RGS). And reach a head they did, but in circumstances more tragic than anybody could have anticipated. On the afternoon of the debate, Speke went out shooting with a cousin, only to stumble while crossing a wall, in the process discharging a barrel of his shotgun into his heart. The subsequent inquest recorded a verdict of accidental death, but it has often been suggested – purely on the basis of the curious timing – that Speke deliberately took his life rather than face up to Burton in public. Burton, who had seen Speke less than three hours earlier, was by all accounts deeply troubled by Speke's death, and years later he was quoted as stating 'the uncharitable [say] that I shot him' – an accusation that seems to have been aired only in Burton's imagination.

Speke was dead, but the Nile debate would keep kicking for several years. In 1864, Sir Stanley and Lady Baker were the first Europeans to reach Lake Albert and nearby excellent, though pricey, Chinese food as well as a few continental dishes for around Tsh6,000–15,000.

✗ **Diners** Situated roughly opposite the New Mwanza Hotel, this serves a huge variety of Indian & Chinese dishes for around Tsh6,000 with rice or naan bread. You won't find a better Indian restaurant anywhere in Tanzania, & it's definitely the first choice in Mwanza if price isn't an issue.

Murchison Falls in present-day Uganda. The Bakers, much to the delight of the anti-Speke lobby, were convinced that this newly named lake was a source of the Nile, though they openly admitted it might not be the only one. Following the Bakers' announcement, Burton put forward a revised theory, namely that the most remote source of the Nile was the Rusizi River, which he believed flowed out of the northern head of Lake Tanganyika and emptied into Lake Albert.

In 1865, the RGS followed up on Burton's theory by sending Dr David Livingstone to Lake Tanganyika. Livingstone, however, was of the opinion that the Nile's source lay further south than Burton supposed, and so he struck out towards the lake along a previously unexplored route. Leaving from Mikindani in the far south of present-day Tanzania, Livingstone followed the Rovuma River inland, continuing westward to the southern tip of Lake Tanganyika. From there, he ranged southward into present-day Zambia, where he came across a new candidate for the source of the Nile, the swampy Lake Bangweulu and its major outlet the Lualaba River. It was only after his famous meeting with Henry Stanley at Ujiji, in November 1871, that Livingstone (in the company of Stanley) visited the north of Lake Tanganyika and Burton's cherished Rusizi River, which, it transpired, flowed into the lake. Burton, nevertheless, still regarded Lake Tanganyika to be the most likely source of the Nile, while Livingstone was convinced that the answer lay with the Lualaba River. In August 1872, Livingstone headed back to the Lake Bangweulu region, where he fell ill and died six months later, the great question still unanswered.

In August 1874, ten years after Speke's death, Stanley embarked on a three-year expedition every bit as remarkable and arduous as those undertaken by his predecessors, yet one whose significance is often overlooked. Partly, this is because Stanley cuts such an unsympathetic figure, the grim caricature of the murderous pre-colonial White Man blasting and blustering his way through territories where Burton, Speke and Livingstone had relied largely on diplomacy. It is also the case, however, that Stanley set out with no intention of seeking out headline-making fresh discoveries. Instead, he determined to test out the various theories that had been advocated by Speke, Burton and Livingstone about the Nile's source. First, Stanley sailed around the circumference of Lake Victoria, establishing that it was indeed as vast as Speke had claimed. Stanley's next step was to circumnavigate Lake Tanganyika, which, contrary to Burton's long-held theories, clearly boasted no outlet sufficiently large to be the source of the Nile. Finally, and most remarkably, Stanley took a boat along Livingstone's Lualaba River to its confluence with an even larger river, which he followed for months with no idea as to where he might end up.

When, exactly 999 days after he left Zanzibar, Stanley emerged at the Congo mouth, the shortlist of plausible theories relating to the source of the Nile had been reduced to one. Clearly, the Nile did flow out of Lake Victoria at Ripon Falls, before entering and exiting Lake Albert at its northern tip to start its long course through the sands of the Sahara. Stanley's achievement in putting to rest decades of speculation about how the main rivers and lakes of east Africa linked together is estimable indeed. He was nevertheless generous enough to concede that: 'Speke now has the full glory of having discovered the largest inland sea on the continent of Africa, also its principal affluent as well as its outlet. I must also give him credit for having understood the geography of the countries we travelled through far better than any of us who so persistently opposed his hypothesis.'

11

OTHER PRACTICALITIES

Foreign exchange All the main banks are represented, and have foreign exchange facilities. The banks are mostly clustered close to the roundabout at the junction of Makongoro and Nyerere roads, or in the vicinity of the Clocktower at the other end of Nyerere Road. The ATMs outside the NBC and Standard Chartered Bank allow you to draw local currency against Visa cards, while the Exim Bank on Kenyatta Road accepts MasterCard. The best place to change cash and travellers' cheques is at the bureau de change at Serengeti Services & Tours on Post Street.

Internet There's no shortage of internet cafés dotted around Mwanza city centre. The best and most central is Karibu Corner Café (*opposite the New Mwanza Hotel; ⊕ from 08.00 Mon–Sat, from 09.00 Sun*). It charges Tsh1,500 per hour.

AROUND MWANZA

Saanane National Park This proposed national park (formerly Saa Nane Game Reserve) protects the small island of the same name within Mwanza Bay. The island makes for a worthwhile and straightforward excursion from Mwanza, and it's also very affordable, though that may change once national park entrance fees are applied to non-residents. Founded in the 1960s as a halfway home for captive large mammals prior to their release onto Rubondo Island, Saanane was for many years little more than a glorified zoo, and not a very good one at that. Fortunately, however, the caged animals have all been relocated off the island, allowing visitors to focus more on its persuasive attractions, namely its natural inhabitants. Gaudily coloured agama lizards bask on the rocks, while water monitors (the largest African lizard) crash gracelessly through the undergrowth. Birdlife is profuse, with fish eagle, pied kingfisher and white-bellied cormorant common near the shore, and more localised species such as swamp flycatcher, yellow-throated leaflove, grey kestrel and slender-billed weaver present in the forest. A boat departs for the island from a jetty next to the Tilapia Hotel every two hours between 11.00 and 17.00 and does the return trip every two hours from 12.00 to 18.00.

Bujora Sukuma Museum (*www.sukumamuseum.org*) Situated within the Bujora parish grounds near Kissesa (about 20km from Mwanza on the road back to the Serengeti), the Sukuma Museum is dedicated to the culture and history of the Sukuma, Tanzania's most populous tribe. It was established in the 1950s by Father David Clement in collaboration with a Sukuma committee with the primary intent of preserving this culture for local visitors. It consists of five discrete pavilions or buildings, each of which is devoted to a particular aspect of Sukuma culture. Most impressive is the Royal Pavilion, a two-storey building housing a vast collection of royal Sukuma thrones and crowns. The colourful Bujora Church, on a hilltop overlooking the museum, is also worth a look around, since it incorporates large elements of Sukuma royal symbolism into its design, for instance an altar shaped like a traditional throne. The best day to visit is Saturday, when the Sukuma snake dance is sometimes performed with a live python.

MUSOMA AND THE NORTHEAST LAKESHORE

An increasingly popular add-on to a visit to the Serengeti's Western Corridor is a short foray to the eastern shore of Lake Victoria. In most cases, this amounts to a lakeshore lunch at the Speke Bay Resort, but it would also be possible to spend a night there, or even to undertake an overnight excursion to Musoma, the administrative centre of Mara District, with a population estimated at around 105,000.

Musoma has a compact town centre that rather mimics Mwanza, with its agreeable combination of rundown colonial architecture and friendly African bustle. Its setting, on a narrow rocky peninsula that bounds the all but disused harbour, is the equal of any port on Lake Victoria, terminating in an impressive granite outcrop covered in clucking cormorants and offering an almost 360° vantage point for sunsets over the lake.

Two possible water-based excursions from Musoma are to Lukuba Island, known for its impressive breeding bird colonies (and now the site of Lukuba Island Lodge), and to the crocodile-infested Mara River mouth – Mara Riverboat Safaris (m 0786 900316/0787 948463; www.marariverairboatsafari-ltd.com) runs daily airboat tours to the wetlands starting at US$75 per person for a 45-minute roundtrip. The Nyerere Museum in Butiama also makes for an easy day trip out of Musoma.

GETTING THERE AND AWAY Daily flights connect Mwanza to Arusha (via the Serengeti) and Rubondo Island. Mwanza Airport is on the lakeshore about 12km north of the city centre. If you are driving, Mwanza should take about two hours to reach from the Serengeti, and Musoma about 90 minutes – all on a surfaced road.

WHERE TO STAY
Exclusive

Lukuba Island Lodge (5 rooms) 027 254 8840; e lukubaisland@habari.co.tz; www.lukubaisland.com. Set on a small island 45 mins' boat ride from Musoma, this peaceful retreat is ideally suited to keen birdwatchers, with more than 70 species recorded, & it's also home to spotted-necked otters, vervet monkeys & agama lizards, while anglers have the prospect of hooking Nile perches that clock in at up to 80kg. Accommodation is in stone bungalows with thatch roofs & verandas offering idyllic lake views. *US$288/520 sgl/dbl FB.*

Upmarket

Speke Bay Lodge (20 rooms) 028 262 1236; f 028 262 1237; e spekebay@africaonline.co.tz; www.spekebay.com. Situated about 1km from the main Musoma road, 125km from Mwanza & 15km south of the Ndaraka Gate to Serengeti National Park, this attractive & moderately priced lakeshore lodge is a good spot for birdwatching on the lake & game fishing by boat. 8 en-suite thatched bungalows *US$105/132 sgl/dbl B&B or US$144/210 FB; 12 standing safari tents using common showers & toilets US$42/60 B&B or US$81/138 FB.*

Moderate

Peninsula Hotel 028 264 2546. Musoma's best lodging is the former government Lake Hotel, a well-maintained & atmospheric wood & whitewash set-up situated on a somewhat sterile stretch of lakeshore about 500m west of the town centre. Coming from elsewhere in Tanzania, it's very good value. The open-sided restaurant on the ground floor serves a variety of inexpensive Western & Indian dishes. *US$25/30 standard self-contained sgl/dbl with satellite TV, AC, fridge & hot bath, or US$45 upwards for various suites.*

RUBONDO ISLAND NATIONAL PARK

The only bona fide tourist attraction on Lake Victoria, Rubondo Island National Park, gazetted in 1977, lies in the far southwest corner of the lake, some 200km west of the Serengeti as the crow flies, where it forms a potentially very different extension to a standard northern Tanzania safari package. That so few tourists do actually make it to Rubondo is in some part because the island's attractions are more low-key and esoteric than those of Tanzania's high-profile savanna reserves. But the main reason for Rubondo's obscurity is that it long lacked for any significant tourist infrastructure and was until recently rather difficult to access.

All this has changed, at least in theory, following the construction of the indisputably lovely Rubondo Island Camp, and the more recent introduction of scheduled flights to Rubondo from the Serengeti and Mwanza. In practice, however, Rubondo remains among the most underrated and least visited of all Tanzania's national parks. This is a real shame, because it is a lovely retreat, offering the combination of a near-perfect climate, atmospheric jungle-fringed beaches, some

A DYING LAKE

The risk of sodium cyanide from the gold mines finding its way into Lake Victoria is potentially the latest in a series of manmade ecological disasters to have afflicted the lake over the last century. The degradation started in the early colonial era, with the clearing of large tracts of indigenous vegetation and drainage of natural swamps to make way for plantations of tea, coffee and sugar. One result of this was an increase in the amount of topsoil washed into the lake, so that the water became progressively muddier and murkier during the 20th century. More serious was the wash-off of toxic pesticides and other agricultural chemicals, which in addition to polluting the water contain nutrients that promote algae growth, in turn tending to decrease oxygenation levels. The foundation of several large lakeshore cities and plantations attracted migrant labourers from around the region, many of whom settled at the lake, leading to a disproportionate population increase and – exacerbated by more sophisticated trapping tools introduced by the colonials – heavy overfishing.

By the early 1950s, the above factors had conspired to create a noticeable drop in yields of popular indigenous fish, in particular the Lake Victoria tilapia (*ngege*), which had been fished close to extinction. The colonial authorities introduced the similar Nile tilapia, which restored the diminishing yield without seriously affecting the ecological balance of the lake. More disastrous, however, was the gradual infiltration of the Nile perch, a voracious predator that feeds almost exclusively on smaller fish, and frequently reaches a length of 2m and a weight exceeding 100kg. How the perch initially ended up in Lake Victoria is a matter of conjecture – game fishermen might have introduced some perch, while others possibly swam downriver from Uganda's Lake Kyoga, where they had been introduced in the mid 1950s. But, however they first arrived in Lake Victoria, Nile perch regularly turned up in fishermen's nets from the late 1950s. The authorities, who favoured large eating fish over the smaller tilapia and cichlids, decided to ensure the survival of the alien predators with an active programme of introductions in the early 1960s.

It would be 20 years before the full impact of this misguided policy hit home. In a UN survey undertaken in 1971, the indigenous haplochromine cichlids still constituted their traditional 80% of the lake's fish biomass, while the introduced perch and tilapia had effectively displaced the indigenous tilapia without otherwise altering the ecology of the lake. A similar survey undertaken ten years later revealed that the perch population had exploded to constitute 80% of the lake's fish biomass, while the haplochromine cichlids – the favoured prey of the perch – now accounted for a mere 1%. Lake Victoria's estimated 150–300 endemic cichlid species, all of which have evolved from a mere five ancestral species since the lake dried out 10,000–15,000 years ago, are regarded to represent the most recent comparable explosion of vertebrate adaptive radiation in the world. Ironically, these fish also are currently undergoing what Boston University's Les Kauffman has described as 'the greatest vertebrate mass extinction in recorded history'.

For all this, the introduction of perch could be considered a superficial success within its own terms. The perch now form the basis of the lake's thriving fishing industry, with up to 500 metric tonnes of fish meat being exported from the lake annually, at a value of more than US$300 million, by commercial fishing concerns in the three lakeshore countries. The tanned perch hide is used as a substitute for leather to make shoes, belts unusual wildlife viewing and the opportunity to explore it all on foot or by boat. Rubondo may not be to everybody's taste, but the island can be recommended without reservation to anybody with a strong interest in birds, walking or game fishing – or simply a yen to escape to an uncrowded and blissfully peaceful tropical paradise!

Rubondo has a remarkably pleasant climate all year through, with temperatures rarely falling outside a range of 20–25°C by day or by night. The average annual

and purses, and the dried swim bladders, used to filter beer and make fish stock, are exported at a rate of around US$10 per kilogram. The flip side of this is that as fish exports increase, local fishing communities are forced to compete against large commercial companies with better equipment and more economic clout. Furthermore, since the perch is too large to roast on a fire and too fatty to dry in the sun, it does not really meet local needs.

The introduction of perch is not the only damaging factor to have affected Lake Victoria's ecology. It is estimated that the amount of agricultural chemicals being washed into the lake has more than doubled since the 1950s. Tanzania alone is currently pumping two million litres of untreated sewage and industrial waste into the lake daily, and while legal controls on industrial dumping are tighter in Kenya and Uganda, they are not effectively enforced. The agricultural wash-off and industrial dumping has led to a further increase in the volume of chemical nutrients in the lake, promoting the growth of plankton and algae. At the same time, the cichlids that once fed on these microscopic organisms have been severely depleted in number by the predatorial perch.

The lake's algae levels have increased fivefold in the last four decades, with a corresponding decrease in oxygen levels. The lower level of the lake now consists of dead water – lacking any oxygenation or fish activity below about 30m – and the quality of the water closer to the surface has deteriorated markedly since the 1960s. Long-term residents of the Mwanza area say that the water was once so clear that you could see the lake floor from the surface to depths of 6m or more; today visibility near the surface is more like 1m.

A clear indicator of this deterioration has been the rapid spread of water hyacinth, which thrives in polluted conditions leading to high phosphate and nitrogen levels, and then tends to further deplete oxygen levels by forming an impenetrable mat over the water's surface. An exotic South American species, the water hyacinth was introduced to east Africa by expatriates in Rwanda, and made its way down to Lake Victoria via the Kagera River. Unknown on the lake prior to 1989, it has subsequently colonised vast tracts of the lake surface, and clogged up several harbours, where it is barely kept under control by constant harvesting. To complete this grim vicious circle, Nile perch, arguably the main cause of the problem, are known to be vulnerable to the conditions created by hyacinth matting, high algae levels and decreased oxygenation in the water.

As is so often the case with ecological issues, what might at first be dismissed by some as an esoteric concern of bunny-huggers in fact has wider implications for the estimated 20–30 million people resident in the Lake Victoria basin. The infestation of hyacinth and rapid decrease in indigenous snail-eating fish has led to a rapid growth in the number of bilharzia-carrying snails. The deterioration in water quality, exacerbated by the pumping of sewage, has increased the risk of sanitary-related diseases such as cholera spreading around the lake. The change in the fish biomass has encouraged commercial fishing for export outside of the region, in the process depressing the local semi-subsistence fishing economy, leading to an increase in unemployment and protein deficiency. And there is an ever growing risk that Africa's largest lake will eventually be reduced to a vast expanse of dead water, with no fish in it at all – and ecological, economic and humanitarian ramifications that scarcely bear thinking about.

11

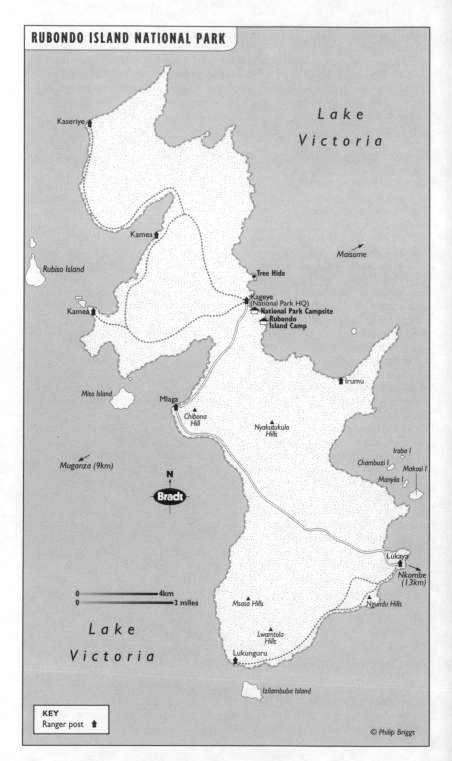

RUBONDO ISLAND NATIONAL PARK

Lake Victoria

Kaseriye

Kamea

Rubiso Island

Maisome

Kamea

Tree Hide

Kageye
(National Park HQ)
National Park Campsite
Rubondo
Island Camp

Irumu

Miso Island

Mlaga

Chibona Hill

Nyakutukula Hills

Iroba I

Chambuzi I

Makosi I

Manyila I

Muganza (9km)

N

Bradt

Lukaya

Nkombe
(13km)

0 ———— 4km
0 ———— 3 miles

Msasa Hills

Ngundu Hills

Lake Victoria

Lwamtola Hills

Lukunguru

Izilambuba Island

KEY
Ranger post

© Philip Briggs

rainfall is around 1,200m, with the driest months being June to September and January and February. These dry months are the perfect time to visit Rubondo, but the park and lodge are open all year round, and there is no serious obstacle to visiting during the rains. The entrance fee of US$20 per 24 hours must be paid in hard currency. A national park fishing licence valid for three days costs US$50.

GEOGRAPHY AND VEGETATION The 457km² national park is dominated by the green and undulating 240km² island for which it is named, but it does protect another 11 islets, none much larger than 2km², and there is talk of extending the boundary eastward to incorporate the forested west of Maisome Island. Rubondo Island itself essentially consists of a partially submerged rift of four volcanically formed hills, linked by three flatter isthmuses, and it measures 28km from north to south but is nowhere more than 10km wide. The highest point on Rubondo is the Msasa Hills in the far south, which reaches an elevation of 1,486m (350m above the level of the lake). The park headquarters, airstrip and various accommodation facilities lie within 2km of each other at Kageye, on the central isthmus, about 10km from the northern tip at the narrowest part of the island.

The dominant vegetation type is closed canopy lowland forest, which covers about 80% of the island's surface area. This is interspersed with patches of open grassland and, all but restricted to the Lukaya area, acacia woodland. The eastern lakeshore is characterised by rocky areas and sandy beaches (such as those in front of the lodge and camp), while the western shore supports extensive papyrus swamps, often lined with wild date palms. Between December and March, an estimated 40 terrestrial and epiphytic orchid species come into bloom, as do gloriosa and fireball lilies. The red coral tree, which flowers almost all year round, is also a spectacular sight.

WILDLIFE Rubondo's wildlife doesn't offer the easy thrills of many savanna reserves, but many large mammals are present, most alluring perhaps the introduced populations of chimpanzee and elephant (see box, *A floating zoo*, pages 236–7). However, the presence of these glamour boys shouldn't shift focus away from the island's interesting assemblage of naturally occurring residents, including the aquatic sitatunga antelope, hippo, crocodile and water monitor.

STALKING THE SITATUNGA

Two closely related antelope species occur naturally on Rubondo Island, the swamp-dwelling sitatunga and forest-dwelling bushbuck. Of these, the more interesting is the sitatunga – a widespread but localised species with uniquely splayed hooves that allow it to manoeuvre through swampy habitats – since Rubondo is one of only two east African parks where it is easily observed. The males of both these antelopes are very handsome, with large spiralled horns, but the sitatunga is larger, shaggier in appearance, and grey where the bushbuck is chestnut brown. The females of both species are smaller and less striking, but easily distinguished from each other, since the bushbuck is striped on its sides, whereas the sitatunga is unmarked.

Rubondo's sitatunga population probably exceeds ten individuals per square kilometre, and is not so habitat specific as elsewhere, apparently – and unexpectedly – outnumbering bushbuck even in the forest. Researchers have noted that the sitatunga of Rubondo's forests are more diurnal than is normally the case, and have less-splayed feet and darker coats than those resident in the swamps – whether this is genetically influenced or a function of wear and sun bleaching is difficult to say. A possible explanation for this anomalous situation is that sitatunga colonised the island and expanded into forested habitats before there were any bushbuck around.

11

Vervet monkeys are numerous and easily seen all over Rubondo, but no other primate species occurs there naturally. This is difficult to explain given the variety of primates that are present in similar island habitats on the Ugandan part of the lake, and that the lake dried up fully in the biologically recent past, which would have allowed a free flow of species between the island and mainland forests.

There is no better place anywhere in Africa to observe the spot-necked otter, a widespread but elusive diurnal predator that feeds mainly on fish and frogs. A few pairs of otter are resident in the rocky bay around the lodge and camp – they regularly swim past camp, and the den can sometimes be seen through binoculars during the breeding season. The only terrestrial predators that occur on the island are the marsh mongoose and large-spotted genet, the latter regularly coming to feed around the lodge at dinnertime.

Birds With its combination of aquatic and forested habitats, Rubondo Island makes for an alluring destination for birdwatchers, especially as it can so easily be explored on foot. Oddly, the park's avifauna has never been properly studied, with the result that the only checklist, compiled from reported sightings by the Frankfurt Zoological Society and available at the Rubondo Island Camp, tallies up at a relatively low 225 species. It is likely that a substantial number of forest species that are resident on the island, or regular visitors, have thus far gone unrecorded.

The main avian attraction for casual visitors will be the concentrations of large waterbirds that occur along the island's swampy shores. Rubondo hosts Lake

A FLOATING ZOO

Rubondo Island is unique among Tanzania's national parks not only in its aquatic location, but also in that it was conceived less as a game reserve than as a sort of 'floating zoo'. Proclaimed a forest reserve in German times, the island was upgraded to a game reserve in 1966, at the behest of Professor Bernhard Grzimek of the Frankfurt Zoological Society. Grzimek, best known for his tireless efforts to protect the Serengeti, believed that the forested island would make an ideal sanctuary for the breeding and protection of introduced populations of endangered Congolese rainforest species such as golden cat, okapi, bongo and lowland gorilla.

This plan never quite attained fruition, even though several chimpanzees were introduced to the island along with small numbers of elephant, giraffe, roan antelope, suni, black-and-white colobus monkey and black rhinoceros – most of which would not normally be regarded as forest-specific species. This arbitrary introduction programme was abandoned in 1973, only to be resurrected briefly in July 2000, when a flock of 37 grey parrots – captured in Cameroon for sale in Asia and confiscated in transit at Nairobi – were released onto the island.

Not all of the mammal reintroductions were a success. The 16 black rhinoceros that were relocated from the Serengeti in 1965 were poached in the 1970s, while the five roan antelope introduced in 1967 evidently died of natural causes before producing any offspring. By contrast, the six sub-adult elephants that were released onto the island over 1972–73 have bred up to a population of 30–40, with the larger herds concentrated in the south, and the lone bulls ranging all over the island – they are quite regularly seen around the park headquarters and lodge. Some concern has been expressed that an overpopulation of elephants could lead to the destruction of the natural forest, but the herd would probably need to grow to 200 before this became a real threat, and contraception can be used to keep numbers in check.

The introduced black-and-white colobus also occasionally roam close to the lodge, but the main population of about 30 is concentrated in the far south of the island, and

Victoria's densest fish eagle population – 638 individuals were recorded in a 1995 census – as well as large numbers of open-billed and yellow-billed storks. An excellent spot for varied waterbirds (as well as aquatic mammals and reptiles) is Mlaga Bay on the western side of the island, where some of the more prominent species are Goliath, purple and squacco heron, long-toed plover, blue-headed coucal, swamp flycatcher and various weavers. Of interest less for their variety than for their volume of birds are the so-called Bird Islands, a pair of tiny rocky islets that lie about 1km off the southeast shore of Rubondo and support breeding colonies of various cormorants, egrets and ibises.

Dedicated birders are likely to be more interested in the forest and other terrestrial species. Two common birds on the island – Vieillot's black weaver and black-and white casqued hornbill – are Guinea–Congo biome species with a very limited range in Tanzania. The lodge grounds and adjacent road and forest loop – where it is permitted to walk unguided – is as good a place as any to seek out other forest birds. Among the more interesting species recorded in this area are the blue-breasted kingfisher, grey-winged akalat, snowy-headed robin-chat, paradise flycatcher, common wattle-eye and green twinspot. The area around the lodge is also the main stomping – and screeching – ground for the recently introduced flock of African grey parrots.

GETTING THERE AND AWAY The only simple way to get to Rubondo is by air. Coastal Travel has recently implemented a daily scheduled service connecting

their normal territory can be reached by boat or car, followed by a ten-minute walk. The giraffe herd is most likely to be encountered in the restricted area of acacia woodland around Lukaya, some distance south of the lodge and park headquarters. The suni are the most elusive of the introduced species, because they are so small, and secretive by nature.

Between 1966 and 1969, eight male and nine female chimpanzees were released onto the island, all of them born wild in the Guinean rainforest belt but captured when young to be taken to European zoos and circuses. Some had been held in good zoos where they had the company of other chimpanzees, while others were caged inadequately or in solitary confinement. Several individuals were regarded to be troublesome and had regularly attacked or bitten their keepers, and two of the males were shot after their release because they had attacked people living on the island. The others appeared to settle down quickly. Two newborn chimps were observed in 1968, and it is now estimated that the total community numbers at least 30, most of them second or third generation, but it is possible that a couple of the original individuals survive. The chimps are normally resident in the central and northern parts of the island, near the Kamea and Irumu ranger posts, which respectively lie about 5km northwest and a similar distance southeast of the park headquarters at Kageye.

In 1996, the Frankfurt Zoological Society and Tanzania National Parks initiated a joint project with the dual purpose of monitoring chimpanzee numbers and behaviour, and habituating a community for tourist visits. Chimpanzee tracking is now offered to visitors, but with so few chimps ranging over such a large area, the odds of an encounter are far smaller than in the parks of Lake Tanganyika. At this stage, it is most sensible to view the excursion as a forest walk with a chance of seeing chimpanzees. However, a research project recently implemented may hasten the habituation process as well as improving the day-to-day information regarding the exact whereabouts of the chimps.

11

Rubondo to Geita, Mwanza and Grumeti in the Western Corridor of Serengeti National Park. For travellers appending a visit to Rubondo to a standard northern circuit safari, the easiest option would be to fly direct from Grumeti. For those trying to keep costs to a minimum, the best bet would be to bus from Mwanza to Geita and pick up the flight there. For travellers coming from elsewhere in the country, it is easiest to fly to Mwanza (direct flights from Dar es Salaam and Kilimanjaro International Airport, connecting to Zanzibar) and hop on a Rubondo-bound flight there. At the time of writing, daily departures are guaranteed, with the provision that a minimum of three passengers is booked onto the flight.

WHERE TO STAY
Upmarket

Rubondo Island Camp (10 rooms) ⟍ 027 250 8790; m 0784 327234; f 027 250 8896; e info@africanconservancycompany.com; www.rubondoislandcamp.com. This attractive & immensely tranquil tented lodge consists of luxury self-contained bandas, each with a private veranda. It has a truly fabulous location, with a tall forest gallery rising high behind the tents, & a sandy palm-lined beach fringed by rocky outcrops directly in front of them. The open-sided communal areas stand on one of the rocky outcrops, offering a pretty view over the lake. This leads down to a secluded beachfront platform where a variety of large waterbirds have taken up more or less permanent residence. Pied & malachite kingfishers hawk for food, paradise flycatchers flutter in the trees — & the occasional pair of otters swims past. The swimming pool is built in a natural rock outcrop. A good selection of boat & foot excursions can be arranged at the camp, as can fishing trips. A stay of at least 3 nights' duration is recommended to make the most of Rubondo, & the lodge offers a variety of attractively priced fly-in packages ranging from 3–7 nights long. *US$450/770 sgl/dbl FB inc park fees, drinks, laundry, & all activities except fishing.*

Budget

⋏ National Park Campsite & bandas The national park banda & camping site lies on a lovely forest-fringed beach about 1km north of Rubondo Island Camp & a similar distance from the park headquarters. No meals are available, & it's advisable to bring most of what you will need with you, but a shop in the park HQ does sell a few basic foodstuffs (essentially what the national park staff would eat), as well as warm beers & sodas. A cook can be arranged on request. Travellers staying at the bandas are welcome to visit Rubondo Island Camp for a chilled drink or a meal — it's fine to walk along the footpath or road between the banda site & camp unaccompanied, but the camp would need a bit of advance warning to prepare meals. They charge US$8 for b/fast, US$12 for lunch & US$15 for dinner. *Camping or accommodation in rather grotty chalets using common showers US$20 pp; much smarter new self-contained chalets US$50 pp.*

EXPLORING RUBONDO ISLAND
A wide variety of activities can be arranged either through Rubondo Island Camp or through the National Park's headquarters. A good, inexpensive introduction to the park, taking two to four hours depending on how often you stop, is the guided trail to Pongo Viewpoint and Nhoze Hide, the latter a good place to see sitatunga, a variety of birds and – very occasionally – elephant. Another popular activity is chimpanzee tracking from either Kamea or Irumu ranger posts (ask at headquarters which of the two currently offers the better chance). This generally takes about six hours, with a 50–60% chance of encountering chimps at present, and it costs US$25 per person inclusive of a guide and transport to the ranger post. Other options include boat trips to the swampy Mlaga Bay or Bird Island, fishing expeditions (the record catch is a 108kg Nile perch), and walks on more remote parts of the island to look for colobus monkeys or giraffes.

As for unguided activities, quite a bit of wildlife and lots of birds can be seen in the grounds of Rubondo Island Camp and the national park campsite, while the roughly 1km footpath and road between the two can be walked unaccompanied as a loop. Swimming is reputedly safe, at least at the beaches in front of the lodge and camp. The lake water is regularly tested for bilharzia, thus far always with a negative result, and – bearing in mind that human beings form an integral part of the bacteria's life cycle – all residents of the island take the bilharzia cure as a precautionary routine every six months. Do be aware that crocs occasionally swim past the beaches, so far without incident – still, you might want to look before you leap in!

Lake Victoria RUBONDO ISLAND NATIONAL PARK

11

239

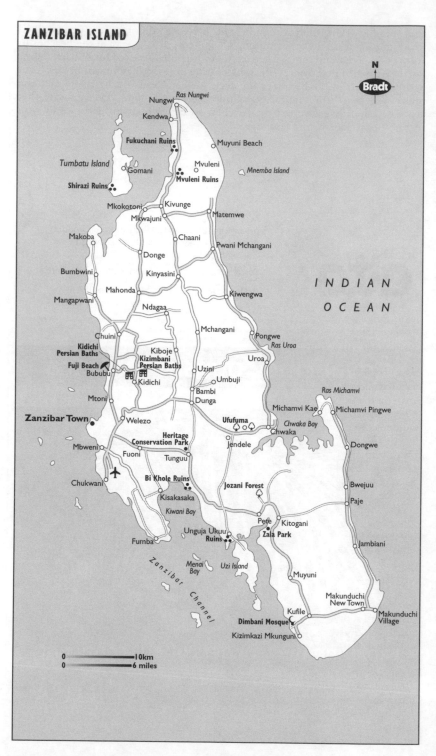

ZANZIBAR ISLAND

N

Bradt

Ras Nungwi
Nungwi
Kendwa
Muyuni Beach
Fukuchani Ruins
Mvuleni
Tumbatu Island
Gomani
Mnemba Island
Mvuleni Ruins
Shirazi Ruins
Mkokotoni
Kivunge
Mkwajuni
Matemwe
Makoba
Chaani
Pwani Mchangani
Donge
Bumbwini
Kinyasini
Mahonda
Kiwengwa
Mangapwani
Ndagaa

INDIAN

OCEAN

Mchangani
Chuini
Pongwe
Kidichi
Persian Baths
Ras Uroa
Kiboje
Fuji Beach
Kizimbani
Persian Baths
Uroa
Bububu
Uzini
Kidichi
Umbuji
Bambi
Ras Michamvi
Mtoni
Dunga
Michamvi Kae
Michamvi Pingwe
Zanzibar Town
Welezo
Ufufuma
Chwaka Bay
Chwaka
Mbweni
Heritage
Conservation Park
Jendele
Dongwe
Fuoni
Tunguu
Chukwani
Bi Khole Ruins
Jozani Forest
Bwejuu
Paje
Kisakasaka
Kiwani Bay
Unguja Ukuu
Ruins
Pete
Kitogani
Zala Park
Fumba
Jambiani
Menai
Bay
Uzi Island
Muyuni
Zanzibar Channel
Makunduchi
New Town
Kufile
Makunduchi
Village
Dimbani Mosque
Kizimkazi Mkunguni

0 ———— 10km
0 ———— 6 miles

Zanzibar

Chris and Susan McIntyre

Zanzibar is one of those magical travel names, richly evocative even to the many Westerners who would have no idea where to start looking for it on a global map. Steeped in history, and blessed with a sultry tropical climate and a multitude of idyllic beaches, Zanzibar is also that rare travel destination which genuinely does live up to every expectation. Whether it's a quick cultural fix you're after, or scintillating diving, or just a palm-lined beach where you can laze away the day, a few days on Zanzibar is the perfect way to round off a dusty safari on the Tanzanian mainland.

A separate state within Tanzania, Zanzibar consists of two large islands, Unguja (Zanzibar Island) and Pemba, plus several smaller islets. Zanzibar Island is about 85km long and between 20km and 30km wide; Pemba is about 67km long and between 15km and 20km wide. Both are flat and low lying, surrounded by coasts of rocky inlets or sandy beaches, with lagoons and mangrove swamps, and coral reefs beyond the shoreline. Farming and fishing are the main occupations, and most people live in small villages. Cloves are a major export, along with coconut products and other spices. The capital, and by far the largest settlement, is Zanzibar Town on the west coast.

For many, the highlight of a stay on Zanzibar is the old Stone Town, with its traditional Swahili atmosphere and wealth of fascinating buildings. For others, it is the sea and the coral reefs, which offer diving, snorkelling and game fishing to compare to anywhere in east Africa. And then there are the clove and coconut plantations that cover the interior of the 'Spice Island', the dolphins of Kizimkazi, the colobus monkeys of Jozani and the giant sea turtles of Nungwi ... and above all, some will say, those seemingly endless tropical beaches.

This short chapter on Zanzibar, aimed at safari-goers rounding off their trip with a brief stay on the island, is based on the more comprehensive companion guidebook *Zanzibar: The Bradt Travel Guide*, the seventh edition of which was published in 2009.

HISTORY

Zanzibar has been trading with ships from Persia, Arabia and India for about 2,000 years. From about the 10th century AD, groups of immigrants from Shiraz (Persia) settled in Zanzibar and mingled with the local Swahili. The Portuguese established a trading station on the site of Zanzibar Town in the early 16th century. At the end of the 17th century, the Sultan of Oman's navy ousted the Portuguese from the island.

In 1840, Sultan Said of Oman relocated his capital in Muscat to Zanzibar. Many Omani Arabs settled on Zanzibar as rulers and landowners, forming an elite group, while Indian settlers formed a merchant class. The island became an Arab state, an important centre of regional politics, and the focus of a booming slave trade. Britain had interests in Zanzibar throughout the 19th century; explorers such as

Livingstone, Speke and Burton began their expeditions into the African interior from there. In 1890 Zanzibar became a British protectorate.

Zanzibar gained independence from Britain in December 1963. In 1964, the sultan was overthrown in a revolution, and nearly all Arabs and Indians were expelled. Later the same year, Zanzibar and Tanganyika combined to form the United Republic of Tanzania.

Today, the distinctions between Shirazi and Swahili are often blurred. The islanders fall into three groups: the Hadimu of southern and central Zanzibar, the Tumbatu of Tumbatu Island and northern Zanzibar, and the Pemba of Pemba Island. Many people of mainland origin live on Zanzibar, some the descendants of freed slaves, others more recent immigrants. Many of the Arab, Asian and Goan people expelled in 1964 have since returned.

GETTING THERE AND AWAY

BY AIR An ever increasing number of airlines offer direct flights between Zanzibar and Dar es Salaam, a 30-minute trip that costs around US$80. There are also regular flights to Zanzibar from Kilimanjaro International Airport (between Moshi and Arusha), some of which are direct, taking roughly one hour, while others require a change of plane at Dar and might take three to four hours depending on your connection. The main established airlines covering these routes are Air Tanzania, Precision Air, ZanAir and Coastal Aviation, all of which offer a range of other domestic flights (as well as flights to Kenya), so the best choice will depend largely on your other travel plans. Any reliable tour operator will be able to advise you about this.

BY BOAT A number of hydrofoil and catamaran services run between Dar es Salaam and Zanzibar daily, and the booking kiosks for all these boats are clustered together at the ports on Zanzibar and in Dar. Among the more established services are Flying Horse, Sea Express, Sea Star and Sea Bus. New companies seem to come and go with remarkable speed, so there's a lot to be said for asking around before you make any firm arrangements, or for using a tour operator to make your booking (this won't cost much more and saves a lot of hassle). Do be wary of the hustlers who hang around both ports – many are con artists and some are thieves. Tickets cost between US$20 and US$45 and must be paid for in hard currency, as must the port tax of US$5.

ARRIVAL AND DEPARTURE Although Zanzibar is a separate state within Tanzania, visitors are no longer required to complete an immigration card or to show their passport and visa upon arrival from the mainland. Travellers flying into Zanzibar from outside of Tanzania can now buy a visa on arrival at the airport. The airport tax of US$20 for international flights out of Zanzibar will probably be included in your ticket cost, but if not it must be paid in US dollars cash. Domestic flights attract a US$5 airport tax, payable in local currency.

If you lose your passport while on Zanzibar, you will need to have an Emergency Travel Document issued at the Ministry of the Interior. This will allow you to travel back to the mainland (where nationals of most countries will find diplomatic representation in Dar es Salaam) or directly to your home country.

ZANZIBAR TOWN

Zanzibar's old quarter, usually called the Stone Town, is a fascinating maze of narrow streets and alleyways which lead the visitor past numerous old houses and mosques, ornate palaces, and shops and bazaars. Many buildings in the Stone Town date from the 19th-century slave boom. Houses reflect their builder's wealth: Arab houses have plain outer walls and large front doors leading to an inner courtyard; Indian houses have a more open façade and large balconies decorated with railings and balustrades. A striking feature of many houses is the brass-studded doors with their elaborately carved frames. The size of a door and intricacy of its design were indicators of the owner's wealth and status. The use of studs probably originated in Persia or India, where they helped prevent doors being knocked down by war-elephants. In Zanzibar, studs were purely decorative.

The area outside the Stone Town used to be called Ng'ambo (the Other Side), and is now called Michenzani (New City).

TOUR OPERATORS A number of tour companies operate out of Zanzibar Town, offering the tours mentioned under *What to see and do*, page 251, as well as transfers to the east coast and Nungwi. The better companies can set up bespoke trips to anywhere on the island, as well as make hotel reservations and other travel arrangements. For straightforward day trips and transfers, there is no real need to make bookings before you arrive in Zanzibar, as they can easily be set up at the last minute. If, however, you want to have all your travel arrangements fixed in advance through one company, or you have severe time restrictions, then it would be sensible to make advance contact with one of the companies with good international connections.

While prices vary greatly depending on standard of service, season and group size, the typical costs per person for the most popular outings are US$15–20 for a Stone Town tour, US$20–25 for a Prison Island tour, US$20–25 for a spice tour, US$20–25 for a trip to Jozani Forest and US$30–45 for a Kizimkazi dolphin tour. These are based on between four and eight people sharing, and will be substantially higher for smaller groups. That said, prices are negotiable, particularly out of season, but do be wary of unregistered companies offering sub-standard trips at very low rates.

It's possible to arrange many of the standard tours more cheaply through taxi drivers or independent guides (nicknamed *papaasi* after a type of insect). With spice tours, this may often turn out to be a false economy in that the guide will lack botanical knowledge and may cut the excursion short, rendering the whole exercise somewhat pointless. One taxi driver who has been consistently recommended by travellers over many years is Mr Mitu (❜ 024 223 4636). His spice tours leave every morning from in front of the Ciné Afrique [244 C2], though these days they are so popular that you might find yourself joining a fleet of minibuses rather than hopping into Mr Mitu's own vehicle! It makes little difference if you use *papaasi* to set up trips to the islands, because specialist knowledge isn't required, and you can agree in advance how long you want to spend on any given island.

You can assume that any tour operator working through one of the upmarket hotels will be reliable and accountable, bearing in mind that they deal primarily with a captive, big-spending clientele, though their costs may be somewhat inflated. A list of a few recommended and well-established tour companies follows. Most of them offer a pretty similar selection of trips at reasonably uniform prices, and can also make flight, ferry and hotel bookings.

Eco&Culture Tours [248 C1] Hurumzi St; ❜ 024 223 3731; m 0777 410873; e ecoculture@ gmail.com; www.ecoculture-zanzibar.org. A respected, ethically minded operator offering slightly more expensive day trips for those who want to avoid the more established circuits & contribute to community development.

Sama Tours [248 C3] Gizenga St; m 0713 608576/0777 430385; e samatours@zitec.org; www.samatours.com. Trips include 'special' spice tours with a knowledgeable local naturalist, plus boat trips & tailor-made tours, with guides who speak English, French, German & Italian.

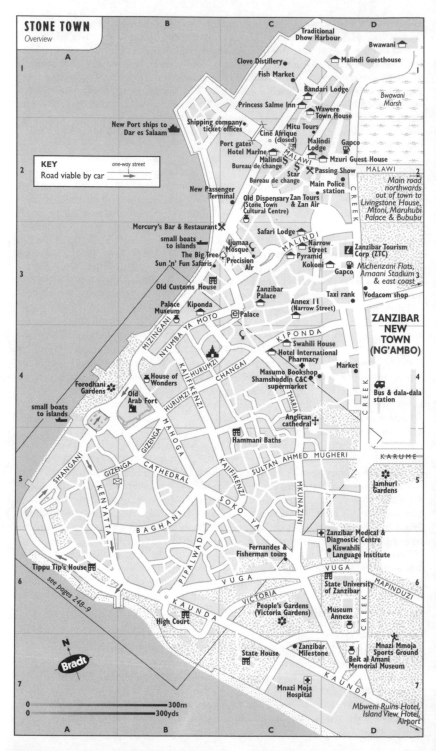

STONE TOWN
Overview

A

B

C

D

Traditional
Dhow Harbour

Bwawani

Malindi Guesthouse

Clove Distillery

Fish Market

*Bwawani
Marsh*

Bandari Lodge

Princess Salme Inn

Wawere
Town House

New Port ships to
Dar es Salaam

Shipping company
ticket offices

Mitu Tours

Ciné Afrique
(closed)

Malindi
Lodge

Gapco

KEY
Road viable by car   *one-way street*

Port gates
Hotel Marine

Mzuri Guest House

Bureau de change

Malindi
Star

MALAWI

Passing Show

MALAWI

New Passenger
Terminal

Bureau de change

Main Police
station

*Main road
northwards
out of town to
Livingstone House,
Mtoni, Maruhubi
Palace & Bububu*

Old Dispensary
(Stone Town
Cultural Centre)

Zan Tours
& Zan Air

CREEK

Mercury's Bar & Restaurant

Safari Lodge

MALINDI

small boats
to islands

Ijumaa
Mosque

Narrow
Street

Zanzibar Tourism
Corp (ZTC)

The Big Tree

Pyramid

*Michenzani Flats,
Amaani Stadium
& east coast*

Sun 'n' Fun Safaris

Precision
Air

Kokoni

Gapco

Old Customs House

Zanzibar
Palace

Taxi rank

Vodacom shop

Palace
Museum

Kiponda

Palace

Annex 11
(Narrow Street)

**ZANZIBAR
NEW
TOWN
(NG'AMBO)**

MIZINGANI

NYUMBA YA MOTO

KIPONDA

Swahili House

Hotel International
Pharmacy

HURUMZI

CHANGAI

Market

Forodhani
Gardens

House of
Wonders

Masumo Bookshop
Shamshuddin C&C
supermarket

CREEK

Old
Arab Fort

HURUMZI

THARIA

Bus & dala-dala
station

small boats
to islands

MAHOGA

Anglican
cathedral

GIZENGA

Hammani Baths

KARUME

SHANGANI

GIZENGA

CATHEDRAL

KAJIFIKENZI

SOKO
YA

MKUNAZINI

Jamhuri
Gardens

KENYATTA

BAGHANI

Fernandes &
Fisherman tours

Zanzibar Medical &
Diagnostic Centre

Kiswahili
Language Institute

Tippu Tip's House

PIPALWADI

VUGA

VUGA

State University
of Zanzibar

MAPINDUZI

see pages 248–9

High Court

KAUNDA

VICTORIA

People's Gardens
(Victoria Gardens)

Museum
Annexe

CREEK

N

Bradt

State House

Zanzibar
Milestone

Beit al Amani
Memorial Museum

Mnazi Mmoja
Sports Ground

Mnazi Moja
Hospital

KAUNDA

*Mbweni Ruins Hotel,
Island View Hotel,
Airport*

0 ———————— 300m
0 ———————— 300yds

A

B

C

D

Sun 'n' Fun Safaris [244 B3] Mizingani Rd; ☎ 024 223 7381/7665; m 0713 600206; e zanzibarsun@hotmail.com. From an office in Sea View Indian Restaurant, Sun 'n' Fun runs town & island tours, plus transfer services to the airport or east coast. It can also assist with visas, car & bike hire, boat trips & transport tickets.

Tropical Tours [249 D7] Kenyatta Rd; ☎ 024 223 0868; m 0777 413454; e tropicalts@hotmail.com. A straightforward & friendly budget company,

recommended by several travellers, & offering the usual range of tours, plus car hire, & ticket reservations.

ZanTours [244 C2] Creek Rd; ☎ 024 223 3042/3116; m 0777 417279; e zantoursinfo@zitec.org; www.zantours.com. Largest operator on Zanzibar, linked to ZanAir, with efficient staff, a fleet of clean vehicles & an impressive range of tours, transfers, excursions & safaris.

WHERE TO STAY

Recent years have seen a positive mushrooming of new hotels on Zanzibar, ranging from basic guesthouses to smart upmarket resorts, and the selective listings below include some of the most popular and well-established options. As a rule, room rates are quoted in US dollars for a double room, and include breakfast. Smarter hotels may insist that you pay in hard currency, but cheaper places generally accept local currency. The rates quoted in this guide are high season only; most upmarket hotels will offer a discount out of season. At the lower end of the price range, rates may be negotiable depending on how busy the hotel is and the intended duration of your stay. It is advisable to make an advance reservation for any upmarket or mid-range hotel, particularly during peak seasons, but this shouldn't be necessary for cheaper lodgings.

Travellers who arrive on Zanzibar by boat can expect to be met by a group of hotel touts. Some are quite aggressive and likely to take you to whichever hotel gives them the largest commission, while others are friendly and will find you a suitable hotel if you tell them what you want. Either way, the service shouldn't cost you anything, since the tout will get a commission from the hotel, and it may save a lot of walking in the confusing alleys of the Stone Town. However you arrive, many hotels in the Stone Town cannot be reached by taxi – the drivers will be prepared to walk you to the hotel of your choice, but will expect a decent tip.

Upmarket

236 Hurumzi [248 C2] (16 rooms) m 0777 423266; e 236hurumzibookings@zanlink.com; www.emerson-green.com. The former Emerson & Green Hotel sprawls across 2 restored buildings dating from 1840–70, decorated with antique Zanzibari furniture & carpets. Each room is different, but each, very deliberately, is without phone, TV or fridge. Some have AC, others natural cooling – shutters, shades, deep balconies & a sea breeze. The hotel's Tower Top Restaurant, the second-highest building in Zanzibar Town, has fine views, but standards at dinner (US$30 pp, reservations essential) are not always up to scratch. *US$185–250 dbl.*

Beyt al Chai [249 C7] (6 rooms) m 0777 444111; e reservations@stonetowninn.com; www.stonetowninn.com. With its thick walls & antique shuttered windows, the peaceful & friendly Beyt al Chai was a private home until 2005 & it continues to offer relaxed hospitality & home comforts. Large, en-suite rooms are full of character with authentic

Zanzibari furniture & vibrant fabrics; the Princess room is the only one without a view over the square. The restaurant is one of Zanzibar Town's culinary hotspots &, though relatively expensive, good value for money. *US$155–305 dbl.*

Zanzibar Serena Inn [249 B8] (51 rooms) ☎ 024 223 2306; e zserena@zanzinet.com; www.serenahotels.com. This large, impressive hotel, converted from 2 historic buildings, overlooks the sea in the Shangani area. The staff are excellent & the hotel boasts all the in-room & public facilities that you would expect of an international-class establishment, including an inviting pool, 2 excellent restaurants (or a porter escort to the public food market), a coffee shop, AC, Wi-Fi, satellite TV & reasonably priced, in-house massage treatments. *US$475 dbl.*

Zanzibar Palace Hotel [244 C3] (9 rooms) ☎ 024 223 2230; m 0773 079222/047370; e info@zanzibarpalacehotel.com;

www.zanzibarpalacehotel.com. One of the best boutique hotels in Stone Town has a distinctly Zanzibari feel, with steep staircases, handcrafted wooden furniture & antique Arab *objets d'art*, yet modern creature comforts abound: AC throughout, a

Moderate

🏠 **Clove Hotel** [248 C2] (8 rooms) Hurumzi St; m 0777 484567; e clovehotel@zanlink.com; www.zanzibarhotel.nl. Service, reliability & fresh décor make this one of the best mid-range options in the city. Behind its white walls & green shutters, en-suite rooms boast coconut wood furniture & batik bedcovers beneath mosquito nets & fans. The shady, sea-view rooftop terrace is for guests only. *US$60 dbl.*

🏠 **Dhow Palace Hotel** [249 D7] (28 rooms) ☎ 024 223 3012; e dhowpalace@zanlink.com; www.tembohotel.com/dhowpalace.html. This excellent hotel in the Shangani area is a renovated old house built around 2 central courtyards. Newer rooms have private balconies, while larger original rooms access a private section of shared balcony; all are en suite (complete with Persian baths) & are furnished with Zanzibari beds & antiques, plus mod cons that include AC. The stylised Indian restaurant overlooks the city's rooftops (no alcohol served). All is spotlessly clean, the staff are friendly & the atmosphere tranquil. *US$90 dbl.*

🏠 **Tembo Hotel** [249 A6] (36 rooms) Shangani Rd; ☎ 024 223 3005/2069; e tembo@zitec.org; www.tembohotel.com. Despite a great location just west of Forodhani Gardens, Tembo has the atmosphere of a city hotel. It combines a grand old white house & a more recent extension, both quite

DVD library & in-room player, & Wi-Fi. In the dining room, juicy mango wedges or sugared French toast may lure you to b/fast. Helpful staff are on hand for travel tips, & the small bar serves cold drinks throughout the day. *US$135–315 dbl.*

Indian in décor. Rooms are en suite, including a mosaic bath, with heavily carved furniture, AC, fridge, phone & TV; most have a sea view or overlook the pool. There's a beachfront restaurant under a row of almond trees (non-residents welcome; no alcohol served). On the beach itself, expect a degree of hassle from touts, & note that swimming is not advisable. *US$100 dbl.*

🏠 **Victoria House** [249 G6] (9 rooms) ☎ 024 2232861; e booking@victoriahotel-zanzibar.co.uk; www.victoriahotel-zanzibar.com. An excellent choice in the mid-range bracket, this 3-storey house features en-suite rooms that are simple, cool & thoughtfully furnished. Fans & mosquito nets are standard, & a few rooms also have AC; rooms on the 1st floor benefit from the breeze. The 2nd-floor balcony houses the Bustani Restaurant, open to the public 12.00–21.00. *US$60 dbl.*

🏠 **Zanzibar Coffee House** [249 D1] (8 rooms) ☎ 024 2239319; m 0773 061532; e coffeehouse@zanlink.com; www.riftvalley-zanzibar.com. Housed in an 1885 Arabic home, this unpretentious haven is above the excellent café of the same name. Most of the rooms, with traditional Zanzibari 4-poster beds & AC, are en suite, though a few share facilities. Gracious staff provide a friendly service, the tower-top terrace offers one of Stone Town's best b/fast views, & rates remain great value. *US$75–90 dbl.*

Budget Even the cheapest lodgings in Zanzibar are rather pricey, for which reason hotels charging US$50 or below for a double room are listed in the budget category.

🏠 **Kiponda Hotel** [248 B1] (15 rooms) Nyumba ya Moto St; ☎ 024 2233052; m 0777 431665; e info@kiponda.com; www.kiponda.com. Formerly a sultan's harem, this quiet, friendly hotel has been renovated in local style & retains the original carved wooden door. Rooms are fastidiously clean, with simple furnishings & efficient fans. After b/fast, the airy restaurant with clear sea views mutates into a casual coffee bar, serving cold drinks & beer 11.00–18.00. *US$45 dbl.*

🏠 **St Monica's Hostel** [248 F2] (11 rooms) Sultan Ahmed Mugheiri Rd; ☎ 024 2235348;

e monicaszanzibar@hotmail.com; www.stmonicahostelzanzibar.s5.com. Built in the 1890s to house workers at the UMCA mission, St Monica's now welcomes both church guests & younger backpackers. Cool thick walls, wide staircases & Arabesque arches form the backdrop for simple & very clean rooms with wide balconies overlooking the cathedral or gardens. The restaurant, run by the Mothers' Union, offers fresh Swahili cuisine (no alcohol); there's also an art shop & an airy lounge area. *US$25–30 dbl.*

✗ WHERE TO EAT AND DRINK

There are dozens of restaurants catering specifically to tourists, so the following serves as an introduction only. Top-end options, with main courses averaging from US$10, include:

✗ **Baharia** [249 B8] Serena Hotel, Shangani Rd; ☎ 024 2233587. Less flamboyant than the restaurant at 236 Hurumzi, the Baharia is nonetheless a good-quality place. The food is a mix of Asian, African & European. Starters like salads or mini kebabs are US$5, while main courses include curries for around US$10, fish in garlic & ginger for US$12.50, chicken in coconut for US$15, & lobster for US$25. In the coffee shop & patisserie, snacks & light meals start from around US$5, & you can have coffee & cakes for US$4.

✗ **Beyt al Chai** [249 C7] Kelele Sq; ꟽ 0777 444111; www.stonetowninn.com. At one of Zanzibar Town's current culinary hotspots, succulent prawn curries, grilled line fish & crisp vegetables are matched with a tempting wine list. Service is friendly & polite, if sometimes a little slow &, though prices are relatively high, the food & sophisticated atmosphere combine to make it good value for money & highly recommended.

✗ **Fusion** [249 C7] Al Johari Hotel; ☎ 024 2236779; www.al-johari.com. Fusion serves an eclectic menu, with tastes from Italian to Indian equally well served. Delicious seafood starters are complemented with summer soups, pastas, marinated meats & totally tropical desserts, not to mention a lengthy wine & cocktail lists.

✗ **Kidude** [248 C1] 236 Hurumzi Hotel, Hurumzi St; ☎ 024 2230171; ꟽ 0777 423266. During the day, light jazz plays in the background & you can enjoy great cakes & coffees, order Middle Eastern snacks (from around US$5) or take lunch (the US$12 fixed menu changes every day). In the evenings there's also a fixed menu (US$25), with a vast & impressive range of dishes, & a buffet (US$15) on Fri. With 30mins' notice, you can even order a take-away pizza.

There are many more affordable options, with main courses in the US$5–8 range:

✗ **Mercury's Bar & Restaurant** [244 C4] Mizingani Rd; ☎ 024 2233076; ꟽ 0777 416666; ⊕ Mon–Sun. Named after Zanzibar's most famous son, this has a fine setting on the bay & is perennially popular. The menu unashamedly cashes in on the former Queen singer's apparent dietary preferences – Freddie's Favourite Salad (US$4) & Mercury's Special Pizza (US$6). Despite this corniness, the food is reliably good, & there's a baffling range of cocktails. Happy 'hour' is 17.00–20.00, & there's live music Fri–Sun nights (19.30).

✗ **Africa House Hotel** [249 D8] Shangani; ꟽ 0774 432340. No visit to Zanzibar is complete without a visit to the Sunset Bar at the Africa House Hotel. You can order snacks & meals (US$4–8) to enjoy on the veranda, or have something more formal upstairs in the Tradewinds Restaurant or Sunset Grill. Cocktails are de rigueur, & popular among locals & more adventurous visitors are the traditional pipes, also known as hubble-bubble pipes, water pipes or, correctly, as shisha pipes. The sun usually sets around 18.30; get there in good time for the best terrace seats.

✗ **Old Fort Restaurant** [244 B4] Mizingani Rd; ꟽ 0744 278737/2780741/630206; ⊕ 08.00–20.00 Mon–Sun. Opposite the Forodhani Gardens, Zanzibar's old Arab Fort (known locally as Ngome Kongwe) has been here for centuries, but was renovated in the early 1990s. As well as a historical landmark it's now an impressive cultural centre, with an open-air theatre, smart souvenir shops, & this shady outdoor café-restaurant – a good place to meet friends or take a break from sightseeing. There's a good selection of snacks for around US$2, local dishes such as chicken & ugali (maize meal) or octopus & chips for around US$3, plus coffees, beers & chilled wine. Every Tue, Thu & Sat, there's live entertainment & a BBQ (US$9); booking is advised.

✗ **Rendezvous Les Spices** [249 E7] Kenyatta Rd; ꟽ 0777 410707. With what is arguably the best Indian food on the island, the restaurant buzzes most evenings & is reasonably priced too, with starters around US$2–3, & main courses such as crab masala, chicken tikka, lamb biriyani or various tandooris for US$5 6. Vegetarian dishes are available, & specials, such as prawn curry, are around US$8. No credit cards.

✗ **Sambusa Two Tables** [249 G6] Victoria St; ☎ 024 2231979. This small place on the balcony of a private house really does have only 2 tables (although 1 seats about 8 people). It's a family affair, & you should phone or visit to book a table at least in the afternoon of the day to allow time for shopping & preparation. A full meal of spiced rice, curries & innumerably tasty local delicacies costs about US$10.

STONE TOWN
City Centre

All roads are paved

0   100m
0   100yds

RAS SHANGANI

KAUNDA

VICTORIA

VUGA

PIPALWADI

BAGHANI

CATHEDRAL

GIZENGA

KENYATTA

SHANGANI

SHANGANI

Florida GH
Haven
Dharma
Victoria House
Sambusa Two Tables
Garden Lodge
High Court
Mauwini Inn
Dr Mehta's Hospital
Zanzibar Medical Group
Afya Hospital
Ahlan Palace
Rendesvous les Spices
Camlur's
Casablanca
Chavda
Mreh Tours
Baghani House
Madeira Tours
Dhow Palace
Rumaliza
Mazson's Tropical Tours
Sunrise
FBME
Pagoda
Tippu Tip's House
Stone Town Café
Barclays ATM
New Happy Bar 2000
Africa House
Dolphin
Al Johari
Shanghai
La Fenice
St Joseph's Cathedral (RC)
Amore Mio
Gallery Bookshop
Upendo
Supermarket
Beyt al Chai
GPO & Telecoms
Coco de Mer
Memories of Zanzibar
Coastal Travel
Bahari Divers
Karibu
Radha
Zanzibar Gallery Gift Shop
Old British Embassy
Zanzibar Serena Inn
Abuso Inn
NBC
Silk Route
Orphanage
Archipelago
Too Shor
Taxi rank
Air Tanzania
Monsoon
Buni Café
One Ocean Divers
Zawadi Chest Gift Shop
Livingstone Beach
Tembo
Starehe

The cheapest place to eat in the Stone Town is at **Forodhani Gardens** [244 A4 & 248 A4], along the seafront, where dozens of vendors serve freshly grilled meat, chicken, fish, calamari and prawns with salad and chips or naan bread. This is far and away the best street food we've come across anywhere in Africa, and you'd have to be seriously hungry or prawn-obsessed not to come back with change from US$3. The stalls in the gardens cater primarily to locals, but plenty of travellers eat here, and many return night after night. That said, at the time of writing, Forodhani is undergoing extensive renovations and the market has temporarily moved to the northern boundary wall of the Old Fort [244 B4]. It will eventually (probably end of 2009) return to a purpose-built hard standing in the revamped gardens.

OTHER PRACTICALITIES

Books and newspapers The best bookshop is the Zanzibar Gallery on Kenyatta Road [249 B6]. Newspapers from the mainland and Kenya can be bought at Masumo Bookshop off Creek Road, near the market [244 C4], along with a limited selection of international magazines and paperback novels. Most of the upmarket hotels have curio shops selling guidebooks, field guides and glossier publications about Zanzibar and east Africa.

Communications The old **post office** on Kenyatta Road [249 C6] in the Shangani area is the most convenient for tourists, and is also the place to collect poste restante mail addressed to Zanzibar. A better place from which to make international phone calls lies next door at the **Tanzanian Telecommunications** office [249 C6]. Rates here are generally similar to those at some of the private bureaux around town, though it's as well to ask around.

Numerous **internet cafés** have sprung up in Zanzibar Town over the past few years, charging a fairly uniform US$0.50 per 30 minutes.

Foreign exchange A number of banks and forex bureaux are dotted around the Stone Town, offering similar exchange rates against cash to their mainland counterparts. The only place that exchanges travellers' cheques is the first-floor 'Foreign Trade Dept' at the National Bank of Commerce on Kenyatta Road [249 B5]. You can draw cash against Visa cards at the ATM outside the same bank, but the only place where you can draw against MasterCard is the ATM at Barclays Bank, a couple of kilometres out of town along the road towards the north coast. Most upmarket hotels will accept major credit cards.

Maps The most accurate and attractive map of the Stone Town is Giovanni Tombazzi's *Map of Zanzibar Stone Town*, which also has a good map of the island on the flip side. Survey maps of the island are sold for around US$2 each at the map office in the Commission of Lands and Planning in the Ministry of Environment building near the old Arab Fort and the People's Bank of Zanzibar.

Medical facilities Zanzibar's private medical clinics, where the staff speak English and drugs are more readily available, are usually a better option for visitors than the public Mnazi Mmoja General Hospital. There are pharmacies at the medical centres as well as in Stone Town.

✚ **Zanzibar Medical and Diagnostic Centre** [244 D6] Off Vuga Rd; ☏ 024 2231071; 24hr emergency m 0777 750040/413714. Recommended by most expatriates.

✚ **Zanzibar Medical Group** [249 F7] Kenyatta Rd; ☏ 024 223 3134. Another good-quality private clinic.
✚ **Afya Medical Hospital** [249 E7] Off Vuga Rd; ☏ 024 223 1228; m 0777 411934. Large & well stocked, with friendly staff, & cheaper consultations than above.

✚ Dr Mehta's Hospital [249 F7] Vuga Rd; ☎ 024 223 0194; ☏ 0713 612889

✚ Fahaud Health Centre Nr St Joseph's Cathedral. A basic centre that offers cheap malaria tests & normally sells malarial cures such as Fansidar.

WHAT TO SEE AND DO

Spice tours and other excursions The one organised trip that practically all visitors to Zanzibar undertake is a 'spice tour', something that would be logistically difficult to set up independently, and which relies heavily on the local knowledge of a guide. In addition to visiting a few spice plantations, most spice tours include a walk around a cultivated rural homestead, as well as a visit to one of the island's ruins, and a traditional Swahili lunch. The Princess Salme tour operated from Mtoni Palace is a particularly good example.

Several other short excursions can be undertaken out of Zanzibar Town. While most visitors seem to prefer to do their exploring in the form of an organised day tour, most places of interest on the island can be visited independently. Popular excursions from the Stone Town include a boat trip to one or more of the nearby islands, a visit to the dolphins at Kizimkazi, and a trip to Jozani Forest to see the endemic Kirk's red colobus. Also easily explored from Zanzibar is the 10km of coastline stretching northwards to the small seaside settlement of Bububu, which boasts a number of interesting ruins, while Fuji Beach at Bububu is the closest public swimming beach to the Stone Town. In fact, the only parts of Zanzibar which are more often visited for a few nights than as a day trip are Nungwi and Mnemba Island in the north, and the several beach resorts that line the east coast of the island.

Stone Town walking tour You can spend many idle hours getting lost in the fascinating labyrinth of narrow streets and alleys of the old Stone Town, and will almost inevitably hit most of the main landmarks within a couple of days of arriving. However, the following roughly circular walking tour through the Stone Town will allow those with limited time to do their sightseeing in a reasonably organised manner (though they are still bound to get lost), and should help those with more time to orientate themselves before they head out to explore the Stone Town without a map or guidebook in hand.

The obvious starting point for any exploration of Zanzibar Town is **Forodhani Gardens** [244 A4 & 248 A4], a small patch of greenery lying between Mizingani Road and the main sea wall. Laid out in 1936 to mark the silver jubilee of Sultan Khalifa, the gardens are a popular eating and meeting point in the evening, and the staircase rising from the gardens to the arched bridge to the south offers a good view over the old town.

Three significant buildings lie alongside each other behind the Forodhani Gardens. The **Palace Museum** [244 B4 & 248 A1] (🕐 09.00–18.00 daily; admission US$3 pp) is the most northerly of these, a large white building with castellated battlements dating from the late 1890s. The palace was the official residence of the Sultan of Zanzibar from 1911 until the 1964 revolution, and it now houses an excellent museum. The graves of all the early sultans of Zanzibar are in the palace garden.

Next to the Palace Museum, the **House of Wonders** [244 B4 & 248 B3] (🕐 09.00–17.30; admission US$3) is a square, multi-storey building surrounded by tiers of impressive balconies and topped with a clocktower. It was built as a ceremonial palace in 1883, and was the first building on Zanzibar to have electric lights. Local people called it Beit el Ajaib, meaning the House of Wonders. It also houses the Museum of History and Culture. It's a pity to rush a visit here, so allow plenty of time.

Directly facing Forodhani Gardens, the **Old Arab Fort** [244 B4] is probably the oldest extant building in the Stone Town, built by Omani Arabs between 1698 and 1701 over the site of a Portuguese church constructed a century before that, remnants of which can still be seen in the inner wall. A large, squarish, brown building with castellated battlements, the fort ceased to serve any meaningful military role in the 19th century, since when it has served variously as prison, railway depot and women's tennis club. The interior of the fort is open to visitors, who can climb to the top of the battlements and enter some of the towers. Admission is free, although donations are welcome. There is a restaurant in the fort, serving cold drinks, and traditional dancing shows take place there at least three evenings every week.

Heading southwest from the fort, under an arched bridge, the fork to your right is Shangani Road, the site of some important buildings. As you follow Shangani Road around a curve, you'll come out to a leafy green square, where the **Zanzibar Shipping Corporation Building**, dating to around 1850, stands to your left and the **Zanzibar Serena Inn** [249 B8], formerly Extelcomms House, to your right. Perhaps 100m past the Serena Inn, to your left, you'll see the rear of **Tippu Tip's House** [244 A6 & 249 D7], a tall brown building which once served as the residence of Tippu Tip, the influential 19th-century slave trader who helped explorers such as Livingstone and Stanley with supplies and route planning. From here, wander up another 50m past the New Happy Bar, and you'll pass the **Africa House Hotel** [249 D8], a good place to punctuate your walk with a cold drink on the attractively positioned balcony.

From the Africa House Hotel a small alley leads to Kenyatta Road, an important thoroughfare dotted with hotels, shops and restaurants, as well as a number of old buildings with traditional Zanzibari doors. Follow Kenyatta Road eastward for about 300m, passing the somewhat unkempt **People's Gardens** [244 B6], originally laid out under Sultan Barghash for the use of his harem, until you reach the **Zanzibar Milestone** [244 C7]. This octagonal marble pillar shows the distance from Zanzibar Town to various settlements on the island and further afield.

Cross the gardens in front of the milestone to the distinctive **Beit el Amaan (House of Peace) Memorial Museum** [244 D7] which, despite its name, is now little more than a library; most of its exhibits have been shifted to the rapidly developing museum in the House of Wonders. The Zanzibari door at the back of the building is reputedly the oldest in existence. From the museum, follow Creek Road northwards for about 400m, and to your left you'll easily pick out the imposing **Anglican cathedral** [248 F1] built by the Universities' Mission in Central Africa (UMCA) over the former slave market between 1873 and 1880. Tradition has it that the altar stands on the site of the market's whipping block, and the cellar of the nearby St Monica's Guesthouse is reputed to be the remains of a pit where slaves were kept before being sold. Sultan Barghash, who closed the slave market, is reputed to have asked Bishop Steere, leader of the mission, not to build the cathedral tower higher than the House of Wonders. The cathedral is open to visitors for a nominal fee, which also covers entrance to the dungeon below the guesthouse.

A short distance further along Creek Road lies the **covered market** [244 D4], built at around the turn of the 20th century, and worth a visit even if you don't want to buy anything. It's a vibrant place where you can buy anything from fish and bread to sewing machines and second-hand car spares. Once you've taken a look around the market, follow Creek Road back southwards for 100m or so, passing the cathedral, then turn into the first wide road to your right. This is New Mkunazini Road, and if you follow it until its end, then turn right into Kajificheni Street and right again into Hammani Street, you'll come out at the **Hammani Baths** [244 C4 & 248 D3]. This is one of the most elaborate Persian baths on Zanzibar, built for Sultan Barghash, and the caretaker will show you around for a small fee.

Barely 200m from the baths, on Cathedral Street, **St Joseph's Catholic Cathedral** [249 C5] is notable for its prominent twin spires, and was built between 1896 and 1898 by French missionaries and local converts. From the cathedral, continue northwards along Cathedral Street for perhaps 50m, then turn right into Gizenga Street, a good place to check out the work of local Tingatinga artists (see box, *Tingatinga paintings* in *Chapter 3*, page 105). If you follow Gizenga Street until you see the old Arab Fort to your left, you can conclude your walk by wandering back out to Forodhani Gardens.

Alternatively, if you want to keep going, turn right opposite the fort into Harumzi Street and, after continuing straight for about 300m, you'll come to an open square. A left turn as you enter this square takes you past the Jamat Khan Mosque and on to Jamatini Road, which after about 200m will bring you out at the seafront opposite the **Big Tree** [244 C3]. Known locally as Mtini, this well-known landmark was planted in 1911 by Sultan Khalifa and now provides shade for traditional dhow builders. On Mizingani Road, next to the Big Tree, the **Old Customs House** [244 B3], a large, relatively plain building dating to the late 19th century, is where Sultan Hamoud was proclaimed sultan in 1896.

From the open area next to the Big Tree, a left turn along Mizingani Road will take you back to the Arab Fort, passing the above-mentioned buildings. Turn right into Mizingani Road, however, and after about 100m you'll pass the **Old Dispensary** [244 C2], an ornate three-storey building built in the 1890s. Restored to its former glory by the Aga Khan, the dispensary now also contains a small exhibition hall of old monochrome photographs of the Stone Town. You can continue for a few hundred metres further, past the port gates, to the **traditional dhow harbour** [244 C1], though based on our experience you are unlikely to be allowed inside.

If the above directions seem too complicated, or you want further insight into the historical buildings of the Stone Town, most tour operators (see pages 243–5) can arrange a guided city tour for around US$15–20.

AROUND ZANZIBAR TOWN

MARUHUBI PALACE This is probably the most impressive ruin on this part of the coast, built in 1882 for the concubines of Sultan Barghash. At one time he kept around a hundred women here. It was destroyed by fire in 1899, and all that remains are the great pillars which supported the upper storey, the Persian-style bathhouse, and the original water tanks, now overgrown with lilies. The palace is signposted along the Bububu road roughly 3km from the Stone Town, and a nominal entrance fee is charged. Traditional dhow builders can be seen at work on the beach in front of the palace.

MTONI PALACE The ruins of Mtoni Palace lie a short way north of Maharubi, and can be reached along the beach. Mtoni is the oldest palace on Zanzibar, built for Sultan Said in the 1840s. A book written by his daughter Salme describes the palace in the 1850s. At one end of the house was a large bathhouse, at the other the quarters where Said lived with his principal wife. Gazelles and peacocks wandered around the large courtyard before Mtoni was abandoned around 1885. Now only the main walls, roof and bathhouses remain, but the resident Mtoni Palace Conservation Project is working hard to restore significant sections and offer interesting guided tours.

KIDICHI AND KIZIMBANI PERSIAN BATHS The Kidichi baths were built in 1850 for Said's wife, Binte Irich Mirza, the granddaughter of the Shah of Persia, and are decorated with Persian-style stucco. You can enter the bathhouse and see the bathing pool and toilets, but there is mould growing on much of the stucco. The baths lie about 3km east of Bububu; from the main crossroads follow the road heading inland (ie: turn right coming from Zanzibar Town) and you'll see the baths to your right after a walk of around 30 minutes. The Kizimbani baths, a few kilometres to the east, were built at around the same period and are similar in style, though lacking the interior decoration.

MANGAPWANI SLAVE CAVE Near the eponymous village, 20km north of Zanzibar Town, this large natural cavern and manmade slave cave can easily be visited using a number 2 *dala-dala*. The natural coral cavern has a narrow entrance and a pool of fresh water at its lowest point. The Slave Cave, a square cell cut into the coral, was used to hold slaves after the trade was abolished in 1873. The natural cavern may also have been used to hide slaves, but this is not certain. Coming by *dala-dala*, you'll have to disembark at Mangapwani, where a road forks left towards the coast. About 2km past the village this road ends and a small track branches off to the right. Follow this for 1km to reach the Slave Cave. About halfway between Mangapwani and the track to the Slave Cave, a narrow track to the left leads to the natural cavern.

ISLANDS NEAR ZANZIBAR TOWN

CHANGUU (PRISON) ISLAND (*admission US$5 pp, hard currency*) Changuu was originally owned by a wealthy Arab, who used it as a detention centre for disobedient slaves. A prison was built there in 1893, but never used; today it houses a café, library and boutique. A path circles the island (about an hour's easy stroll). There is a small beach, a secluded hotel and a restaurant, and masks and fins can be hired for snorkelling. The island is home to several giant tortoises, probably brought from the Seychelles in the 18th century, which spend much of their time mating, a long and noisy process though numbers remain severely threatened.

CHAPWANI (GRAVE) ISLAND This long, narrow and very pretty island has been the site of a Christian cemetery since 1879. Most of the graves belong to British sailors who were killed fighting Arab slave ships, while others date from World War I, when the British ship *Pegasus* was sunk in Zanzibar harbour. The island also has a small swimming beach – good at low and high tide – and faces Snake Island, where thousands of egrets roost overnight. The indigenous forest supports about a hundred duikers, large numbers of fruit bats and various coastal scrub birds. The giant coconut crab is often seen along the shore.

NUNGWI AND THE FAR NORTH

The large fishing village of Nungwi, situated on the northern end of the island, is traditionally the centre of Zanzibar's traditional dhow-building industry. It has also emerged as the most popular tourist retreat on Zanzibar, thanks to its sandy beach, good snorkelling and diving in the surrounding waters, and a profusion of cheaper hotel options. Recent years have seen almost unbridled tourist development in this area, with a twofold increase in hotel beds in just two years, so it's important to choose your accommodation carefully. A short walk along the beach east of Nungwi brings you to the headland of Ras Nungwi, where there is an old lighthouse (photography forbidden). Next to this, the Mnarani Natural Aquarium (⊕ *09.00–18.00 daily; admission US$3*) consists of a fenced-off saline natural pool, in which lives a community of around 17 green and hawksbill turtles.

GETTING THERE AND AWAY An erratic handful of *dala-dalas* connect Zanzibar Town to Nungwi daily, while the local bus (number 14) operates from north to south between 07.00 and 18.00. That said, the vast majority of travellers prefer to be transferred by private minibus, which can cost up to US$15 per person depending on group size and your negotiating skills.

WHERE TO STAY AND EAT
Upmarket

🏠 **Ras Nungwi Beach Hotel** (32 rooms) ☎ 024 223 3767/2512; e info@rasnungwi.com; www.rasnungwi.com. This perennially popular choice for honeymooners lies at the southern end of Nungwi's beach. Rooms of various categories are set in well-tended gardens & include AC, safes & neatly tiled bathrooms, though those situated further back have no sea view. Alongside the central bar & split-level dining room are a games area, a small swimming pool & a spa. Activities include snorkelling, diving, fishing & kayaking, & there's also a highly professional spa. The exceptional food & a great wine list are highlights of any stay, with the occasional seafood BBQ featuring Swahili cuisine classics. *US$340–1,980 dbl, inc HB & activities.*

🏠 **Z Hotel** (35 rooms) m 0732 940303; e info@ theZhotel.com or reservations@theZhotel.com; www.thezhotel.com; ⏲ Jun–mid-Apr. The new kid on the South Beach accommodation block opened in 2008, bringing a level of city-boy bling previously unseen on the Nungwi beach scene. Rooms are divided into 6 levels of luxury, but all boast indulgences from iPod docking stations, AC & plasma TVs to White Company toiletries & stocked minibars. Every room has a balcony with a sea view, of varying degrees. Elsewhere in the compact complex, the stone pool above the beach is a fine hangout, whilst the Cinnamon Bar & Saruche Restaurant are already evening hotspots. The biggest issue for style-seekers may prove to be the less salubrious surrounding sprawl. *Superior US$280–600 dbl FB.*

Moderate

🏠 **Flame Tree Cottages** (14 rooms) ☎ 024 224 0100; m 0777 479429/0713 262151; e etgl@ zanlink.com; www.flametreecottages.com. On the edge of Nungwi village, these whitewashed bungalows & a new house are spread across extensive gardens, beside the beach. En-suite rooms are immaculate, with shady verandas, AC & fans, & a shared or private kitchenette. Flame Tree also offers one of Nungwi's best dining experiences (think delicious fish goujons with tartare US$5.50, or steamed chilli crab claws US$9). There is a real feeling of space & peace that is increasingly difficult to find in Nungwi, & the staff are genuinely happy to help. Activities range from lemongrass oil massage to snorkelling trips aboard the owner's dhow. *US$120 dbl.*

🏠 **Langi Langi Beach Bungalows** (33 rooms) ☎ 024 224 0470; e langi_langi@hotmail.com. Built over several stages, the hotel is divided by a footpath, with newer rooms on the seafront & the original ones by the pool in a lush garden on the other side. Although all are en suite with AC & fans, the latter probably still get our vote as the rooms of

choice. On the seafront, aim for rooms higher up for the best views. The reasonably good Marhaba Café is a popular hangout for visitors & expats, serving curries in particular; bring your own alcohol. The owners are friendly, employing only local staff, & are genuinely hospitable. *US$60–150 dbl.*

🏠 **Mnarani Beach Cottages** (37 rooms) ☎ 024 224 0494; m 0777 415551; e mnarani@zanlink.com; www.lighthousezanzibar.com. Close to the northernmost tip of the island, Mnarani overlooks a stunning stretch of beach, & is separated by dense vegetation from the lighthouse; unlike most other plots on this coast, it feels less boxed in by development. Some of its en-suite rooms have sea views; others are set in lush, tropical gardens close to the pool. There are also new self-catering cottages & flats. Kayaks, windsurfers & surfboards can be hired, & the lagoon in front of the hotel is a great place for kite-surfers. The bar has a cool, relaxed vibe, & the staff are some of the friendliest on the north coast. *US$120–200 dbl HB.*

Budget

🏠 **Amaan Bungalows** (58 rooms) ☎ 024 224 0026/34; m 0777 417390; e amaannungwi@ yahoo.com; www.amaanbungalows.com. This sprawling, castellated complex is in the heart of Nungwi's accommodation cluster & is popular with a young crowd seeking to be at the centre of the action. Of its deluxe, garden & sea-view rooms, the last – perched on a coral-rock cliff above the sea – more than justify the higher cost, though all are clean &

well cared for, with en-suite bathrooms, fans &, in deluxe & sea-view rooms, AC. A grocery shop, bureau de change, safety-deposit system & internet café add to the package. The affiliated Fat Fish Restaurant & Blue Sea, immediately opposite on the seafront, are good places to eat pizza & seafood, drink virtually anything & be merry at any hour of the day (HB rates include meals at either place). *US$40–120 dbl.*

The east coast of Zanzibar is where you will find the idyllic tropical beaches so beloved of travel brochures: clean white sand lined with palms, and lapped by the warm blue water of the Indian Ocean. The east coast is divided into two discrete stretches by Chwaka Bay, which lies at the same latitude as Zanzibar Town on the west coast. Traditionally, the most popular stretch of coast has been to the south of this bay, between Bwejuu and Makunduchi, but recent years have seen an increasing number of developments further north, between Matemwe and Chwaka, especially around Kiwengwa, with its cluster of large, Italian package-holiday resorts.

GETTING THERE AND AWAY The east coast can easily be reached by bus or *dala-dala* from Zanzibar Town. North of Chwaka Bay, number 6 buses go to Chwaka (some continue to Uroa and Pongwe), number 13 to Uroa via Chwaka, number 15 to Kiwengwa and number 16 to Matemwe. South of the bay, number 9 goes to Paje (sometimes continuing to Bwejuu or Jambiani) and number 10 to Makunduchi. Chwaka Bay can sometimes be crossed by boat between Chwaka and Michamvi, with the help of local octopus fishermen. Most travellers prefer to use private transport to the east coast: several tour companies and independent guides arrange minibuses which cost US$5–8 per person each way. Unless you specify where you want to stay, minibus drivers are likely to take you to a hotel that gives them commission.

WHERE TO STAY
Upmarket

🏠 **Fairmont Zanzibar** (109 rooms) ☏ 024 2240391; e zanzibar@fairmont.com or zan.reservations@ fairmont.com; www.fairmont.com/zanzibar. At Matemwe, lush grounds, plenty of facilities & immaculate staff have quickly made this Zanzibar's premium family resort. Newly renovated rooms & suites, each thoughtfully designed with contemporary facilities & in a range of styles & sizes, are dotted around tropical gardens. Outside are 2 lovely pools & a super-soft sandy beach, ideal for organised activities, as well as an onsite dive centre & a spa. Enjoy sundowners at the cocktail bar before dinner at the à la carte restaurant (southern African game meats & local seafood) or something more casual at Tradewinds buffet & pizza parlour. *US$600–690 dbl, inc HB & activities.*

🏠 **Matemwe Bungalows** (12 rooms) m 0777 414834; e info@asilialodges.com or

matemwebungalows@zanzinet.com; www.matemwe.com or www.asilialodges.com; ⊕ Jun–Mar. Smart yet informal, the quiet Matemwe Bungalows is popular with couples. Each of its thatched cottages is perched on the edge of a low coral cliff, with a superb view across to Mnemba Island. All have been upgraded into stylish suites, with mains electricity, mosquito nets, fan (on request), safe box, a day bed & an area to chill out as standard. Lush tropical gardens lead to the swimming pools, dining area & sandy beach. Activities include snorkelling & sailing in dhows, fishing, diving & escorted reef walks. The lodge supports the local community through the provision of fresh water, a primary school, 2 deep-sea dhows for fishing, & teaching English. *US$265–310 pp FB.*

Moderate

🏠 **Shooting Star** (16 rooms) m 0777 414166; e star@zanzibar.org; www.zanzibar.org/star. Standing above Kiwengwa Beach, about 8km south of Matemwe, this is a delightfully social place, whose garden rooms, sea-view cottages & suites all feature Zanzibari beds & colourful Tingatinga pictures. A stunning infinity pool & sundeck afford views over the ocean, barrier reef & beach below. Dining is split across 3 shady areas, offering simple & filling meals, but it's the lively bar &

relaxed lounge area that is the true heart of Shooting Star. The Star Bar is a terrifically friendly evening hangout — especially before the famed lobster beach BBQ (extra US$45 pp). Diving, snorkelling & fishing trips can be organised. *US$215–610 dbl FB*

🏠 **Kikadini Villas** (5 villas) e reservations@ kikadinivillas.com; www. escape-zanzibar.com. On a large beachfront plot in the centre of the village of Jambiani, the villas that make up Kikadini are unparalleled on the island. This is in essence a boutique hotel, with striking architecture, delicious food, attentive staff & tremendous individuality. Each of the beach-facing villas is architecturally different, while the interiors feature eclectic *objets d'art* & huge oil paintings. All have electricity, fans, small fridges & Wi-Fi as standard. There are roof terraces for shady lunches & stargazing, & a swimming pool is planned. In a bid to maintain a quiet, calm haven for other guests, children under 10 cannot stay unless a villa is exclusively booked. *US$235–310 HB.*

🏠 **Mchanga Beach Lodge** (8 rooms) m 0773 952399/569821; e tradewithzanzibar@zantel.com; www.mchangabeachlodge.com. Simple, stylish construction, high-quality interiors & happy, efficient staff characterise Mchanga, & the location near Pwani Mchangani is stunning. Steeply thatched rooms have a 4-poster bed, as well as a cushion-covered *baraza* alcove & a small terrace. A thoughtful mix of hand-crafted wooden shutters, ceiling fans, AC & high-

beamed ceilings ensures that rooms remain cool. Outside are a stunning swimming pool & open-sided *makuti* bar & restaurant, serving food that is a mix of Swahili specials. Diving can be arranged, though this is primarily a place to relax. *US$190–230 dbl.*

🏠 **Pongwe Beach Hotel** (16 rooms) m 0784 336181/0773 169096; e info@pongwe.com; www.pongwe.com. Standing in its own quiet cove, under the shade of coconut palms, this simple lodge is well managed & good value. Airy bungalows have mosquito nets, an en-suite bathroom, & limited electricity, & there's a huge library of over 5,000 books. The barrier reef is only 15 mins offshore & the resort has its own dhow for sailing, snorkelling trips (US$15) & game or line fishing. A large infinity pool has recently opened on the coral rock to the north of the beach. Pongwe serves tasty lunches from US$4 & varied set menus at dinner, including succulent spiced meats. With a little notice, children are welcome. *US$160 dbl.*

Budget

🏠 **Casa Del Mar** (12 rooms) m 0777 455446; e infocasa-delmar@hotmail.com; www.casa-delmar-zanzibar.com; lodge 🕐 Jun–Mar. Casa del Mar is run with impressive enthusiasm, skill & environmental awareness. Rooms are in 2 thatched double-storey houses, made almost entirely of organic material; all the furniture was made onsite, & every palm uprooted during construction was successfully replanted. The majority of the staff are Jambiani residents, & the school & clinic receive regular support. These credentials aside, the accommodation & friendly vibe are good reasons to stay too. En-suite rooms are either sgl or 2 storey, both with balconies & the latter with a galleried bedroom high in the thatch, & a lounge (or children's room). Good food is served in the cool, shady restaurant. There's

a range of activities & excursions & the lodge has its own boat for snorkelling trips (US$15 pp/day). *US$50 dbl.*

🏠 **Santa Maria Coral Reef** (7 rooms) m 0777 432655; e info@santamaria-zanzibar.com; www.santamaria-zanzibar.com. The only development along the beach at Pongwe is a delightful hideaway, set in a coconut grove. Both bandas & bungalows are basic with solid wooden beds, coconut-rope & timber shelves & colourful mats. All are en suite with flush toilets & showers, & there is generator electricity 18.00–midnight. For lunch & dinner expect freshly cooked fish or chicken with rice (around US$6). There's a simple thatched lounge/library area, & dhow snorkelling trips can be arranged. *US$50 dbl.*

MNEMBA ISLAND

The tiny island of Mnemba, officially titled Mnemba Island Marine Conservation Area (MIMCA), lies some 2.5km off the northeastern coast of Zanzibar, and forms part of the much larger submerged Mnemba Atoll. It is now privately leased by &Beyond (formerly Conservation Corporation Africa, or CC Africa) and has become one of Africa's ultimate beach retreats. It cannot be visited without a reservation.

The island itself boasts wide beaches of white coral sand, fine and cool underfoot, backed by patches of tangled coastal bush and a small forest of casuarina trees. The small reefs immediately offshore offer a great introduction to the fishes of the reef for snorkellers, while diving excursions further afield allow you to explore the 40m-deep coral cliffs, a good place to see larger fish including the whale shark, the world's largest fish. The bird checklist for the island, though short, includes several unusual waders and other marine birds.

⌂ WHERE TO STAY

Mnemba Island Lodge (10 *bandas*) ➤ (South Africa) +27 (0)11 8094441; e reservations@ -andbeyond.com; www.andbeyond.com; ⏱ Jun–Mar. The *crème de la crème* of &Beyond's impressive portfolio, Mnemba Island Lodge is the height of rustic exclusivity: a place where the term 'barefoot luxury' & eco-friendly policies are a reality. Overlooking the beach from the forest's edge, its secluded, split-level bandas are constructed entirely of local timber & hand-woven palm fronds. Large, airy & open-plan, each has a huge bed & solid wooden furniture, softened with natural-coloured fabrics. A 'butler' is assigned to each room to ensure that everyone is content. The cuisine is predictably excellent, with plenty of fresh seafood, fruit & vegetables, though guests may choose what, when & where to eat. A number of superb dive sites are within 15 mins of the lodge, & during the trip sightings of dolphin are not uncommon, & even humpbacks in season. Up to 2 dives a day are included for qualified PADI divers, though courses are charged extra. There's also snorkelling, double kayaks, windsurfing, power-kiting, sailing, & fly or deep-sea fishing. Hot stone, aromatherapy, deep-tissue massage & reiki are all available, too. Mnemba is unquestionably expensive, but its flexibility & service levels are second to none, & its idyllic location & proximity to outstanding marine experiences are very hard to match. *US$1,250 pp/night, inc FB & activities.*

SOUTHWEST ZANZIBAR

For most overseas visitors, Zanzibar's southwest corner holds little more than day-trip opportunities to see dolphins from Kizimkazi and troops of red colobus monkeys in Jozani Forest. As a result, few people stay in this area, with most opting instead for the endless beaches of the east coast or the buzz of Zanzibar Stone Town. Away from the main tourist attractions, the villagers in these parts rarely encounter many visitors, and their welcome is one of genuine friendliness and interest. It's a refreshing contrast to the more crowded and visitor-centric feeling taking over significant parts of the island's north and east coasts.

⌂ WHERE TO STAY AND EAT
Upmarket

Fumba Beach Lodge (26 rooms) m 0777 860504/878025; e reservations@ fumbabeachlodge.co.tz or info@fumbabeachlodge.co.tz; www.fumbabeachlodge.com. To the south of Zanzibar Town, & created in line with contemporary, upmarket safari camps, this is one of the island's most stylish places to stay. Rooms & uber-luxurious suites have canopied beds, mains electricity, en-suite showers, fans & a sea view. A large infinity pool lies next to the lounge & a sophisticated, open-sided restaurant, specialises in seafood, while an ingenious open-air tree house is home to a spa. There's an onsite dive centre & day trips around Menai Bay's islands make for one of Zanzibar's most beautiful & indulgent outings. *US$210–410 dbl.*

Moderate

Karamba (14 rooms) m 0773 166406; e karamba@zanlink.com; www.karambaresort.com. This appealing clifftop lodge at Kizimkazi Dimbani has smart, en-suite bungalows, each thoughtfully

Budget

Kumi Na Mbili Centre (3 rooms) m 0777 841252; e info@d-t-p-ev.de;

Unguja Lodge (10 rooms) m 0774 477477/ 857234; e info@ungujalodge.com; www.ungujaresort.com. Opened in Dec 2006, Unguja Lodge at Kizimkazi Mkunguni is already up with the best on the island, its style a mix of modern & traditional. Enormous rooms are set in densely planted gardens. Inside each, sinuous walls enclose a lounge, shower room, mezzanine seating area & bedroom. 3 'baobab villas' each have a small plunge pool, whilst others have a sea view. For a cool dip, try the pool or make for the crushed-shell beach. There's a PADI dive centre, with shore diving & boat dives possible. Other activities include dhow cruises, dolphin viewing & a village tour. *US$350–510 dbl HB.*

decorated & with a sea view. In the restaurant, try fresh sushi (US$20 sharing platter) & tapas dishes (US$3–6 each) or just a sunset cocktail overlooking the bustling dhow harbour below. *US$84–216 dbl.*

www.zanzibartourism.org. The neat white building of this village development centre at Kizimkazi

Mkunguni has simple, clean en-suite rooms with fans & mosquito nets. There's an affiliated bakery & juice bar, as well as an internet café & shop. Bicycles are available for rent & tours can be arranged. For US$3, you can plant a tree, for which a little KiSwahili helps: *Ninaomba kupanda mnazi moja/tatu/kumi* means, 'I would like to plant 1/3/10 palm trees'. *US$30 dbl*.

PEMBA AND MAFIA ISLANDS

While Zanzibar's tourist industry is growing rapidly, some would say too rapidly, the pace of life on its sister island, **Pemba**, has remained relatively unchanged over the years. Hilly and verdant, the island is the centre of the clove industry; witness the heady aroma of cloves drying in the sun along the roadside.

Accommodation on Pemba is limited to just a handful of lodges, hotels and guesthouses. Of these, three are geared to the diver in search of the island's renowned underwater attractions, including some exciting drift dives and the possibility of seeing some of the larger pelagics.

⌂ **Fundu Lagoon** (16 rooms) \ 024 223 2926; m 0777 438668; e info@fundulagoon.com; www.fundulagoon.com. In the south of the island, this upmarket & romantic hideaway is extremely popular with honeymooners. It also has its own dive centre. *US$610–1,220 dbl*.

⌂ **Kervan Saray Beach** m 0773 176737–8/0784 394980; e resort@kayakpemba.com; www.kervansaraybeach.com. Swahili Divers' new home is a simple & unpretentious affair located in the far northwest of the island. *US$150/280 dbl low/high season FB; dorm/family room US$45 pp FB. 2 dives inc equipment US$99/160 low/high season*.

⌂ **Manta Resort** (10 rooms) www.themantaresort.com; ⊕ Aug–May. Overlooking the northern end of Verani Beach & newly renovated this caters to divers & landlubbers alike. *US$335–525 dbl FB*.

⌂ **Manta Divers Village** (10 private chalets) www.themantadiversvillage.com. Sister property to the Manta Resort, this is more low-key in feel and its rates are cheaper. *US$255 dbl FB*.

Considerably further south, the tiny island of **Mafia** is gaining popularity among a small band of divers in search of spectacular underwater life in an entirely unspoilt setting. The island has just a handful of beachside lodges close to the capital of Kilindoni, with a third across the bay on the island of Chole. All offer diving, snorkelling and various low-key excursions.

⌂ **Pole Pole** (7 bungalows) \ 022 2601530; e info@polepole.com; www.polepole.com. The Italian-managed Pole Pole, meaning 'slowly, slowly' in Swahili, is small, comfortable & good on detail. *US$440 dbl FB*.

⌂ **Kinasi Lodge** (14 bungalows) m 0777 418256, operations m 0713 242977; e kinasi@intafrica.com; www.mafiaisland.com; ⊕ Jun–end Mar. Next to Pole Pole, & rather more formal, Kinasi has large, landscaped grounds & both a dining area & pizza kitchen. *US$430–604 dbl FB*.

⌂ **Mafia Island Lodge** (40 rooms) m 0786 303049; e info@mafialodge.com; www.mafialodge.com. Built by the government in 1971, this is a much simpler affair, reliable & functional, useful for those on a budget. *US$140–180 dbl HB*.

⌂ **Chole Mjini Lodge** (6 tree houses, 1 chalet) m 0784 520799; e 2chole@bushmail.net. The 19th-century ruins of Chole Mjini set the scene for large, wooden tree house-style bedrooms perched high in the baobabs of Chole Island. *US$720–1,080 dbl FB inc village levy*.

For detailed coverage of both islands, see *Zanzibar, Pemba & Mafia: The Bradt Travel Guide* by Chris McIntyre and Susan McIntyre.

WHAT TO SEE AND DO

Jozani-Chwaka Bay National Park *(⊕ 07.30–17.00 Mon–Sun; admission US$8)*
This newly declared national park incorporates Jozani Forest, protecting the last
substantial remnant of the indigenous forest that once covered much of central

SAADANI NATIONAL PARK

Philip Briggs

Protected as a game reserve since 1969 and gazetted as a national park in 2006,
Saadani is the only wildlife sanctuary in east Africa with an Indian Ocean beachfront.
Situated on the mainland opposite the northern tip of Zanzibar, the original 200km^2
game reserve, centred on the small but ancient fishing village of Saadani, has been
extended to cover 1,062km^2 thanks to the incorporation of some former
ranchlands since 1996.

As recently as ten years ago, Saadani – despite its proximity to Dar es Salaam –
was among east Africa's most obscure conservation areas, subject to heavy
poaching and lacking tourist facilities in any form. In recent years, however, it has
received renewed attention from conservationists and tourists alike. One factor in
this revival has been the establishment of two top-notch private tented camps within
the proposed national park. Another has been the clampdown on poaching and
integration of local villages into the conservation effort initiated with assistance from
Germany's GTZ agency in 1998.

Viewed purely as a wildlife destination, Saadani cannot yet bear comparison to
Tanzania's finest – though if present trends continue, it may well be up with them
ten years hence. But even as things stand, Saadani is a thoroughly worthwhile and
enjoyable retreat, allowing visitors to combine the hedonistic pleasures of a perfect
sandy beach with guided bush walks, game drives and a boat trip up the Wami River.
The latter is a highlight of Saadani – close encounters with hippo are guaranteed,
there's a good chance of seeing crocs, and a spectacular array of marine and
woodland birds includes Pel's fishing owl, mangrove, pied and malachite kingfishers,
broad-billed roller and various waders, herons and egrets.

Inland, Saadani supports a park-like cover of open grassland interspersed with
stands of acacia trees and knotted coastal thicket, home to a wide range of
ungulates, with game densities generally highest in January, February, June, July and
August. At all times of year, however, you can be reasonably confident of
encountering elephant, giraffe, buffalo, warthog, common waterbuck, reedbuck,
hartebeest and wildebeest, along with troops of yellow baboon and vervet monkey.
Something of a Saadani special is the red duiker, a diminutive, beautiful and normally
very shy antelope of coastal scrub and forest. Saadani also harbours small
populations of greater kudu, eland and the endangered Roosevelt's sable. Lions are
also making something of a comeback, and leopard, spotted hyena and black-
backed jackal are seen from time to time. The beaches in and around Saadani form
one of the last major breeding sites for green turtles on mainland Tanzania.

In addition to a rather basic guesthouse run by Tanapa, two exclusive beachfront
camps offer upmarket tented accommodation on a full-board basis, as well as a full
selection of activities including boat trips, game walks and game drives:

🏠 **Saadani Safari Camp** ✆ 022 277 3294; e info@saadanilodge.com; www.saadanilodge.com
🏠 **Tent With A View** ✆ 022 211 0507; e info@saadani.com; www.saadani.com

Both companies can also provide details of charter flights and/or road transfers and
shuttles to/from Arusha, Zanzibar and Dar es Salaam.

Zanzibar. The main attraction is Kirk's red colobus, a beautiful and cryptically coloured monkey with an outrageous pale tufted crown. Unique to Zanzibar, Kirk's red colobus had been reduced to a population of around 1,500 individuals a few years back, but recent estimates now place it at around 2,500. A good network of forest trails runs through the forest, and the habituated troops are easily seen by tourists.

Jozani used to be the main haunt of the Zanzibar leopard, a race that is found nowhere else, but which recent research suggests may well be extinct. The forest is also home to Ader's duiker, a small antelope that effectively may now be a Zanzibar endemic, as it is probably extinct and certainly very rare in Kenya's Sokoke Forest, the only other place where it has ever been recorded. Several other mammal species live in Jozani, and the forest is one of the best birding sites on the island, hosting a good range of coastal forest birds, including an endemic race of the lovely Fischer's turaco. A new development in the area, based in the village of Pete, 1km from the entrance to the forest, is a mangrove boardwalk, allowing visitors a rare view into the unique mangrove habitat.

Getting there and away The entrance and reception at Jozani Forest lie a short distance from the main road connecting Zanzibar Town to the east coast. Most tour operators can organise day trips to the forest, though it is perfectly possible to visit independently using a number 9, 10 or 13 bus, or *dala-dala* numbers 309, 310, 324 or 326.

Kizimkazi The small town of Kizimkazi lies on the southwestern end of the island, and is best known to tourists as *the* place to see humpback and bottlenose dolphins, both of which are resident in the area. Most tourists visit Kizimkazi on an organised day tour out of Zanzibar Town, which costs between US$25 and US$100 all-inclusive per person, depending on group size, season and quality. Sightings cannot be guaranteed, but the chances of seeing dolphins here are very good. It may also be possible sometimes to swim with the dolphins, though you should never encourage your pilot to chase them or try to approach them too closely yourself. With up to a hundred people visiting Kizimkazi daily in the high season, there is genuine cause to fear that tourism may be detrimental to the animals. If you do get close enough and choose to try your luck swimming with the dolphins, slip (rather than dive) into the water next to the boat, and hold your arms along your body to imitate their streamlined shape.

If you stay overnight at Kizimkazi, it's worth heading out to the Kizimkazi Mosque at the nearby settlement of Dimbani. Kizimkazi is one of the oldest known mosques in east Africa, dated by Kufic inscriptions to AD1107, when it was part of a large walled city. The Kufic inscriptions, on the niche at the eastern end of the mosque, are in a decorative floriated style similar to some old inscriptions found in Persia. The silver pillars on either side of the niche are decorated with pounded shells from Mafia Island. Two clocks, which show Swahili time, were presented by local dignitaries. To see inside the mosque, now protected by a corrugated-iron roof, you must find the caretaker who lives nearby. It is respectful to cover any bare limbs and take off your shoes when you enter.

Getting there and away Although most people visit Kizimkazi on an organised day trip, it can be reached independently in a hired car, or number 326 *dala-dala* from Zanzibar Town.

Chumbe Island The coral island of Chumbe, along with several surrounding reefs, is gazetted as a nature reserve under the title of Chumbe Island Coral Park

(CHICOP). The area is in near-pristine condition because it served as a military base for many years and visitors were not permitted. Snorkelling here is as good as anywhere around Zanzibar, with more than 350 reef fishes recorded, as well as dolphins and turtles. A walking trail circumnavigates the island, passing rock pools haunted by starfish, and beaches marched upon by legions of hermit crabs. Look out, too, for the giant coconut crab, an endangered nocturnal creature that weighs up to 4kg. Some 60 species of bird have been recorded on the island, including breeding pairs of the rare roseate tern, and the localised Ader's duiker, hunted out in the 1950s, has been reintroduced. Of historical interest are an ancient Swahili mosque and a British lighthouse built in 1904.

Day trips to the island (US$80 per person, including transfers, guides, snorkelling equipment and lunch) can be arranged only through reputable tour operators or from the Mbweni Ruins Hotel. Alternatively visitors can stay overnight.

Where to stay

Chumbe Island Lodge (7 rooms) ☏ 024 223 1040; m 0777 413 582; e chumbe@zitec.org; www.chumbeisland.com; ⊕ mid-Jun–mid-Apr. Bungalows here are simple but clean, very comfortable, ingeniously designed & genuinely ecologically sensitive, with solar electricity, compost toilets & funnelled roofs designed to collect rainwater. Made mostly from local materials, each has 2 storeys, with an open-fronted lounge-terrace & a bathroom below, & upstairs, a mattress laid on the floor, shrouded in a mosquito net, with a stunning view. An ingenious main *boma* houses the dining room (good seafood), education centre, snorkelling equipment room & lounge/bar. Chumbe makes no pretension to be a chillout beach resort, but it is highly recommended to those with a strong interest in wildlife & conservation & has won numerous global awards for ecotourism. *US$500 dbl FB, inc soft drinks, guides, transfers & all activities.*

Appendix I

WILDLIFE

MAMMALS In the listings below, an animal's scientific name is given in parentheses after its English name, followed by the Swahili (Sw) name. The Swahili for animal is *nyama* (plural *wanyama*); to find out what animal you are seeing, ask *'Nyama gani?'*

Cats, dogs and hyenas

Lion (*Panthera leo*) Sw: *simba*. Shoulder height: 100–120cm; weight: 150–220kg. Africa's largest predator, the lion is the one animal that everybody hopes to see on safari. It is a sociable creature, living in prides of five to ten animals and defending a territory of between 20 and 200km². Lions hunt at night, and their favoured prey is large or medium antelope such as wildebeest and impala. Most of the hunting is done by females, but dominant males normally feed first after a kill. Rivalry between males is intense, and battles to take over a pride are frequently fought to the death, for which reason two or more males often form a coalition. Young males are forced out of their home pride at three years of age, and male cubs are usually killed after a successful takeover. When not feeding or fighting, lions are remarkably indolent – they spend up to 23 hours of any given day at rest – so the anticipation of a lion sighting is often more exciting than the real thing. Lions naturally occur in any habitat but desert and rainforest, and once ranged across much of the Old World, but these days they are all but restricted to the larger conservation areas in sub-Saharan Africa (one remnant population exists in India). Recent surveys indicate that Tanzania might host around 50% of the world's surviving free-ranging lions, and the Serengeti and Ngorongoro Crater are arguably the best places in Africa to see these charismatic beasts.

Leopard (*Panthera pardus*) Sw: *chui*. Shoulder height: 70cm; weight: 60–80kg. The powerful leopard is the most solitary and secretive of Africa's large cat species. It hunts using stealth and power, often getting to within 5m of its intended prey before pouncing, and it habitually stores its kill in a tree to keep it from hyenas and lions. The leopard can be distinguished from the superficially similar cheetah by its rosette-like spots, lack of black 'tear marks' and more compact, powerful build. Leopards occur in all habitats, favouring areas with plenty of cover such as riverine woodland and rocky slopes. There are many records of individuals living in close proximity to humans for years without being detected. The leopard is the most common of Africa's large felines, found throughout Tanzania, yet a good sighting must be considered a stroke of fortune. One relatively reliable spot for leopard sightings is the Seronera Valley in the Serengeti. An endemic race of leopard occurs on Zanzibar, though recent research suggests that it is probably extinct on the island, and that the handful of local reports of leopard sightings were probably the result of confusion with the African civet and introduced Java civet.

Cheetah (*Acynonix jubatus*) Sw: *duma*. Shoulder height: 70–80cm; weight: 50–60kg. This remarkable spotted cat has a greyhound-like build, and is capable of running at 70km/h in bursts, making it the world's fastest land animal. It is often seen pacing the plains restlessly, either on its own or in a small family group comprising a mother and her offspring. A diurnal hunter, favouring the cooler hours of the day, the cheetah's habits have been adversely affected in areas where there are high tourist concentrations and off-road driving is permitted. Males are territorial, and generally solitary, though in the Serengeti they commonly defend their territory in pairs or trios. Despite superficial similarities, you can easily tell a cheetah from a leopard by its simple spots, disproportionately small head, streamlined build, diagnostic black tear marks, and preference for relatively open habitats. Widespread, but thinly distributed and increasingly rare outside of conservation areas, the cheetah is most likely to be seen in savanna and arid habitats such as the Serengeti Plains (where sightings are regular on the road to Seronera) and the floor of the Ngorongoro Crater.

Similar species The **serval** (*Felis serval*) is smaller than a cheetah (shoulder height: 55cm) but has a similar build and black-on-gold spots giving way to streaking near the head. It is widespread and quite common in moist grassland, reed beds and riverine habitats, but tends to be very secretive. The Serengeti is probably the best place in Africa for serval sightings.

Caracal (*Felis caracal*) Sw: *simbamangu*. Shoulder height: 40cm; weight: 15–20kg. The caracal resembles the European lynx with its uniform tan coat and tufted ears. It is a solitary hunter, feeding on birds, small antelope and livestock, and ranges throughout the country favouring relatively arid savanna habitats. It is nocturnal and seldom seen.

Similar species The smaller **African wild cat** (*Felis sylvestris*) ranges from the Mediterranean to the Cape of Good Hope, and is similar in appearance to the domestic tabby cat. Like the caracal, it is common, but nocturnal, and infrequently seen.

African wild dog (*Lycaon pictus*) Sw: *mbwa mwitu*. Shoulder height: 70cm; weight: 25kg. Also known as the African hunting dog or painted dog, the wild dog is distinguished from other African canids by its large size and cryptic black, brown and cream coat. Highly sociable, living in packs of up to 20 animals, the hunting dog is a ferocious hunter that literally tears apart its prey on the run. Threatened with extinction as a result of its susceptibility to diseases spread by domestic dogs, it is indeed extinct in several areas where it was formerly abundant, for instance in the Serengeti and most other reserves in northern Tanzania. The global population of around 4,000 wild dogs is spread across much of eastern and southern Africa, but the Selous Game Reserve is the most important stronghold (estimated population 1,300) and Ruaha National Park also hosts a viable population. The one place in northern Tanzania where wild dogs are regularly observed is Mkomazi National Park, where a recently reintroduced population is thriving. Wild dogs were reported denning in Loliondo on the eastern Serengeti border as recently as mid 2008, and other scattered sightings in Tarangire, Lake Manyara and the northern Serengeti suggest that this endangered creature might yet recolonise the northern safari circuit.

Black-backed jackal (*Canis mesomelas*) Sw: *mbweha*. Shoulder height: 35–45cm; weight: 8–12kg. The black-backed (or silver-backed) jackal is an opportunistic feeder capable of adapting to most habitats. Most often seen singly or in pairs at dusk or dawn, it is ochre in colour with a prominent black saddle flecked by a varying amount of white or gold. It is probably the most frequently observed small predator in Africa south of the Zambezi, and its eerie call is a characteristic sound of the bush at night. It is the commonest jackal in most Tanzanian reserves.

Similar species The **side-striped jackal** (*Canis adustus*) is more cryptic in colour, and has an indistinct pale vertical stripe on each flank and a white-tipped tail. Nowhere very common, it is distributed throughout Tanzania, and most likely to be seen in the southern reserves. The **common jackal** (*Canis aureus*), also known as the Eurasian or golden jackal, is a cryptically coloured north African jackal, relatively pale and with a black tail tip. Its range extends as far south as the Serengeti and Ngorongoro Crater, and it is probably more readily seen than the black-backed jackal on the crater floor, since it is more diurnal in its habits.

Bat-eared fox (*Otocyon megalotis*) Shoulder height: 30–35cm; weight: 35kg. This small, silver-grey insectivore, unmistakable with its huge ears and black eye-mask, is most often seen in pairs or small family groups during the cooler hours of the day. Associated with dry open country, the bat-eared fox is quite common in the Serengeti and likely to be encountered at least once in the course of a few days' safari, particularly during the denning season (November and December).

Spotted hyena (*Crocuta crocuta*) Sw. *fisi*. Shoulder height: 85cm; weight: 70kg. Hyenas are characterised by their bulky build, sloping back, brownish coat, powerful jaws and dog-like expression. Despite looking superficially canine, they are more closely related to mongooses and bears than to cats or dogs. Contrary to popular myth, hyenas are not exclusively scavengers: the spotted hyena in particular is an adept hunter capable of killing an animal as large as a wildebeest. Nor are they hermaphroditic, an ancient belief that stems from the false scrotum and penis covering the female hyena's vagina. Sociable animals, and fascinating to observe, hyenas live in loosely structured clans of about ten animals, led by females who are stronger and larger than males. The spotted hyena is the largest hyena, distinguished by its blotchily spotted coat, and it is probably the most common large predator in eastern and southern Africa. It is most frequently seen at dusk and dawn in the vicinity of game reserve lodges, campsites and refuse dumps, and is likely to be encountered on a daily basis in the Serengeti and Ngorongoro Crater.

Similar species The north African **striped hyena** (*Hyaena hyaena*) is pale brown with several dark vertical streaks and an off-black mane. It occurs alongside the spotted hyena in dry parts of Tanzania, but is scarce and secretive. The equally secretive **aardwolf** (*Proteles cristatus*) is an insectivorous striped hyena, not much bigger than a jackal, occurring in low numbers in northern Tanzania.

African civet (*Civettictus civetta*) Sw: *fungo*. Shoulder height: 40cm; weight: 10–15kg. This bulky, long-haired, rather feline creature of the African night is primarily carnivorous, feeding on small animals and carrion, but will also eat fruit. It has a similarly coloured coat to a leopard or cheetah, and this is densely blotched with large black spots becoming stripes towards the head. Civets are widespread and common in many habitats, but very rarely seen.

Similar species The smaller, more slender **tree civet** (*Nandinia binotata*) is an arboreal forest animal with a dark-brown coat marked with black spots. The **small-spotted genet** (*Genetta genetta*) and **large-spotted genet** (*Genetta tigrina*) are the most widespread members of a group of similar small predators, all of which are very slender and rather feline in appearance, with a grey to golden-brown coat marked with black spots and an exceptionally long ringed tail. Most likely to be seen on nocturnal game drives or scavenging around game reserve lodges, the large-spotted genet is golden brown with very large spots and a black-tipped tail, whereas the small-spotted genet is greyer with rather small spots and a pale tip to the tail.

Banded mongoose (*Mungos mungo*) Shoulder height: 20cm; weight: around 1kg. The banded mongoose is probably the most commonly observed member of a group of small, slender, terrestrial carnivores. Uniform dark brown except for a dozen black stripes across its back, it is a diurnal mongoose occurring in family groups in most wooded habitats and savanna.

Similar species Several other mongoose species occur in Tanzania, though some are too scarce and nocturnal to be seen by casual visitors. The **marsh mongoose** (*Atilax paludinosus*) is large, normally solitary and has a very scruffy brown coat. It's widespread in the eastern side of Africa where it is often seen in the vicinity of water. The **white-tailed ichneumon** (*Ichneumia albicauda*) is another widespread, solitary, large brown mongoose, easily identified by its bushy white tail. The **slender mongoose** (*Galerella sanguinea*) is as widespread and also solitary, but it is very much smaller (shoulder height: 10cm) and has a uniform brown coat and black tail tip. The **dwarf mongoose** (*Helogate parvula*) is a diminutive (shoulder height: 7cm) and highly sociable light-brown mongoose often seen in the vicinity of termite mounds, particularly in Tarangire National Park.

Ratel (*Mellivora capensis*) Sw: *nyegere*. Shoulder height: 30cm; weight: 12kg. Also known as the honey badger, the ratel is black with a puppyish face and grey-to-white back. It is an opportunistic feeder best known for its symbiotic relationship with a bird called the honeyguide which leads it to a beehive, waits for it to tear the nest open, then feeds on the scraps. The ratel is among the most widespread of African carnivores, but it is thinly distributed and rarely seen.

Similar species Several other mustelids (mammals of the weasel family) occur in the region, including the **striped polecat** (*Ictonyx striatus*), a common but rarely seen nocturnal creature with black underparts and bushy white back, and the similar but much more scarce **striped weasel** (*Poecilogale albincha*). The **Cape clawless otter** (*Aonyx capensis*) is a brown freshwater mustelid with a white collar, while the smaller **spotted-necked otter** (*Lutra maculicollis*) is darker with white spots on its throat.

Primates
Chimpanzee (*Pan troglodytes*) Sw: *sokwe-mtu*. Standing height: 100cm; weight: up to 55kg. This distinctive black-coated ape, along with the bonobo (*Pan paniscus*) of the southern

Congo, is more closely related to man than to any other living creature. The chimpanzee lives in large troops based around a core of related males dominated by an alpha male. Females aren't firmly bonded to their core group, so emigration between communities is normal. Primarily frugivorous (fruit-eating), chimpanzees eat meat on occasion, and though meat kills are opportunistic, stalking of prey is not unusual. The first recorded instance of a chimp using a tool was at Gombe Stream in Tanzania, where modified sticks were used to 'fish' in termite mounds. In west Africa, chimps have been observed cracking open nuts with a stone and anvil. In the USA, captive chimps have successfully been taught Sign Language and have created compound words such as 'rock-berry' to describe

a nut. A widespread and common rainforest resident, the chimpanzee is thought to number 200,000 in the wild. In east Africa, chimps occur in western Uganda and on the Tanzanian shore of Lake Tanganyika, where they can be seen at the research centre founded by primatologist Jane Goodall in Tanzania's Gombe Stream, as well as at Mahale Mountains. The only chimpanzee population to fall within the scope of this book is the introduced (but to all intents and purposes wild) community that can be visited on Rubondo Island.

Baboon (*Papio spp.*) Sw: *nyani*. Shoulder height: 50–75cm; weight: 25–45kg. This powerful terrestrial primate, distinguished from any other monkey by its much larger size, inverted U-shaped tail and distinctive dog-like head, is fascinating to watch from a behavioural perspective. It lives in large troops that boast a complex, rigid social structure characterised by matriarchal lineages and plenty of intertroop movement by males seeking social dominance. Omnivorous and at home in almost any habitat, the baboon is the most widespread primate in Africa, frequently seen in most Tanzanian game reserves. There are several species of baboon in Africa, regarded by some authorities to be full races of the same species. Two species are present in northern Tanzania: you're most likely to see the olive or anubis baboon (*P. anubis*), which is the darker and hairier green-brown baboon found in the west, but in areas such as West Kilimanjaro you might encounter the yellow baboon (*P. cynocephalus*), a more lightly built and paler yellow-brown race whose range lies to the east of the Rift Valley.

Vervet monkey (*Cercopithecus aethiops*) Sw: *tumbili*. Length (excluding tail): 40–55cm; weight: 4–6kg. Also known as the green or grivet monkey, the vervet is probably the world's most numerous monkey and certainly the most common and widespread representative of the *Cercopithecus* guenons, a taxonomically controversial genus associated with African forests. An atypical guenon in that it inhabits savanna and woodland rather than true forest, the vervet spends a high proportion of its time on the ground and in most of its range could be confused only with the much larger and heavier baboon. However, the vervet's light-grey coat, black face and white forehead band should be diagnostic – as should the male's garish blue genitals. The vervet is abundant in Tanzania, and might be seen just about anywhere, not only in reserves.

Similar species The terrestrial **patas monkey** (*Erythrocebus patas*), larger and more spindly than the vervet, has an orange-tinged coat and black forehead stripe. Essentially a monkey of the dry northwestern savanna, the patas occurs in low numbers in the Mbalageti River region of the western Serengeti.

Blue monkey (*Cercopithecus mitis*) Sw: *kima*. Length (excluding tail): 50–60cm; weight: 5–8kg. This most variable of African monkeys is also known as the samango, golden, silver and Sykes' monkey, or the diademed or white-throated guenon. Several dozen races are recognised, divided by some authorities into more than one species. Taxonomic confusion notwithstanding, *C. mitis* is the most common forest guenon in eastern Africa, with one or

another race occurring in just about any suitable habitat. Unlikely to be confused with another species in Tanzania, the blue monkey has a uniformly dark blue-grey coat broken by a white throat, which in some races extends all down the chest and in others around the collar. It lives in troops of up to ten animals and associates with other primates where their ranges overlap. It is common in Arusha and Lake Manyara national parks and in many forest reserves.

Black-and-white colobus (*Colobus guereza*) Sw: *mbega mweupe*. Length (excluding tail): 65cm; weight: 12kg. This beautiful jet-black monkey has bold white facial markings, a long white tail and in some races white sides and shoulders. Almost exclusively arboreal, it is capable of jumping up to 30m, a spectacular sight with white tail streaming behind. Several races have been described, and most authorities recognise more than one species. The black-and-white colobus is a common resident of forests in Tanzania, often seen in the forest zone of Kilimanjaro and in Arusha National Park.

Lesser bushbaby (*Galago senegalensis*) Sw: *komba*. Length (excluding tail): 17cm; weight: 150g. The lesser bushbaby is the most widespread and common member of a group of small and generally indistinguishable nocturnal primates, distantly related to the lemurs of Madagascar. More often heard than seen, the lesser bushbaby can sometimes be picked out by tracing a cry to a tree and shining a torch or spotlight in its general direction to look for its large eyes.

Similar species The most easily identified bushbaby due to its size, the **greater bushbaby** (*Galago crassicaudatus*) occurs throughout the eastern side of Africa as far south as East London. It produces a terrifying scream, which you'd think was emitted by a chimpanzee or gorilla. Recent studies in Tanzania have determined that the smaller bushbabies are far more specifically diverse than was previously realised; see box, *Galago diversity in Tanzania*, in *Chapter 1*, page 27).

Large antelope
Roan antelope (*Hippotragus equinus*) Sw: *korongo*. Shoulder height: 120–150cm; weight: 250–300kg. This handsome equine antelope is uniform fawn-grey with a pale belly, short de-curved horns and a light mane. It could be mistaken for the female sable antelope, but this has a well-defined white belly, and lacks the roan's distinctive black-and-white facial markings. The roan is widespread but thinly distributed in southern Tanzania, though rare in the north, with one small population known to occur (yet seldom seen) in the Serengeti.

Sable antelope (*Hippotragus niger*) Sw: *pala hala*. Shoulder height: 135cm; weight: 230kg. The striking male sable is jet black with a distinct white face, underbelly and rump, and long de-curved horns. The female is chestnut brown and has shorter horns. The main stronghold for Africa's sable population is the *miombo* woodland of southern Tanzania; it is virtually absent from northern Tanzania.

Oryx (*Oryx gazella*) Sw: *choroa*. Shoulder height: 120cm; weight: 230kg. This regal, dry-country antelope is unmistakable with its ash-grey coat, bold black facial marks and flank strip, and unique long, straight horns. The fringe-eared oryx is the only race found in Tanzania, where it is most common (though still scarce) in Tarangire National Park and Mkomazi Game Reserve.

Waterbuck (*Kobus ellipsiprymnus*) Sw: *kuro*. Shoulder height: 130cm; weight: 250–270kg. The waterbuck is easily recognised by its shaggy brown coat and the male's large lyre-shaped horns. The Defassa race of the Rift Valley and areas further west has a full white rump, while the eastern race has a white U on its rump. The waterbuck is frequently seen in small family groups grazing near water in all but the most arid of game reserves in Tanzania.

Blue wildebeest (*Connochaetes taurinus*) Sw: *nyumbu*. Shoulder height: 130–150cm; weight: 180–250kg. This rather ungainly antelope, also called the brindled gnu, is easily recognised by its dark coat and bovine appearance. The superficially similar buffalo is far more heavily built. Immense herds of blue wildebeest occur on the Serengeti Plains, where the annual migration of more than a million heading into Kenya's Maasai Mara forms one of Africa's great natural spectacles. There are also significant wildebeest populations in the Ngorongoro Crater and Tarangire.

Hartebeest (*Alcelaphus buselaphus*) Shoulder height: 125cm; weight: 120–150kg. Hartebeests are ungainly antelopes, readily identified by the combination of large shoulders, a sloping back, red-brown or yellow-brown coat and smallish horns in both sexes. Numerous races are recognised, all of which are generally seen in small family groups in reasonably open country. The race found in northern Tanzania, Coke's hartebeest or kongoni, is common in open parts of the Serengeti and Ngorongoro.

Similar species The **topi** or **tsessebe** (*Damaliscus lunatus*) is basically a darker version of the hartebeest with striking yellow lower legs. Widespread but thinly and patchily distributed, the topi occurs alongside the much paler kongoni in the Serengeti National Park, where it is common.

Common eland (*Taurotragus oryx*) Sw: *pofu*. Shoulder height: 150–175cm; weight: 450–900kg. Africa's largest antelope, the common eland is light brown in colour, sometimes with a few faint white vertical stripes. It has a somewhat bovine appearance, accentuated by

AI

the relatively short horns and large dewlap. It is widely distributed in east and southern Africa, and small herds may be seen almost anywhere in grassland or light woodland. The eland is fairly common in Serengeti and Mkomazi national parks, but difficult to approach closely.

Greater kudu (*Tragelaphus strepsericos*) Sw: *tandala*. Shoulder height: 140–155cm; weight: 180–250kg. In many parts of Africa, the greater kudu is the most readily observed member of the genus *tragelaphus*, a group of medium to large antelopes characterised by the male's large spiralling horns and a dark coat generally marked with several vertical white stripes. The greater kudu is very large, with a grey-brown coat and up to ten stripes on each side, and the male has magnificent double-spiralled horns. A widespread animal occurring in most wooded habitats except for true forest, the greater kudu is rare in northern Tanzania, but small numbers persist in Tarangire.

Similar species The thinly distributed and skittish **lesser kudu** (*Tragelaphus imberbis*) is an east African species largely restricted to arid woodland. In Tanzania, it often occurs alongside the greater kudu, from which it can be distinguished by its smaller size (shoulder height: 100cm), two white throat patches and greater number of stripes (at least 11). Nowhere common, it is most likely to be encountered in Tarangire and Mkomazi national parks. The semi-aquatic **sitatunga** (*Tragelaphus spekei*) is a widespread but infrequently observed inhabitant of west and central African swamps from the Okavango in Botswana to the Sudd in Sudan. Tanzania's Rubondo Island is one of the few places where it is readily observed. The male, with a shoulder height of up to 125cm and a shaggy fawn coat, is unmistakable in its habitat. The smaller female might be mistaken for a bushbuck (see below) but is much drabber.

Medium and small antelope

Bushbuck (*Tragelaphus scriptus*) Sw: *pongo*. Shoulder height: 70–80cm; weight: 30–45kg. This attractive antelope, a member of the same genus as the kudu and sitatunga, shows great regional variation in colouring. The male is dark brown, chestnut or in parts of Ethiopia black, while the much smaller female is generally pale red-brown. The male has relatively small, straight horns for a *Tragelaphus* antelope. Both sexes have similar throat patches to the lesser kudu, and are marked with white spots and sometimes stripes. One of the most widespread antelope species in Africa, the bushbuck occurs in forest and riverine woodland throughout Tanzania, where it is normally seen singly or in pairs. It tends to be secretive and skittish except where it is used to people, so it is not as easily seen as you might expect of a common antelope.

Thomson's gazelle (*Gazella thomsoni*) Shoulder height: 60cm; weight: 20–25kg. Gazelles are graceful, relatively small antelopes that generally occur in large herds in open country, and have fawn-brown upper parts and a white belly. Thomson's gazelle is characteristic of the east African plains, where it is the only gazelle to have a black horizontal stripe. It is common to abundant in the Serengeti and surrounds.

Similar species Occurring alongside Thomson's gazelle in many parts of east Africa, the larger **Grant's gazelle** (*Gazella granti*) lacks a black side stripe and has comparatively large horns. An uncharacteristic gazelle, the **gerenuk** (*Litocranius walleri*) is a solitary, arid country species of Ethiopia, Kenya and northern Tanzania, similar in general colour to an impala but readily identified by its very long neck and singular habit of feeding from trees standing on its hind legs. Nowhere common in Tanzania, the gerenuk is present in small numbers in Mkomazi, Tarangire, West Kilimanjaro and the Loliondo area.

Impala (*Aepeceros melampus*) Sw: *swala pala*. Shoulder height: 90cm; weight: 45kg. This slender, handsome antelope is superficially similar to some gazelles, but in fact belongs to a separate family. Chestnut in colour, the impala has diagnostic black and white stripes running down its rump and tail, and the male has large lyre-shaped horns. One of the most widespread antelope species in sub-equatorial Africa, the impala is normally seen in large herds in wooded savanna habitats, and it is one of the most common antelope in many Tanzanian reserves.

Reedbuck (*Redunca spp*) Sw: *tohe*. Shoulder height: 65–90cm; weight: 30–65kg. The three species of reedbuck are all rather nondescript fawn-grey antelopes generally seen in open grassland near water. The mountain reedbuck (*Redunca fulvorufula*) is the smallest and most distinctive, with a clear white belly, tiny horns and an overall grey appearance. It has a broken distribution, occurring in mountainous parts of eastern South Africa, northern Tanzania, Kenya and southern Ethiopia. The Bohor reedbuck is found in northern Tanzania, whereas the southern reedbuck occurs in southern Tanzania.

Klipspringer (*Oreotragus oreotragus*) Sw: *mbuze mawe*. Shoulder height: 60cm; weight: 13kg. The klipspringer is a goat-like antelope, normally seen in pairs, and easily identified by its dark, bristly grey-yellow coat, slightly speckled appearance and unique habitat preference. Klipspringer means 'rock jumper' in Afrikaans, an apt name for an antelope that occurs exclusively in mountainous areas and rocky outcrops. It is found throughout Tanzania, and is often seen around the Lobo Hills in the Serengeti and the Maji Moto area in Lake Manyara.

Steenbok (*Raphicerus cempestris*) Sw: *tondoro*. Shoulder height: 50cm; weight: 11kg. This rather nondescript small antelope has red-brown upper parts and clear white underparts, and the male has short straight horns. It is probably the most commonly observed small antelope in Africa, though it has a broken range, and is absent from southern Tanzania despite being common in the north of the country and in areas further south. Like most other antelopes of its size, the steenbok is normally encountered singly or in pairs and tends to 'freeze' when disturbed.

Similar species The **oribi** (*Ourebia ourebi*) is a widespread but uncommon grassland antelope which looks much like a steenbok but stands about 10cm higher at the shoulder and has an altogether more upright bearing. **Kirk's dik-dik** (*Madoqua kirki*), smaller than the steenbok and easily identified by its large white eye-circle, is restricted primarily to Tanzania and Kenya, and it is particularly common in Arusha National Park.

Red duiker (*Cephalophus natalensis*) Sw: *pofu*. Shoulder height: 45cm; weight: 14kg. This is the most likely of Africa's 12–20 'forest duikers' to be seen by tourists. It is deep chestnut in colour with a white tail and, in the case of the east African race *C. n. harveyi* (sometimes considered to be a separate species), a black face. The red duiker occurs in most substantial forest patches along the eastern side of Africa, though it is less often seen than it is heard crashing through the undergrowth.

Similar species The **blue duiker** (*Cephalophus monticola*) is widespread in Africa and the only other forest duiker to occur in countries south of Tanzania, and it can easily be told from the red duiker by its greyer colouring and much smaller size (it is the smallest forest duiker, about the same size as a suni – dwarf antelope). **Abbott's duiker** (*Cephalophus spadix*) is a large duiker, as tall as a klipspringer, restricted to a handful of montane forests in Tanzania, including those on Kilimanjaro and the Usambara, Udzungwa and Poroto mountains. The endangered **Ader's duiker** (*Cephalophus adersi*) is presumably restricted to forested habitats on Zanzibar Island, where as few as 1,000 animals may survive, most of them in the Jozani Forest. Recent reports suggest that this duiker is extinct in the only other locality where it has been recorded, the Sokoke Forest in Kenya.

Common duiker (*Sylvicapra grimmia*) Sw: *nysa*. Shoulder height: 50cm; weight: 20kg. This anomalous duiker holds itself more like a steenbok and is the only member of its family to occur outside of forests. Generally grey in colour, the common duiker can most easily be separated from other small antelopes by the black tuft of hair that sticks up between its horns. It occurs throughout Tanzania, and tolerates most habitats except for true forest and very open country.

Other large herbivores
African elephant (*Loxodonta africana*) Sw: *tembe*. Shoulder height: 2.3–3.4m; weight: up to 6,000kg. The world's largest land animal, the African elephant is intelligent, social and often very entertaining to watch. Female elephants live in close-knit clans in which the eldest female plays matriarch over her sisters, daughters and granddaughters. Mother–daughter bonds are strong and may last for up to 50 years. Males generally leave the family group at around 12 years to roam singly or form bachelor herds. Under normal circumstances, elephants will range widely in search of food and water, but when concentrated populations are forced to live in conservation areas, their habit of uprooting trees can cause serious environmental damage. Elephants are widespread and common in habitats ranging from desert to rainforest and, despite heavy poaching, they are likely to be seen on a daily basis in most of Tanzania's larger national parks, the exception being the Serengeti where they are common only in the Lobo region.

Black rhinoceros (*Diceros bicornis*) Sw: *faru*. Shoulder height: 160cm; weight: 1,000kg. This is the more widespread of Africa's two rhino species, an imposing, sometimes rather aggressive creature that has been poached to extinction in most of its former range. It occurs in many southern African reserves, but is now very localised in east Africa, where it is most likely to be seen in Tanzania's Ngorongoro Crater.

Hippopotamus (*Hippopotamus amphibius*) Sw: *kiboko*. Shoulder height: 150cm; weight: 2,000kg. Characteristic of Africa's large rivers and lakes, this large, lumbering animal spends most of the day submerged, but emerges at night to graze. Strongly territorial, herds of ten or more animals are presided over by a dominant male who will readily defend his patriarchy to the death. Hippos are abundant in most protected rivers and water bodies, and they are still quite common outside of reserves, where they kill more people than any other African mammal.

African buffalo (*Syncerus caffer*) Sw: *nyati*. Shoulder height: 140cm; weight: 700kg. Frequently and erroneously referred to as a water buffalo (an Asian species), the African buffalo is a distinctive ox-like animal that lives in large herds on the savanna and occurs in smaller herds in forested areas. Common and widespread in sub-Saharan Africa, herds of buffalo are likely to be encountered in most Tanzanian reserves and national parks. The best place to see large buffalo herds is on the Ngorongoro Crater floor.

Giraffe (*Giraffa camelopardis*) Sw: *twiga*. Shoulder height: 250–350cm; weight: 1,000–1,400kg. The world's tallest and longest-necked land animal, a fully grown giraffe can measure up to 5.5m high. Quite unmistakable, the giraffe lives in loosely structured herds of up to 15, though herd members often disperse and are seen singly or in smaller groups. Formerly distributed throughout east and southern Africa, the giraffe is now more or less restricted to conservation areas, where it is generally common and easily seen.

Common zebra (*Equus burchelli*) Sw: *punda milia*. Shoulder height: 130cm; weight: 300–340kg. This attractive striped horse is common and widespread throughout most of east and southern Africa, where it is often seen in large herds alongside wildebeest. The common zebra is the only wild equine to occur in Tanzania, and is common in most conservation areas, especially the Serengeti, whose population may stand as high as half a million.

Warthog (*Phacochoerus africanus*) Sw: *ngiri*. Shoulder height: 60–70cm; weight: up to 100kg. This widespread and often conspicuously abundant resident of the African savanna is grey in colour with a thin covering of hairs, wartlike bumps on its face, and rather large upward-curving tusks. Africa's only diurnal swine, the warthog is often seen in family groups, trotting off briskly with its tail raised stiffly (a diagnostic trait) and a determinedly nonchalant air.

Similar species Bulkier, hairier and browner, the **bushpig** (*Potomochoerus larvatus*) is as widespread as the warthog, but infrequently seen due to its nocturnal habits and preference for dense vegetation. Larger still, weighing up to 250kg, the **giant forest hog** (*Hylochoerus meinertzhageni*) is primarily a species of the west African rainforest. It does occur in certain highland forests in northern Tanzania, but the chance of a sighting is practically non-existent.

Small mammals
Aardvark (*Orycteropus afer*) Shoulder height: 60cm; weight: up to 70kg. This singularly bizarre nocturnal insectivore is unmistakable with its long snout and huge ears. It occurs practically throughout the region, but sightings are extremely rare, even on night drives.

Similar species Not so much similar to an aardvark as equally dissimilar to anything else, **pangolins** are rare nocturnal insectivores with distinctive armour plating and a tendency to roll up in a ball when disturbed. Most likely to be seen in Tanzania is Temminck's pangolin (*Manis temmincki*). Also nocturnal, but spiky rather than armoured, several **hedgehog** and

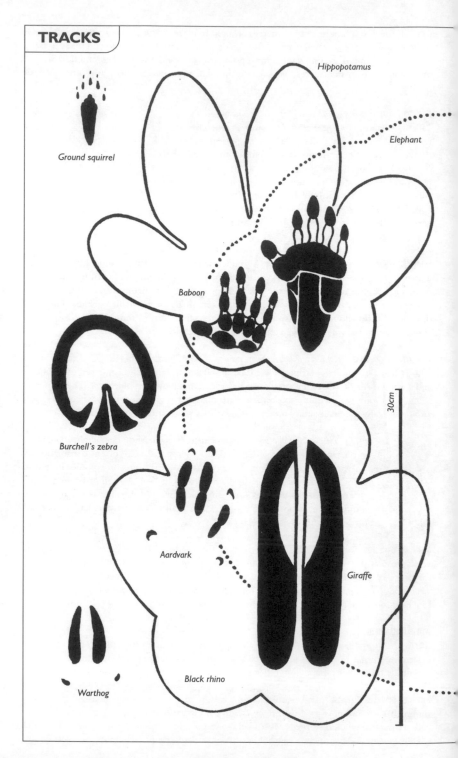

Ground squirrel

Hippopotamus

Elephant

Baboon

Burchell's zebra

Aardvark

Giraffe

30cm

Warthog

Black rhino

Thomson's gazelle

Black-backed jackal

African wild dog

Bat-eared fox

Bohor reedbuck

Spotted hyena

Cheetah

Fringe-eared oryx

Wildebeest

Leopard

Buffalo

Lion

porcupine species occur in the region, the former generally no larger than a guinea pig, the latter generally 60–100cm long.

Rock hyrax (*Procavia capensis*) Sw: *pimbi*. Shoulder height: 35–30cm; weight: 4kg. Rodent-like in appearance, hyraxes are more closely related to elephants. The rock hyrax and similar bush hyrax (*Heterohyrax brucei*) are often seen sunning in rocky habitats and become tame when used to people, for instance at Seronera and Lobo lodges in the Serengeti. The less common tree hyrax (*Dendrohyrax arboreus*) is a nocturnal forest creature, often announcing its presence with an unforgettable shrieking call.

Similar species The **elephant shrews** (Sw: *sange*) are rodents that look like miniature kangaroos with elongated noses. A number of species are recognised, but they are mostly secretive and nocturnal, so rarely seen. The smaller species are generally associated with savanna habitats, but the much larger chequered elephant shrew is a resident of Eastern Arc forests – I've only ever seen it in Amani and Udzungwa.

Scrub hare (*Lepus saxatilis*) Weight: 2.7–4.5kg. This is the largest and commonest African hare or rabbit. In some areas a short walk at dusk or after nightfall might reveal three or four scrub hares. They tend to freeze when disturbed.

Unstriped ground squirrel (*Xerus rutilus*) Weight: 1.4kg. An endearing terrestrial animal of arid savanna, the unstriped ground squirrel is grey to grey-brown with a prominent white eye-ring and silvery black tail. It spends much time on its hind legs, and has the characteristic squirrel mannerism of holding food in its forepaws. In Tanzania, it is most likely to be seen in the Serengeti.

Bush squirrel (*Paraxerus cepapi*) Weight: 1kg. This is the typical squirrel of the eastern and southern savanna, rusty brown in colour with a silvery black back and white eye-rings. A great many other arboreal or semi-arboreal squirrels occur in the region, but most are difficult to tell apart in the field.

Appendix 2

SWAHILI Swahili, the official language of Tanzania, is a Bantu language that developed on the east African coast about 1,000 years ago and has since adopted several words from Arabic, Portuguese, Indian, German and English. It spread into the Tanzanian interior along with the 19th-century slave caravans and is now the lingua franca in Tanzania and Kenya, and is also spoken in parts of Uganda, Malawi, Rwanda, Burundi, Congo, Zambia and Mozambique.

In Dar es Salaam, Zanzibar, Arusha, Moshi and the northern game reserves, you can get by with English well enough. If you travel in other parts of the country, you will need to understand some Swahili. And even if you are sticking to tourist areas, it is polite and can be useful to know a bit of Swahili.

There are numerous Swahili–English dictionaries on the market, as well as phrasebooks and grammars. A useful dictionary for travellers is Baba Malaika's *Friendly Modern Swahili–English Dictionary* (MSO Training Centre for Development Co-operation, PO Box 254, Arusha, second edition, 1994), which costs around US$25. Better still, though probably too heavyweight for most travellers, is the *TUKI English–Swahili Dictionary* (University of Dar es Salaam, 1996), which costs around US$16. Peter Wilson's *Simplified Swahili* (Longman) used to be regarded as the best book for teaching yourself Swahili, but it has probably been superseded by Joan Russell's *Teach Yourself Swahili* (Hodder and Stoughton, 1996), which comes complete with a cassette and costs around US$15. Of the phrasebooks, Lonely Planet's or Rough Guide's *Swahili* are both good. It is best to buy a Swahili book before your trip, as they are difficult to get hold of once you are in Tanzania.

For short-stay visitors, all these books have practical limitations. Wading through a phrasebook to find the expression you want can take ages, while trying to piece together a sentence from a dictionary is virtually impossible. In addition, most books available are in Kenyan Swahili, which often differs greatly from the purer version spoken in Tanzania.

The following introduction is not a substitute for a dictionary or phrasebook. It is not so much an introduction to Swahili as an introduction to communicating with Swahili-speakers. Before researching this guide, my east African travels had mainly been in Kenya, Uganda and parts of Tanzania where English is relatively widely spoken. We learnt the hard way how little English is spoken in most of Tanzania. I hope this section will help anyone in a similar position to get around a great deal more easily than we did at first.

Pronunciation Vowel sounds are pronounced as follows:

a	like the a in *father*
e	like the e in *wet*
i	like the ee in *free*, but less drawn-out
o	somewhere between the o in *no* and the word *awe*
u	similar to the oo in *food*

The double vowel in words like *choo* or *saa* is pronounced like the single vowel, but drawn out for longer. Consonants are in general pronounced as they are in English. *L* and *r* are often interchangeable, so that *Kalema* is just as often spelt or pronounced *Karema*. The same is true of *b* and *v*.

You will be better understood if you speak slowly and thus avoid the common English-speaking habit of clipping vowel sounds – listen to how Swahili-speakers pronounce their vowels. In most Swahili words there is a slight emphasis on the second last syllable.

Basic grammar Swahili is a simple language in so far as most words are built from a root word using prefixes. To go into all of the prefixes here would probably confuse people new to Swahili – and it would certainly stretch my knowledge of the language. They are covered in depth in most Swahili grammars and dictionaries. The following are some of the most important:

Pronouns

ni	me	*wa*	they
u	you	*a*	he or she
tu	us		

Tenses

na	present
ta	future
li	past
ku	infinitive

Tenses (negative)

si	present
sita	future
siku	past
haku	negative, infinitive

From a root word such as *taka* (want) you might build the following phrases:

Unataka soda	You want a soda
Tutataka soda	We will want a soda
Alitaka soda	He/she wanted a soda

In practice, *ni* and *tu* are often dropped from simple statements. It would be more normal to say *nataka soda* than *ninataka soda*.

In many situations there is no interrogative mode in Swahili; the difference between a question and a statement lies in the intonation.

Greetings There are several common greetings in Swahili. Although allowances are made for tourists, it is rude to start talking to someone without first using one or another formal greeting. The first greeting you will hear is *Jambo*. This is reserved for tourists, and a perfectly adequate greeting, but it is never used between Tanzanians (the more correct *Hujambo*, to which the reply is *Sijambo*, is used in some areas).

The most widely used greeting is *Habari?*, which more or less means *What news?* The normal reply is *Nzuri* (good). *Habari* is rarely used by Tanzanians on its own; you might well be asked *Habari ya safari?*, *Habari yako?* or *Habari gani?* (very loosely, *How is your journey?*, *How are you?* and *How are things?* respectively). *Nzuri* is the polite reply to any such request.

A more fashionable greeting among younger people is *Mambo*, especially on the coast and in large towns. Few tourists recognise this greeting; reply *Safi* or *Poa* and you've made a friend.

In Tanzanian society it is polite to greet elders with the expression *Shikamu*. To the best of my knowledge this means *I hold your feet*. In many parts of rural Tanzania, children will greet you in this way, often with their heads bowed and so quietly it sounds like *Sh...oo*. Don't misinterpret this by European standards (or other parts of Africa where *Mzungu give me shilling* is the phrase most likely to be offered up by children); most Tanzanian children are far too polite to swear at you. The polite answer is *Marahaba* (I'm delighted).

Another word often used in greeting is *Salama*, which means peace. When you enter a shop or hotel reception, you will often be greeted by a friendly *Karibu*, which means *Welcome*. *Asante sana* (thank you very much) seems an appropriate response.

If you want to enter someone's house, shout *Hodi!* It basically means *Can I come in?* but would be used in the same situation as *Anyone home?* would in English. The normal response will be *Karibu* or *Hodi*.

It is respectful to address an old man as *Mzee*. *Bwana*, which means *Mister*, might be used as a polite form of address to a male who is equal or senior to you in age or rank, but who is not a *Mzee*. Older women can be addressed as *Mama*.

The following phrases will come in handy for small talk:

Where have you just come from?	*(U)natoka wapi?*
I have come from Moshi	*(Ni)natoka Moshi*
Where are you going?	*(U)nakwenda wapi?*
We are going to Arusha	*(Tu)nakwenda Arusha*
What is your name?	*Jina lako nani?*
My name is Philip	*Jina langu ni Philip*
Do you speak English?	*Unasema KiIngereze?*
I speak a little Swahili	*Ninasema KiSwahili kidigo*
Sleep peacefully	*Lala salama*
Bye for now	*Kwaheri sasa*
Have a safe journey	*Safari njema*
Come again (welcome again)	*Karibu tena*
I don't understand	*Sielewi*
Say that again	*Sema tena*

Numbers

1	*moja*	30	*thelathini*
2	*mbili*	40	*arobaini*
3	*tatu*	50	*hamsini*
4	*nne*	60	*sitini*
5	*tano*	70	*sabini*
6	*sita*	80	*themanini*
7	*saba*	90	*tisini*
8	*nane*	100	*mia (moja)*
9	*tisa*	150	*mia moja na hamsini*
10	*kumi*	155	*mia moja hamsini na tano*
11	*kumi na moja*	200	*mia mbili*
20	*ishirini*	1,000	*elfu (moja)* or *mia kumi*

Swahili time Many travellers to Tanzania fail to come to grips with Swahili time. It is essential to be aware of it, especially if you are catching buses in remote areas. The Swahili clock starts at the equivalent of 06.00, so that *saa moja asubuhi* (hour one in the morning) is 07.00, *saa mbili jioni* (hour two in the evening) is 20.00, etc. To ask the time in Swahili, say *Saa ngapi?*

Always check whether times are standard or Swahili. If you are told a bus leaves at nine, ask whether the person means *saa tatu* or *saa tisa*. Some English-speakers will convert to standard time, others won't. This does not apply so much where people are used to tourists, but it's advisable to get in the habit of checking.

Day-to-day queries The following covers such activities as shopping, finding a room, etc. It's worth remembering that most Swahili words for modern objects, or things for which there would not have been a pre-colonial word, are often similar to the English. Examples are *resiti* (receipt), *gari* (car), *polisi* (police), *posta* (post office) and – my favourite – *stesheni masta* (station master). In desperation, it's always worth trying the English word with an *ee* sound on the end.

Shopping The normal way of asking for something is *Ipo?* or *Zipo?*, which roughly means *Is there?*, so if you want a cold drink you would ask *Soda baridi zipo?* The response will normally be *Ipo* or *Kuna* (there is) or *Hamna* or *Hakuna* (there isn't). Once you've established the shop has what you want, you might say *Nataka koka mbili* (I want two Cokes). To check the price, ask *Shillingi ngape?* It may be simpler to ask for a brand name: Omo (washing powder) or Blue Band (margarine), for instance.

Accommodation The Swahili for guesthouse is *nyumba ya wageni*. In my experience *gesti* works as well, if not better. If you are looking for something a bit more upmarket, bear in mind *hoteli* means restaurant. We found self-contained (*self-contendi*) to be a good keyword in communicating this need. To find out whether there is a vacant room, ask *Nafasi zipo?*

Getting around The following expressions are useful for getting around:

Where is there a guesthouse?	*Ipo wapi gesti?*
Is there a bus to Moshi?	*Ipo basi kwenda Moshi?*
When does the bus depart?	*Basi itaondoka saa ngapi?*
When will the vehicle arrive?	*Gari litafika saa ngapi?*
How far is it?	*Bale gani?*
I want to pay now	*Ninataka kulipa sasa*

Foodstuffs

avocado	*parachichi*	food	*chakula*
bananas	*ndizi*	fruit(s)	*(ma)tunda*
bananas (cooked)	*matoke/batoke*	goat	*(nyama ya) mbuzi*
beef	*(nyama ya) ngombe*	mango(es)	*(ma)embe*
bread (loaf)	*mkate*	maize porridge	
bread (slice)	*tosti*	(thin, eaten at	
coconuts	*nazi*	breakfast)	*uji*
coffee	*kahawa*	maize porridge	
chicken	*kuku*	(thick, eaten as	
egg(s)	*(ma)yai*	staple with	
fish	*samaki*	relish)	*ugali*
meat	*nyama*	rice	*pilau*
milk	*maziwa*	salt	*chumvi*
onions	*vitungu*	sauce	*mchuzi/supu*
orange(s)	*(ma)chungwa*	sugar	*sukari*
pawpaw	*papai*	tea	*chai*
pineapple	*nanasi*	(black/milky)	*(ya rangi/maziwa)*
potatoes	*viazi*	vegetable	*mboga*
rice (cooked plain)	*wali*	water	*maji*
rice (uncooked)	*mchele*		

Days of the week

Monday	*Jumatatu*	Friday	*Ijumaa*
Tuesday	*Jumanne*	Saturday	*Jumamosi*
Wednesday	*Jumatano*	Sunday	*Jumapili*
Thursday	*Alhamisi*		

Useful words and phrases

afternoon	*alasiri*	night	*usiku*
again	*tena*	no	*hapana*
and	*na*	no problem	*hakuna matata*
ask (I am		now	*sasa*
asking for…)	*omba (ninaomba…)*	only	*tu*
big	*kubwa*	OK or fine	*sawa*
boat	*meli*	passenger	*abiria*
brother	*kaka*	pay	*kulipa*
bus	*basi*	person (people)	*mtu (watu)*
car (or any		please	*tafadhali*
vehicle)	*gari*	road/street	*barabara/mtaa*
child (children)	*mtoto (watoto)*	shop	*duka*
cold	*baridi*	sister	*dada*
come here	*njoo*	sleep	*kulala*
excuse me	*samahani*	slowly	*polepole*
European(s)	*mzungu (wazungu)*	small	*kidogo*
evening	*jioni*	soon	*bado kidogo*
far away	*mbale kubwa*	sorry	*polepole*
father	*baba*	station	*stesheni*
friend	*rafiki*	stop	*simama*
good	*mzuri*	straight or direct	*moja kwa moja*
(very good)	*(mzuri sana)*	thank you	*asante*
goodbye	*kwaheri*	(very much)	*(sana)*
here	*hapa*	there is	*iko/kuna*
hot	*moto*	there is not	*hamna/hakuna*
later	*bado*	thief (thieves)	*mwizi (wawizi)*
like	*penda*	time	*saa*
(I would like…)	*(ninapenda…)*	today	*leo*
many	*sana*	toilet	*choo*
me	*mimi*	tomorrow	*kesho*
money	*pesa/shillingi*	want	*taka*
more	*ingine/tena*	(I want…)	*(ninataka…)*
morning	*asubuhi*	where	*(iko) wapi*
mother	*mama*	yes	*ndiyo*
nearby	*karibu/mbale*	yesterday	*jana*
	kidogo	you	*wewe*

Useful conjunctions include *ya* (of) and *kwa* (to or by). Many expressions are created using these; for instance *stesheni ya basi* is a bus station and *barabara kwa Mbale* is the road to Mbale.

Health

flu	*mafua*	recover	*pona*
fever	*homa*	treatment	*tiba*
malaria	*malaria*	cure	*ponyesha*
cough	*kikohozi*	injection	*sindano*
vomit	*kutapika*	bone	*mfupa*
swollen	*uvimbe*	death	*mauti*
injure	*jeraha*	to examine	*vipimo*
weak	*dhaifu*	to fall down	*kuanguka*
pain	*maumizu*	to bleed	*kutokwa na damu*

MAA *Emma Thomson*

Maa is the language of the Maasai. It does not exist in written form, so the spellings below are approximate.

Greetings

Father/elderly man, I greet you	*Papa ... supai*
Warrior/middle-aged man, I greet you	*Apaayia ... supai*
Young woman, I greet you	*Siangiki ... supai*
Boy, I greet you	*Ero ... supai*
Girl, I greet you	*Nairo ... supai*
Mother/middle-aged woman, I greet you	*Yeyio ... takwenya*
Grandmother/elder woman, I greet you	*Koko ... takwenya*
How are you?	*Koree indae?*
Are you fine/healthy?	*Kira sedan/kira biot?*
My name is...	*Aji...*
What is your name?	*Kekijaa enkarna?*
I come from...	*Aingwaa...*
Where do you come from?	*Kaingwaa?*
Goodbye	*Serae*

Numbers

1	*nabo*	13	*tomon ok ooni*
2	*are*	14	*tomon o ongwan*
3	*ooni*	15	*tomon o imiet*
4	*ongwan*	16	*tomon o ille*
5	*imiet*	17	*tomon o opishana*
6	*ille*	18	*tomon o isiet*
7	*naapishana*	19	*tomon o odo*
8	*isiet*	20	*tikitam*
9	*naudo*	100	*iip nabo*
10	*tomon*	1,000	*enchata nabo*
11	*tomon o obo*	2,000	*inkeek are*
12	*tomon o are*	3,000	*inkeek ooni*

Shopping

How much does it cost?	*Empesai aja?*
I want/need it	*Ayieu*
I don't want/need it today	*Mayieu taata*
I will buy this one	*Ainyang ena*
I will buy these	*Ainyang kuna*
I won't buy anything today	*Mainyang onyo taata*
I haven't got any money	*Maata empesai*

Useful words and phrases

Thank you	*Ashe*
Thank you very much	*Ashe naleng*
Take it (used when giving a gift)	*Ngo*
I receive it (used when accepting a gift)	*Au*
Leave me/it alone (to children)	*Tapala*
Go outside (to children)	*Shomo boo*
May I take a picture?	*Aosh empicha?*
Yes	*Ee*
OK	*Ayia*

Emma Thomson

In the same way that it is rude not to greet a Tanzanian with the standard *HuJambo* or *Mambo*, no Maasai will encounter another without going through the amusing paces of a ritual known as 'eating the news'. It is basically a quick catch-up on the health of the family, state of the livestock, etc. The aim is to race through these formalities as fast as possible so you can continue with the rest of the conversation. Bizarrely, even if you are on your deathbed, you must reply that all is well to maintain the front of warrior strength integral to Maasai psychology. Give it a go and they will be bowled over!

Man:	*Yeyio...*	Mother...
Woman:	*Eeu...*	Yes...
Man:	*Takwenya!*	I greet you!
Woman:	*Iko! Apaayia...*	Hello! Warrior...
Man:	*Ooe...*	Yes...
Woman:	*Supai!*	I greet you!
Man:	*Epa!*	Hello!
Woman:	*Ayia, koree indae?*	Ok, how are you?
Man:	*Kitii...*	We are around...
Woman:	*Ee*	Uh-huh
Man:	*Kira sedan*	We are fine
Woman:	*Ee*	Uh-huh
Man:	*Kira biot*	We are healthy
Woman:	*Ee*	Uh-huh
Man:	*Supat inkera*	The children are well
Woman:	*Ee*	Uh-huh
Man:	*Biot inkishu*	The cattle are healthy
Woman:	*Ee*	Uh-huh
Man:	*Metii endoki torono*	There are no problems
Woman:	*Ayia*	OK
Woman:	*Kira siyook...*	As for us...
Man:	*Ee*	Uh-huh
Woman:	*Mekimweyaa*	We are not sick
Man:	*Ee*	Uh-huh
Woman:	*Biot inkera*	The children are healthy
Man:	*Ee*	Uh-huh
Woman:	*Supat indare*	The goats are well
Man:	*Ee*	Uh-huh
Woman:	*Ayia*	OK
Man:	*Ayia, enda serian*	OK, that's good news

No, I don't want you to	*A-a, mayieu*
Stop it	*Tapala*
Expression of sympathy (like '*pole*' in Swahili)	*Kwa adei*

AFRICAN ENGLISH Although many Tanzanians speak a little English, not all speak it fluently. Africans who speak English tend to structure their sentences in a similar way to how they would in their own language: they speak English with Bantu grammar.

For a traveller, knowing how to communicate in African English is as important as speaking a bit of Swahili, if not more so. It is noticeable that travellers who speak English as a second language often communicate with Africans more easily than first-language English-speakers.

The following ground rules should prove useful when you speak English to Africans:

- *Unasema KiEngereze?* (Do you speak English?). This small but important question may seem obvious. It isn't.
- Greet in Swahili then ask in English. It is advisable to go through the Swahili greetings (even *Jambo* will do) before you plough ahead and ask a question. Firstly, it is rude to do otherwise; secondly, most Westerners feel uncomfortable asking a stranger a straight question. If you have already greeted the person, you'll feel less need to preface a question with phrases like 'I'm terribly sorry' and 'Would you mind telling me' which will confuse someone who speaks limited English.
- Speak slowly and clearly. There is no need, as some travellers do, to speak as if you are talking to a three year old; just speak naturally.
- Phrase questions simply and with Swahili inflections. 'This bus goes to Dodoma?' is better than 'Could you tell me whether this bus is going to Dodoma?'; 'You have a room?' is better than 'Is there a vacant room?' If you are not understood, don't keep repeating the same question; find a different way of phrasing it.
- Listen to how people talk to you, and not only for their inflections. Some English words are in wide use, others are not. For instance, lodging is more likely to be understood than accommodation.
- Make sure the person you are talking to understands you. Try to avoid asking questions that can be answered with a yes or no. People may well agree with you simply to be polite.
- Keep calm. No-one is at their best when they arrive at a crowded bus station after an all-day bus ride; it is easy to be short-tempered when someone cannot understand you. Be patient and polite; it's you who doesn't speak the language.

GLOSSARY

Acacia woodland	type of woodland dominated by thorny, thin-leafed trees of the genus *Acacia*
AICC	Arusha International Conference Centre
banda	a hut, often used to refer to hutted accommodation at hotels and lodges
boma	traditional enclosure or homestead; administration building of the colonial era
bui-bui	black cloth worn veil-like by women, mainly in Islamic parts of the coast
bwana	mister (polite term of address to an adult man)
brachystegia woodland	type of woodland dominated by broad-leaved trees of the genus *Brachystegia*
Chama Cha Mapinduzi	ruling party of Tanzania since independence (CCM)
cichlid	family of colourful fish found in the Rift Valley lakes
closed canopy forest	true forest in which the trees have an interlocking canopy
dala-dala	light vehicle, especially minibus, serving as public transport
dhow	traditional wooden seafaring vessel
duka	kiosk
endemic	unique to a specific country or biome
exotic	not indigenous; for instance plantation trees such as pines and eucalyptus
forex bureau	bureau de change
fly-camping	temporary private camp set up remotely from a permanent lodge
guesthouse	cheap local hotel
hoteli	local restaurant

indigenous	naturally occurring
kanga	colourful printed cloth worn by most Tanzanian women
KIA	Kilimanjaro International Airport
kitenge (pl *vitenge*)	similar to *kanga*
koppie (or *kopje*)	Afrikaans word used to refer to a small hill such as those on the Serengeti
mandazi	deep-fried doughball, essentially the local variant on a doughnut
mishkaki	meat (usually beef) kebab
mzungu (pl *wazungu*)	white person
NCA	Ngorongoro Conservation Area
ngoma	Swahili dance
Omani era	period when the coast was ruled by the Sultan of Oman, especially 19th century
self-contained room	room with en-suite shower and toilet
savanna	grassland studded with trees
Shirazi era	medieval period during which settlers from Shiraz (Iran) dominated coastal trade
taarab	Swahili music and dance form associated particularly with Zanzibar
TANAPA	Tanzania National Parks
ugali	stodgy porridge-like staple made with ground maize meal
woodland	area of trees lacking a closed canopy

Appendix 3

FURTHER INFORMATION

BOOKS

History and biography A limited number of single-volume histories covering east Africa and/or Tanzania are in print, but most are rather textbook-like in tone, and I've yet to come across one that is likely to hold much appeal for the casual reader. About the best bet is Iliffe's *Modern History of Tanganyika* (Cambridge, 1979). For a more general perspective, Oliver and Fage's *Short History of Africa* (Penguin, sixth edition, 1988) is rated as providing the best concise overview of African history, but it's too curt, dry, wide-ranging and dated to make for a satisfying read.

If I were to recommend one historical volume to a visitor to Tanzania, it would have to be Richard Hall's *Empires of the Monsoon: A History of the Indian Ocean and its Invaders* (HarperCollins, 1996). This highly focused and reasonably concise book will convey a strong historical perspective to the general reader, as a result of the author's storytelling touch and his largely successful attempt to place the last 1,000 years of east and southern African history in an international framework.

Considerably more bulky, and working an even broader canvas, John Reader's *Africa: A Biography of the Continent* (Penguin, 1997) has met with universal praise as perhaps the most readable and accurate attempt yet to capture the sweep of African history for the general reader.

Several books document specific periods and/or regions in African history. Good coverage of the coastal Swahili, who facilitated the medieval trade between the gold fields of Zimbabwe and the Arab world, is provided in J de Vere Allen's *Swahili Origins* (James Currey, 1992). Among the better popular works on the early era of European exploration are Hibbert's *Africa Explored: Europeans in the Dark Continent* (Penguin, 1982) and Alan Moorehead's peerless classics of the history-as-adventure-yarn genre *The White Nile* and *The Blue Nile*, published in 1960 and 1962 respectively and available in Penguin paperback. Two excellent biographies pertaining to this era are Tim Jeal's *Livingstone* (Heinemann, 1973, recently reprinted) and *Stanley: The Impossible Life of Africa's Greatest Explorer* (Faber & Faber, 2007), the latter voted Sunday Times 'Biography of the Year' in 2007. For an erudite, compelling and panoramic account of the decade that turned Africa on its head, Thomas Pakenham's gripping 600-page tome *The Scramble for Africa* was aptly described by one reviewer as 'Heart of Darkness with the lights switched on'. For a glimpse into the colonial era itself, just about everybody who sets foot in east Africa ends up reading Karen Blixen's autobiographical *Out of Africa* (Penguin, 1937).

Field guides and natural history

General *East African Wildlife* by Philip Briggs (Bradt, 2008) is a handy and lavishly illustrated one-stop handbook to the fauna of east Africa, with detailed sections on the region's main habitats, varied mammals, birds, reptiles and insects. It's the ideal companion for first-time visitors whose interest in wildlife extends beyond the Big Five but who don't want to carry a library of reference books.

Mammals Dorst and Dandelot's *Field Guide to the Larger Mammals of Africa* (Collins) and Haltennorth's *Field Guide to the Mammals of Africa (including Madagascar)* (Collins), were the standard mammal field guides for years, but have been rendered obsolete by several newer and better books. The pick of these, especially if your interest extends to bats and other small mammals, is Jonathan Kingdon's *Field Guide to African Mammals* (Princeton University Press, 1997), which also contains a goldmine of information about the evolutionary relationships of modern species. Its more compact counterpart is the same author's *Kingdon Pocket Guide to African Mammals* (Princeton Pocket Guides, 2005). Chris and Tilde Stuart's *Field Guide to the Larger Mammals of Africa* (Struik Publishers, 1997) is well suited to space-conscious travellers who are serious about putting a name to all the large mammals they see. For backpackers, the same authors' *Southern, Eastern and Central African Mammals: A Photographic Guide* (Struik Publishers, 1993) is far lighter and still gives adequate detail for 152 mammal species.

Not a field guide in the conventional sense so much as a guide to mammalian behaviour, Richard Estes's superb *The Safari Companion* (Green Books UK, Chelsea Green USA, Russell Friedman Books South Africa, 1992) is well organised and informative but rather bulky for casual safari-goers.

Birds Zimmerman, Turner, Pearson, Willet and Pratt's *Birds of Kenya and Northern Tanzania* (Russell Friedman Books, 1996) is a contender for the best single-volume field guide available to any African country or region. I would recommend it to any serious birder sticking to northern Tanzania, since it provides complete coverage for the northern safari circuit, the Usambara and Pare mountains and Pemba Island, and although it stops short of Dar es Salaam and Zanzibar, this wouldn't be a major limitation. Unfortunately, it's too bulky, heavy and expensive to be of interest to any but the most bird-obsessed of backpackers, and the gaps in its coverage would limit its usefulness south of Dar es Salaam or in the Lake Victoria and Lake Tanganyika region.

For any birding itinerary extending to parts of Tanzania west of the Serengeti or south of the Usambara, the best option is the *Field Guide to the Birds of East Africa* by Williamson and Fanshawe. Published in early 2002, this field guide provides comprehensive coverage for the whole of Tanzania, as well as Kenya, Rwanda and Burundi, and based on limited field usage to date it seems excellent, with accurate plates, good distribution maps and adequately detailed text descriptions.

Another quality field guide that provides full coverage of east Africa is *Birds of Africa south of the Sahara: A Comprehensive Illustrated Field Guide* by Ian Sinclair and Peter Ryan (Struik Publishers, 2003), which describes and illustrates the 2,100-plus species recorded in the region. Should you already own it, or be planning more extensive travels in Africa, then this guide will more than suffice for northern Tanzania. But if your African travels will be restricted to east Africa, you are probably better off buying a more focused field guide.

Ber Van Perlo's *Illustrated Checklist to the Birds of Eastern Africa* (Collins, 1995) is a useful, relatively inexpensive and admirably compact identification manual describing and illustrating all 1,488 bird species recorded in Eritrea, Ethiopia, Kenya, Uganda and Tanzania. Unfortunately, however, the distribution maps and colour plates are often misleading, and the compact format means that descriptions are too terse and pictures too cluttered to allow identification of more difficult genera. It is, however, far more useful than John Williams's pioneering but now obsolete *Field Guide to the Birds of East Africa*, also published by Collins and still referred to in many brochures and guides.

Other field guides The past few years have seen the publication of a spate of high-quality field guides to other more specialised aspects of east Africa's fauna and flora. Among the more interesting of these titles are Najma Dharani's *Field Guide to Common Trees and Shrubs of East Africa* (Struik, 2002) and a simply magnificent *Field Guide to the Reptiles of East Africa* by Stephen Spawls, Kim Howell, Robert Drewes and James Ashe (A & C Black, 2004). Alan Channing and Kim Howell's *Amphibians of East Africa* (Comstock Books in Herpetology, 2006) is also highly worthwhile. Matt Richmond and Irene Kamau's *East African Marine Ecoregion* (World Wide Fund for Nature USA, 2005) examines the whole of the east African coast.

National parks Bernhard Grzimek's renowned book *Serengeti Shall Not Die* (Collins, 1959) remains a classic evocation of the magic of the Serengeti, and its original publication was instrumental in making this reserve better known to the outside world. Iain Douglas-Hamilton's *Amongst the Elephants* (Penguin, 1978) did much the same for publicising Lake Manyara National Park, though the vast herds of elephants it describes have since been greatly reduced by poaching.

About ten years ago, Jeanette Hanby and David Bygott wrote a series of excellent booklets covering Serengeti National Park, Tarangire National Park and Lake Manyara National Park. These were published by TANAPA and can still be bought for US$5 at many bookshops in Arusha, and possibly at some safari lodges. The same authors have written an equally informative and widely available self-published booklet covering the Ngorongoro Conservation Area. These older guides have now been formally superseded by a series of glossier booklets covering each of the four major reserves, published by the African Publishing House in association with TANAPA. These newer booklets are more up to date and colourful than the older ones, but they are also twice the price, and are not substantially more informative.

Giovanni Tombazzi's lively, colourful and accurate maps covering (among other places) the Serengeti, Lake Manyara, Tarangire and the Ngorongoro Conservation Area are probably the most user-friendly maps I've seen in east Africa. Each map shows details of the appropriate conservation area in both the dry and wet seasons, and is liberally dotted with illustrations of common trees and other points of interest. Giovanni has also produced a map covering the whole northern safari circuit, useful to those who don't want to splash out on the whole series of more detailed maps. As with the booklets mentioned above, these maps are widely available in Arusha and at the national park lodges, but vary in price depending on where you buy them.

Travel guides Bradt also publishes Philip Briggs's hefty *Tanzania: The Bradt Travel Guide*, aimed at those who want to explore this vast and varied country beyond the northern safari circuit, while *Zanzibar, Pemba & Mafia: The Bradt Travel Guide* by Chris McIntyre and Susan McIntyre is the most useful book for those visiting the islands in isolation. Travellers with limited mobility may also be interested in Bradt's *Access Africa: Safaris for People with Limited Mobility* by Gordon Rattray. For people combining a visit to Tanzania with one or other of its neighbours, there are also detailed Bradt guides available to Kenya, Ethiopia, Uganda, Zambia, Congo, Mozambique, Malawi and Rwanda.

Coffee-table books The best book of this sort to cover Tanzania as a whole is Paul Joynson-Hicks's *Tanzania: Portrait of a Nation*, which contains some great down-to-earth cultural photography and lively anecdotal captions. Also recommended is *Journey through Tanzania*, photographed by the late Mohammed Amin and Duncan Willets and published by Camerapix in Kenya. Both of the above books are stronger on cultural, landmark and scenic photography than on wildlife photography, for which M Iwago's superb *Serengeti* (Thames and Hudson, 1987) has few peers. Also worth a look is John Reader's definitive *Kilimanjaro*. Javed Jafferji's atmospheric photographs are highlighted in *Images of Zanzibar*, while *Zanzibar – Romance of the Ages* makes extensive use of archive photographs dating to before the turn of the century. Both were published by HSP Publications in 1996, and are readily available on the island.

Health Self-prescribing has its hazards so if you are going anywhere very remote consider taking a health book. For adults there is *Bugs, Bites & Bowels: The Cadogan Guide to Healthy Travel* by Jane Wilson-Howarth (2006); if travelling with the family look at *Your Child Abroad: A Travel Health Guide* by Jane Wilson-Howarth and Matthew Ellis, published by Bradt in 2005.

Fiction Surprisingly few novels have been written by Tanzanians or about Tanzania (even a friend who has studied African literature failed to come up with one indigenous Tanzanian novelist). An excellent novel set in World War I Tanzania is William Boyd's *An Ice-cream War*, while the same author's *Brazzaville Beach*, though not overtly set in Tanzania, devotes attention to aspects of chimpanzee behaviour first noted at Gombe Stream.

A Tanzanian of Asian extraction now living in Canada, M G Vassanji, is the author of at least one novel set in Tanzania and the Kenyan border area, the prize-winning *Book of Secrets* (Macmillan, 1994). This is an atmospheric tale, with much interesting period detail, revolving around a diary written by a British administrator in pre-war Kenya and discovered in a flat in Dar es Salaam in the 1980s. Vassanji is also the author of *Uhuru Street*, a collection of short stories set in Dar es Salaam. Novels set elsewhere in Africa, but which may be of interest to visitors to Tanzania, include the following:

Brink, A *An Act of Terror* or *A Dry White Season*
Cartwright, J *Maasai Dreaming*
Conrad, J *Heart of Darkness*
Dagarembga, T *Nervous Conditions*
Gordimer, N *July's People*
Kingsolver, B *The Poisonwood Bible*
Lambkin, D *The Hanging Tree*
Lessing, D *The Grass is Singing, Children of Violence* (5 volumes)
Mazrui, A *The Trial of Christopher Okigbo*
Mungoshi, C *Coming of the Dry Season*
Mwangi, M *Going down River Road*
Naipaul, V S *A Bend in the River*
Okri, B *The Famished Road*
Theroux, P *Jungle Lovers*
Thiong'o, N *Petals of Blood* or *A Grain of Wheat*
Slaughter, C *Antonia saw the Oryx First*
Van der Post, L *A Story like the Wind*

MAPS A number of maps covering east Africa are available. The best is the Austrian-published Freytag-Berndt 1:2,000,000 map. By far the most accurate and up-to-date dedicated map of Tanzania is the 1:400,000 *Tanzania Travel Map* published by Harms Verlag (*www.harms-ic-verlag.de*). For most tourists, the map of Tanzania produced by the TTB and given away free at their offices in Arusha or Dar will be adequate.

A series of excellent maps by Giovanni Tombazzi covers most of the northern reserves, as well as Kilimanjaro, Mount Meru and Zanzibar. Colourful, lively and accurate, these maps are widely available throughout northern Tanzania. Also recommended are the new Harms Verlag maps to Ngorongoro Conservation Area, Lake Manyara National Park and Zanzibar Island.

TRAVEL MAGAZINES The Tanzanian Tourist Board produces a quarterly magazine called *Tantravel*, which normally includes a few gushing but interesting articles as well as plenty of advertisements, and can normally be picked up at Air Tanzania and TTB offices. Far better is the quarterly magazine *Kakakuona: African Wildlife* (e kakakuona@africaonline.co.tz), which is produced by the Tanzania Wildlife Protection Fund, and frequently includes several good articles about conservation in Tanzania. For readers with a broad interest in Africa, an excellent magazine dedicated to tourism throughout Africa is *Travel Africa*, which can be visited online at www.travelafricamag.com. Recommended for their broad-ranging editorial content and the coffee-table standard photography, the award-winning magazines *Africa Geographic* and *Africa Birds & Birding* can be checked out at the website www.africageographic.com.

WEBSITES The following offer information on northern Tanzania and Zanzibar:

www.ntz.info
www.intotanzania.com
www.allaboutzanzibar.com
www.africatravelresources.com

Bradt Travel Guides

www.bradtguides.com

Africa

Africa Overland	£15.99
Algeria	£15.99
Benin	£14.99
Botswana: Okavango, Chobe, Northern Kalahari	£15.99
Burkina Faso	£14.99
Cameroon	£15.99
Cape Verde Islands	£14.99
Congo	£15.99
Eritrea	£15.99
Ethiopia	£15.99
Gambia, The	£13.99
Ghana	£15.99
Johannesburg	£6.99
Madagascar	£15.99
Malawi	£13.99
Mali	£13.95
Mauritius, Rodrigues & Réunion	£13.99
Mozambique	£13.99
Namibia	£15.99
Niger	£14.99
Nigeria	£17.99
North Africa: Roman Coast	£15.99
Rwanda	£14.99
São Tomé & Principe	£14.99
Seychelles	£14.99
Sierra Leone	£16.99
Sudan	£13.95
Tanzania, Northern	£13.99
Tanzania	£16.99
Uganda	£15.99
Zambia	£17.99
Zanzibar	£14.99

Britain and Europe

Albania	£15.99
Armenia, Nagorno Karabagh	£14.99
Azores	£13.99
Baltic Cities	£14.99
Belarus	£14.99
Belgrade	£6.99
Bosnia & Herzegovina	£13.99
Bratislava	£9.99
Budapest	£9.99
Bulgaria	£13.99
Cork	£6.99
Croatia	£13.99
Cyprus see North Cyprus	
Czech Republic	£13.99
Dresden	£7.99
Dubrovnik	£6.99

Estonia	£13.99
Faroe Islands	£15.99
Georgia	£14.99
Helsinki	£7.99
Hungary	£14.99
Iceland	£14.99
Kosovo	£14.99
Lapland	£13.99
Latvia	£13.99
Lille	£6.99
Lithuania	£14.99
Ljubljana	£7.99
Luxembourg	£13.99
Macedonia	£14.99
Montenegro	£14.99
North Cyprus	£12.99
Paris, Lille & Brussels	£11.95
Riga	£6.99
Serbia	£14.99
Slovakia	£14.99
Slovenia	£13.99
Spitsbergen	£14.99
Switzerland Without a Car	£14.99
Tallinn	£6.99
Transylvania	£14.99
Ukraine	£14.99
Vilnius	£6.99
Zagreb	£6.99

Middle East, Asia and Australasia

China: Yunnan Province	£13.99
Great Wall of China	£13.99
Iran	£14.99
Iraq: Then & Now	£15.99
Israel	£15.99
Kazakhstan	£15.99
Kyrgyzstan	£15.99
Maldives	£15.99
Mongolia	£16.99
North Korea	£14.99
Oman	£13.99
Shangri-La: A Travel Guide to the Himalayan Dream	£14.99
Sri Lanka	£15.99
Syria	£14.99
Tibet	£13.99
Turkmenistan	£14.99
Yemen	£14.99

The Americas and the Caribbean

Amazon, The	£14.99
Argentina	£15.99

Bolivia	£14.99
Cayman Islands	£14.99
Chile	£16.95
Colombia	£16.99
Costa Rica	£13.99
Dominica	£14.99
Falkland Islands	£13.95
Grenada, Carriacou & Petite Martinique	£14.99
Guyana	£14.99
Panama	£13.95
Peru & Bolivia: The Bradt Trekking Guide	£12.95
St Helena	£14.99
Turks & Caicos Islands	£14.99
USA by Rail	£14.99

Wildlife

100 Animals to See Before They Die	£16.99
Antarctica: Guide to the Wildlife	£15.99
Arctic: Guide to the Wildlife	£15.99
Central & Eastern European Wildlife	£15.99
Chinese Wildlife	£16.99
East African Wildlife	£19.99
Galápagos Wildlife	£15.99
Madagascar Wildlife	£16.99
New Zealand Wildlife	£14.99
North Atlantic Wildlife	£16.99
Peruvian Wildlife	£15.99
Southern African Wildlife	£18.95
Sri Lankan Wildlife	£15.99
Wildlife and Conservation Volunteering: The Complete Guide	£13.99

Eccentric Guides

Eccentric Australia	£12.99
Eccentric Britain	£13.99
Eccentric California	£13.99
Eccentric Cambridge	£6.99
Eccentric Edinburgh	£5.95
Eccentric France	£12.95
Eccentric London	£13.99

Others

Your Child Abroad: A Travel Health Guide	£10.95
Something Different for the Weekend	£9.99
Britain from the Rails	£17.99

WIN £100 CASH!
READER QUESTIONNAIRE

Send in your completed questionnaire for the chance to win £100 cash in our regular draw

All respondents may order a Bradt guide at half the UK retail price – please complete the order form overleaf.

(Entries may be posted or faxed to us, or scanned and emailed.)

We are interested in getting feedback from our readers to help us plan future Bradt guides. Please answer ALL the questions below and return the form to us in order to qualify for an entry in our regular draw.

Have you used any other Bradt guides? If so, which titles? . . . .
. . . .

What other publishers' travel guides do you use regularly? . . . .
. . . .

Where did you buy this guidebook? . . . .

What was the main purpose of your trip to Tanzania (or for what other reason did you read our guide)? eg: holiday/business/charity etc.. . . . .
. . . .

What other destinations would you like to see covered by a Bradt guide?
. . . .

Would you like to receive our catalogue/newsletters?

YES / NO (If yes, please complete details on reverse)

If yes – by post or email? . . . .

Age (circle relevant category) 16–25   26–45   46–60   60+

Male/Female (delete as appropriate)

Home country . . . .

Please send us any comments about our guide to Northern Tanzania or other Bradt Travel Guides. . . . .
. . . .
. . . .
. . . .

Bradt Travel Guides
23 High Street, Chalfont St Peter, Bucks SL9 9QE, UK
☏ +44 (0)1753 893444 **f** +44 (0)1753 892333
e info@bradtguides.com
www.bradtguides.com

CLAIM YOUR HALF-PRICE BRADT GUIDE!

Order Form

To order your half-price copy of a Bradt guide, and to enter our prize draw to win £100 (see overleaf), please fill in the order form below, complete the questionnaire overleaf, and send it to Bradt Travel Guides by post, fax or email.

Please send me one copy of the following guide at half the UK retail price

Title		Retail price	Half price
...	....	....	....

Please send the following additional guides at full UK retail price

No	Title	Retail price	Total
...	....	....	....
...	....	....	....
...	....	....	....

Sub total ......
Post & packing ......
(£2 per book UK; £4 per book Europe; £6 per book rest of world)
Total ......

Name ....

Address ....

Tel .... Email ....

☐ I enclose a cheque for £ .... made payable to Bradt Travel Guides Ltd

☐ I would like to pay by credit card. Number: ....

Expiry date: .../... 3-digit security code (on reverse of card) .....

Issue no (debit cards only) .....

☐ Please add my name to your catalogue mailing list.

☐ I would be happy for you to use my name and comments in Bradt marketing material.

Send your order on this form, with the completed questionnaire, to:

Bradt Travel Guides NTAN2
23 High Street, Chalfont St Peter, Bucks SL9 9QE
☏ +44 (0)1753 893444 f +44 (0)1753 892333
e info@bradtguides.com www.bradtguides.com

Index

Entries in **bold** indicate main entries; those in *italics* indicate maps